Process and Outcome in Peer Relationships

DEVELOPMENTAL PSYCHOLOGY SERIES

SERIES EDITOR
Harry Beilin

Developmental Psychology Program
City University of New York Graduate School
New York, New York

A complete list of titles in this series is available from the publisher.

PROCESS AND OUTCOME
IN PEER RELATIONSHIPS

Edited by

EDWARD C. MUELLER

Department of Psychology
Boston University
Boston, Massachusetts

CATHERINE R. COOPER

Department of Child Development
College of Home Economics
University of Texas
Austin, Texas

1986

ACADEMIC PRESS, INC.
(Harcourt Brace Jovanovich, Publishers)
Orlando   San Diego   New York   Austin
London   Montreal   Sydney   Tokyo   Toronto

ACADEMIC PRESS, INC.
Orlando, Florida 32887

United Kingdom Edition published by
ACADEMIC PRESS, INC. (LONDON) LTD.
24–28 Oval Road, London NW1 7DX

LIBRARY OF CONGRESS CATALOGING IN PUBLICATION DATA

Main entry under title:

Process and outcome in peer relationships.

Includes index.
1. Social interaction—Addresses, essays, lectures.
2. Interpersonal relationships—Addresses, essays,
lectures.   3. Age groups—Addresses, essays, lectures.
4. Child development—Addresses, essays, lectures.
5. Friendship—Addresses, essays, lectures.   I. Mueller,
Edward C.   II. Cooper, Catherine R.
HQ783.P76   1985   302   85-1263

ISBN 0-12-509560-0 (alk. paper)
ISBN 0-12-509561-9 (paperback)

PRINTED IN THE UNITED STATES OF AMERICA

86 87 88 89   9 8 7 6 5 4 3 2 1

This book is dedicated to Richard Jung and William L. Faust,
whose examples provide us with continuing inspiration.

CONTENTS

PART II. PROCESS IN PEER
AND FAMILY RELATIONSHIPS   55

3. Infant–Mother Attachment and Early Peer Relations: The Assessment of Behavior in an Interactive Context
Joseph L. Jacobson, Robin L. Tianen, Diane E. Wille, and Donald M. Aytch

4. The Effect of Experience on Peer Relationships
Beatrice Blyth Whiting

9. Organization of Social Play among Toddlers: An Ecological Approach

Mira Stambak and Mina Verba

10. "Frame Talk": A Dramatistic Analysis of Children's Fantasy Play

David Forbes, Mary Maxwell Katz, and Barry Paul

V. PROCESS IN LEARNING   267

11. Four Perspectives on Peer Learning among Elementary School Children

Catherine R. Cooper, Angela Marquis, and Deborah Edward

12. Problem Solving in Children's Management of Instruction
Shari Ellis and Barbara Rogoff

VI. REFLECTIONS AND NEW DIRECTIONS   327

13. Peer Relations and the Growth of Communication
Catherine Garvey

CONTRIBUTORS

Numbers in parentheses indicate the pages on which the authors' contributions begin.

Donald M. Aytch (57), Department of Psychology, Wayne State University, Detroit, Michigan 48202

Thomas J. Berndt (105), Department of Psychological Sciences, Purdue University, West Lafayette, Indiana 47907

Barbara Bokus (189), Uniwersytet Warszawski, Instyut Psychologii, Warszawa, ul. Stawki 5/7, Poland

Deborah Cohen (161), Department of Psychology, Boston University, Boston, Massachusetts 02215

Catherine R. Cooper (3, 269), Department of Home Economics, University of Texas, Austin, Texas 78712

Deborah Edward (269), The Austin Children's Museum, Inc., Austin, Texas 78701

Shari Ellis[1] (301), Department of Psychology, University of Utah, Salt Lake City, Utah 84112

Joyce L. Epstein (129), Center for Social Organization of Schools, Johns Hopkins University, Baltimore, Maryland 21218

David Forbes (249), Harvard Graduate School of Education, Cambridge, Massachusetts 02138

Catherine Garvey (329), Department of Psychology, University of Maine, Orono, Maine 04469

Joseph L. Jacobson (57), Department of Psychology, Wayne State University, Detroit, Michigan 48202

Mary Maxwell Katz (249), Harvard Graduate School of Education, Cambridge, Massachusetts 02138

---

[1] Present address: 85 Hawthorne Road, Williamstown, Massachusetts 02167

Angela Marquis (269), Stephens County Guidance Center, Duncan, Oklahoma 73533

Edward C. Mueller (3, 161), Department of Psychology, Boston University, Boston, Massachusetts 02215

Tullia Musatti (25), Istituto di Psicologia, Consiglio Nazional delle Ricerche, 00182 Roma, Italy

Barry Paul (249), Harvard Graduate School of Education, Cambridge, Massachusetts 02138

Barbara Rogoff (301), Department of Psychology, University of Utah, Salt Lake City, Utah 84112

Grace Wales Shugar (189), Uniwersytet Warszawski, Instyut Psychologii, Warszawa, ul. Stawki 5/7, Poland

Mira Stambak (229), CRESAS, 75005 Paris, France

Robin L. Tianen (57), Department of Psychology, Wayne State University, Detroit, Michigan 48202

Mini Verba (229), C.N.R.S., Paris, CRESAS, 75005 Paris, France

Beatrice Blyth Whiting (79), Harvard Graduate School of Education, Cambridge, Massachusetts 02138

Diane E. Wille (57), Department of Psychology, Wayne State University, Detroit, Michigan 48202

PREFACE

Current studies of children's peer relations have often shown more exuberance than coherence. In fact, recent publications and conference papers on peer relations seem to indicate that its study is in conceptual and theoretical disarray. The goal of this volume is to integrate a variety of research programs focused on the study of peer relations. It represents a further step in considering peer research from a developmental perspective. Pursuing this approach leads to the realization that to understand the contribution of children's peer relationships to their development, one must examine the processes involved in these relationships. Rather than seeing peer relations as one isolated area of development, the contributors view these relationships as significant for development in many areas, including friendships, play, and learning. For example, the child who effectively negotiates an appropriate social role in a classroom learning group is one who gains academically from that group. This developmental approach also delineates the process through which experiences in peer relationships foster these diverse ends. It represents an advance over studies which look only at process or outcome, or which simply compare adult and peer relationships as though each constituted a homogeneous set of experiences for children.

Although the contributors to this volume come from varied disciplines and are interested in different aspects of peer relations at varying ages, they all have employed this integrated developmental orientation in their research. All have studied both the direct dynamics of peer encounters and related the process of interaction to the functional importance of peer relations in some period of childhood. The participant's work converges on the following four issues:

1. What is the nature of our understanding of the *process* of peer interaction?

2. What are the key *developmental changes* in peer relationships?
3. What *contextual variables* affect these developments?
4. What significance do peer relations have for children's emotional and cognitive development? That is, what *developmental outcomes* do they affect?

In selecting the individuals to address these questions, we sought diversity both in terms of geography and discipline. As a result, this is the first volume on peer research to strike some balance between European and North American research. In terms of academic discipline, scholars from sociology, anthropology, psycholinguistics, and developmental psychology are included. The results illustrate the wide range of impact of peer experience in children's development. Peer relations play a role in areas as diverse as infant's symbolic skills and sixth-graders' academic performance; they affect emotional health as well as the acquisition of skills.

This book both illustrates the diversity of current peer research and provides a framework for ordering that diversity. The introductory chapter considers four root metaphors that underlie the approaches to the study of peer relations and suggests that an appreciation of these assumptions and their implications will contribute to integrating and differentiating current work. Following a second chapter that offers perspective on Vygotsky and Piaget, the subsequent chapters are grouped according to the domains of development in which peer relationships are considered: Peer and Family Relationships, Friendships, Play, and Learning. Catherine Garvey contributes a final chapter that offers perspectives on the questions of development, context, and outcome in the study of peer process.

We would like to express our appreciation to the contributors and other participants at the conference and to the editors and staff at Academic Press for their support and encouragement in the preparation of this volume. We also acknowledge the generous support of the Society for Research in Child Development and the Foundation for Child Development, who funded a meeting among the contributors at Osgood Hill, North Andover, Massachusetts, as the chapters for this volume were being prepared.

PART I

CONCEPTUAL FOUNDATIONS

A newcomer to the field of peer relations would be struck by the number of theoretical frameworks in use. The conceptual foundations of peer research spring from no single source. Early work drew upon psychoanalytic concerns with compensating for deficient parent–child relationships, or social-psychological interest in group structure. Cognitive developmentalists have regarded the relatively egalitarian distribution of power and maturity in peer relations as an asset in the development of symbolic skills. Research conducted from the perspectives of social learning theory, sociolinguistics, ethology, and ego psychology have also examined the contribution of peer experience to development. Can these approaches be understood within some common framework?

In Chapter 1, "On Conceptualizing Peer Research," Mueller and Cooper consider the definition of peer relations as formulated by the contributors to this volume, as well as by other investigators in the field. As a way of clarifying the current conceptual disarray in the field, as well as to help individual researchers proceed more thoughtfully, these authors present a framework, developed by philosopher Stephen Pepper, of four fundamental metaphors that have formed the basis for scientific investigations through the

1

centuries. Peer research exemplifying all four metaphors is then used to illustrate the distinctive contribution of each.

Musatti, in "Early Peer Relations: The Perspectives of Piaget and Vygotsky" (Chapter 2, this volume), provides an incisive review of these two key theoretical views, including a clarification of the often misunderstood controversy between the two scholars. Integrating work in cognitive development with findings from object-related and peer-related behavior, as well as with studies of play and representation, Musatti proposes a model which offers the basis for integrated research in the development of toddler peer relations.

Other theoretical approaches, including those of Sullivan, Bowlby, Sroufe, Lamb, Goffman, Burke, and Bem, are also utilized in various papers in this volume to characterize aspects of process, developmental outcome, and context in peer functioning. By considering this array of conceptual approaches, we do not argue for the superiority of any one for addressing the diverse questions in the field. Rather, following Pepper, we encourage investigators to see the implications of their own choices in the context of a wider conceptual perspective on peer research.

CHAPTER 1

On Conceptualizing Peer Research

Edward C. Mueller and Catherine R. Cooper

*I am pretty sure these four keys will
open any closet now built that is worth opening.*
(Pepper, 1942)

Introduction

What can be done about the theoretical disarray in studies of peer relations? One solution, often tried in the history of our science, is to follow a "great theorist." Freud and Piaget, for example, both theorized about peer relations. Freud stressed the role of peer contact in developing the conflict-free sphere of the ego (see Chapter 7, this volume), and Piaget stressed the role of peers in moral development (see Chapter 5, this volume). However, neither Piaget nor Freud can be said to dominate modern peer research. Indeed there is no great theorist of peer research uniting current efforts in this area.

In the present chapter we develop the thesis that this state of affairs is exactly as it should be. Great theorists, it is argued, narrow research too far. There is no *one* best approach.

Another solution is for researchers to imitate Charles Darwin's approach by trying to forge a creative synthesis based on their own evidence without too much concern for the ideas of others. Although this would be intellectual anarchy, it is not so different from the current situation.

Yet there must be some middle ground between allegiance to a great theorist and intellectual chaos. The thesis of this chapter, borrowed from Pepper (1942), is that intellectual history has yielded but four great frameworks for theorizing about peer relations. Our purpose is to use Pepper's four scaffolds to organize the current disarray in research on peer relations. The field of peer research is conceptually confusing because we remain unclear about the four equally useful models that already guide us. Claims for these models are strong: They are justified both by Western intellectual history and by the beliefs that we each invoke in our efforts to understand things.

Before developing these points, it should be understood that this position is quite different from the ever-popular stance called "pure empiricism." The empiricist argues that theory should be avoided entirely in the initial fact-gathering phase of research on a topic. Because peer research is a new endeavor, argues the empiricist, no theory is possible or even desirable. This chapter exposes the naivete in this position, showing that behind all current peer research are simple theories about how things works.

It is impossible, we submit, even to define peer relations without invoking such assumptions or models. The problem of definition has concerned the contributors to this volume, and we asked them to share with us their thoughts about it. From their responses, it seems that most contributors are dissatisfied with the traditional *near agemates* definition. Before turning to our main goal, we pause briefly to consider their reflections.

Definition of Peer Relations

Shugar introduces the problem in this way:

> It would be useful to be clearer as to our understanding of peerhood (or a peer relation as opposed to a nonpeer one). Is the peer relation a formal one, of contemporaneousness, of an arbitrary age bracketing within given limits, of co-generation membership? Or is it one of quality and function, and if so, in terms of what characteristics? Can we envisage a peer relationship turning into a nonpeer relation? That is, is there a dynamic involved? some basic social process? Further, we need to be clear whether we are dealing with a researcher's construct, or whether people perceive each other as peers or nonpeers, and if so, under what conditions. (G. W. Shugar, personal communication, August 11, 1982)

Jacobson approaches one of Shugar's questions by stressing one "quality and function" of peer relations:

> When we try to integrate the perspectives of the European and North American research traditions, it seems that equality and dominance are two especially frequent foci of peer relations research. *Perhaps what is unique in the peer situation is the fact that no hierarchial relationship is defined in advance.* It is therefore of

particular interest to investigate the degree to which the relationship that emerges is characterized either by dominance on the one hand or cooperation based on equality on the other. If so, the defining characteristic of peer relations is not age similarity per se but rather the absence of an obvious predetermined basis for asymmetry or inequality. This lack of a preestablished hierarchy explains why even inherently asymmetrical relations (parent–child, employer–employee) are considered "peer-like" when the participants attempt to approach the ideal of equality. (J. L. Jacobson, personal communication, August 5, 1982)

While symmetry or equality seem central in peer relations, is it a potential equality, as Jacobson et al. suggests, or an achieved equality? Shugar develops the latter position:

One might say that in general terms what unites peers is to belong to the same world (not only a "found" world, given by predecessors, shaped and accessed by elders), in terms not only of setting and behavior, but also of similar ways of perceiving it. The peer process—in the long perspective—would be to act upon this world, to re-shape social orders, to transform what exists, by an intermeshing or clash of goals.

Peer process is ongoing, like any process, and it is up to researchers to find ways of segmenting it so that the outcome can be identified, so that we may see what changes the individual has wrought upon the world as participant in the peer process, and what changes this process has wrought upon him or her. In this line of thinking, it is not dominance vs. submission that characterizes a peer process, but the working out of mutual rights and responsibilities so that a potential equality becomes a negotiated quality. (G. W. Shugar, personal communication, August 11, 1982)

For Shugar, then, peer relations are those where children seek to work on the world, either to understand it, thereby generating shared meaning or to alter it, yielding shared mastery. In addition, children do not work only on the world; they also work on themselves, on their personal needs and feelings, and they do so with others with whom they have achieved a "negotiated equality" or friendship.

This view of children's peer relations as reshaping what they experience is crucial to the definition of peer relations for several contributors. It affects not only their actual definition but also their view of the "context" of peer relations. For example, Musatti noted:

In research on the child's social behavior and its development the main question no longer should be, "How is the child adapted to the context" but should rather be "How is the context adapted to the child?". This would mean studying not only the contextual determinants of the child's behavior, but also the organization of the physical and social environment and *how* it is dynamically related to the child's behavior. . . . A famous example of the problem can be found in the debate about the effects of infant day-care centers on the child's social and cognitive development. Quite often the effects of the infant day-care center on the child's behavior are evaluated without analyzing the actual organization of the social and physical environment in the center. More specific studies, like the Oxford Preschool Project

(Sylva, Ray, & Painter, 1980), found a close relation between the infant's or toddler's behavior and the day-care organization in its educational, social, and psychological features. (T. Musatti, personal communication, September 2, 1982)

In summary, terms like "peer relations" and its "context" remain problematic. Should beginning researchers use age similarity or must they deal with issues like potential versus achieved equality? Our answer is that there are several equally useful definitions, each stemming from basically different conceptualizations. To state these definitions, it is necessary first to consider the four distinct approaches that utilize them.

The problem with an exercise of this sort is that no one likes to be "pigeon-holed," but remember that it is the approach to the work that is being classified, not the workers. There is an important difference. During their careers, researchers' views change. They are likely to contribute research stemming from more than one approach, especially if their basic interest is in the topic itself rather than in a given methodological stance. Also many studies are themselves eclectic, combining several approaches in seeking to understand a single problem in peer research.

Pepper's Root Metaphors and World Theories

The question then arises: If peer research is often eclectic, in what sense could four approaches exist as separate entities? Pepper (1942) develops two kinds of reasons for believing in the integrity of each approach that he had identified. His first claim is that each approach has remained distinct across centuries of Western thought; if any had been distinctly less adequate than the others, it would have been discarded long ago. If any had been merely a version of a different one, it would not have remained so distinct across the years. Furthermore, each one is consistent with the thought of great philosophers. Thus, if one's research follows from any single approach, one can feel sure that one's thinking is consistent with the thoughts of the major philosophers, most probably either Plato, Locke, Hegel or William James. Consequently one's research can be read and understood readily by anyone versed in the traditions of Western epistemological thought.

Pepper's second claim relates more to the psychology of mind than the history of thought. He proposes that each of us, in our efforts to explain things, stumbles across objects or events that we subsequently take as prototypes for explaining other things. Some prototypes are simple objects, like water, or simple concepts, like similarity; others are harder to label, like the experience of a dynamic, dramatic event. Pepper calls these prototypes "root metaphors."

Lacking their own Darwin, Pepper implies that peer researchers have turned to whichever of these implicit metaphors predominated in their own past attempts to understand their world, or perhaps to the metaphors of their teachers. Researchers then apply this metaphor in their own conceptual and methodological decisions as they plan their peer studies.

In Pepper's analysis of the history of philosophy and science, only seven or eight root metaphors have proven useful in constructing general theories. And, of these metaphors, only four have been found durable and continue to generate theories; these are presented in Table 1.1. Each is thought to have passed the test of "unlimited scope." That is, each is about equally powerful in its ability to serve as a model for building theories *about anything*. The root metaphors are (1) the developing organism, (2) the machine, (3) the intuition of alikeness, and (4) the purposive, meaningful act. Although people have constructed many metaphors, Pepper argues that only these four have turned out to be of durable use to philosophers and to scientists in developing theories of humanity and of the universe.

World theories is the term Pepper gives to the general theories of nature that have been constructed by philosophers from these metaphors. One could also call them the enduring schools of philosophy and the enduring

Table 1.1

Pepper's Root Metaphors and World Theories Expressed in
Philosophy and Social Science

Root metaphor	Derivative world theory	Sources in philosophy (approximate time of origin)	Twentieth century expressions in social sciences
Objects that are –similar –expressions of a plan	Formism (Platonic idealism)	Socrates, Plato, Aristotle (400 B.C.)	Noam Chomsky Carl Jung
The machine	Mechanism	Democritus (450 B.C.) John Locke (1650)	John B. Watson Kurt Lewin B. F. Skinner
The immediate meaningful event	Contextualism[a] (Pragmatism)	William James John Dewey George Herbert Mead (1875)	Erving Goffman Gregory Bateson
The integrated organism	Organicism[b] (Absolute or objective idealism)	Schelling Hegel (1800)	Jean Piaget

[a]All world theories must consider *context*. There is no commonly accepted alternative name, so this chapter retains Pepper's label.

[b]Alternative names that may come closer to the essence of the world view are *constructivism* and *integrationism*.

scientific epistemologies. In an effort to add some immediate meaning to the metaphors and world theories, Table 1.1 also lists some of the philosophers contributing to the development of each world theory and some representative expressions among modern social scientists.

Pepper sees the world theories as divisible into two groups, depending on whether discrete elements or complexes are taken as the beginning point of theory building. Both ancient world theories, *formism* and *mechanism,* are analytical in nature; they begin with discrete elements. Both relatively recent theories, *contextualism* and *organicism,* are synthetic theories; they begin with complexes or integrated wholes. In the more recent theories, items of data are meaningful and interpretable only in the larger context or totality.

The four world theories also can be combined in a second way that pairs ancient with modern: mechanism and organicism are both *integrative* theories. Integrative theories reject cosmic novelty or chance and insist that all features of the universe have a determinate order. In contrast, formism and contextualism are *dispersive* theories:

> Facts are taken one by one from whatever source they come and are interpreted as they come and so are left. The universe has for these theories the general effect of multitudes of facts rather loosely scattered about and not necessarily determining one another to any considerable degree. The cosmos for these theories is not in the end highly systematic—the very word "cosmos" is not exactly appropriate. (Pepper, 1942, pp. 142–143)

In other words, contextualism and formism do not lead to deterministic, closed explanations, so there is a special tolerance for uncertainty in knowledge in these approaches.

We cannot go into further detail about Pepper's ideas, considered only in the abstract. His important message is that each world hypothesis is about equally powerful, otherwise it would have been discarded in the long course of intellectual history. Another of his major ideas is that no world hypothesis is refutable in the categories of a different hypothesis. One example of this situation occurred several years ago in a series of debates between Chomsky and Piaget (Gardner, 1979). Given their classification in Table 1.1 as spokespersons for different metaphors, Pepper would probably predict that they would "talk past" each other because of the different basic metaphors and categories underlying their ideas.

For each of the four world theories, we will attempt the following: (1) to present a representative past study from the literature on peer relations that exemplifies a given approach in practice; (2) to show that each study yields something so fundamental to our current understanding of peer process or outcome that it is impossible to ignore or discount the underlying approach; and (3) to suggest how the chapters in the present volume continue to further each of the approaches. Finally, we will argue for the necessity of an informed eclecticism (i.e., the use of multiple theories) in properly assessing the state of knowledge in peer research.

Let us state at the outset that classifying empirical studies into the four approaches was done with a bias toward the conceptualizations underlying each study rather than towards the particular methodologies adapted in them.

Formism in Peer Research

Formism was the first relatively adequate world hypothesis to reach its full expression in philosophy. Thus, there is some poetic justice in its underlying the first systematic study of peer relations (Bühler, 1927). Bühler's central interest was in personality types, a subject today more often labeled "temperament" or "the psychology of individual differences." Formist theorists such as Bühler believe that the goal of science is to infer the natural "forms" or "laws" that produce the regularity or orderliness in nature. Through careful observation, Bühler's hope was to deduce the natural social dispositions of infants. Prior to 1927, she had examined adolescent diaries in an attempt to solve the same problem, but in teenagers she found the basic dispositions to be too confounded by the earlier experiences of childhood. By 1933, in the second edition of Murchison's *Handbook of Child Psychology,* she was ready with her solution to the problem:

> [I] observed and described *three types* of social behavior in babies of this age. These types were called the *socially blind,* the *socially dependent,* and the *socially independent* . . . The criteria are the following: (a) The socially blind infant behaves in the presence of another child as if nobody were present . . . (b) the socially dependent infant, on the contrary, is deeply impressed by the other's presence and activities . . . (c) the third type is still different. The socially independent child is one who—though aware of the other's presence and responsive to his behavior—does not seem dependent on him, is neither intimidated nor inspired. (1933, p. 393)

Bühler was developing a theory of the natural and lawful personality types. What better place to look for these than in first social expression among unacquainted infant peers? Notice that formist theory does not require any given child perfectly to embody any of the three types. Formists believe that scientists infer the laws by which nature operates. Although nature seeks to produce these three ideal forms, it rarely succeeds perfectly. Just as there is a "norm" or "law" of the ideal oak tree, so there is a norm of the ideal "socially dependent" child. A given child may not perfectly embody this ideal because of interfering factors in normal development. The idea that development has a natural course that becomes "distorted" by the environment is a formist view.

Buhler's theory of social types did not gain widespread acceptance in this century. It yielded to a different set of categories (e.g., hysterical, compulsive personality) that derive from a different Viennese theory and from different world hypotheses. In peer work, however, educational psychologists may have remained faithful to a formistic approach in the research tradition called "sociometry." Here the effort has focused on identifying and characterizing, for example, the popular, rejected, and peer-isolated child (see Epstein, Chapter 6, this volume).

In developmental psychology, the formist effort has largely shifted away from the types of social character to the types of social behavior. Perhaps there is a natural additive sequence in which the infant's socially relevant behaviors emerge, for example, visual regard and crying before smiling, touching, and so forth; this sequence would then be expressed simultaneously both in parent–infant and early peer relations. Support for this idea is found in research by Vandell and her colleagues (e.g., Vandell & Wilson, 1982).

Thus, current peer research reveals an indispensible contribution of formism to our understanding of peer relations, namely the idea that there are natural ideal forms of peer relations both in terms of the social qualities of participants and in terms of the specific behaviors they produce. To our knowledge, no peer researchers as yet have sought to extend formistic thinking to the laws governing interactions when the various individual types of children combine in actual dyadic interactions, although several investigators have reported important consequences of pairing high- and low-status types (Furman, Rahe, & Hartup, 1979).

In the present volume, Shugar and Bokus's contribution (Chapter 8) is a most productive example of formistic thought. For centuries the two essential forms in all formistic theories have been time and space. As Pepper (1942) states: "All concrete existences participate in the laws of time and space, whatever other forms they may also participate in" (p. 174). Shugar and Bokus propose structural forms for describing both the temporal and spatial organization of children's activities in preschool play. Children are shown to structure their time in terms of "action lines" which can be either "dominant," "submissive to another," or "shared with another." Note that the nature of the particular activity, in other words the content of the play, is used mainly to determine whose line of play predominates. A detailed description of content is beside the point here; instead it is the form of the relationship that counts.

In continuing the logic of a formistic analysis, Shugar and Bokus arrive at an intriguing idea, a proposal describing the forms of spatial organization in peer relations: Preschoolers, it appears, attribute spatial "action fields" both to themselves and their playmates, and these spatial organizations influence the character of peer interaction that occurs in them. The method used to support this idea as well as the idea itself is new in the peer relations literature illustrating the continuing generativity of formist approaches, despite their ancient origins in the thought of Plato and Aristotle.

While Shugar and Bokus stress a formistic approach, they also borrow some central concepts from contextualism, especially the concept of "agency." Our purpose is to highlight the different approaches used today, not to assert that any given chapter is a pure exemplar of a single theory.

Mechanism in Peer Research

Mechanism was the predominant world theory in the growth of experimental psychology (Boring, 1950), and it continues to be a major guiding theory in the natural sciences. A traditional mechanist believes that valid explanations require specification of the properties of matter and energy in motion. For example, in explaining why the boy hits another child, the mechanist might invoke testosterone (the material or inherent cause) and its movement from the testes to the brain plus its chemical effect on the brain (the efficient or eliciting causes). In addition, mechanists tend to believe in *elementism,* the belief that things are best understood in terms of the action of their elementary parts. The founder of experimental psychology, Wundt, used to be called a "brick and mortar psychologist" by his critics. The *bricks* were his mental elements and the *mortar* was his association processes. The extension of mechanism to psychology, except for its physiological aspect, has always required some stretching of the mechanistic world theory in the sense that one cannot locate associations and sensations in the same way one can locate testosterone.

Peer relations, or any other social relations, provide still further problems since one is no longer dealing with even a single machine. However, one aspect of social interaction, its mutually elicited, back-and-forth quality, lends itself nicely to analysis in terms of the mechanists' material and efficient causes. For example, a baby's sudden cry causes comforting behavior by the parent. The material cause of comforting response is the baby and the efficient cause is the sound of its cry traveling through the air and impacting on the parents ears.

An example of mechanistic peer research focusing on exactly this problem of response elicitation among preschoolers was conducted by Mueller (1972). Largely disregarding the content of messages, he demonstrated the power of communication features like attention and proximity in eliciting verbal responses. He showed, for example, that the listener's paying attention at the time of the message was of central importance in the speaker's receiving a verbal response. In contrast, the physical proximity of the participants was of little eliciting strength in this situation. Considering all elements together in multivariate prediction, Mueller showed that preschool children could ensure or make determinate (i.e., with probability = 1.00) a verbal response to their verbal initiations. This work showed that skilled children, in principle, can time their messages so that listeners are in a receptive state and can select message properties in ways that ensure verbal replies, even from unfamiliar peers.

This research, like that of Shugar and Bokus, tells us very little about the content or topic of the conversations. However, its high predictive power confirms the value of conceiving of peer relations in terms of the mechanistic model. The effective communicator seems to set up a kind of magnetic force field which the listener cannot resist; he or she must respond. Even very young communicators mutually elicit responses from each other and do so with skills of known efficiency. It is as if the efficiency of peer communication in eliciting responses is a knowable quantity, just like the efficiency of a physical machine.

Traditionally, mechanism provided the basis for much of what is called ecological and ethological psychology. The two movements differ mainly in stressing the environmental forces on behavior in the former and the endogenous, material sources of behavior in the latter. But each complements the other because they share a single world view. Fine examples of this research tradition in peer relations seem especially abundant in the homeland of John Locke (e.g., Blurton Jones, 1972; McGrew, 1972).

In the present volume, the research of Jacobson, et al. (Chapter 3, this volume) derives from the ethological tradition while Epstein's (Chapter 6, this volume) approach can be taken as an example of ecological research. Jacobson and his colleagues relate something called the *attachment system* to early peer relations. What is this attachment system? For the ethologist, as Jacobson, Tianen, Wille, and Aytch note, it is a "genetically specified set of behavioral propensities" (Chapter 3, this volume). Genes are the material cause that leads the child to seek proximity to the caregiver when the child is made apprehensive by unfamiliar or startling stimuli. Furthermore, the adequacy of parental responding to the child's security needs can cause the child to become securely versus insecurely attached. As in all mechanistic theories, we see material (genes) and efficient (parental response contingencies) causes acting together in producing an effect that is inevitable, given sufficient knowledge of the causes.

As is often the case, the claim here is that the primary thrust of the Jacobson et al. study is mechanistic, not that every concept in the chapter is. For example, in their effort to develop a wide ranging code for both the cognitive and emotional expressions of early social development, Jacobson et al. borrow from organicism and other traditions. However, the central idea underlying the research, the connection between parent–child attachment and subsequent peer interaction, is consistent with the mechanistic world theory.

Epstein (Chapter 6, this volume) shows that an analysis similar to Mueller's on dyadic communication can be performed at a macro-level for the outcomes of peer affiliation in schools. The key influences in understanding who associates with whom are the task structure of classroom, the reward structure for instrumental performance, and the authority structure in decision making in the class. Epstein's results, like Mueller's, are powerful: A given child's cross-race peer relations and academic grades depend heavily on the classroom's structural features and on friendship choices. For example, peer teaching programs improve cross-race peer relations and friendship choices influence grades.

Mechanistic thinking long has stressed reward contingencies in controlling behavior, including peer relations. Like Epstein, Berndt (Chapter 5, this volume) stresses the role of rewards in assessing the determinants of sharing as a kind of altruism between friends. For Berndt there are two essential determinants of sharing: (1) internal motivation states (material causes), which are themselves influenced by (2) costs and rewards in the task structure (efficient causes). The task is the ecological determinant while the motivational state is the internal determinant. Berndt refers to the curious finding that in some tasks friends compete more with each other than with neutral classmates. A mechanist might view such a result as reaffirming the belief that reward structure is a more powerful determinant of motivational state and social behavior than is any declaration of mutual liking among children.

Contextualism in Peer Research

For Pepper the root metaphor of contextualism is the immediate dramatic event; it is a meaningful purposive act seen in its full, rich situational detail. When social scientists speak in favor of "letting intent and purpose back in" as research categories, they are calling for a shift in basic approach from mechanism to contextualism.

In no other theory do the basic universal structural features of nature remain so indeterminate. The only ineradicable categories of contextualism are *change* and *novelty*. At first, peer relations might not seem analyzable at all in such a theory; contextualism seems headed toward utter skepticism. Seeking to avoid complete uncertainty, the contextualist latches firmly onto the particular event, seeking to describe it in all its detail and trying to understand its connections only to nearby events.

Events for the contextualist have the properties of *quality* and *texture*. Take as an example the writing of an English sentence, such as this one. Its quality corresponds roughly to its total meaning and its texture to its component words and grammatical relations. Yet do not let this example be misleading: The contextualist seeks no universals either of grammar or meaning. To the contrary, the meaningful utterances of each culture are taken on their own terms and related to their present historical circumstances. There can be no universal theory of peer relations because the functional importance of peer relations probably varies from culture to culture. Without doing systematic research, there is no way to tell.

From its foundation in the work of William James, contextualism has relied heavily on utility or successful functioning in formulating its theory. This is portrayed as "goal attainment" or the kind of "steady state equilibrium" of well-adapted individuals and societies. But these goals and utilities are conceived rather narrowly for the particular context assessed. This week's goals may not be the same as next week's. In an every-changing world, who is to say what situations will present themselves? Change is the fundamental reality, but people impose order on it with the purpose of making living meaningful.

Among the leading twentieth century social scientists developing contextualistic theories we might list Malinowski, Bateson, and with special purity, Goffman. *Frame Analysis* (1974) represents Goffman's attempt to systematize the inherently mysterious processes of his own contextualistic research. Although these major theorists of contextualism do not consider children's peer relations, some ethnographic peer work in this genre has been reported (e.g., Cook-Gumperz, 1977; Corsaro, 1979).

The contextualist world theory underlies more research in the present volume than any other approach. Historically this peer work has often been couched as research on "play" rather than on peer relations per se. Why should this be? Perhaps for the contextualist the very idea of peer relations sounds rather formist and static. By contrast, play is something active, dynamic, and paradoxical, thus made to order for the contextualist.

Play is very much at the heart of Geertz's (1972) description of the socioemotional importance of the Balinese cockfight. Although the paper does not concern children, it surely does concern one aspect of peer relations. For Geertz the dramatic sports-like events surrounding the battle of two cocks is *deep play*. The term derives from the English philosopher Jeremy Bentham who noted that people engage in games where the stakes are so high that it is irrational to participate at all. In the size of their bets on the outcome, the participants seemingly are "in over their heads." Yet Geertz's thesis is that Bentham, at least in part, missed the point: that deep play, while irrational, serves a crucial cultural function. To understand this function one must know something about the rigid hierarchical caste-like social status system in Bali. Not only is social mobility nearly impossible, but the Balinese spend inordinate amounts of time in affirming these social arrangements "in a haze of etiquette, a thick cloud of euphemism and ceremony, gesture and allusion" (p. 673). In the cockfight, the cultural message is that status relations are matters of life and death. The fight is over only when the losing cock dies: "The slaughter of the cock is not a depiction of how things literally are among men, but, what is almost worse, of how, from a particular angle, they imaginatively are" (p. 673).

While the Balinese care about winning and losing money as much as anyone, Geertz argues that across many cockfights, the money evens out and actual status or social position never really changes. Thus a focus on the betting outcomes misses the more important function of the fight, which is the depiction of a ritual story the Balinese have created about the social arrangements of their own culture:

> As any art form—for that finally is what we are dealing with—the cockfight renders ordinary, everyday experience comprehensible by presenting it in terms of acts and objects which have had their practical consequences removed and been reduced (or, if you prefer, raised) to the level of sheer appearances, where their meaning can be more powerfully articulated and more exactly perceived (p. 670–671). . . . [The cockfight] is interpretive: it is a Balinese reading of Balinese experience; a story they tell themselves about themselves. (p. 674)

Here, clearly articulated, is the contextualist contribution to peer research. More than in any other metaphor, contextualists see peer relations as attempts to infuse human experience with meaning. Further than any other theory, they articulate how those meanings differ with culture and with age. While describing the Balinese view of life, Geertz also captures one quality of his own contextualist theory: "Their life as they arrange it and perceive it, is less a flow, a directional movement out of the past, through the present, toward the future than an on–off pulsation of meaning and vacuity" (p. 670). The same may be said of contextualism. While the ultimate direction or purpose of peer relations remains unknown, much can be said about its immediate goals and functions. No other theory expresses this appreciation of the role of meaning and purpose in peer relations—its shared quality and its cultural relativity—as clearly as does this one.

In this volume, contextualism has many advocates. Across the past decade Garvey has played a central role in developing the contextualist theory as applied to peer relations; she has done so with openness to the research of other approaches. Such openness to other views is almost a principle of contextualism. Pepper (1942) states this point:

> The categories [of contextualism] must be so framed as not to exclude from the world any degree of order it may be found to have . . . order being defined in any

way you please, *so long as it does not deny the possibility of disorder or another order in nature also.* (p. 234)

Such openness to divergent views of peer relations placed Garvey in a good position to discuss this volume (Chapter 13).

The chapters by Whiting (Chapter 4, this volume), and Forbes, Katz, and Paul (Chapter 10, this volume) provide a sampling of the new contextualistic contribution to peer research. Whiting adopts the metaphor of a theatrical production with a "cultural script," a "stage on which all relationships are played out," a "cast of characters," and the "activities in progress when a given interaction occurs." Forbes and his colleagues, adopting similar categories, have as their central thesis the idea that the various parts of the play become integrated and that this integration gives pretend play its crucial role in enculturation.

Whiting has at her disposal the largest, quantitatively most precise cross-cultural sample of children's social relations extant. When such data are found to support cross-cultural universals in family life, they seem especially convincing precisely because they are what the contextualist least expects. Yet Whiting finds that in all societies girls play a greater role than boys in the care of infants and toddlers. In addition, maternal communication style seems to be connected closely to maternal workload and family supports across all societies. The universal in this finding is the relationship itself rather than either the mother's workload or her communication styles. Such laws suggest a movement in Whiting's thought away from strict contextualism and toward theories more compatible with universals such as formism.

Forbes et al. focus on the traditional contextualist topic of children's play. Nearly all features of their chapter—the focus on shared meaning as the key feature of children's communication, the development of a detailed set of categories suggesting that a whole complex of variables can be understood in a dramaturgical conception, and the demonstration of their utility in detailed examples of actual play—are exceptionally pure contextualism.

Organicism in Peer Research

Of the universially acclaimed twentieth century social theorists, only one, Piaget, was deeply interested in childhood peer relations. And he was an organicist.

As in contextualism, the starting point here is a concern with organized complexes rather than on units or pieces. But the emphasis in organicism is on the discovery of fully integrated systems. Not since mechanism have we seen an approach so certain of the universal functioning of its categories.

At heart a rationalist (i.e., holding a belief in the power of mind and reason to understand all experience), the organicist not only thinks the world is made of integrated systems but can even tell us where each system is headed—its "absolute ideal," not that this state is ever achieved in actual biological or social systems. Newton's law of universal gravitation comprises merely one "stage" in our knowledge of the properties of matter and Einstein's theory is but a more exact approximation of the ideal. Like other world theories, organicistic theory has been applied to any and all progressions in culture (Levi–Strauss), in historical analysis (Hegel), and in child development and pathology (Werner).

In his peer work, Piaget's goal was to show the progressive stages in the development of the child's morality. As an organicist, Piaget was sure of his ideal developmental endpoint both for all societies and for all individuals: "The morality of good develops progressively and constitutes, in relation to society, a form of ideal equilibrium, as it were, which rises above the false and unstable equilibria which are based on constraint" (1965, p. 333). In arriving at his theory of moral development, Piaget begins with the theory of Emile Durkheim, the great French sociologist. Piaget accepted Durkheim's view that "the individual is unable of himself to create morality" (p. 370). But he could not accept Durkheim's attempt to turn society itself into an organism: "Not content with showing that *the main key to human psychology is to be found in social life,* Durkheim tries to make of society a whole, a being" (p. 360, italics added). For Piaget the solution rests instead in the organicist commitment to the study of relationships: "One may conceive of cooperation as constituting the ideal form of equilibrium to which society tends when compulsory conformity comes to break down . . . , although the movement between the two forms is continuous" (p. 346–347). For Piaget, the ideal of cooperation is achieved by the individual chiefly through the instrumentality of peer relations across childhood. The child moves from an early stage of morality based on duty to a later stage of morality based on cooperation. This change is effected because the child increasingly participates as an equal with peers. Here, understanding of the equalitarian nature of rules changes: "The good [comes to] constitute the law of perspective and the rule of reciprocity which aim at bringing about mutual understanding" (p. 352). Peer relations constitutes the central dynamic process by which children anywhere achieve a moral understanding based on reciprocity and equality.

The logic of Piaget's theory would imply that the sooner a child can establish peer relations, the sooner he or she can establish a cooperative morality. Yet Piaget believed that there were cognitive limitations in the young children (egocentrism) that set strict lower limits on intellectual cooperation with others. Is the Piagetian concept of egocentrism compatible with the frequent demonstration of infant and toddler communication in the 1970s? Musatti (Chapter 2, this volume) answers this question in the affirmative. First she notes that Piaget's revised thinking on the nature of egocentrism is not even included in some commonly cited editions of *The Language and Thought of the Child.* Any serious student of egocentrism should read Piaget's revised view included as Chapter 6 of the third edition of this book (1959). Using this source, Musatti stresses that egocentrism in no way precludes early childhood sociability. Indeed Piaget himself appreciated the role of peers in overcoming egocentrism *even in the preoperational* (preschool) *period.* Musatti's synthesis of the Piagetian theory with the relatively atheoretical recent literature on early peer relations should be read carefully by anyone seeking to understand the relations between Piaget's theory of early cognitive growth and the actual interactions that occur among young children. There is no comparably developed organismic integration of early peer research elsewhere in the modern literature.

Musatti considers the organismic perspective more fully than do the authors of other chapters in this volume. However, the work presented by both Ellis and Rogoff (Chapter 12, this volume) and Mueller and Cohen (Chapter 7, this volume) may be treated here as well. Both chapters reflect an organismic perspective.

Ellis and Rogoff find that adults are much more effective in teaching classification problems to 8- or 9-year-old children than are their peers. While the authors' goal is chiefly a detailed description of the quality of child–child communication, their interpretation of their results is couched in organicism. Specifically, they find that children of these ages are unable to coordinate the demands of the social–instructional task itself with the equally demanding requirements of the classification task. This stress on communication skill as a gradual integration or coordination of previously separate skills is very much an organicist approach to peer process. Indeed, we might see the progressive construction of more elaborate and better coordinated schemas as the hallmark of organicism when applied to descriptions of process in peer relations.

Mueller and Cohen describe approaches to psychotherapy with elementary school children utilizing peer relations. Most of the work described, as well as Mueller's and Cohen's own proposal for a "little latency," is couched in psychoanalytic theory. Thus the problem of understanding the underlying approach of their chapter is the same as classifying psychoanalytic theory. This is difficult because Freud was such an eclectic theorist. While the point cannot be developed here, surely there is mechanism, organicism, and formism in his thought. As an organicist, Freud stressed the general "stage boundedness" of development and the differentiation of ego and superego from libido. His stages emphasized the waxing and waning of the child's emotional security as family attachments grew and changed. This belief in alternating periods of emotional equilibrium and conflict within the family is an organicist viewpoint and is precisely the one Mueller and Cohen seek to extend to the toddler period. Freud's "anal stage" concerned this same period in development, but had a mechanistic flavor. Mueller and Cohen examine this period within an organicist framework, one that Freud stressed more heavily only for the older stages in his age series. According to Mueller and Cohen, it is the equilibrium of the initial attachment that frees the child for the autonomy striving and peer friendships of the "little latency."

Eclecticism

Given four approaches to peer research, why not combine them? At first glance Pepper simply opposed electicism in building research and theory. He put the matter bluntly: "Eclecticism is confusing" (p. 104).

In understanding Pepper's stance, it is useful to see his (1942) work itself as part formist and part contextualist. On his formist side, he holds that the four world theories are so naturally distinct that one's thinking must inevitably get muddled when combining them: "There are an infinity of ways of garbling a theory, but only a few . . . of stating it . . . adequately" (p. 340). World theories, he continues: "just naturally seek out their own distinct lines of . . . corroboration, gathering their categories together into distinct clusters which reject one another [i.e., across theories] . . . that is the only way to keep our thinking and the interrelations of our evidence clear" (1942, p. 341). There is little doubt but that Pepper's formist side prevailed in the 1942 volume. His call for "eclecticism in practice" in the same volume is simply his understanding that a balanced view of the knowledge on any subject requires that we examine it from all four perspectives. Yet given his nondogmatic approach, one can ask if he has carried his contextualist thought far enough in forming his views on the possible interrelatedness of the world theories. Perhaps his analytic–synthetic, integrative–dispersive categories forced a "four-cell table" view of the world theories upon him when the truth is otherwise. Perhaps the rapid growth of computers has forged new root metaphors half way between machines and organisms. Whatever the current reality, one's stance toward eclecticism itself is probably related to one's own world theory, with formists acting conservatively, not wishing to change the historically clear and well-developed theories, and contextualists ever ready to embrace eclectic combinations.

In this volume, the chapters by Stamback and Verba (Chapter 9) and by

Cooper, Marquis, and Edward (Chapter 11) can be viewed as the clearest instances of eclecticism. As might have been expected, contextualism plays a major role in both chapters. Yet in each case, there is a second theory that receives nearly equal weight.

Stambak and Verba base their approach on the contextualist ideas of children's proposals, interactions, and shared meanings. Social roles are also emphasized, as seen in role taking and role complementarity. Organicist themes play an important secondary part in this work, as seen in the stress on toddlers' interactive construction of peer play. The mechanist approach is evidenced by the interest in specifying the effects of particular physical objects in stimulating particular activities and in eliciting peer responses. (Formist themes are not apparent).

Cooper, Marquis, and Edward also base their work on contextualist ideas, as they emphasize the meaningful resources offered by the network of children's peer relationships and view students as having learning goals and purposes. The secondary world theory used in this research is formistic, as seen in the research goal of discovering the natural classes of peer learning interactions, such as teacher–learner, collaborative, etc., and the use of sociometric designations such as best work friend and best play friend. A mechanistic focus on efficient cause is evidenced in the interest in the power of directives and questions in eliciting effective performance on a standardized cognitive task. Yet Cooper and her colleagues also predict the utility of organicist ideas when they acknowledge the importance of studying the coordination and integration of viewpoints in peer communication. Like several other authors in the volume, the chapters by Stambak and Verba, and Cooper et al. indicate that some cycling through the world theories may reflect a scholars' progress in long-term reseach on the issues of peer relationships.

Comparing the Four Approaches

Having outlined the four approaches, and the eclectic combinations, we can offer a solution to the problem of the definition of peer relations introduced earlier. The world hypotheses view is that there are four equally useful definitions of peer relations, one stemming from the basic categories of each world theory. Of course there is no *one* way to write each of these definitions. For example, some mechanists would only recognize environmental elicitors of behavior while others recognize only neuro-physiological elicitors. Yet the point remains that only a definition of peers compatible with peer process in terms of efficient and material cause would be acceptable to them.

- For *formists,* the problem of definition is insoluble until one is sure that peer relations are in fact a natural and distinct category different from other types of relationships. If personality types exist, then perhaps peer relations types could also exist, for example the aggressive child with a submissive child, or a younger precocious child with an older less advanced child.
- For *mechanists,* peer relations are sequences of response elicitation among agemates. Among the causes of peer relations are stimulus factors, and internal states of each participant.
- For *contextualists,* peer relations are whatever a given culture thinks they are. Like all aspects of culture, they will be analyzed as indicative of the shared beliefs and purposes useful to a given culture at a given time.
- For *organicists,* peer relations are those social relationships which aid children or adults in jointly developing the ideals of personal cooperative moralities and democratic social institutions. The relative ages of the participants are wholly irrelevant.

No further amalgamation of definition is possible because the four theories derive from different root metaphors, focusing on different aspects of our common experience.

The studies in this volume attempt to relate peer processes to the outcomes of participation in peer relations. While all world theories must deal with both process and outcome, they do not emphasize both equally. It appears, in fact, that each world theory involves significant imbalance, some emphasizing process and others outcome. This imbalance is depicted in Table 1.2 with arrows pointing toward the emphasized aspect of a given theory. In mechanism, outcomes are simply the irreversible result of long series of particular peer interactions, which are themselves, in turn, influenced by the drive states of participants. In this sense, outcome is completely subordinated to process in mechanism.

The same subordination of outcome to process occurs in contextualism but for different reasons. The focus here is on how people achieve their goals and purposes. Such purposes are never knowable in any ultimate sense. Instead, they are always contingent on particular historical and cultural contexts or situations. Thus little can be said about outcomes that is not already implicit in immediate purposes. The goal of peer relations then is the purpose implicit in a child saying to her friend "Let's play Uno!" The outcome is implicit right inside the act.

In organicism the emphasis is on outcomes. In describing the stages of development, the organicist is describing optimal or ideal structures in a progression that itself moves towards always more complete differentiation

Table 1.2

The Relation of Process and Outcome in Each of the Four World Theories

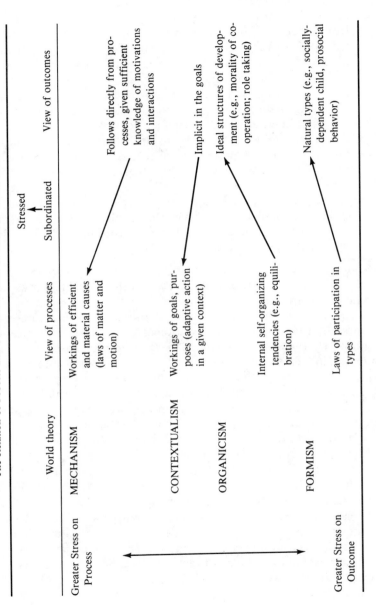

World theory	View of processes		View of outcomes
		Stressed ← Subordinated	
Greater Stress on Process	MECHANISM	Workings of efficient and material causes (laws of matter and motion)	Follows directly from processes, given sufficient knowledge of motivations and interactions
	CONTEXTUALISM	Workings of goals, purposes (adaptive action in a given context)	Implicit in the goals
	ORGANICISM	Internal self-organizing tendencies (e.g., equilibration)	Ideal structures of development (e.g., morality of co-operation; role taking)
Greater Stress on Outcome	FORMISM	Laws of participation in types	Natural types (e.g., socially-dependent child, prosocial behavior)

and integration. It is these structures about which the organicist is the most definite. While processes are considered, they are depicted rather abstractly (e.g., equilibration, assimilation) and always in the service of building a structure (like the morality of cooperation) that is both specified in advance and universally applicable.

Like organists, formists are the more definite about outcomes in the natural order of things, as natural types, than they are about processes. Pepper suggests that in this world theory process reduces to "participation in" the natural types. For example, in explaining why one child stays apart from others on the playground, it is enough to say that this child participates in the essence of being a "socially withdrawn personality type." It is the typology therefore that ultimately matters because process boils down to classifying cases as exemplars of this or that natural type.

Note that if each world hypothesis is as imbalanced between process and outcome as Table 1.2 suggests, then the pressure for eclecticism becomes very strong indeed. It is almost irresistible to select one's outcomes from organicism or formism and one's processes from contextualism or mechanism. A researcher, for example, might describe mechanistic helping interaction processes that explain the growth of a cooperative morality. Pepper (1942), as we have seen, opposes such combinations on the grounds of intellectual clarity. Whatever this particular researcher may mean by a "morality of cooperation," the term takes its meaning from a metaphor that focuses on the internal self-organizing processes within the child rather than one stressing interactional contingencies as determinative.

Summary

In the preceding sections, we have attempted to orient the reader toward the peer literature, both as it is expressed in this volume as well as in past work. Our thesis has been that to be a fully educated student of peer relations requires considerable cognitive and epistemological training. Like the juggler who can keep four balls in the air at once, the student of peer relations is asked to acquire four keys, because our knowledge of peer relations is kept in four different closets.

In conclusion, recall that Pepper's (1942) argument against eclecticism extends only to the conduct of research and to theory building. When our research is complete and we come together as peers to share our views regarding the progress made, we must "seek on the matter in question, the judgment supplied from each of these relatively adequate world theories" (p. 330). Then:

Having done all that we can do rationally to organize the evidence . . . , and finding as a rule that there are four equally justifiable hypotheses explaining the nature of the subject, we shall have the wisdom not to conclude that we know nothing about the topic, but, on the contrary, that we have four alternative theories about it, which supply us with a great deal more information than any one of them alone could have done. (p. 331)

This we believe is the state of our knowledge of peer relations. Let's open the closets.

References

Blurton Jones, N. (1972). *Ethological studies of child behavior.* New York: Cambridge University Press.

Boring, E. (1950). *A history of experimental psychology* (2nd ed.). New York: Appleton Century Crofts.

Bühler, C. (1927). Die ersten sozialen (Verhaltungsweisen des Kindes. [The first social relationships among children.] In C. Bühler, H. Hetzer & B. Tudor-Hart (Eds.), *Soziologische und psychologische Studien uber das erste Lebensjahr.* Jena: Gustav Fischer.

Bühler C. (1933). The social behavior of children. In C. Murchison (Ed.), *Handbook of child psychology* (2nd ed.). Worcester, MA: Clark University Press.

Cook-Gumperz, J. (1977). Situated instructions: Language socialization of school age children. In S. Ervin-Tripp & C. Mitchell-Kernan (Eds.), *Child discourse.* New York: Academic Press.

Corsaro, W. A. (1979). "We're friends, right?": Children's use of access rituals in a nursery school. *Language in Society, 8,* 315–336.

Furman, W., Rahe, D. F., & Hartup, W. W. (1979). Rehabilitation of socially-withdrawn preschool children through mixed-age and same-age socialization. *Child Development, 50,* 915–922.

Gardner, H. (1979). Encounter at Royaumont. *Psychology Today, 13*(2), 14–17.

Geertz, C. (1976). Deep play: A description of the Balinese cockfight. In J. Bruner, A. Jolly & J. Sylva (Eds.), *Play: Its role in development and evolution.* New York: Basic Books. (Original work published in *Daedalus,* 1972, *101,* 1–37)

Goffman, E. (1974). *Frame analysis.* New York: Harper & Row.

McGrew, W. C. (1972). *An ethological study of children's behavior.* New York: Academic Press.

Mueller, E. (1972). The maintenance of verbal exchanges between young children. *Child Development, 43,* 930–938.

Pepper, S. P. (1942). *World hypotheses.* Berkeley: University of California Press.

Piaget, J. (1959). *The language and thought of the child* (3rd ed.). London: Routledge & Kagan. (Original work published in 1923)

Piaget, J. (1965). *The moral judgment of the child.* New York: The Free Press. (Original work published in 1932)

Sylva, K., Ray, C., & Painter, M. (1980). *Childwatching at playgroup and nursery school.* Ypsilanti, MI: High/Scope.

Vandell, A. L. & Wilson, K. S. (1982). Social interaction in the first year: Infant's social skills with peers versus mother. In K. H. Rubin and H. S. Ross (Eds.), *Peer relationships and social skills in childhood.* New York: Springer-Verlag.

CHAPTER 2

Early Peer Relations: The Perspectives of Piaget and Vygotsky

Tullia Musatti

Introduction

The integration of the study of children's social behavior with other aspects of their behavior seems to be an ongoing process. Since the 1930s, the most relevant theories in developmental psychology have been formulated in terms of this perspective. Both Vygotsky (1931/1960) and Piaget (1936/1954) stressed that children learn and develop their thinking processes by interacting with both objects and people. Until recently, however, developmental psychology has been characterized mainly by separate studies of children's behavior related to persons (social behavior) and objects (cognitive performance).

In developmental cognitive psychology, there is a large-scale convergence of researchers from different theoretical and methodological backgrounds who are trying not so much to identify stages of development as to focus on the developmental process itself. As expressed by El'konin (1972), this focus on the process of development must include a unitary perspective of the two processes of children's interaction with both objects and persons. Current research claims that the environmental and social context in which children's cognitive performance occurs should be considered a relevant variable of performance itself rather than an independent factor. The gap between the study of communicative and social aspects of children's behavior and its cognitive structure thus seems to be narrowing.

Likewise, studies of children's social behavior and relations are being progressively integrated with the study of the cognitive skills inherent in social behavior. Thus, a developmental social cognition, with its own specific theories and methodologies, is emerging. The study of how children come to know other persons and their behavior is also being extended to infants. Sherrod and Lamb (1981) assert that research into infants' social behavior must include the study of cognitive aspects. Also studies of social cognitive development are mostly focused on the origin and nature of developmental changes, rather than just on the sequence of developmental acquisitions. Damon (1981) stressed the need to combine the study of children's ability to understand social experience with the study of their thinking during actual social interaction. According to Damon, it is important to study both how social interaction affects the acquisition of knowledge and how the acquisition of knowledge is involved in social interaction.

Flavell and Ross (1981) warned about the dangers of bringing the almost exclusively cognitive emphasis of current social psychology into developmental research. They envisaged the danger of reducing the fields of *feeling* and *acting* to *thinking* alone (the traditional cognitive–conative–affective trinity). This danger exists for the developmental social psychologist attempting a unitary approach to the study of behavior, and the dangers for the developmental cognitive psychologist are just as great. In fact, in studying children's cognitive performance during socialization, there is a great risk of losing sight of both the trends and the meaning of the developmental process. Many of these difficulties could be avoided if the theoretical and methodological problems peculiar to the study of social behavior and cognitive development could be considered in terms of a general theory of child development and if, within this theory, both developmental processes could be explained as well.

The study of early peer relations involves all these problems in an even more dramatic form. First, do peer relations form part of a general system of the child's socialization with which they share adaptive processes and developmental sequences? Or do they form a subsystem of social relations separate from the process of the child's socialization in the world of adults? In this case, how do early peer relations interact with the development of these other social relations? During the first years of life, children not only accumulate knowledge concerning the physical and social world, but they also acquire cognitive structures and processes. Is this process of both *knowing what* and *knowing how* shared by both physical and social knowledge, or is the latter processed in different ways and in different periods? What is the role played by early peer relations in this process?

The close relation between the various aspects of the child's behavior and developmental process during the first years of life calls for a functional approach in the treatment of these questions. As Lewis, Young, Brooks, and Michalson (1975) have pointed out, the study of the functional aspects of early peer relations is essential in order to explore their role in the process of acquiring social skills. To an even greater extent, a functional approach to the study of the relationship between early peer relations and cognitive processes is essential for understanding the role of the social relations in the development of cognitive processes in infancy and toddlerhood. The present work is an attempt to contribute to the definition of such an approach by examining results of current research on early peer relations within the framework of Piaget's and Vygotsky's theories of children's cognitive development.

Early Studies of Peer Relations in Infancy

The study of the relationship between early peer relations and cognitive development in infancy and toddlerhood is a comparatively unexplored field, fraught with both theoretical and methodological hazards of historical and theoretical origin. Until recently, it was rare for infants and toddlers to be observed with peers. There was not much occasion for them to meet, and any meetings took place mostly in environments such as orphanages or welfare institutions, which were generally organized to discourage any effective and prolonged peer contact.

For decades, developmental psychology considered peer relations mainly as an index of the development of certain aspects of social behavior. During adolescence, peers were considered as possibly triggering aggressive factors or stimulating certain aspects of sexual development. But for infants or toddlers, the question was even more basic: Can peer contact stimulate any aspect of social behavior and, if so, which ones? This question was raised in the first pilot studies in the 1930s and again in the last decade, after the problem had fallen into oblivion for nearly 40 years. Research on early peer relations was for many years thought a battlefield concerned with whether a battle actually existed, that is, whether peers are a factor of stimulation in children's behavior. The battle to define which behaviors are stimulated by peers has only just begun.

Early studies on peer relations (Bridges, 1933; Buhler, 1931) were deeply influenced by Gesell's theory of development (Mueller, 1978). According to Gesell, unity among various aspects of behavior is inherent in the maturational process. Thus, no attempt was made in these early studies to consider the relationship between the development of social behavior with peers and other aspects of development. Such a viewpoint also explains why in these earlier investigations, as in many recent ones based on them, the study of early peer relations consists of studying the child's capacity to form relations and interact with another child rather than examining whether and how these peer-directed social behaviors were organized into actual social relations. It is not surprising that the only research from this perspective arose out of the meeting between a historically and tragically dated social experience (World War II) and psychoanalysis. Anna Freud (Burlingham & Freud, 1965; Freud & Dann, 1951) twice considered if and how the group upbringing of children without their parents can adequately substitute for certain functions of parent–child relations. This was perhaps the first time that social behavior with peers was studied as the development of actual social relations and the problems of their effect on children's development. Subsequently, however, these points were not incorporated in any actual developmental theory, even by workers following the same psychoanalytical approach.

Theoretical reasons are also evident in the delays and difficulties in focusing attention on the relationship between cognitive development and early peer relations. For a long time, developmental psychologists' basic disregard for the cognitive processes in early infancy was offset only by Piaget's observational studies (1936/1954; 1937/1954; 1945/1962). Piaget's work also represents the theoretical framework for much recent research on early cognitive development both in Europe (Sinclair, Stambak, Lezine, Rayna, & Verba, 1982) and the United States (Uzgiris, 1973). Together with work on developmental psycholinguistics, these studies have shown the *knowing* nature of the young child, whose interactions with the world are expressed in elementary behavioral patterns but reflect fairly complex mental operations. What relationship exists between social and cognitive aspects of infants' and toddlers' development? The social basis of language acquisition has been extensively treated by developmental psycholinguistics (Bates, 1982). More general questions can also be raised. What cognitive processes are involved in social interaction? How does social interaction affect cognitive processes, and how is it affected by cognitive development? Are the relationships between social interaction and cognitive processes different when the child interacts with different partners, such as adults or peers? Both Vygotsky's and Piaget's works provide some answers to these questions and integrating their analyses in a unitary perspective can be an appealing challenge.

Piaget's Conception of Egocentrism

Piaget's position on the relationship between social interaction and interaction with objects is closely connected with his conception of egocentrism and the controversy related to it. The concept of egocentrism was first formulated by Piaget in 1923 and has had mixed success in the studies on preschool children's interaction and, more generally, on the relationship among cognition, language, and social interaction. The controversy over this concept is part of the unrecorded history of psychological research. Its implications for the analysis of verbal interaction between preschoolers have been redefined in several studies (Garvey & Hogan, 1973; Mueller, 1972). The study of the relationship among cognition, language, and social interaction has mostly taken other directions. Nevertheless, a fresh analysis of this notion in Piaget's work is necessary to point out what hypotheses concerning the role of early peer relations in cognitive development in infancy and toddlerhood can be advanced within the framework of Piaget's work.

Piaget made several references to Bühler's studies. Being a thorough and up-to-date reader of the literature on child psychology, Piaget revealed on more than one occasion that he immediately used and appreciated precisely those results that Buhler had obtained on early peer-directed behavior. Piaget's early studies on children's thinking (1923/1959, 1924) were also read and appreciated by contemporary researchers on children's social behavior. We must thank Bridges (1933) for one of the best definitions of the Piagetian notion of egocentrism and its implications for the study of early social behavior. She noted that Piaget (1923/1959) observed that although the language of young children is largely "egocentric" in form and reference and that speech becomes more "socialized" with advancing years, social communication with voice and gesture occurs before any skills in the use of articulated language (Bridges, 1933). Bridges thus stressed that the term "egocentrism" refers to a phenomenon of language use in communication and is situated in a definite period of cognitive development. In fact, in Piaget's formulation, verbal egocentrism, corresponds to a certain relationship between cognition, as actual ability to know the world, and verbal communication, as displayed during certain times in certain activities by preschool children. During certain activities and with certain partners, preschool children describe their own activities or express opinions in ways that are not purposefully directed towards information exchange with their partners. Thus, the egocentric child is not incapable of adapting his or her speech to the listener, since only part of his or her utterances are egocentric, and then only at certain times. Since verbal egocentrism is a "functional" phenomenon that depends both on the child's stage of cognitive development and on the environment in which it is displayed, it is not possible to obtain any measure of the child's cognitive egocentrism from his/her egocentric verbal production. If this is Piaget's definition of egocentrism, why was there so much subsequent controversy over this concept, and why did its discussion include wider issues involving a social psychology of the child, or, as Piaget (1963) preferred to call it, a "psycho-sociology" of the child? On several occasions Piaget expressed deep regret in having chosen the term egocentrism (Piaget, 1945/1962; Piaget, 1951; Piaget & Inhelder, 1966/1969); most of a new chapter added to the third French edition (1945) of

"Language and thought of the child" (the present Chapter 6 of the English translation[1]) is devoted to clarifying the implications of this term in the child's verbal, intellectual, and social development. Actually, egocentrism is a cognitive phenomenon typical of preschool thought and is not involved only in the use of language for communication (verbal egocentrism). It is also noted in social (social egocentrism) and intellectual interactions (logical egocentrism). Egocentrism corresponds to a specific relationship between the structure and the functioning of the child's knowledge and the world of things and persons. Social egocentrism is thus only a special case of cognitive egocentrism, not its determinant nor its consequence. The child's sociability before, during, and after the egocentric period was thus not questioned by Piaget. In answer to Buhler, who rejected the notion of egocentrism, Piaget insisted that, to the extent to which this notion denotes an epistemic confusion between subject and object, egocentrism and the feeling of community (or sociability) in the child are so consonant that they often correspond to the same phenomenon (1923, 3rd ed./1959).

The Piagetian child constructs his or her cognitive structures through interaction with the social world although these cognitive structures change during development. In the egocentric period, they result from an unbalanced relationship between individual knowledge and socially shared knowledge. During the egocentric period, the child's subjective point of view emerges both in the interaction of his/her own actions or mental operations with those of others and in his/her cognitive operations on social relations. Piaget wrote that children confuse their own egos with their representation of others as well as with that of physical objects (1923, 3rd ed./1959). So, to use more recent terminology, egocentrism could be said to be involved both with aspects of social cognition and aspects of social understanding. In both aspects of the developmental process of acquiring knowledge and socialization, Piaget viewed egocentrism as corresponding to an intermediate stage. The egocentric child is still a "presocial" child (Piaget, 1932/1962) precisely in the sense that he or she is incapable of mastering cognitive abilities in interaction with others, that is, of socializing his or her operations. Conversely, in another sense, the pre-egocentric child is a highly social child, making no basic distinction between individual and social cognitive processes. Thus, a discussion on egocentrism involves basic issues related to the development of mastery over knowledge (or, to use

[1]This chapter, entitled "The measure of ego-centric language in verbal communication between the adult and the child and in verbal exchanges between children," was written in collaboration with Mme A. Leuzinger–Schuler. It does not seem to be reported in most of the English versions of the book, that are still based on its 2nd. edition. The English version published by Routledge and Kegan in 1959 is based on the 3rd edition of 1945 (revised and enlarged) and reports the new chapter as Chapter 7.

Piagetian terms, of the grasp of consciousness of one's own knowing activity), as well as to the development of the socialization process.

Egocentrism and Cooperation in Peer Interaction

As Sinclair has pointed out (1981), two main statements in Piaget's work concerning the relationship between the child's language and thought are original and pave the way for important subsequent research. The first has already been discussed, that is, analyzing the function of verbal utterances in social interaction. The other, according to Piaget, is that the egocentric dimension of thought is a functional phenomenon, since it is displayed to a different degree in the process of socialization between adult and child than between peers. The social relation between adult and child is quite different from that established between peers, and this difference is reflected in both the quality and the quantity of egocentrism as well as in the child's social development as a whole (Piaget, 1923/1959).

The relationship between adult and child is characterized by unequal power and knowledge. The child feels dominated by a superior mental organization that totally understands him or her. In interactions with adults, children experience greater difficulty in recognizing the differences between their own cognitive activity and that of others. They are less stimulated to clarify their own points-of-view by comparing them with those of others, because the adults' views dominate. On the contrary, the peer relationship is characterized by cognitive and power equality. Peer interaction is more likely to involve verifying and comparing points of view and, therefore, stimulates the attainment of cooperation. The interrelation between cognitive acts and social reciprocity and the overcoming of egocentrism is the very essence of the process of socialization with peers (Piaget, 1923, 3rd ed./1959). Peers thus stimulate the socialization of knowledge because in peer interaction the grasp of consciousness of the mechanisms operating in interpersonal cooperation is elicited. This function of stimulation is inherent in the equality between peers, although it can be adequately given also in adult-child interaction, when an adult displays a nonauthoritarian attitude towards the child. The quality of the peer relation thus affects the actual dimension and duration of egocentrism.

Piaget's and Vygotsky's Perspectives: Some Questions about Peer Interaction

Vygotsky's criticism (1934/1962) of Piaget's interpretation of verbal egocentrism is well known. Piaget (1962), replying to Vygotsky, expressed regret about having to answer the criticism of a dead colleague, which was, in any case, based solely on a first version of his notion of egocentrism. Piaget (1962) pointed out that his real concern was with a point never addressed by Vygotsky—the understanding of individual and interpersonal cooperation mechanisms, that is, the way in which activities performed by a single child or by different children are coordinated and organized during development. Unfortunately, Piaget, was able only to read Vygotsky's *Thought and language* and not the essays that describe in detail (again in disagreement with Piaget) the role of education and learning in mental development (Vygotsky, 1934/1972; 1978). Direct discussion between the two authors would certainly have been illuminating since both touched upon two important, although different, points in the relationship between the social and cognitive aspects of development: Piaget meant to describe the mechanisms of actual interaction among the cognitive performance of several subjects; Vygotsky stressed that historically determined human culture becomes the very driving force of development via the educational process.

According to Vygotsky (1931/1960), individuals produced systems of complex psychological relations (i.e., signs) in the course of social interactions. These signs mediate both interpersonal and individual processes. As children acquire systems of signs by social interaction (education), they become able to control their own thinking and assign new meanings to their own behavior. Thus Vygotsky (1931/1960) asserted that social interaction deeply affects development, since it provides children with systems of signs and cultural meanings.

Investigating the role of peers in the developmental process raises interesting but different questions from both Piaget's and Vygotsky's perspectives. Piaget points out how peer interaction stimulates the overcoming of egocentrism in the preoperational period. Egocentrism is situated midway between a state of confusion over the subject's individual and social self and the child's consciousness of the relations that exist between him or herself, both as a social and as a knowing subject. Egocentrism results from the relationship between a certain type of social interaction and the cognitive processes in the preoperational period. The quality of the child's relationships, in particular the condition of equality with peers, affects the actual dimension and duration of egocentrism. From this Piagetian perspective, what is the role of peer interaction in earlier periods of development? In Vygotsky's work, the role of adult as an educator, providing the child with the cultural means of knowledge, seems to emerge clearly. Vygotsky does not appear to have been specifically concerned with the role of peer interaction in the child's developmental and educational process. Nevertheless, investigating the role of peers from Vygotsky's perspective can raise a new and interesting question: What is the role of a peer in a child's acquisition of the cultural means of knowledge?

Sensorimotor Intelligence and the Process of Socialization

From birth until the child is capable of intellectual cooperation with others, the developmental process is long and complex. Human intelligence is influenced by social life from the first day of life to the last (Piaget, 1951), although different socialization processes correspond to different levels of intelligence. At the sensorimotor level, socialization consists of the interdependence of the child's activities with those of others. A basic step in development consists of the acquisition of representational abilities by which the child can recall persons and objects in their absence (Piaget & Inhelder, 1966/1969) as well as acquire a system of interpersonal signs. Thus the child can share a system of meanings that will permit concepts to be elaborated upon during social interaction (Piaget, 1945/1962). The interrelation between the acquisition of representational abilities and the process of socialization is one of the most relevant and unexplored areas in child psychology. The acquisition of representational abilities is a slow developmental process that occurs in the second year of life and can be viewed as the most relevant result of early cognitive development. From birth, children increasingly organize their cognitive activity by means of sensorimotor schemes (Piaget, 1936/1954). Two basic developmental processes can be identified in the sensorimotor period: the increasing coordination of schemes by their differentiation and integration, and the increasing number of intermediaries between the stimulus of the child's action and its result (primary, secondary, tertiary circular action). The representational act results from the developmental synthesis of these two processes. Through it, the actual knowledge is coordinated with that of the past and future, and intermediary means (signs, symbols or images) can be the actual stimuli of the action. The first evidence of the acquisition of representational abilities is seen in the child's symbolic play, deferred imitation, and use of language (Piaget, 1945/1962). The acquisition of representational abilities marks the attainment of sensori-motor intelligence and the transition to operational thought. Recent research has provided new evidence of these developmental processes in the first years of life both in the child's systematic exploration of relations between objects, (Sinclair et al., 1982) and in the child's play (Bates, Benigni, Bretherton, Camaioni, & Volterra, 1979; Inhelder, Lezine, Sinclair, & Stambak, 1972; Fenson, Kagan, Kearsley, & Zelazo, 1976; Largo & Howard, 1979; Nicolich, 1977; Watson & Fischer, 1977).

Piaget (1945/1962) identified both a *structural heterogeneity* and a *functional continuity* between sensorimotor thinking and operational thinking. The differences in the child's cognitive acts during the sensorimotor and the representational periods correspond to four functional conditions that mark the transition from one period to another:

F-1. A general acceleration of actions that provides the child with the ability to merge single actions into a whole and to have anticipatory drafts of it.

F-2. Awareness and consciousness of ongoing operations that permit the replacement of practical success with observation and explanation.

F-3. Acquisition of a system of signs that allows the construction of general concepts.

F-4. The socialization that accompanies the use of a system of signs to integrate individual thinking in shared and objective reality.

These four functional conditions correspond to two developmental processes; (1) conditions F.1 and F.2 relate to the achievement of a system of mobile reversible mental operations, and (2) conditions F.3 and F.4 pertain to the process of interpersonal coordination of mental operations. Piaget stresses that these two processes, one referring to intraindividual cognitive organization, and the other to interpersonal cognitive organization, are interdependent. Cooperation elicits judgments by the child, while the development of general concepts elicits the interpersonal coordination of the operations. Thus the child's search for truth, which represents the stimulus and aim of the cognitive process at the operational level, and the socialization of thought are linked (Piaget, 1936/1954).

Research on the relationship between social relations and cognitive development in infancy and toddlerhood may find a theoretical framework in this Piagetian perspective. We may ask whether the developmental trends identified by Piaget during the sensorimotor period can be identified also in peer relations. Furthermore, the relationships among the various transitional conditions to the operational period and different social relations can be different. We may then ask what conditions are more closely connected with peer relations. It is our view that recent research on early peer social relations has provided some answers to these questions.

Play, Representational Abilities, and the Process of Socialization among Peers

The relationship between the development of play and the development of representational abilities was supported theoretically by both Piaget (1945/1962) and Vygotsky (1933/1967), although with differences in interpretation. Both authors identified some fundamental aspects in children's play: (1) in play children exercise the ability to master things and persons cognitively since their activity is performed for its own sake and is outside the appropriate context; (2) in play children express their subjective points-of-view of the world and, therefore; (3) the expression of affect is an essential part of play.

The acquisition of representational abilities, that is, the capacity to reproduce an activity out of context and attribute a new meaning to it, is inherent in the development of play and transforms it from sensorimotor to symbolic in character. However, the meanings stemming from play behavior seem to be of a particular sort. In fact, the meanings attributed by children to their play activities are subjective (Piaget, 1945/1962) and related to the expression of intimate (Piaget, 1945/1962), although generalized (Vygotsky, 1933/1967) affect. Piaget (1963) noted that symbolic play and egocentrism in the preschool child seem to be closely related. Just as egocentric children express a subjective point of view in social interaction, so in symbolic play they express their personal concerns. Piaget (1963) also suggested that just as peer interaction reduces the degree of egocentrism, symbolic play with peers probably facilitates the overcoming of the more subjective features of the child's play activity. According to Piaget (1963), socialization both of affect and of symbolic thought seem to be involved in symbolic play since children must share a system meaning. From this perspective, research on play between toddlers is of special relevance for understanding the relationship between the acquisition of representational abilities and the process of socialization with peers.

According to Vygotsky (1933/1967) play creates a zone of proximal development, that is, stimulates the child's overcoming of cognitive limitations. Thus, play seems to affect the child's development even more than education. In fact, in play children become conscious both of their own actions and of the meanings of objects. From this perspective, research on play between peers seems crucial for understanding the role of peers in the child's development.

Peer-Directed Behavior and Cognitive Processes in Infancy and Toddlerhood

Whether early peer-directed behavior is social and when such behavior is first produced were explored in the first studies in the 1930s. Buhler (1931) stressed the need to distinguish between social behavior as a response to a person perceived as such, and behavior aimed at attracting a person's attention. Smiling, which Buhler considered to be the most elementary social behavior, is produced by children younger than 6 months in response to the adult. Eventually, the child who meets the gaze of a peer may also react by smiling, but usually only a 6-month-old child can attract a peer's attention. Bridges (1933) made similar distinctions in her description of early social behavior, but reported these behaviors as occurring earlier. According to both authors, the following behaviors occur at successive developmental stages: awareness of the peer's presence, or attention to the peer, which corresponds to an ability to recognize the peer's behavior as a specific stimulus; exhibition of even elementary social behavior in response to such behavior by the peer, which corresponds to the ability to select a response appropriate to the received stimulus; and active solicitation of the partner's attention, which corresponds to the ability to produce a behavior appropriate to the social nature of the object it is directed to.

In more recent research, only a few studies have involved peer-directed behavior in early infancy. However, the pattern described by both Buhler (1931) and Bridges (1933) does not seem to have been confirmed. In a study that stimulated a series of studies on early peer social behavior and interaction, Vincze (1971) stressed that awareness of the peer's presence, as deduced from the intense gazes directed to him by the 2- to 3-month-old child, is closely related to the peer's availability. In fact, reciprocal position plays a crucial role in the 2- to 3-month-old child's ability to focus attention on a peer. Dubon, Josse, & Lezine (1981) have found not only peer-directed gazing, but actual eye captures (accrochages) in 2- to 3-month-old infants facing each other. At the same age, these investigators claim that peer gazing could also be accompanied by gross motor behavior (peer-directed body rigidity) or by facial expressions or attracting mimicry (raise eyebrows, chin jutting forward, mouth open) and possibly smiling. In these cases, the child's intention of directing behavior to the peer is more evident. However, neither gazing, smiling, nor other expressive elements can strictly be considered as indicative of the child's recognition of the peer as a social agent. It is the mutuality of these behaviors that indicates social intention to the observer and actually reinforces it in the child. Mutual smiling and gazing have been found between 3- to 4-month-old infants by Dubon et al. (1981) and in 6-month-olds by Vincze (1971).

The intentionality of peer-directed behavior is more clearly evident in the single child's behavior when it results from the coordination of a motor or verbal act with a look directed to the peer (Mueller & Lucas, 1975). Mueller and Brenner (1977) provided the nomenclature of early socially-directed behavior (SDB) and social interaction, in order to analyze the cognitive processes involved in them. Behavior socially directed to peers, (that is, the child's display of a motor or verbal act accompanied by a look directed to the peer), can be considered as the coordination of two (*simple* SDB) or more (*coordinated* SDB) sensorimotor schemes. Social interaction, the successive exhibition of two related SDBs by two children, can be considered as the interpersonal coordination of action schemes. The number of SDBs produced alternatively during interaction between children provides a measure of social interaction. Among a group of toddlers meeting daily in a play group, the number of *isolated* SDBs, that is, those produced outside an interaction, did not vary substantially between 12 and 18 months; while SDBs, both simple and coordinated, produced during peer interaction increased significantly, as well as short (composed of 2 SDBs) and long (several SDBs) social interactions. The authors wondered whether these changes were due to a developmental process or to peer experience in the play group. Two groups of toddlers (16 to 17 months and 18 to 19 months) were compared, one group with 4½ months of peer experience and the other with only 15 days. Although children from the two groups seemed equally capable of and motivated towards behavior socially directed to peers (number of simple SDBs) and interaction with peers (number of short social interactions), peer experience significantly affected the production of more complex social behavior (coordinated SDBs) and longer interactions. Peer experience in the play group thus seems to consolidate the child's ability to direct behavior to the peer as a social partner. It is notable that children in both groups succeeded in and were motivated to produce peer-directed behavior and to engage in peer interaction as soon as the occasion arose at 12 and 17 months (the time of first entry to the play group).

In further research, Vandell (1980) observed both simple and coordinated SDBs in previously unacquainted infants from the age of 6 months and found that their frequency was lower than that reported for toddlers by Mueller and Brenner (1977), and that frequency did not differ significantly between 6 and 12 months. Also, social interactions were less frequent, although they consisted mostly of the interpersonal coordination of only two SDBs. The variability of these results as a function of peer experience was not investigated. Knowledge of the peer (familiarity of friendship among children) was also found to have both a quantitative and a qualitative effect on social behavior between toddlers (Becker, 1977; Bronson, 1974; Lewis et al., 1975; Vincze, 1971). As described by Mueller and Vandell (1979) peer experience and familiarity are not the only influences on the production of peer-directed social behavior and its coordination in interaction. The institutional and environmental setting, as well as group size, also seem to affect peer interaction to different degrees, at least at the performance level.

Thus, at an early age the child seems able to direct behavior deliberately to a peer, if the latter is available and if the child is allowed to do so by contextual conditions. The child is increasingly able to coordinate two or more actions into socially directed behavior and to interpersonally coordinate them with the peer's in sequences of varying lengths. This ability seems to be affected both by developmental changes and peer experience.

The child's exhibition of peer-directed behavior and the mutual exchange of actions between children seem to co-occur in the development.

Mother-Related and Peer-Related Social Behavior

Both Buhler (1931) and Bridges (1933) reported a difference of several weeks in the appearance of the same social behavior, depending upon whether it was directed towards an adult or a peer. However, recent studies (Dubon et al., 1981; Vincze, 1971) seem to cast doubt on this developmental progression. Furthermore, findings on the quality and organization of the first peer-directed behaviors (eye contacts and smiles) do not seem to differ from those reported for early adult–child interaction (Schaffer, 1971). What is clearly found to differ is the adult's role as a partner in which intention to interact is clearly expressed, thus compensating for the child's distractability. In mother–child interaction, the adult directs frequent (more than 70% of the total) and long (about 20 seconds) glances at the child, a pattern quite different from adult–adult interaction (Stern, 1977). It may be hypothesized that when a child under 6 months directs a look or some other elementary communicative act vis-à-vis a peer or an adult, the same perceptual and cognitive abilities are being challenged, although in conditions of different complexity. In infants from 6 to 12 months, Vandell (1980) found a basic similarity between the number of smiles and looks directed to the mother or the peer. This relation does not seem to be affected by individual differences nor by environmental variations (presence of toys).

The hypothesis that there is a general consistency in the infant's social behavior directed toward different partners thus seems to be confirmed, without excluding the possibility of future differentiation as a function of involvement in different social relations. These different social relations with adults and peers may also differently affect the child's cognitive processes. Bronson (1974) asserted that the ability to control the partner's behavior is challenged to a greater extent in peer interactions. Mueller and Vandell (1979) hypothesized that while in mother–child interaction the infant's interest seems to be focused on social interaction by the mother's constant attention, in peer interaction children's reciprocal interest seems to be mediated by objects. A detailed analysis of the relationships between object-related behavior and peer-related behavior is thus pertinent to this problem.

Peer-Related Behavior and Object-Related Behavior

The acquisition of reference to objects in adult–child interaction seems to be a basic step in toddler's communicative development (Lock, 1978). Integration of peer-related behavior with behavior related to objects also seems to be significant. What are the cognitive demands made on toddlers' cognitive processes when they must relate their behavior both to objects and peers?

Agreement is widespread concerning the increasing relevance of objects in peer interactions among 1-year-olds. A specific object-exchange activity has often been observed in chldren of this age (Brenner & Mueller, 1982; Bronson, 1975; Dubon et al., 1981; Musatti & Panni, 1981; Vincze, 1971). What are the cognitive processes involved in toddlers' behavior in these cases? Bronson (1975) observed that toddlers' simple gestures of offering objects to peers are very frequent, and he postulated that "to perceive the relationship between the object and the agemate and to make an inference about the peer's intent" (1975, p. 150) seem to be the cognitive prerequisites of an offer-gesture directed to the peer, and seem to correspond to the child's ability to play the peer's role. In object exchange between peers, the behavior of the offering child is coordinated with that of the receiving child. The expressions often accompanying these behaviors and the repeated object exchanges in the same interactive sequence show that both children have mastered the object–peer relationship (Musatti & Panni, 1981).

An awareness of the possible relationship between object and peer appear to exist in "blind" (i.e., not accompanied by any look) gestures of offering an object among younger children (Musatti & Panni, 1981; Vincze, 1971). Such behavior seems to result from a difficulty encountered in coordinating peer-related behavior with object-related behavior to form a socially directed behavior (SDB). Difficulties of coordinating object-related behavior and social behavior with an unacquainted peer could also explain the finding of Ramey, Finkelstein, and O'Brien (1976) that object activity does not occur with peer social contact in 6½- to 11½-month-olds, as well as the results of Vandell, Wilson, and Buchanan (1980) that SDBs in 6- to 12-month-olds are more frequent in the absence of toys, even though actions with objects are increasingly involved in peer interactions.

Mueller and Lucas (1975) observed that integration of activities with objects in interaction between 1-year-old peers seem to result in a particular interaction structure, in which children alternately manipulate the same object in long sequences of activity without exhibiting any SDB to the peer. Eckerman and Whatley (1977) also reported that between unacquainted children of 10-12 and 22-24 months, the presence of toys affects the frequency of social interactions, although at the same time it provides the opportunity for new types of interactions focused on object manipulation and exchange. According to Mueller and Brenner (1977), most social interactions between toddlers aged 12 to 18 months occur while engaged in object-focused activities. In larger groups of 6 children, objects seem to support clustering among children (Mueller & Rich, 1976).

In sum, younger or unacquainted children seem to have trouble coordinating object-related and peer-related behavior. Interaction with objects does not appear to be an alternative to peer interaction but, in some ways, seems to elicit it. A direct relationship between sharing attention to an object between peers and interpersonally coordinating social behaviors directed to each other seems to result.

Activities with Objects and Peer Interaction

The studies reported refer to the child's ability to coordinate peer-related behavior and object-related behavior, both internally and interpersonally, that is, to integrate activity with objects in social interaction. Just how is this coordination achieved, how do activities with objects and peer-related behavior or peer interaction affect each other? The types of objects used by children seem to affect the integration of their activities during peer interaction. De Stefano and Mueller (1982) found that object size affected the frequency of peer interactions between toddlers. In addition, the type of activity that can be performed with objects seems to affect peer interaction. When toddlers perform specific activities with objects, the interpersonal coordination of these activities affects the structure of their interaction. Stambak, Barriere, Bonica, Maisonnet, Musatti, Rayna, and Verba (1983) found that activities elicited by different objects (exploration of the objects, gross motor activities, pretend play) corresponded to different structures of social interaction in small groups of toddlers.

Conversely, peer interaction affects the type of activities toddlers engage in with objects. The cognitive processes involved in the interpersonal coordination of the activities with objects seems to be equivalent to those observed in the sequential coordination of the single child's activities with the same objects. Verba, Stambak, and Sinclair (1982) analyzed the cognitive processes involved in the interpersonal coordination of activities, in imitative interaction sequences in small groups of children during physical exploration, and in building with objects. Analysis of the activities successively performed by two or more children around a table suggested three procedures used by children to assimilate the peer's behavior: (1) repetition of the peer's action with a different object; (2) combination of two successive peer's actions into a single one; and (3) understanding of the peer's unsuccessful trials to solve a problem, as it was expressed by their performing the action that corresponds to the correct solution. All three seem to involve a process of abstraction as described by Piaget in the single child's activities. Verba et al. argue that, in this case, the peer's actions provide both a synchronic and diachronic accumulation of cognitive experience which the single child can only achieve diachronically.

Musatti and Verba (1982), observing small groups of 1- to 2-year-olds with two different types of objects, analyzed the child's mechanisms coordinating peer-related behavior and activities. Two patterns were found: (1) one child's activity is elicited by a peer's action, and the child performs a similar action with either different or the same objects, and (2) a child proposes that the peer perform an action with the objects relating to one of his or her own actions. Thus, even in toddlerhood, the peer can elicit a specific activity with objects in two ways: by eliciting a cognitive performance related to objects, or by eliciting the interpersonal coordination of activities with objects. In other words, the child's thinking seems to be stimulated by different foci, that is, the possible actions with objects and the possible logical coordination of actions with objects. The authors suggest that the mechanisms regulating the interpersonal coordination of toddlers' activities seem to correspond to the two procedures of the grasp of consciousness that, according to Piaget (1974/1977, 1975), regulate cognitive processes related to objects or actions.

In sum, toddlers' coordination of activities with objects with peer-related behavior seems to affect both cognitive processes related to objects and social cognitive processes. These processes do not appear to be competitive in the child's actual behavior but seem to be *similar* and *mutually functional*. Second, the peer elicits not only social behavior in the child but also cognitive acts related to objects and to the relationships between various activities with objects. Third, children show a basic cognitive identification between their own actions and those of peers. This identification may allow or stimulate the actualization of the same cognitive processes regulating the single child's activity in the interpersonal coordination of activities. Conversely, the peer seems to be an organizer of the child's cognitive processes, since in several ways he or she elicits the child's reflections about possible activities with objects and possible ways of coordinating them. In conclusion, the fact that many social interactions among children occur via objects could be explained both by the fact that the object focuses the coordination of socially directed behaviors in a social interaction, and the fact that the peer focuses the child's attention on activities with objects.

Most studies on the coordination of activities with objects and peer-related behavior concern toddlers. In fact, in this period, the child's ability to differentiate and coordinate object-related activities undergoes crucial developmental growth. The acquisition of representational abilities slowly comes into play and modifies the child's cognitive processes. Again, the interpersonal sharing of meaning systems structures and modifies adult–child interaction. Is the acquisition of representational abilities involved in peer-related behavior and peer interaction? Research on peer interaction during play may answer some of these questions.

Play and Representational Abilities
in Early Peer Relations

The sequence of cognitive abilities involved in the toddler's play was described by Piaget (1945) and then by Inhelder, Lezine, Sinclair, and Stambak (1972), and Nicolich (1977). These include (1) the ability to perform activities appropriate to the conventional use of objects (e.g., pretending to sleep on a cushion), then to repeat these activities with inappropriate objects (e.g., pretending to sleep on a rag doll); (2) the grasp of consciousness of the pretense of actions (e.g., pretending to sleep on a cushion, then laughing); (3) the ability to coordinate and plan several pretend activities related to the same theme. Can these developmental processes be found also in the social play between toddlers?

Eckerman, Whatley, and Kutz (1975), observing unacquainted home-reared children (10–12, 16–18 and 22–24 month-olds), found that social play increases greatly between 16–18 and 22–24 months. Unfortunately, these authors defined social play as occurring whenever the child involves a peer in his or her own activity with objects, but they failed to consider whether the activity was characterized by nonliteralness and playfulness. In describing social play centered on large objects in 18- to 26-month-olds, (e.g., peekaboo, run-chase, rhythmic banging) Maisonnet and Stambak (1983) stressed how the sharing of gross motor play activities is accompanied by expressions of particular playfulness and positive affect, which is unusual during the sharing of object-exploring activities. According to Goldman and Ross (1978), nonliteralness is one of the basic features (together with mutual involvement, alternation of turns, repetition, and absence of negative affect) distinguishing games from other sequences of social interaction between toddlers. In their study, 28 games of different content (with or without objects) were identified in 32 dyads of unacquainted children (12–18 and 18–24 months). According to these authors, the expression of non-literalness through smiles and laughter and irrelevant or repeated behavior, together with the highly familiar content of certain games (e.g., ball games), has a metacommunicative function in initiating play with an unacquainted peer in the absence of speech. The sharing of a play ritual between familiar toddlers in an infant day-care center was described by Musatti and Panni (1981).

The existence of shared meanings in both play and nonplay social interactions between toddlers is strongly supported by Brenner and Mueller (1982). These shared meanings or themes support the interactions between 12- to 23-month-olds meeting daily in a playgroup. A repertoire of 12 themes was identified involving both gross motor activities and activities with objects, but not implying object transformation, that is, of the meaning of the objects involved. An increase in the frequency and variety of shared meanings between 12 and 19 months was found. Although the children seem to be capable of long sequences of social interaction even before the onset of the various shared meanings, the integration of a shared meaning in the social interaction supported its longer duration. The notion of shared meaning tends to express not the fact that the child succeeds in sharing an activity with a peer, but the fact that a child can understand what he or she is doing together with the peer.

The sharing of meanings by children, which they refer to during interaction, somehow involves knowledge which the single child can refer to even outside interaction. From this perspective, Musatti and Mueller (in press) have examined developmental changes in peer-related play behavior corresponding to the acquisition of representational abilities as planning and coordinating a sequence of acts. Peer-related behavior concerning a list of play themes adapted from Brenner and Mueller (1982) was investigated in 12- to 18-month old toddlers. Dramatic developmental changes in the ability of planning both the theme and the peer's involvement and in the ability to coordinate sequentially more communicative aids directed to the peer with the expression of the play theme were found between 12 and 18 months.

These studies provide evidence that during toddlerhood, in peer-related behavior and interaction (particularly in play), abilities involved in social play among preschoolers (Garvey, 1974) seem to emerge developmentally, that is, the ability (1) to abstract rules concerning peer interaction (copying, complementarity, alternation); (2) to refer to shared themes during peer interaction; and (3) to express the nonliteral feature of the play theme with the peer. These studies also demonstrate that the development of representational abilities found in object-related toddler play occur in peer-related play as well.

As seen in these studies, peer-related play behavior can integrate object-related behavior (e.g., a ball game) or may consist solely of gross motor activities (e.g., rough-and-tumble play). In both cases, the peer-related play behavior is closely related to the actual context of social interaction. The shared meanings are meaningful only in the social interaction or in the single child's play that directly refers to the interactive context. Any generalization of these meanings among different populations of toddlers or from peer interactions to adult–child interaction (or vice versa) seems to result from contextual constraints (the similarity of the toddlers' performance and environmental elements; Brenner & Mueller, 1982), and does not imply any conventionalization of the meanings themselves in wider social systems. Second, the nonliteralness of the play behavior is expressed only in the context of the actual social interaction by the use of metacommunicative cues directed to peers (Hay, Ross, & Goldman, 1979). In conclusion, during the play interactions described in these studies, the toddlers do not use a system of general interpersonal meanings. They share meanings in play but do not share play on meanings.

This different level of representational abilities seems to be challenged in social play involving pretend activities with conventional objects between children from 18 to 32 months (Musatti, 1983). As early as 18 months, children succeed in sharing the meaning of the pretend activity with objects. Subsequently (30–32 months) they attribute meanings to their actual social interactions (role play), referring to conventionalized social relations (such as, Mommy and Baby). It thus seems that the transition from shared meanings to the sharing of meanings in early peer relations is supported by the reference to increasingly wide systems of meanings (conventional use of objects, social roles, etc.) that are conventional and all related to the area of social relations.

In conclusion, the development of representational abilities seems to be involved in peer interactions throughout the period of transition from sensory-motor intelligence to representational intelligence. The development of representational abilities that refer to the social interaction itself is noted. Some systems of meanings, notably those related to social understanding, in particular, seem to appear in interactions between children. The play interactions are those more closely related to the two developmental processes of the socialization of meanings and the acquisition of social meanings.

Conclusions

From this review, early peer relations and cognitive developmental process appear to be closely related. The evidence for this relationship will be summarized in a set of statements. The general considerations implied by these statements will be developed, and the relationships between them and the major questions raised from both Piaget's and Vygotsky's perspectives will be discussed. Since cognitive skills at different levels of complexity seem to be involved in peer-related behavior and peer interaction, some of the specific cognitive processes involved will also be considered.

1. *In peer-related behavior the same cognitive processes are involved as in object-related behavior.* No specific cognitive competence seems to be acquired by children in order for them to relate behavior to a peer and to coordinate that behavior with his/her own peer-related behavior. Children seem capable of relating their own behavior to the peer in different ways according to their general cognitive competence. The relationships between

this level of cognitive competence and the level of cognitive performance expressed in peer-related behavior obviously must be explored in greater detail. However, sufficient evidence already exists to relate this issue to a more general discussion of the homogeneity versus heterogeneity of human cognitive development (Flavell, 1982) rather than consider this issue as a matter of relationships between different behaviors (i.e., social vs. cognitive). If this is true, no cognitive prerequisites for the various social behaviors will need to be discovered. Above all, experiential variables affecting peer-related behavior (e.g., familiarity and peer experience) and contextual conditions (e.g., peer availability, group size, behavioral setting) seem relevant in determining the heterogeneity of peer-directed behavior among children at the same cognitive level. This would, however, have to be explored further if the peer elicits behavior that is cognitively homogeneous or heterogeneous with respect to other behavior by the same child. This question involves the more general issue of the relationship between motivation and cognition.

With regard to the problem of differences and similarities between adult-related and peer-related behavior, the question of the relationships between affective and cognitive aspects of behavior arises. It has, in fact, been suggested that these differences and similarities can be explained as a function of experiential variables (different social relations in which the social behavior is exhibited) and contextual variables (greater availability of adults and support of child's attention during the social interaction). A specific role of attachment in supporting the child's attention during social interaction was postulated by Mueller and Vandell (1979). Affective and cognitive aspects seem to be intrinsically connected in social interaction. This connection appears to be different and to have different effects among different relationships.

The relationship between peer-related behavior and object-related behavior has received greater attention in research. The question of the temporal relation between the child's ability to exhibit peer-related and object-related behavior certainly requires further research. In any case, it seems that object-related behavior is not an alternative to, or competitive with, peer-related behavior in a general sense. The interest in objects seems to be competitive with interest in the peer only at certain times and as a function of experiential and contextual aspects. In fact, at least from about the end of the first year, the child's attention seems to be mutually elicited in both the object–peer and peer–object directions. The peer not only elicits behavior directed towards him or herself, but also somehow stimulates the partner's integration of this behavior with an object-related behavior. In particular, the peer's present or previous action with the object seems to elicit directly the child's behavior with objects according to imitative or cooperative processes.

The increasing coordination of sensorimotor schemes is a major developmental trend in the sensorimotor period. Does a similar developmental trend occur in peer-related behavior in this period? This question can be considered in two senses. First, with regard to the single child's behavior, an increasing coordination of peer-related behaviors and their increasing integration with object-related behavior was observed. The same question can be raised with respect to the interpersonal organization of peer-related behaviors. Also, the interpersonal coordination of different children's peer-related behaviors, that is, social interaction, seems to be organized in increasingly long sequences. From available data, it does not seem possible to hypothesize a linear development from the single child's peer-related behavior to the interpersonal coordination with another child's behavior, for the single child's peer-related behaviors and their interchange between children occur at the same age. Indeed, the production of the child's peer-related behavior seems to be strongly related to mutuality with the peer's behavior at all ages. Damon (1981) postulates that this aspect of mutuality is what makes social events differ from physical events, engendering and requiring a special type of understanding. On the other hand, a process of cognitive identification seems intrinsic in the coordination of activities with objects among peers both to motivate and to support coordination itself.

2. *In the interpersonal coordination of the child's activities with their peer's activities, the cognitive processes involved in the dyachronic coordination of the single child's activities are displayed synchronously.* The hypothesis of Piaget (1923, 3rd ed./1959) that peer relations are based on equality and influence, and that they stimulate the interpersonal coordination of mental operations appears valid during the sensorimotor period. Although this equality may resemble a total identification with the peer, as Piaget himself pointed out, it stimulates the coordination of activities between children.

3. *The coordination of activities with the peer's elicits the child's consciousness of cognitive processes.* In the sensorimotor period the interpersonal coordination of activities with objects seems to be regulated by two separate mechanisms, which respectively stimulate the child's thinking about activities with objects and their coordination. It was postulated that in this way the coordination of the child's activities with the peer's enhances the grasp of consciousness as described by Piaget (1974/1977; 1975). The condition of equality in peer relations thus seems to play a role not only in attracting the child's attention and in eliciting cognitive performance related to objects. It seems also to play a part in eliciting the cognitive processing of the activity performed itself, both as the peer's activity is unfolded syn-

chronically before the child's attention, and as the child's activity appears to be coordinated with a peer's.

The second major trend of cognitive development during the sensorimotor period, that is, the acquisition of representational abilities, was found to be involved in peer-related behavior and deeply related to early peer relations. On the one hand, evidence was reported of rehearsal of shared activities in peer interactions, which seems to suggest shared meanings already at the level of sensorimotor activity. The strong contextual bounds exhibited by these meanings seem to depend on both children's performance level and the paucity of their cognitive storage capacity during this period. Even when children are not using wider meaning systems, they share a sort of knowledge constructed around sensorimotor activities. Thus,

4. *A process of socialization of meanings is involved in early peer relations.* During peer interaction, whenever the children have the opportunity or the capacity to refer to meaning systems conventionalized within more general social relations (conventional use of objects, social relations systems, language), some meaning systems seem to be preferred and peculiar to peer interactions, that is, those referring to aspects of social life rather than those referring to the processing of object-related knowledge. Meanings related to the area of social understanding seem to be most often involved in the shared construction of meaning systems between peers. Thus,

5. *The acquisition of systems of meanings referring to the social life are peculiarly involved in peer relations.*

One crucial point with regard to the question of early peer socialization and the acquisition of meaning systems is that the relation between play behavior and the acquisition of representational abilities (found by Piaget (1945/1962) and Vygotsky (1933/1967) seems to be enhanced by the special relation between peer and play behavior (Mueller and Vandell, 1979). It therefore appears to be no coincidence that the process of socialization of meanings and of acquisition of meaning systems are related mainly to behaviors in the peer-play situation, rather than to other behaviors in peer interaction. With regard to this point Vygotsky's assertion that play plays an important role in stimulating the child's development provides a new view of the role of peer relations in the child's development and acquisition of cultural means of knowledge.

It is also relevant to note that although play behavior occurs frequently during peer interaction, it is certainly stimulated whenever the interactions occur between peer friends. Future research on the sharing of meanings among children would have to consider that play has mostly been observed between children having permanent relations with each other. A special connection between peer play and friendship has been identified by Vandell and Mueller (1980). The observation that in play a representation of children's affect emerges has been supported by Vygotsky (1933/1967). It will be interesting to investigate which affective meanings are built up in social play between friends.

Finally, several other more general remarks can be made. The distinctions among social behavior, social interaction, and social relations made by Hinde (1979) need to be retained—also with respect to early peer relationships. It seems necessary to consider all these three levels of social organization of behavior, even when only one of them is being analyzed. The quality of social relation occurring among children was found to affect both peer-related behavior and peer interaction. The connections between peer-directed behavior and peer interaction seem equally relevant. Yet, research and theoretical and methodological discussion have increased rapidly in recent years only on early peer-directed behavior and early peer interaction. Future research must necessarily also make a more thorough analysis of early peer social relations.

So far, several hypotheses concerning the role of early peer relations in development during infancy and toddlerhood can be formulated. Despite some reservations (Bronson, 1981), early peer relations seem to play a positive, specific role in the development process, although further research and analysis are obviously required. Statement number 1 allows us to consider that the same paradigms can be applied to developmental processes involved in peer relations as in other aspects of behavior. As Table 2.1 shows, the comparison between Statements 2–5 and Piaget's interpretation of functional changes occurring in the transition from the sensorimotor period to representational intelligence yields very interesting theoretical perspectives. Early peer relations are apparently closely related to all four functional developmental changes occurring during this period and are affected by the developmental process as much as they themselves affect it. More specifically, a particular role of peer relations in child development during this period can be hypothesized. The interdependence of the development of mental operations and the socialization process claimed by Piaget (1945) seems to be also valid with regard to the child's process of socialization with peers. Functional changes F.1 and F.2 seem to be deeply involved in peer relations. In fact, on the basis of recent research (e.g., S.2 in Table 2.1), it can be postulated that, since in peer interactions different actions occur simultaneously, the child's ability to coordinate more actions and produce anticipatory schemes is stimulated. Statement three (see S.3 in Table 2.1) points to an important role of peer-related behavior in the "grasp of consciousness" of cognitive processes.

The other two functional changes, F.3 and F.4, referring to the acquisition and socialization of systems of meanings, also seem to be related to peer relations, although in a peculiar way. In fact, on the basis of S.4 it

Table 2.1

Comparison between Piaget's Functional Conditions and Recent Research
on Early Peer Relations

Functional conditions		Statements	
F.1.	General acceleration of actions that provides the child with the ability to merge single actions into a whole and to have anticipatory drafts of it.	S.2	In the interpersonal coordination of the child's activities with the peer's, the cognitive processes involved in the dyachronic coordination of the single child's activities are displayed synchronously.
F.2.	Awareness and consciousness of on-going operations so as to replace practical success by observation and explanation.	S.3.	The coordination of activities with the peer's elicits the child's consciousness of the cognitive processes.
F.3.	Acquisition of systems of signs to allow the construction of general concepts.	S.5.	The acquisition of systems of meanings referring to the social life are peculiarly involved in peer relations.
F.4.	Socialization that goes with the use of a system of signs to integrate individual thought in shared and objective reality.	S.4.	A process of socialization of meanings is involved in early peer relations.

can be postulated that since a process of socialization of meanings is involved in peer relations, the single child's activity can be increasingly integrated in a shared reality (F.4). But, while Piaget's functional condition F.3 stresses the relevance of the acquisition of a system of signs to encourage the child's logical development, S.5 points out that the system of meanings involved in peer relations seem to especially favor the acquisition of knowledge about social relations. Thus, S.5 asserts a positive role of peer relations in the acquisition of a cultural knowledge as social understanding, but it is not concerned with the child's acquisition of a system of signs as language. Actually, the role of early peer relations in the different aspects of a toddler's language acquisition does not seem to have received sufficient attention in recent research.

In light of this fact, Piaget's hypothesis (1923, 3rd ed./1959) regarding special character of the process of peer socialization suggests new directions for future research. Furthermore, Vygotsky's assertion (1931/1960; 1934/1962) of the role of social interaction in the child's acquisition of cultural means of knowledge can be usefully integrated within this perspective. In toddlerhood, which cultural means of knowledge are peculiarly acquired in social interaction with adults or peers? Perhaps in answering this question on early peer relations, theoretical perspectives previously considered divergent can be integrated to form a multifaceted interpretation. Is not the integration of Piaget's and Vygotsky's perspectives also a problem of relations between peers?

Acknowledgements

I would like to thank Hermine Sinclair for suggesting some of the ideas underlying this paper, though their expression remains the full responsibility of the author. I also express my thanks to Edward Mueller and Franco Robustelli who patiently read and discussed the manuscript.

References

Bates, E., Benigni, L., Bretherton, I., Camaioni, L., & Volterra, V. (1979). Cognition and communication from nine to thirteen months: Correlational findings. In E. Bates (Ed.), *The emergence of symbols: Cognition and communication in infancy.* New York: Academic Press.

Bates, E., Bretherton, I., Beeghly–Smith, M., & McNew, S. (1982). Social bases of language development: A reassessment. In H. W. Reese & L. P. Lipsitt (Eds.), *Advances in child development and behavior,* (Vol. 16, pp. 8–75). New York: Academic Press.

Becker, J. (1977). A learning analysis of the development of peer-oriented behavior in nine-month-old infants. *Developmental Psychology, 48,* 481–491.

Brenner, J., & Mueller, E. (1982). Shared meaning in boy toddlers' peer relations. *Child Development, 53,* 380–391.

Bridges, K. M. B. (1933). A study of social development in early infancy. *Child Development, 4,* 36–49.

Bronson, W. C. (1974). Mother–toddler interaction: A perspective on studying the development of competence. *Merrill–Palmer Quarterly, 20,* 275–301.

Bronson, W. C. (1975). Development in behavior with age mates during the second year of life. In M. Lewis & L. A. Rosenblum (Eds.), *Friendship and peer relations* (pp. 131–152). New York: Wiley.

Bronson, W. C. (1981). *Toddlers' behaviors with agemates: Issues of interaction, cognition, and affect.* Norwood, NJ: Ablex.

Buhler, C. (1931). The social behavior of the child. In C. Murchison (Ed.), *Handbook of child psychology* (pp. 374–416). Worcester, Mass.: Clark University.

Burlingham, D., & Freud, A. (1965). *Infants without families.* London: George Allen and Unwin.

Damon, W. (1981). Exploring children's social cognition on two fronts. In J. H. Flavell & L. Ross (Eds.), *Social cognitive development* (pp. 154–175). Cambridge: Cambridge University Press.

De Stefano, C. T., & Mueller, E. (1982). Environmental determinants of peer social activity in 18-months-old males. *Infant Behavior and Development, 5,* 175–183.

Dubon, D. C., Josse D., & Lezine, I. (1981). Evolution des échanges entre enfants au cours des deux premières années de la vie. [Evolution of the exchanges among children during the first two years of life.] *Neuropsychiatrie de l'enfance, 29,* 273–290.

Eckerman, C. O., & Whatley, J. L. (1977). Toys and social interaction between infant peers. *Child Development, 48,* 1645–1656.

Eckerman, C. O., Whatley, J. L. & Kutz, S. L. (1975). Growth of social play with peers during the second year of life. *Developmental Psychology, 11,* 42–48.

El'konin, D. B. (1972). Toward the problem of stages in the mental development of the child, *Soviet Psychology, 2,* 225–251.

Fenson, L., Kagan, J., Kearsley, R. B., & Zelazo, P. R. (1976). The developmental progression of manipulative play in the first two years. *Child Development, 47,* 232–236.

Flavell, J. H. (1982). On cognitive development. *Child Development, 53,* 1–10.

Flavell, J. H., & Ross, L. (1981). Concluding remarks. In J. H. Flavell & L. Ross (Eds.), *Social cognitive development* (pp. 306–316). Cambridge: Cambridge University.

Freud, A., & Dann, S. (1951). An experiment in group upbringing. *Psychoanalytic Study of the Child,* 127–168.

Garvey, C. (1974). Some properties of social play. *Merrill–Palmer Quarterly, 20,* 163–180.

Garvey, C., & Hogan, R. (1973). Social speech and social interaction: Egocentrism revisited. *Child Development, 44,* 562–568.

Goldman, B. D., & Ross, H. S. (1978). Social skills in action: An analysis of early peer games. In J. Glick & K. A. Clarke-Stewart (Eds.), *The development of social understanding* (pp. 177–212). New York: Gardner Press.

Hay, F. D., Ross, H. S., & Goldman, B. D. (1979). Social games in infancy. In B. Sutton-Smith (Ed.), *Play and learning* (pp. 83–107). New York: Gardner Press.

Hinde, R. A. (1979). *Towards understanding relationships.* London: Academic Press.

Inhelder, B., Lezine, I., Sinclair, H., & Stambak, M. (1972). Les débuts de la fonction symbolique. [The beginnings of symbolic function.] *Archives de psychologie, 163,* 187–243.

Largo, R. H., & Howard, J. A. (1979). Developmental progression in play behavior of children between nine and thirty months. I: Spontaneous play and imitation. *Developmental Medicine and Child Neurology, 21,* 299–310.

Lewis, M., Young, G., Brooks, J., & Michalson, L. (1975). The beginning of friendship. In M. Lewis & L. A. Rosenblum (Eds)., *Friendship and peer relations* (pp. 27–66). New York: Wiley.

Lock, A. (Ed.) (1978). *Action, gesture and symbol: The emergence of language.* London: Academic Press.

Maisonnet, R., & Stambak, M. (1983). Echanges dans une situation de jeux moteurs. [Peer interaction in motor play.] In M. Stambak, M. Barriere, L. Bonica, R. Maisonnet, T. Musatti, S. Rayna, & M. Verba, *Les bébés entre eux.* [Among babies.] (pp. 17–56). Paris: Presses Universitaires de France.

Mueller, E. (1972). The maintenance of verbal exchange between young children. *Child Development, 43,* 930–938.

Mueller, E. (1978). *Early studies on peer relations and the lost history of social development.* Unpublished manuscript, Boston University.

Mueller, E., & Brenner, J. (1977). The origins of social skills and interactions among play-group toddlers. *Child Development, 48,* 854–861.

Mueller, E., & Lucas, T. (1975). A developmental analysis of peer interaction among toddlers. In M. Lewis & L. A. Rosenblum (Eds.), *Friendship and peer relations* (pp. 223–257). New York: Wiley.

Mueller, E., & Rich, A. (1976). Clustering and socially-directed behaviors in a toddler's playgroup. *Journal of Child Psychology and Psychiatry, 17,* 315–322.

Mueller, E., & Vandell, D. (1979). Infant–infant interaction. In J. Osofsky (Ed.), *Handbook of Infant Development* (pp. 591–622). New York: Wiley.

Musatti, T. (1983). Echanges dans une situation de faire semblant. [Peer interaction in pretend play.] In M. Stambak, M. Barriere, L. Bonica, R. Maisonnet, T. Musatti, S. Rayna, &

M. Verba, *Les bebes entre eux*. [Among babies.] (pp. 93–134). Paris: Presses Universitaires de France.

Musatti, T., & Mueller, E. (in press). Expressions of representational growth in toddlers' peer communication. *Social Cognition*.

Musatti, T., & Panni, S. (1981). Social behavior and interaction among day-care center toddlers. *Early Child Development and Care, 7*, 5–27.

Musatti, T., & Verba, M. (1982). *Processus cognitifs et role d'autrui dans les activités entre enfants de 1 à 2 ans*. [Cognitive processes and the role of others in activities among children from 1 to 2 years.] Unpublished manuscript, Istituto di Psicologia, CNR, Roma, CRESAS, Paris.

Nicolich McCune, L. (1977). Beyond sensorimotor intelligence: Assessment of symbolic maturity through analysis of pretend play. *Merrill–Palmer Quarterly, 23*, 89–99.

Piaget, J. (1959). *The language and thought of the child*. London: Routledge & Kegan. (Original work published 1923, 3rd ed., 1945).

Piaget, J. (1924). *Le jugement et le raisonnement chez l'enfant*. [Judgment and reasoning in the child.] Neuchâtel: Delachaux & Niestlé.

Piaget, J. (1962). *The moral judgment of the child*. New York: New Press. (Original work published 1932).

Piaget, J. (1954). *The origins of intelligence in children*. New York: Basic Books. (Original work published 1936).

Piaget, J. (1954) *The child's construction of reality*. New York: Basic Books. (Original work published 1937).

Piaget, J. (1962). *Play, dreams and imitation in childhood*. New York: Norton. (Original work published 1945).

Piaget, J. (1951). Pensée egocentrique et pensée sociocentrique. [Egocentric thought and sociocentric thought.] *Cahiers Internationaux de Sociologie, X*, 34–39.

Piaget, J. (1962). *Comments on Vygotsky's critical remarks*. Cambridge: the M.I.T. Press.

Piaget, J. (1963). Problemes de la psycho-sociologie de l'enfance. [Problems of child psychosociology.] In G. Gurvitch (Ed.), *Traite de sociologie* (pp. 229–254). Paris: Presses Universitaires de France.

Piaget, J. (1975). *L'equilibration des structures cognitives*. [Equilibration of cognitive structures.] Presses Universitaires de France.

Piaget, J. (1977). *The grasp of consciousness*. London: Routledge & Kegan. (Original work published 1974).

Piaget, J., & Inhelder, B. (1969). *The psychology of the child*. London: Routledge & Kegan. (Original work published 1966).

Ramey, C. T., Finkelstein, N. W., & O'Brien, C. (1976). Toys and infant behavior in the first year of life. *Journal of Genetic Psychology, 129*, 341–342.

Schaffer, H. R. (1971). *The growth of sociability*. Harmondsworth, Middlesex: Penguin.

Sherrod, L. M., & Lamb, M. E. (1981). Infant social cognition: An introduction. In M. E. Lamb & L. M. Sherrod (Eds.), *Infant social cognition* (pp. 1–36). Hillsdale, N. J.: Erlbaum.

Sinclair, H. (October, 1981). *Developpement cognitif et langage*. [Cognitive development and language.] Conference in honor of Jean Piaget, Rome.

Sinclair, H., Stambak, M., Lezine, L., Rayna, S., & Verba, M. (1982). *Les bébés et les choses: La creativité du developpement cognitif*. [Babies and things: The creativity of cognitive development.] Paris: Presses Universitaires de France.

Stambak, M., Barriere, M., Bonica, L., Maisonnet, R., Musatti, T., Rayna, S., & Verba, M. (1983). *Les bébés entre eux*.[Among babies.] Paris: Presses Universitaires de France.

Stern, D. (1977). *The first relationship: Infant and mother.* London: Fontana/Open Books & Open Books.

Uzgiris, I. C. (1973). Patterns of cognitive development in infancy. *Merrill–Palmer Quarterly, 19,* 181–204.

Vandell, D. L. (1980). Sociability with peer and mother during the first year. *Developmental Psychology, 16,* 355–361.

Vandell, D. L., & Mueller, E. C. (1980). Peer play and friendships during the first two years. In C. Foot, J. Chapman, & J. R. Smith (Eds.), *Friendship and social relations in children* (pp. 181–208). New York: Wiley.

Vandell, D. L., Wilson, K. S., & Buchanan, N. R. (1980). Peer interaction in the first year of life: An examination of its structure, content and sensitivity to toys. *Child Development, 51,* 481–488.

Verba, M., Stambak, M., & Sinclair, H. (1982). Physical knowledge and social interaction in children from 18 to 24 months of age. In G. E. Forman (Ed.), *Action and thought* (pp. 267–296). London, New York: Academic Press.

Vincze, M. (1971). The social contacts of infants and young children reared together. *Early Child Development and Care, 1,* 99–109.

Vygotsky, L. S. (1960). Istorija razvitija vyssih psihiceskih funkcij (History of development of higher psychological functions). In Vygotsky, L. S. Razvitija vyssih psihiceskih funkcij (Development of higher psychological functions). Moscow: Izd. APN RSFSR. (Original work published 1931).

Vygotsky, L. S. (1962). *Thought and language.* Chicago: M.I.T. Press. (Original work published 1934).

Vygotsky, L. S. (1967). Play and its role in the mental development of the child. *Soviet Psychology, 5,* 6–18. (Original work published 1933).

Vygotsky, L. S. (1972). Problema vozrastnoj periodizacij destkogo razvitija (The problem of period identification in child development). *Voprosy Psihologii, 2,* 114–123. (Original work published 1934).

Vygotsky, L. S. (1978). *Mind in society.* Cambridge, MA: Harvard University Press.

Watson, M. W., & Fischer, K. W. (1977). A developmental sequence of agent use in late infancy. *Child Development, 48,* 828–836.

PART II

PROCESS IN PEER AND FAMILY RELATIONSHIPS

Once considered as two antagonistic worlds, children's family and peer relationships are now understood to influence one another in different ways across development and across cultures. Early parent–child relationships are seen as launching children into the peer group, whereas older children's peer experiences may be used as bases for adolescents' expectations of greater mutuality with their parents (Youniss, 1980). To some degree, peer and parents offer distinctive contributions to children's development. Parents transmit the established values and obligations of the culture, whereas peers offer a context in which rules may be negotiated, and thus fairness, justice, and other universal prosocial values may be reinvented by the participants (Damon, 1983). Although these functions can now be differentiated in broad terms, the specific mechanisms of transmission from family to peer systems are under active investigation.

In Chapter 3 (this volume) entitled "Infant–Mother Attachment and Early Peer Relations: The Assessment of Behavior in an Interactive Context," Jacobson, Tianen, Wille, and Aytch consider two different theoretical accounts of

55

the link between family experience and early peer relations. One focuses on social competence and is derived from ethological and constructivist principles. This approach focuses on the influence of parental attachment on the child's development of trust and interactive skills that are generalized to peers. The second approach focuses on the affective qualities of the securely attached child, including enthusiasm, persistence, and confidence, that elicit engagement and friendship from peers. Jacobson and his colleagues find that affective linkages between secure attachment and effective peer relations are most clearly supported in their observations of toddlers.

Whiting presents a cross-cultural survey of 14 societies in Chapter 4 (this volume), entitled "The Effect of Culture on Peer Relationships." By considering a set of process variables, including nurturant, prosocial, egoistic (dependent or dominant), sociable, and training behaviors, Whiting reports distinctive patterns of mother–child interaction across societies grouped by the mothers' workload and their access to other adult females within their households. Whiting then traces continuities in the patterns of interpersonal behavior learned in children's relations with their mothers and in caregiving responsibilities with infants and toddlers to their patterns of interactions with peers. She argues that patterns of family behavior, which vary widely among cultures, have major influences on peer relations within each culture.

The implications for differences in values regarding interaction in one system for behavior in another are quite significant. As Hinde's (1976) work suggests, who is involved in an interaction—whether the father, mother, friend, or stranger—, what group is being considered, and what topic or task is being addressed all have great impact on our inferences regarding the origins of peer relations.

References

Damon, W. (1983). *Social and personality development: Infancy through adolescence.* New York: Norton.

Hinde, R. (1976). On describing relationships. *Journal of Child Psychology and Psychiatry, 17,* 1–19.

Youniss, J. (1980). *Parents and peers in social development: A Sullivan–Piaget perspective.* Chicago: University of Chicago Press.

CHAPTER 3

Infant–Mother Attachment and Early Peer Relations: The Assessment of Behavior in an Interactive Context

Joseph L. Jacobson, Robin L. Tianen,
Diane E. Wille, and Donald M. Aytch

Introduction

Although behavioral codes based on discrete events have dominated research on early peer interaction (e.g., Eckerman, Whatley, & Kutz, 1975; Mueller & Lucas, 1975; Parten, 1932), investigators in other areas of social development have noted that relationships often emerge more clearly when coding is based on rating scales (Bakeman & Brown, 1980; Cairns, 1979; Sroufe & Waters, 1977). Because raters can be more sensitive to the emotional tone of a behavior and to its connotation in a particular interactive context, they are often better able to evaluate its psychological significance. One disadvantage of rating scales, however, is that they typically reveal less detail regarding developmental processes. Because the rater is not required (and is frequently unable) to identify the nuance or contextual connotation that influenced a given rating, the investigator remains largely uninformed regarding such issues.

It is possible to obtain some of the advantages of both rating scales and discrete behavior codes by using a rating scheme whose scale points are defined in discrete behavioral terms. This type of approach has been used successfully by Ainsworth and her associates in coding security of infant–

parent attachment (Ainsworth, Blehar, Waters, & Wall, 1978) and by Brazelton (1973) in assessing neonatal behavior. In this chapter, we present a scheme for coding peer interaction, in which behaviorally grounded rating scales are used to evaluate each social overture and response, as well as each episode of agonistic interaction. This approach, which we call *Episode-Based Rating Scales,* was developed in the context of research on the relation between infant–mother attachment and the development of peer play in toddlers.

Four recent studies have reported a relationship between security of infant–mother attachment and early peer social interaction (Easterbrooks & Lamb, 1979; Lieberman, 1977; Pastor, 1981; Waters, Wippman, & Sroufe, 1979). The authors of these studies differ, however, in their interpretations of the behavioral, cognitive, and affective variables that link these two domains of social behavior. Some stress a cognitive or competence dimension, suggesting that securely attached children have more opportunity to develop interpersonal skills and are therefore more adept at initiating and maintaining interaction with a peer. Others emphasize affective variables, positing that the secure child is not necessarily more skillful but is friendlier, more enthusiastic, and therefore a more attractive playmate. The coding schemes employed in the prior studies are not sufficiently detailed, however, to evaluate the relative importance of interpersonal skill and affective style in linking parental attachment to early peer interaction.

We begin this chapter by reviewing Ainsworth's approach for assessing infant–parent attachment. Ainsworth's work is of interest both because it helps us understand the substantive linkages between attachment and peer relations and because her rating scales are similar to those we are proposing for peer interaction. Next, we outline four alternative interpretations of the relationship between attachment and early peer relations. Two of these interpretations emphasize social competence; two others, affective style. The difficulties involved in relying on either discrete behavioral data or global rating scales to select from among these interpretations are illustrated in a review of the previous studies on attachment and peer play. Finally, we summarize the principal features of our Episode-based Rating Scales and present data from our own research to illustrate this approach.

Patterns of Infant–Parent Attachment

Ainsworth and her associates (see Ainsworth et al., 1978) have developed a laboratory procedure known as the *strange situation* for assessing security of parental attachment at 1 year. Mother and infant are brought into a large playroom equipped with a variety of age-appropriate toys, which the child is free to explore and manipulate. The mother departs from the room twice during the session, leaving the infant with an unfamiliar adult for 3 min during one separation and, later, for 6 min—3 min alone followed by 3 with the stranger. Security of attachment is evaluated on the basis of the infant's behavior when the mother returns to the playroom after each of the separations. The *securely attached* infant greets the mother warmly on her return, shows little anger toward her, and recovers relatively easily from separation distress. The *ambivalent* infant is difficult to comfort on reunion and often mixes contact-seeking behavior with squirming to get down, pushing away, and other signs of contact resistance. The *avoidant* infant appears unperturbed by the mother's departure but actively avoids her attempts to engage him or her when she returns. Both the ambivalent and the avoidant infant are considered *anxiously attached*.

Ainsworth's coding scheme is based primarily on four rating scales, which are grounded more firmly in specific behavioral definitions than rating scales typically used to assess peer social interaction. Scale points are defined by criteria, such as "The baby gives the mother no greeting; the mother strives to gain his attention; after about 15 seconds he gives her his attention but he is fairly unresponsive even then" (Avoidance, scale point 5). It is important to emphasize that the scale point assigned to a particular behavior depends heavily on context. For example, approaching the mother after 30 seconds of avoidance is given less weight than an approach immediately when she re-enters the room. Latencies, intensities, durations, and frequencies of behaviors are all used in defining the various scale points, but the weight accorded to each of these metrics varies across context in an attempt to reflect the psychological significance of the behavior in question. The infant's attachment classification is derived from scores on these four rating scales in a quasi-intuitive fashion. While subjective judgment is important, the scales insure that this judgment is behaviorally based.

In investigating the cross-situational and temporal stability of infant attachment patterns, Sroufe and Waters (1977) suggest that continuity at the level of overt behavior may be relatively rare. Instead, they predict stability at a higher level of behavioral organization. For attachment, they propose that the construct of *felt security* provides the appropriate level of analysis. Behaviors which differ across situation and age become predictable when their significance with regard to the infant's felt security is taken into account. For example, during the first 3 minutes of the strange situation, when the infant and mother are initially alone together in the laboratory playroom, the secure infant explores freely. The ambivalent infant, feeling less secure in the novel situation, remains close to the mother. By contrast, during the reunions the secure infant is likely to seek proximity to the mother in order to recover from separation distress, while the ambivalent infant, who is unable to recover, vacillates between approach and rejection. Thus, although the overt behavior, maternal proximity-seeking, is uncorrelated across episodes of the strange situation, patterns of change across episodes can be predicted with reference to the infant's pattern of attachment.

Kagan (1971) has used the term *heterotypic continuity* to refer to the concept that the overt behaviors expressing an underlying psychological predisposition may vary systematically across age. This principle is illustrated by a finding from research by Matas, Arend, and Sroufe (1978). Avoidant infants are typically aloof and apparently unperturbed during the reunions with their mothers in the strange situation at 18 months. Yet, in the context of a frustrating tool-use task at 24 months, avoidant infants were significantly more impatient, distressed, and aggressive when compared with securely attached infants. The predictability of the avoidant infants' tool-use behavior from their strange situation behavior 6 months earlier provides evidence of continuity. But the continuity is heterotypic since the overt behavior exhibited in the two situations is so different. While Kagan (1971) has emphasized heterotypic continuity across age, this concept can be extended to include cases where the overt behavior associated with a particular attachment pattern also varies systematically across setting.

Linkages to Peer Interaction

SOCIAL COMPETENCE

Two of the studies reporting a relationship between attachment and early peer interaction have interpreted their findings in terms of social competence or skill (Easterbrooks & Lamb, 1979; Lieberman, 1977), while two others have emphasized affective linkages (Pastor, 1981; Waters et al., 1979). Lieberman's social competence interpretation is based on principles derived from both ethological (Bowlby, 1969) and constructivist (Piaget, 1952) theory. For the ethologist, attachment and exploration are seen as complementary behavioral systems. The perception of danger leads the infant to seek the proximity of an attachment figure, thereby reducing exploration. In ethological terms, it is considered adaptive for the anxiously attached infant, who has found the parent nonresponsive (Stayton & Ainsworth, 1973), to limit exploration in order to maximize personal safety.

Competence can be defined as the extent to which the individual "can, through his own activity, control the effect the environment will have on him" (Ainsworth & Bell, 1974). In the context of peer interaction, this definition implies that the toddler possesses the requisite skill to exert influence on the peer's behavior. In a constructivist or Piagetian model, this skill is neither acquired as a result of modeling and reinforcement nor does it emerge spontaneously as a consequence of maturation. Instead, it develops gradually as a result of the child's efforts to deal with and relate to peers. Since the development of peer competence depends on opportunities to exercise newly emerging skills, Lieberman (1977) predicts that the inhibition of exploration by the anxiously attached child will interfere with the development of this competence.

In interpreting the relationship between attachment and early peer interaction, Easterbrooks and Lamb (1979) also emphasize social competence but do so from the perspective of learning theory. They hypothesize that both interactive skills and a basic sense of trust are first acquired in the course of interaction with the parent and later generalized to the peer play context (Lamb, 1978). Trust in the reliability and predictability of the parent's behavior makes the securely attached infant more willing to approach and relate to peers, leading, in turn, to more opportunities to acquire peer skills. Conversely, a tendency to avoid the parent derived from aversive interactive experiences should be associated with a tendency to withdraw from peer interaction.

Easterbrooks and Lamb's interpretation resembles Lieberman's (1977) in its assumption that the securely attached infant will have more opportunities to relate to peers but differs on fundamental motivational issues. While Lieberman assumes that inadequate parenting can interfere with and inhibit exploration, the propensity to explore the environment is considered a biological given (cf. Bowlby, 1969). Lamb (1978), in contrast, suggests that the infant's basic willingness to explore is itself derived from the quality of early experiences with the parent. Lamb differs from the constructivist view (Mueller, 1979) in positing the generalization of particular interactive skills to the peer interaction context. The securely attached infant's warm relationship with his or her parents enhances their salience as behavioral models and increases their potency as reinforcers as they teach interactive skills.

AFFECTIVE STYLE

While Sroufe's (1979) interpretation is similar to Lamb's (1978) in that he too assumes that trust in caretakers is transferred to other potential interactive partners and that some interactive skills may be acquired via modeling, his emphasis is on affective style. The capacity of the securely attached child to be affectively expressive and to deal confidently and effectively with the environment attracts the attention and positive regard of his or her peers (Sroufe & Waters, 1977). Whereas a constructivist would assume that skill at initiating and maintaining interaction enhances the popularity of the securely attached child, Sroufe and Waters make the opposite prediction: affectively attractive children may become skilled more quickly because other children seek them out as interactive partners. Similarly, leadership may either be a function of the child's skill in influencing the behavior of his or her peers; or conversely, leadership skills could develop as a consequence of repeatedly receiving the attention and positive regard of one's peers.

The literature on toddler peer relations demonstrates that peer sociability varies considerably depending on such situational parameters as the familiarity of the setting and the peer (Mueller & Vandell, 1979), the availability of toys (Eckerman & Whatley, 1977), and the type of toys available (DeStefano & Mueller, 1982). Although familiar peers interact less in a novel setting than unacquainted infants (Jacobson, 1981), the greatest frequencies and most sophisticated interaction have been observed among acquainted toddlers at home (Becker, 1977; Rubenstein & Howes, 1976). Since an unfamiliar peer is likely to generate some degree of wariness or uncertainty (Jacobson, 1980; Kagan, Kearsley, & Zelazo, 1975), which might be expected, in turn, to activate the attachment system (cf. Bowlby, 1969), attachment pattern is likely to interact with familiarity of peer in influencing peer sociability. Thus, while securely attached children may be most sociable when playing with a familiar peer at home, this prediction does not necessarily hold for unacquainted toddlers in a laboratory setting.

IMPLICATIONS

The social competence and affective style interpretations differ most sharply in their predictions regarding the earliest stages of peer social interaction. The affective style approach suggests that in the earliest period, before peer skills begin to develop, attachment will primarily influence affective variables. This influence may entail either cross-situational behavioral consistency or heterotypic continuity. Where consistency is predicted, securely attached infants should be friendlier and generally more responsive to their peers; anxiously attached infants, more withdrawn or negative. By contrast, evidence of early skill differences would support a social competence interpretation, which would predict that, even in early peer interaction, securely attached infants will be more adept at eliciting responses from their peers and at maintaining interaction over longer periods of time.

The Assessment of Peer Competence and Affective Style

None of the studies that have reported a relationship between attachment and peer interaction were designed to assess the alternative interpretations that have been advanced to explain this relationship. Two types of peer interaction measures were used in these studies: (1) discrete behavior coding of a focal child, along the lines of the code developed by Eckerman et al. (1975); and (2) qualitative rating scales. Both types of measures demonstrate the existence of relationships between parental attachment and peer play, but neither is sufficiently sensitive to discriminate between social competence and affective style.

DISCRETE BEHAVIOR CODES

Three of the prior studies (Easterbrooks & Lamb, 1979; Lieberman, 1977; Pastor, 1981) used discrete behavior codes similar to those developed by Eckerman et al. (1975). Eckerman et al. code the occurrence of peer-oriented behaviors, such as watch peer, smile at peer, strike peer, and imitate peer. Since only one child is coded at a time, the focus is social behavior rather than interaction. The presence of interaction can be inferred from two relatively global coding categories: coordinate play and struggle over toy. But the degree of competence or skill exhibited during interaction is not assessed.

Mueller and his associates have attempted to go beyond social behavior at the individual level of analysis to code peer interaction from a dyadic perspective. For example, Mueller and Vandell (1979) distinguish short interaction sequences (one peer acts; the other responds) from longer sequences (three acts or longer). They suggest that in the longer sequence the child must be able to respond to a peer behavior while simultaneously anticipating and seeking another. This competence, which they call *bidirectionality,* seems to indicate interpersonal skill. While the measurement of interaction length has proven useful in research on the effects of peer experience and age (e.g., Brownell, 1982; Jacobson, 1981; Mueller & Brenner, 1977), it does not specifically assess the competence of the individual toddler participating in the dyad. In addition, the measurement of interaction length involves no direct assessment of the specific interpersonal skills that promote and sustain interaction. Interaction length is analogous to *mean length utterance* in language acquisition, which indexes the child's developmental level without specifying the competencies that are mastered at each stage.

Whereas secure infant–mother attachment is an attribute of the individual child, peer interaction occurs at the dyadic level of analysis. Research on the relation between these domains should, therefore, assess competence exhibited by the individual child in an interactive context. This approach is exemplified by the concept of *successful initiations* (Finkelstein, Dent, Gallacher, & Ramey, 1978; Holmberg, 1980), defined as those initiations which elicit a response from the peer. This concept measures peer competence directly, since both the individual child's behavior and its effectiveness in influencing the peer's behavior are assessed. Another approach used effectively by Mueller (1979) has been to distinguish between *simple* and *coordinated socially-directed behaviors* (SDBs). In a simple SDB, the toddler coordinates a look toward the peer with one other discrete action (e.g., smiling, banging a toy). In a coordinated SDB, two or more discrete behaviors are coordinated with a look. The assumption that coordinated SDBs indicate greater social skill is supported by the finding that, although frequency of peer interaction is unrelated to peer experience, coordinated SDBs are significantly more prevalent among peer-experienced toddlers.

PRIOR STUDIES

Lieberman (1977) reported correlations between security of attachment assessed at home and peer interaction in unacquainted 3-year-olds observed in a familiar setting. A broad range of peer interaction measures were reduced to three factors in a principal components analysis. *Negative behavior,* which included violent treatment of toys, physical aggression, attempts to leave the room, and crying, was exhibited less frequently by securely attached children, lending support to the prediction of affectively based linkages. Secure attachment was positively associated with a second factor, which Lieberman called *reciprocal interaction.* Although she treated this factor as a measure of peer competence, only one of its items, successful verbal requests, actually indicates interpersonal skill. Other items, such as give or show toy and number of social initiations, merely suggest a positive, friendly attitude toward the peer.

Easterbrooks and Lamb (1979) found a relationship between attachment and peer interaction in unacquainted 18-month-olds in an unfamiliar setting. Because only four of their 66 infants were classified as anxiously attached, they limited their analyses to the securely attached infants. Ainsworth et al. (1978) subdivide securely attached infants into four subgroups according to their behavior during the reunion episodes. B_3 infants, the normative group, actively seek contact with their mothers as they recover from separation distress. B_1 and B_2 infants seek proximity and contact to a lesser degree than B_3's, while B_4 infants cling extensively during the reunions. In Easterbrooks and Lamb's study, the B_1 and B_2 infants also sought less contact with their mothers during the peer play sessions and spent more time than other infants in playing with the peer. The data were interpreted as evidence of cross-situational generalization of the capacity to operate independently of the mother.

Among Easterbrooks and Lamb's (1979) peer interaction measures, the strongest effects are found for *proximity to peer* and *positive interaction.*

Although the authors conclude that their data demonstrate differences in peer competence, it is not clear that either of these measures indicate interpersonal skill. Proximity to peer seems to reflect attitude toward the peer more than competence, since approximately 92% of time spent proximal to the peer involved no interaction or sharing of toys. Positive interaction is a composite of proffer toy, accept toy, smile, laugh, imitate peer, play with same materials, and coordinate play. Since this measure combines sociability measures with indicators of peer skill, it is difficult to determine the relative importance of these dimensions.

Pastor (1981) also studied unacquainted toddlers in an unfamiliar setting. He used six rating scales, four of which indicated more optimal social behavior on the part of the securely attached toddlers. The principal problem with these scales, however, is that each is defined so broadly that it is difficult to identify those aspects of peer relations that are most strongly influenced by attachment pattern. The *overall sociability* scale, for example, mixes diverse affective characteristics with elements of social competence. The highly rated child is described affectively as being friendly, comfortable, and relaxed, relating easily to mother and peers. With regard to competence, he or she has a "good repertoire of initiations" and is persistent "although not in the face of negative response." Finally, the child shows "personal strength . . . in the face of aggression" from the peer, although the behaviors that evidence "personal strength" are not specified.

Pastor also found significant attachment differences on 3 of 13 discrete behavior codes which, in contrast to earlier investigators, he did not attempt to aggregate. One of these measures, *redirection,* is defined in terms of a specific interactive context. Redirection assesses whether, after losing an object struggle, the child immediately directs his or her attention to another activity. Although relatively rare ($M = 1.0$ occurrence per child), this measure yielded a significant effect, possibly because it codes the child's behavior in relation to the peer behavior to which he or she is responding.

Waters et al. (1979) reported a relationship between infant–mother attachment assessed at 15 months and ratings of interaction among familiar peers observed in nursery school classrooms at age 3½. Twelve peer interaction items were taken from a 72-item Q-sort (Baumrind, 1968), which was completed by two independent raters who had observed the children in the preschool setting for 5 weeks. Securely attached children scored significantly higher than anxiously attached children on all but one of these items. The greatest difference was on an attractiveness item ("other children seek his company"), but significant differences were also obtained on items relating to competence ("peer-leader"; "suggests activities") and affect ("sympathetic to peer's distress"; "withdraws from excitement and commotion"). When compared with rating scales, Q-sorts are less susceptible to halo effects, since each child can be rated highly on only a few items. As with rating scales, however, the observer need not specify the particular behaviors that influenced his or her judgment.

Waters et al. (1979) suggest that specific competencies and skills may not be predictable from security of attachment; instead, continuity may be evident only in an overall assessment of the quality of the child's adaptation at each stage of development. If the behavioral manifestations of this adaptation vary considerably among children, then it may be impossible to identify specific linkages between attachment and peer competence. It seems likely, however, that the affective linkages predicted by Sroufe and his associates are mediated by a limited range of specific behaviors. Given the limitations of the measurement schemes used for assessing peer competence to date, a conclusion that behavioral linkages cannot be identified seems premature.

In summary, the results of prior investigations differ according to age of child and setting. In a familiar situation at 3–3½ years, securely attached children appear most friendly and socially competent (Lieberman, 1977; Waters et al., 1979). In an unfamiliar setting at 18–24 months, on the other hand, the results are contradictory. The children Ainsworth considers most securely attached, the B_3's, are more reticent to interact with an unfamiliar peer (Easterbrooks & Lamb, 1979), yet they are rated most positively by Pastor's (1981) adult observers. While most of these studies interpreted their findings with reference to social competence with peers, few direct measures of interpersonal skill were tested. Most of the evidence is based either on composite measures that include affective, attitudinal, and skill components or on *broad-band* assessments (rating scales; Q-sorts) (Waters & Sroufe, in press) that do not specify how the differences associated with attachment pattern are manifest in terms of particular behaviors.

Composite behavioral measures often seem necessary to compensate for the limited frequencies of particular behaviors in a brief laboratory play session. They may also be necessary if the particular behaviors that reveal interpersonal competence or affective style vary among children. Broad-band assessments provide advantages similar to those of composite behavioral measures and, in addition, permit the observer to "look behind" the particular behaviors exhibited in order to assess their psychological significance in context. Frequency counts of individual behaviors have been popular, largely because such behaviors are relatively easy to define and code reliably. Their disadvantage is that discrete acts do not necessarily constitute the appropriate level of analysis. For purposes of the present investigation, for example, they are not sufficiently embedded in an interactive context to measure peer skills and they are usually too insensitive to interpersonal context and communication nuance to indicate affective style.

Episode-Based Rating Scales

The Episode-Based Rating Scales were designed to assess both interpersonal skill and affective tone in the context of the ongoing interactive exchange. Behavior is coded not in terms of type of act (e.g., offer, smile, look) but rather according to its role in promoting or discouraging interaction. Thus, the acceptance of a proffered toy followed by an offer to return the toy to the peer is classified as an *active response* since it invites a further response from the peer, whereas an acceptance of the toy accompanied by no more than a blank stare is coded as a *minimal response* because it does not actively promote continued interaction. A manual for this coding scheme is available from the authors. We will outline its basic structure here, with emphasis on those measures that were designed to distinguish social competence from sociability. Social competence is defined as the ability to elicit an active response from the peer and to resist effectively in an agonistic encounter. Sociability is defined as the affective tone exhibited toward the peer in terms of friendliness or antagonism.

The coding scheme distinguishes between positive (or neutral) interaction, on the one hand, and agonistic interaction, on the other. Because positive interaction is typically brief and difficult for toddlers to maintain, it seems appropriate to code it on an act-by-act basis. Agonistic encounters, on the other hand, especially struggles over toys, seem to be maintained much more easily at this age. For example, in Bronson's (1981) data, a large majority of the *contact bursts* and *contact chains* (i.e., peer interchanges greater than three acts in length) were either partially or completely agonistic, even at the end of the second year. An act-by-act analysis of such interactions typically consists of Child A's tugs on the toy alternating with Child B's tugs on the toy; no subtle timing or interpersonal signalling are required. A rating scale summarizing the performance of each child in each agonistic encounter therefore seems adequate to summarize the degree of competence exhibited.

AGONISTIC ENCOUNTERS VERSUS POSITIVE (OR NEUTRAL) INTERACTION: DEFINITIONS

An *agonistic encounter* is defined as beginning when "one child interferes with the other's possession of a toy or assaults the other child in some fashion, for example, tries to take away a toy, hits, makes a threatening vocalization." Although this definition resembles an Eckerman-type discrete behavior category, it is qualified by two additional sentences which emphasize affective tone:

> Merely reaching for the peer's toy is not sufficient [to constitute the initiation of an agonistic encounter], but strongly lunging for the toy

is. A toy taking that is smooth, relaxed, i.e., without force, is *not* coded as agonistic if it occurs in the course of an otherwise positive interaction or is accompanied by a smile or a positive vocalization.

Note that the attempt here is to use behavioral indicators and context to infer the child's intent to a much greater degree than is possible in most discrete behavior codes. The inference of intent makes the code more difficult to use but, we believe, brings it closer to the way interaction is experienced and interpreted by the participants.

Positive (or neutral) interaction is initiated by a *social overture,* which is defined as "an act clearly directed toward the peer." Following Mueller and Lucas (1975), an act is considered peer-directed if it is accompanied by a look to the peer. Looking is not considered necessary, however, if the child calls the peer by name, tries to give a toy to the peer, or touches him or her in a nonagonistic fashion. Our definition of interaction differs from Mueller and Brenner's (1977) in that, once interaction has been initiated, peer-directed looks are not considered necessary to maintain it. Interaction is assumed to continue so long as the children continue to direct successive acts either toward each other or to an object "toward which the other child has directed an act at some time earlier in the interaction." Thus, Child A may give Child B a piece of a puzzle which B may place onto the puzzle board without looking back at A. B's act is considered responsive to A's overture, even though B doesn't look back.

MEASURES RELATING TO SOCIAL COMPETENCE

Quality of Initiation

Each social overture is rated on a five-point *quality of initiation* scale. This scale was derived from an inspection of pilot videotapes, in which we attempted to identify those behaviors that would lead an adult rater to consider a particular initiation to be competent at this age. In those initiations that appear most competent, the child looks toward the peer both at the beginning of the overture and immediately afterwards. The function of the initial look is to determine that the child has the peer's attention and to signal that the act is directed to the peer. The follow-up look is necessary to ascertain the peer's response. In those initiations that appear somewhat less competent, either the initial or the follow-up look is too brief or the action seems too abrupt in some respect, for example, too sudden or physically awkward. In initiations that appear even less competent, the initial or follow-up look is omitted altogether or the gesture is too brief to allow the peer time to respond, such as when the child offers a toy but withdraws it before the peer has a chance to accept the offer. A *highly skilled* initiation is defined as one in which the child uses either verbal or nonverbal cues to direct or encourage a particular response from the peer.

Proportion of Active Responses Exhibited

Each successive response is rated on the following six-point *degree of responsiveness* scale, which is designed to assess the child's availability for social interaction: (1) ignores initiation; (2) just watches; (3) disruptive response, that is, responds in a way that tends to discourage further interaction; (4) minimal response, that is, minimally encourages the peer to continue to interact; (5) active response, that is, actively encourages an additional response from the peer; (6) sophisticated response. Although developed independently, this scale is very similar to one proposed by Bronson (1981), who used it to evaluate each interactive episode but not each individual response. One of these scale points, *active response,* entails what Mueller and Vandell (1979) call bidirectionality, an act which is not only responsive to the peer but also actively promotes further interaction. Since bidirectionality requires a coordination of behaviors and therefore a certain degree of interpersonal skill, we hypothesized that it might indicate social competence at this age. *Proportion of active responses* is defined as the proportion of nondisruptive (i.e., minimal + active) responses which incorporate bidirectionality. Sophisticated responses, which also require bidirectionality, are combined with active responses in this measure.

Proportion of Active Responses Elicited from the Peer

Social competence can also be assessed in terms of the child's influence on the peer's behavior. Since social initiations are presumably intended to elicit active rather than minimal responses, social competence is indicated, in part, by the degree to which the child is able to elicit active responses from the peer.

Degree of Resistance to Peer Agonism

The child's competence in the context of agonistic encounters is assessed in a six-point *degree of resistance* scale ranging from "no resistance, for example, withdraws without defending self," to "resists strongly and escalates the conflict until the peer gives up, the child establishes him or herself as the winner and withdraws at will, both children withdraw simultaneously, or a mother intervenes." The escalation of aggression is seen as instrumental in this context, where the goal is winning the conflict. Our resistance scale resembles Ainsworth's rating scales in that a child's score may be based either on frequency (number of resistant acts), intensity (strength of resistance), or duration, whichever seems most clearly to indicate degree of resistance. The peer's behavior is also taken into account in that a child can receive a high score for moderately resisting a weak agonistic challenge when strong resistance seems unnecessary. A child's agonism rating is lowered if he or she becomes visibly upset during the encounter, on the theory that visible distress undermines a child's effectiveness in confronting agonistic behavior.

MEASURES OF PEER SOCIABILITY

Initiation Rates

Frequency counts are used to indicate the child's attitude or affective style vis-a-vis the peer. *Number of positive or neutral initiations* indicates the child's inclination to interact with the peer, while *number of initiations of agonistic encounters* reflects an affectively less positive play style. *Proportion of positive initiations* compares the relative frequencies of these two measures by dividing the number of positive or neutral initiations by total number of initiations.

Types of Responses

Each response in the context of positive or neutral interaction is assessed in terms of the six-point responsiveness scale outlined above. The three most common types of response—just watches, minimal, and active—are examined separately for each child. Because sophisticated responses are rare at this age, they are combined with active responses in these frequency counts.

INTEROBSERVER RELIABILITY

Interobserver reliability was assessed for 10 dyads which were coded independently by authors Tianen and Aytch. Percentage agreement was calculated for each of the frequency measures for each child by dividing the smaller of the two observers' scores by the larger and multiplying by 100. Median reliabilities are 96% for positive or neutral initiations; 100% for agonistic initiations; 84% for active responses; 71% for minimal responses; and 88% for just watches. Reliabilities for the rating scales were assessed with Pearson product–moment correlations relating the two observers' scores across the 20 children. Reliabilities are .83 for quality of initiation and .99 for resistance to peer agonism.

SUMMARY

Our Episode-Based Rating Scales are designed to provide measures relating to both social competence and affective style while minimally confounding these two domains. Because of their focus on the effectiveness of a behavior in promoting or discouraging social interaction, these measures are more sensitive than discrete behavior codes to subtle interpersonal cues and behavioral contexts. Yet they are more specific than traditional rating scales because they are grounded in behavior and permit the specification of particular affective and skill characteristics.

Empirical Evidence

SUBJECTS AND PROCEDURE

Twenty-four unacquainted dyads were observed in free play at age 2 years. Each child had been seen in the strange situation (Ainsworth et al., 1978) at 18 months ($M = 18.2$, $SD = 1.0$) and classified as secure, ambivalent, or avoidant by author Jacobson or Wille. Reliability was established between the investigators for 12 of the sample infants and between author Jacobson and Everett Waters, who kindly supplied 12 prescored videotapes for this purpose. Average reliabilities for the four behavior rating scales which form the basis for the attachment classification were .96, .96, .89, and .79 for proximity-seeking, contact maintenance, resistance, and avoidance, respectively. The distribution of maternal attachment patterns was similar to those reported by Ainsworth et al. (1978) at 12 months and Waters (1978) at 12 and 18 months.

Each child returned to the laboratory approximately 6 months later to participate in a 25-minute dyadic free play session. The playroom was large (4.9 by 3.4 m), brightly lit, and carpeted. There were two chairs for the mothers in one corner of the room and 17 age-appropriate toys, including two riding toys, a ball, a tea set, a doll with a bottle, and a wood puzzle. The mothers were asked not to initiate any interaction with the children but to respond naturally if their child seemed to be in any danger or distress. They were also encouraged to converse with each other during the session. Two video cameras, hidden behind curtains at opposite ends of the room, recorded the children's behavior. The camera signals were integrated onto a single videotape by means of a special effects generator.

One member of each dyad was designated as the target child; the other, as the playmate. There were 9 avoidant, 5 secure, and 10 ambivalent target children. All the playmates were securely attached. Eleven of the dyads were male, 13 female. Mean ages were 23.5 months (SD = 1.0) for the target children; 23.4 months (SD = 1.1), for the playmates. Fifty-eight percent of the target children and 54% of the playmates were firstborns. The parents were predominantly upper middle class; 73% of the fathers were employed in professional, technical, or managerial positions, and mean maternal education was 15.4 years (SD = 2.3).

DISCRIMINANT VALIDITY

The peer interaction measures described above were designed to discriminate between social competence or skill, on the one hand, and sociability or affective orientation, on the other. If these measures reflect distinct dimensions in the behavioral organization of the toddler, there should be moderate correlations within each set of measures but minimal correlations across domains (Nunnally, 1978). The data provide evidence of internal consistency for peer sociability although not for peer competence. Number of positive or neutral initiations predicts both degree of responsiveness, r = .50, p < .025, and number of responses, r = .51, p < .025, indicating that the children who initiate interaction most frequently are likely to be most responsive to the overtures of their playmates.

Although designed to tap distinct behavioral domains, the social competence and sociability measures show considerable overlap. For example, the target children who most frequently initiate agonistic encounters are also most effective in resisting the agonism they encounter from the playmate, r = .57, p < .01. Frequency of positive or neutral initiations is correlated with proportion of active responses, r = .47, p < .025, indicating that the target children who are most anxious to initiate interaction are also most likely to respond in a bidirectional fashion to the overtures of their playmates. We infer that a bidirectional response may reflect the target child's eagerness to interact with the playmate, not merely his or her skill in doing so. Finally, frequency of agonistic initiation is negatively correlated with quality of positive initiation, r = -0.41, p < .05. Those toddlers who initiate agonistic encounters are apparently also less likely to make the effort to coordinate behavior with looking when initiating positive interaction.

The overlap between the social competence and sociability measures is perhaps not surprising since children are likely to exhibit their most competent social behaviors when they are most eager to interact with a peer. Moreover, the capacity to coordinate looking with action in the context of an initiation or a bidirectional response has presumably been mastered by this age (cf. Mueller & Brenner, 1977), so that children whose initiations and responses appear unsophisticated may be merely less interested in interacting with the playmate.

PATTERNS OF MUTUAL INFLUENCE

While the foregoing analyses demonstrate some consistency in the target children's sociability and social competence measures, the data for the playmates are less consistent. For example, initiation and response rates, which are significantly intercorrelated for the target children, are unrelated for the playmates (Table 3.1). The playmate's level of responsiveness is predicted by the target child's initiation rate rather than his or her own. This finding is subject to two interpretations. First, given that all 24 playmates are securely attached, they may be more sensitive to the interpersonal cues exhibited by the target children, most of whom are either ambivalent or avoidant. In addition, variability in frequency of initiation is greater for the target children, $SD = 5.3$, than the playmates, $SD = 3.4$, suggesting that the targets represent a broader range in terms of extraversion or gregariousness. A greater range in affective style is not surprising, given the targets' greater diversity in terms of pattern of attachment.

A similar set of relationships can be seen with respect to agonistic encounters. The target child's resistance during such encounters predicts both the target's agonistic initiation rate and that of the playmate (Table 3.1). The securely attached playmates apparently initiate agonistic encounters more frequently with the more resistant target children while leaving the

Table 3.1

Correlations between Initiation Rates and Responses
by Target Children and Playmates[a]

	Target child	Playmate
Positive or neutral initiations		
Positive or neutral responses		
Target child	.51*	.27
Playmate	.79**	−.05
Agonistic initiations		
Resistance to peer agonism		
Target child	.57**	.44*
Playmate	−.12*	.23

[a] $N = 24$ dyads.
*$p < .05$; **$p < .01$; ***$p < .001$.

more submissive ones alone. Again, the affectively more variable target children seem to set the tone. Evidence that the playmates are more attuned to the peer's behavior is provided in Table 3.2. Watching responses by the playmate are predicted by both minimal and active responses from the target child, whereas watching by the target child is unrelated to the playmate's responses.

A second pattern of mutual influence is also evident in Table 3.2. There seems to be some tendency to match the level of responsiveness exhibited by the peer. Thus, frequencies for both the active and minimal response measures are significantly intercorrelated for the two members of the dyad, with a particularly strong relationship for frequency of active responses. Given that most of these toddlers' experience comes from asymmetrical interaction with their parents, one might expect one member of the dyad to be more active while the other child responds minimally. Although this pattern may hold for some interactive episodes, the data suggest a more prevalent tendency for active responses by one child to be matched by active responses from the other. This type of mutual influence pattern, along with the evidence that the playmate's behavior is affected by the target child's affective tone, tend to contradict Bronson's (1981) conclusion that there is little mutual influence in peer interaction at this age.

THE INFLUENCE OF ATTACHMENT PATTERN

The ambivalent toddlers exhibit the greatest sociability toward the novel playmate in the present sample (Table 3.3). They initiate the greatest number of positive or neutral interactions and respond most frequently to the playmate's overtures in a bidirectional fashion. This greater sociability is associated, in turn, with more watching and minimal responses from the

Table 3.2

Intercorrelations among Three Types of Responses for Target Children and Playmates[a]

	Target children		
	Just watches	Minimal response	Active response
Playmates			
Just watches	−.14	.41*	.72***
Minimal response	.12	.60**	.53**
Active response	.18	.51*	.87***

[a]$N = 24$ dyads.
*$p < .05$; **$p < .01$; ***$p < .001$.

Table 3.3
Interactive Behavior by Attachment Pattern

	Attachment pattern				
	Avoidant (N = 9)	Secure (N = 5)	Ambivalent (N = 10)	Overall F(2,21)	Linear F(1,21)
Number of positive initiations					
Target child	3.6	3.6	8.4	2.87*	5.74**
Playmate	4.3	5.0	4.1	<1.00	<1.00
Target child's responses					
Just watches	3.0	5.4	2.6	1.36	<1.00
Minimal response	2.7	2.8	4.0	<1.00	1.72
Active response	2.0	4.2	8.7	2.79*	5.46**
Playmate's responses					
Just watches	2.0	2.4	6.0	4.04**	8.05***
Minimal response	2.2	1.4	4.9	3.07*	4.03*
Active response	2.2	4.4	6.6	1.13	2.25
Number of agonistic initiations					
Target child	3.1	1.8	3.1	<1.00	<1.00
Playmate	2.9	2.2	2.4	<1.00	<1.00
Proportion of initiations that are positive or neutral					
Target child	64.3%	77.3%	71.0%	<1.00	<1.00
Playmate	59.1%	77.5%	46.1%	2.51	3.25*
Resistance to peer agonism					
Target child	2.9	2.0	3.4	1.39	1.81
Playmate	3.7	2.2	1.5	4.91**	6.84**

*p < .10; **p < .05; ***p < .01.

playmate. Although the ambivalent toddlers are most overtly antagonistic in the strange situation reunions with their mothers, they are not more likely to initiate agonistic encounters with a peer. Yet, despite their apparent greater sociability, the ambivalent toddlers are not particularly effective at eliciting positive responses from the playmate. None of the social competence measures differ significantly for the three attachment groups.

The avoidant toddlers resemble the securely attached toddlers on most of the sociability measures. Both attachment patterns are associated with greater reticence or cautiousness in dealing with the novel peer. Yet there are indications in the data that the two groups may differ with respect to social competence and/or attractiveness. The avoidant toddlers elicit the greatest degree of resistance from their playmates during agonistic encounters (Table 3.3), which is consistent with Pastor's (1981) finding that secure playmates engage in a greater number of *object struggles* when paired with avoidant toddlers. The secure infants, by contrast, seem to make more attractive playmates in that they tend to receive the greatest proportion of positive or neutral initiations from the peer.

Our sociability findings are consistent with Easterbrooks and Lamb's (1979) data, although not with their interpretation. The most securely attached toddlers are reticent to interact with the novel peer in both studies. Easterbrooks and Lamb suggest that a greater dependency on the mother leads their B_3 infants to relate less to the playmate. But the avoidant infants in the present study, who exhibit little dependency in the strange situation, are also cautious vis-a-vis the novel peer. An alternative interpretation focuses on the toddler's attachment history. Ainsworth, Bell, & Stayton (1971) report that mothers of B_1 and B_2 infants are inconsistently responsive to their infants' signals and needs. Mothers of ambivalent infants are similar but even more likely to delay in responding to their infants' signals (Ainsworth et al., 1978). One might speculate in the case of the ambivalent toddler (and, to a lesser extent, the B_1 or B_2 toddler) that uncertainty regarding maternal responsiveness may generate anxiety in the child's relations with both parents and peers. This anxiety may, in turn, lead these toddlers to be particularly eager to make contact and elicit a response from the playmate.

Conclusion

A relationship between attachment and early peer interaction has been demonstrated in four prior studies. Our Episode-Based Rating Scales make it possible to evaluate alternative interpretations of this relationship by using distinct measures to assess sociability and peer competence. The data provide the clearest support for interpretations emphasizing affective linkages, which appear more frequently in the form of heterotypic continuity than in the cross-situational generalization of behavior. Thus, securely attached toddlers, who are friendliest to their mothers during the strange situation reunions, are reticent with a novel peer in an unfamiliar setting; whereas ambivalent infants, who are most antagonistic in the Ainsworth strange situation, are most anxious to make contact with the playmate. We cannot infer from the present data that attachment pattern is unrelated to peer competence, since the novel setting may inhibit the expression of competence differences that might otherwise emerge. The data do suggest, however, that in an encounter involving a novel playmate, which is likely to generate uncertainty or wariness at this age, it is affective tone rather than peer competence that is influenced most directly by pattern of attachment.

References

Ainsworth, M. D. S., & Bell, S. M. (1974). Mother–infant interaction and the development of competence. In K. J. Connolly & J. Bruner (Eds.), *The growth of competence.* New York: Academic Press.

Ainsworth, M. D. S., Bell, S. M., & Stayton, D. J. (1971). Individual differences in strange situation behavior of one-year-olds. In H. R. Schaffer (Ed.), *The origins of human social relations.* New York: Academic Press.

Ainsworth, M. D. S., Blehar, M. C., Waters, E., & Wall, S. (1978). *Patterns of attachment: A psychological study of the strange situation.* Hillsdale, NJ: Erlbaum.

Bakeman, R., & Brown, J. V. (1980). Early interactions: Consequences for social and mental development at three years. *Child Development, 51,* 437–447.

Baumrind, D. (1968). *Manual for the preschool behavioral Q-Sort.* Parental Authority research project. Institute of Human Development, University of California, Berkeley.

Becker, J. (1977). A learning analysis of the development of peer oriented behaviors in nine-month-old infants. *Developmental Psychology, 13,* 481–491.

Bowlby, J. (1969). *Attachment.* New York: Basic Books.

Brazelton, T. B. (1973). *Neonatal behavioral assessment scale.* Philadelphia: Lippincott.

Bronson, W. C. (1981). *Toddlers' behaviors with agemates: Issues of interaction, cognition, and affect.* Norwood, NJ: Ablex.

Brownell, C. A. (1982). Effects of age and age-mix on toddler peer interaction and development of role-taking ability in toddlers. Paper presented at the International Conference on Infant Studies, Austin, TX.

Cairns, R. B. (1979). *Social development: The origins of plasticity of interchanges.* San Francisco, CA: Freeman.

DeStefano, C. T., & Mueller, E. (1982). Environmental determinants of peer social activity in 18-month-old males. *Infant Behavior and Development, 5,* 175–183.

Easterbrooks, M. A., & Lamb, M. E. (1979). The relationship between quality of infant–mother attachment and infant competence in initial encounters with peers. *Child Development, 50,* 380–387.

Eckerman, C. O., & Whatley, J. L. (1977). Toys and social interaction between infant peers. *Child Development, 48,* 1645–1656.

Eckerman, C. O., Whatley, J. L., & Kutz, S. L. (1975). Growth of social play with peers during the second year of life. *Developmental Psychology,* 42–49.

Finkelstein, N. W., Dent, C., Gallacher, K., & Ramey, C. T. (1978). Social behavior of infants and toddlers in a day-care environment. *Developmental Psychology, 14,* 257–262.

Holmberg, M. C. (1980). The development of social interchange patterns from 12 to 42 months. *Child Development, 51,* 448–456.

Jacobson, J. L. (1980). Cognitive determinants of wariness toward unfamiliar peers. *Developmental Psychology, 16,* 347–354.

Jacobson, J. L. (1981). The role of inanimate objects in early peer interaction. *Child Development, 52,* 618–626.

Kagan, J. (1971). *Change and continuity in infancy.* New York: Wiley.

Kagan, J., Kearsley, R. B., & Zelazo, P. R. (1975). The emergence of initial apprehension to unfamiliar peers. In M. Lewis & L. Rosenblum (Eds.), *Friendship and peer relations.* New York: Wiley.

Lamb, M. E. (1978). Social interaction in infancy and development of personality. In M. E. Lamb (Ed.), *Social and personality development.* New York: Holt, Rinehart and Winston.

Lieberman, A. F. (1977). Preschoolers' competence with a peer: Relations with attachment and peer experience. *Child Development, 48,* 1277–1287.

Matas, L., Arend, R. A., & Sroufe, L. A. (1978). Continuity of adaptation in the second year: The relationship between quality of attachment and later competence. *Child Development, 49,* 547–556.

Mueller, E. (1979). (Toddlers + toys) = (An autonomous social system). In M. Lewis & L. A. Rosenblum (Eds.), *The child and its family.* New York: Plenum.

Mueller, E., & Brenner, J. (1977). The origins of social skills and interaction among playgroup toddlers. *Child Development, 48,* 854–861.

Mueller, E., & Lucas, T. (1975). A developmental analysis of peer interaction among toddlers. In M. Lewis & L. A. Rosenblum (Eds.), *Friendship and peer relations.* New York: Wiley.

Mueller, E., & Vandell, D. (1979). Infant–infant interaction. In J. D. Osofsky (Ed.), *Handbook of infant development.* New York: Wiley.

Nunnally, J. C. (1978). *Psychometric theory* (2nd ed.). New York: McGraw-Hill.

Parten, M. (1932). Social participation among preschool children. *Journal of Abnormal and Social Psychology, 27,* 243–269.

Pastor, D. L. (1981). The quality of mother–infant attachment and its relationship to toddlers' initial sociability with peers. *Developmental Psychology, 17,* 326–335.

Piaget, J. (1952). *The origins of intelligence in children.* New York: International Universities Press.

Rubinstein, J., & Howes, C. (1976). The effects of peers on toddler interaction with mother and toys. *Child Development, 47,* 597–605.

Sroufe, L. A. (1979). Socio-emotional development. In J. D. Osofsky (Ed.), *Handbook of infant development.* New York: Wiley.

Sroufe, L. A., & Waters, E. (1977). Attachment as an organizational construct. *Child Development, 48,* 1184–1199.

Stayton, D. J., & Ainsworth, M. D. S. (1973). Individual differences in infant responses to brief, everyday separations as related to other infant and material behaviors. *Developmental Psychology, 9,* 226–235.

Waters, E. (1978). The reliability and stability of individual differences in infant–mother attachment. *Child Development, 49,* 483–494.

Waters, E., & Sroufe, L. A. (in press). Social competence as a developmental construct: Perceiving the coherence of individual differences across age, across situations, and across behavioral domains. *Developmental Review.*

Waters, E., Wippman, J., & Sroufe, L. A. (1979). Attachment, positive affect, and competence in the peer group: Two studies in construct validation. *Child Development, 50,* 821–829.

CHAPTER 4

The Effect of Experience
on Peer Relationships

Beatrice Blyth Whiting

Introduction

A child brings to its relationship with peers the experience it has had with its parents, its mother in particular, and with its siblings and other individuals who live in its house. We believe that these experiences influence a child's pattern of interaction with peers. This is certainly not a new hypothesis. It is one that psychoanalysts and all clinicians have documented.

A child's experiences are influenced by the culture in which it grows up. The culture prescribes the settings the child will frequent, the activities the child engages in, and the individuals with whom it interacts. Thus, culture programs the learning environment of styles of social interaction.

Social scientists all recognize that there are differences among the cultures of the world, but few have focused on the details of the culturally determined social environment that affects child development. It is the aim of this paper to explore the environmental variables at the cultural level of analysis. In particular, we are interested in the companions who are available in the growing child's environment and their possible effect on the nature of a child's interpersonal behavior. We want to ask the following questions of our data: What does a child learn in culturally programmed settings? With how many different types of individuals does a child learn to interact? Do children who spend their daily life in their early years with siblings, half-siblings and cousins who are older and younger, differ in be-

79

havioral profile from children who, from early childhood, spend extended periods of time with peers of the same age? What experiences do children bring to peer relationships? Do the children who have little experience with peers have different patterns of interaction that have lasting effects on peer relationships? Does experience with other categories of individuals carry forward and influence one's pattern of interaction with peers?

The comparison of children's lives in different parts of the world functions to alert students of social behavior and relationships to the process variables that program a child's experiences. If researchers limit their studies to individuals who are members of their own culture, they are apt to overlook variables that are important determinants of social behavior. Culture as defined here includes the beliefs, values, and practices of a society, the norms of behavior to the various categories of individuals who play different roles in a society. These norms detail reciprocal role behavior—the expected behavior of individuals when they interact with persons of different gender, age, kin relationship, and status. There must be consensus in a society as to appropriate role behavior, rules governing expectations as to interpersonal behavior.

On a micro level, there must be a consensus among the members of a society as to the intention of certain types of behavior or else meaningful communication would be impossible. We need to know the expectations, beliefs, and values of the interactors in order to understand their behavior. *Setting,* following Barker and Wright, 1955, is defined as the physical and social environment. Studies in our society make use of this cultural knowledge, often completely unaware that the researchers are using it in their interpretations.

During the time when developmental psychologists were devoting the majority of their energy to understanding cognitive development, little attention was given to detailing differences in the social environment. The interest in maternal socialization practices, one of the central concerns of the 1930s, took second place to chronological and developmental age as the most important predictor of behavior. A summary assessment of a family's socioeconomic status was the most typical index variable of the social environment (Warner, Meeker, & Eels, 1949). This macro-level variable leaves much to be desired. It is interesting to note, for example, that it only includes the education of the father, although the mother is the principal caretaker of young children. The household assessment of Rossi, Sampson, Bose, Jasso, & Passel (1974) makes a judgment based on both the husband's and wife's occupation and education.

More recently, studies include a comparison of individuals growing up in different types of households that vary as to the presence of the child's biological and sociological parents and their employment. More rarely, researchers also attempt to include other aspects of the culture of the households. For example, the work of Swanson (1958), Kohn (1969), LeVine (1974), and Radke-Yarrow, Zahn-Waxler, & Chapman (1983) have included assessments of parental goals and expectations. Baltes and Schaie (1973) and Elder (1974, 1979) have explored cohort differences in beliefs, values, and practices associated with the changing economic environment in the United States. Barker and Wright and their followers have explored the effect of the size of populations on behavior (Barker & Gump, 1964). Loo and others have explored the effect of space (1972). Two recent projects have been innovative in including a variety of setting variables, the Family and Stress Project (Belle 1982) and the Family Life Styles Project (Weisner & Martin, 1979; Weisner & Weibel, 1981; Weisner, Bansana, & Kornfein, in press).

In our work, we have attempted to construct a model that includes all the environmental variables (i.e., setting variables) that we have identified in our cross-cultural work (Whiting, B, 1980). We conceive of the culture of a society as detailing the social settings in which the child lives, settings that impose constraints on the child's companions and activities. Although the content of cultures varies, the cultural elements of special import in influencing relationships have many similarities. Culture can be likened to a program that details the physical and social environment that interacts with the genetic characteristics and the physical, cognitive and social skills of the developing child. When we write a program for analyzing relationships, be they mother–child, father–child, sibling–child, or child–child, we must take into account the environmental constraints.

In our thinking, we have used the metaphor of a play rather than a program. The cultural script describes the settings, the stage on which all relationships are played out. Using this metaphor, the scene is detailed, describing the physical characteristics of the space, the cast of characters who frequent the space, and the activities in progress when the interaction between the actors takes place. The program notes tell the audience the country in which the action is to take place and the epoch to be portrayed. Many playwrites include in the program notes a summary of salient attitudes and values that characterize the historical milieu of the setting. The audience is expected to fill in from its knowledge of the relevant period the details of the cultural beliefs and values of the times. The script of the play will include statements by the actors that alert the audience to those attitudes and values that the playwright considers essential for the understanding of the action that unfolds. If the audience is to infer the intention of the actors and the meaning of their speeches, it must be privy to the beliefs, values and expectations of the actors, those variables that we subsume in the concept of culture.

In some ways, the metaphor of a computer program may be more useful than the metaphor of the script of a play. It has the advantage of being easy to revise to encompass individual or group change. In the history of cultures, there is constant change. Cultural programs that do not produce the desired quality of life for a community must be rewritten by its members. The beliefs, values, and practices are modified by the society in an attempt to improve the quality of life, a process known as cultural change. On an individual level, intervention by a therapist or teacher or events, such as those that follow adoption, may lead to changes in the beliefs, values, and practices of a child's socializers, associated with changes in the social behavior of the child. If one uses the metaphor of the play, and the outcome is not pleasing, the playwright must revise the entire script.

The data presented in the following pages summarize the detailed study of 30 to 50 families in 20 sample communities. The data were collected by the original members of the Six Culture Study in the mid-1950s (Whiting & Whiting, 1975) and by 14 colleagues who have collected data in India, South America, Central America, Africa, and the United States (See Footnote 1 for the list of researchers and Table 4.1 and 4.2 for their research sites. The comparative analysis was made possible by a grant from the Ford Foundation [Whiting & Edwards, in preparation]. Data on the setting variables were collected by ethnographic interviews focused on the daily routines of families, daily informal observations of the families by individuals who spent 18 months to 3 years at their field sites, by systematic, randomized spot observations of sample children (see Munroe & Munroe, 1971, and Rogoff, 1978, for descriptions of methodology), and by data collected as an adjunct to the recording of children's interaction. Several of these methods were used in the research sites.

The analysis of the relation between setting variables and the dyadic interaction of children ages 2 to 12 is on a cultural level. The cultures have been divided into culture types on the basis of the clustering of the setting variables. The social interaction behavior has been summarized in dyad types defined by the gender and age of the interactors.

It is customary for anthropologists to stress the uniqueness of cultures. In our studies of child life, we have been impressed by similarities across cultures that appear in areas of the world that share, at a basic minimum, ecological niches, economic pursuits and technological knowledge. The following pages will present the setting variables that we have identified and the clustering that we have labeled cultural types. In reviewing our data, one of the most impressive findings is that in many of the societies of the

[1]The data were collected by Charlene Bolton, Ralph Bolton, Carol Ember, Gerald Erchak, Sara Harkness, Amy Koel, Carold Michelson, Ruth Munroe, R. L. Munroe, Sara Nerlove, Barbara Rogoff, Susan Seymour, Charles Super, and Thomas Weisner.

Third World that are new to the international industrial society, we have few records of interaction between peers as defined by children who are not kin and who are, on an average, the same chronological age. Association with peers, so defined, is fostered by schools, institutions that become essential with the introduction of occupational specialization and the need for literacy. In their younger years, children in many preindustrial societies had little opportunity to interact with children who were not siblings, half-siblings and courtyard cousins.

The industrial revolution has had a far-reaching affect on the lives of children. With the introduction of schools, children spend extended periods of time with companions who are not kindred. When school attendance becomes universal, these companions are also agemates, and in that sense, potentially peers in physical, social, and cognitive skills. It is probable that contact with peers, so defined, is a relatively recent phenomenon in human history.

Are there styles of behavior that characterize the interaction of peers that are not learned in interaction with siblings and relatives that live in daily contact with children? What do children who spend extended time with various aged siblings bring to peer relationships? Do their peer relationships differ from those of children who do not have these experiences? To answer these questions on the cultural level, we must be able to rate societies on the amount of time children spend with various categories of people and assess what the children learn in interaction with these individuals. On an intracultural level, we must be able to compare the history of individual children's experiences with various types of companions.

Cultural Determinants of Styles of Dyadic Interaction

BASIC ECONOMY AND SETTLEMENT PATTERNS

What do we know about the cultural variables that determine the types of category of individuals who will interact frequently with young children? Beginning with the macro variables, the economic base of a society influences the settlement patterns of families, which in turn determines the cast of characters with whom a child interacts. One can trace in broad outline the characteristics of settlement patterns in the evolution of society, from the hunters and gatherers of prehistoric time to the industrial nations of the modern world. Hunters and gatherers tended to live in nomadic bands, often including not more than two or three families during those months of the year when it was necessary to divide up the territory according to its ability to supply adequate game and wild vegetable products. Larger groups formed when an area supplied a special food crop. Thus, the Paiute Indians of Oregon, whom I studied in the 1930s (1950), had wandered in prereservation days in groups of two to four families when gathering spring roots, had gathered in somewhat larger areas for berry picking and salmon fishing, and had wintered in groups as large as 200 around Lake Harney, where there was an abundant fall crop of edible seeds and adequate wood and water for the winter months. Thus, for many months of the year a child's social interaction was limited to adults, siblings, and cousins. Families were small. The play groups were small and multi-aged, similar to those described by Draper (1972, 1973) and Konner (1972) for the Kung Bushmen of the Khalahari Desert of Botswana. Even at the winter camp the Paiute children had little opportunity to interact with a group of same-age peers.

The nomadic herdsmen of East Africa had more opportunity to interact with same-age peers. The population of the settlement was larger. Societies like the Samburu and the Masaii lived in large camps (bomas), including several polygymous men and their children. Age grading was important in structuring interpersonal behavior. At adolescence, the male children were segregated from their families and lived in camps (manyattas) that included groups of young males who had been initiated together and formed an age set. This age graded system allowed for the aggregation of large groups of males of roughly the same age who were of the warrior class, responsible for the care of the herds of cattle and, in particular, for the protection of the animals from the raids by other warrior groups. The girls who spent time with the young warriors were cohorts of preadolescents who, at initiation, which immediately followed menarche, formed an age set. Since at marriage these girls moved to the camp of their husbands, they spent less time with their age set mates than did the boys.

Agricultural societies vary in settlement pattern. Some have nucleated villages, the houses clustered in hamlets, villages or towns surrounded by agricultural land. Other families live in isolated farm households. In societies with shifting agriculture and the seasonal rotation of gardens, the land may be many miles from the villages. In the nucleated villages such as Taira, Okinawa (Maretzki & Maretzki, 1966), depending on size, the child may find agemates as soon as it is allowed out of the house and yard. In the isolated polygynous homesteads, such as those described by LeVine and LeVine (1966) in Nyansongo, the child will associate with siblings, half-siblings and cousins until it is old enough to be allowed to wander away from the homestead—an age which, in our sample, is earlier for boys than for girls.

In industrial societies there is occupational specialization. Since many of the jobs require literacy, schools are introduced to teach the three R's. These educational institutions revolutionized the lives of children. When schools became age graded, they required children of the same age to spend many hours of the day together. These peers were of the same sex in the segregated schools, cross sex when coeducation was permitted. Once schools became established, children of 6 or 7 years of age were in the company of peers. In many societies the absence of the older children who cared for their younger siblings added to the workload of women who were responsible for helping in the economic tasks of the family. This led to the development of nursery schools. In recent times, in societies of the Western World, as more women join in the work force, the introduction of crèches and infant schools permits the association of same-aged children from infancy or toddlerhood.

In sum, the settlement pattern and the educational institutions program the nature of a child's social experience. The availability of males and females of various ages depends on the arrangement of families in space. The rules governing permission to wander beyond the confines of the household further constrain dyadic interaction. The rules themselves reflect the parental generations' beliefs about the capability of children of various ages to take care of themselves. The rules also reflect their trust in the members of the community to see to the well-being of its children.

HOUSEHOLD AND FAMILY COMPOSITION

Household composition defines the available persons with whom a child may interact before leaving the home environment. In the United States, we identify mother–child households, monogamous nuclear households, and three-generational households. More recently, we have divided households on the basis of the marital status of live-in males. In our samples, in addition, we have polygynous households, 4-generational households, and households extended collaterally, including brothers and their respective wives and children. Thus, the developing child in these societies has different amounts of experience with different types of individuals.

Some children, like those in isolated farms in northern Norway, may spend the majority of their time with their parents and siblings until they reach school age. They will enter school with no experience in interacting with children who are not siblings or cousins, or with adults who are not parents or close relatives. They may not even have had much contact with these relatives. The school itself may be small with few children in any one grade. Classrooms may include several grades. The effect of this isolation on cognitive and social skills has been explored by Merida Hollos in a study comparing the isolated farm children with children growing up in Norwegian towns (1974).

The size of the family is another setting variable that influences a child's social experience. This is a variable that has been more widely used in studies in the United States, most frequently as a variable to be controlled rather than explored. As discussed below, in our cross-cultural studies, family size influences the diversity of experience with younger and older same-sex and cross-sex siblings and influences the patterns of dyadic interaction.

The division of labor, the work routine of the adults and children, also acts as a constraint on social interaction. In our program the workload of the mother is an important predictor of mother–child interaction and of the activities of the children. Mothers who work away from the house, responsible for raising food or earning wages, interact with their children in a different style from mothers whose activities are limited to child care and household maintenance. Mothers with heavy workloads expect their children to help by performing chores that may include infant and child care, household maintenance tasks, and farm and animal husbandry tasks. The age at which these chores are assigned, and the degree to which they are assigned according to the child's gender are important predictors of the pattern of dyadic interaction.

The salience of the father, the amount of time he spends with his children, and his assigned responsibilities for the care of his children also affect the social experiences of the child. Research in the United States has been mainly limited to contrasting father-absent and father-present households. The degree of father salience has seldom been used as a variable. Our sample families vary widely in their conception of the father's role in socialization. The fathers of Tarong in the Philippines are the most involved in the care of their children in infancy and early childhood, the fathers of subSaharan Africa the least.

ACTIVITIES AND PARENTAL GOALS

To assess what a child learns in various settings, we need to include an analysis of the activities that are recurrent in a child's life. These include not only the work tasks associated with family living, but school routines and leisure activities, the types of play and organized games that are a part of a child's life.

We are beginning to explore the predictive power of the cultural values of adults and of children of various ages. We have identified types of parental goals that influence social interaction. The attributes of the ideal child desired by parents vary among our communities. The parental goals in turn influence dyadic interaction. The characteristics of the culturally defined ideal relationship of older and younger, same-age and cross-sex siblings are other important variables to be included in our cross-cultural program. To date, we have not included the cultural concepts of an ideal friend, but believe that these are also important in predicting the social relationships of dyads.

SUMMARY

In the development of the child, these cultural variables determine what dyadic partners are available, how much time the child will spend in various types of dyadic interaction, the nature of the space in which the dyadic interaction will take place, the activities in which the child will participate, and the adults and others present while the dyadic interaction is taking place. The attributes of the ideal parent, the ideal child, and the ideal friend will influence feelings, expectations, and behavior. It is obviously impossible to explore the effects of all these variables in any one study. The comparison of samples of dyadic interaction collected in different parts of the world, however, suggests what effects can be expected as a result of these cultural factors.

Cross-Cultural Analysis of Dyadic Interaction

In the cross cultural study of dyadic interaction in 13 communities (Table 4.1), we have analyzed the styles of interpersonal behavior that characterize mother–child and child–child dyads controlling for the gender, age, and kin relationship of the actors. We have discovered some consistent patterns of interaction across all the samples and some differences that are associated with the frequency of interaction and the activities of the children.

DATA BASE

Over a period of 20 years observation of the social interaction of children ranging in age from 2–12 have been collected by a group of anthropologists and psychologists in 13 communities in different parts of the world. The method of observing and recording the dyadic interaction of these children was similar, enabling us to pool the data for cross-cultural analysis. The list of the sample communities, the names of the researchers, and the number of children observed in each sample is presented in Table 4.1. The settings the children frequent in the communities differ along the dimensions described above.

CODING AND ANALYSIS OF DYADIC INTERACTION

The transcultural code of social behavior is a modification of the code used in the Six Culture Study (Whiting, 1968; Whiting & Whiting, 1975). It identifies five summary categories of *mands,* that is, the attempt of one

Table 4.1

Observations of Social Interaction

Location	Field Researcher	Subjects
1. Khalapur, India	Leigh Minturn 1955–56	24 households; 24 children aged 3–10
2. Taira, Okinawa	Thomas Maretzki and Hatsumi Maretzki 1955–56	24 households; 24 children aged 3–10
3. Juxtlahuaca, Mexico	A.K. Romney and Romaine Romney 1955–56	22 households; 22 children aged 3–10
4. Tarong, Philippines	William and Corinne Nydegger 1955–56	24 households; 24 children aged 3–10
5. Nyansongo, Kenya	Robert LeVine and Barbara LeVine 1956–57	16 households; 16 children aged 3–10
6. Orchard Town, U.S.A.	John Fischer and Ann Fischer 1956–57	24 households; 24 children aged 3–10
7. Kien-taa, Liberia	Gerald Erchak 1970–71	15 households; 20 children aged 1–6
8. Ngeca, Kenya	Beatrice Whiting 1968–70 1973	42 homesteads; 104 children aged 2–10
9. Oyugis, Kenya	Carol Ember 1968–69	10 children aged 8–12
10. Kisa, and Kariobangi, Kenya	Thomas Weisner 1970–72	24 urban and rural families matched by age, education, and kinship ties; 68 children aged 2–8
12. Kokwet, Kenya	Sara Harkness and Charles Super 1972–75	Kokwet: 64 children aged 3–10 Uort: 64 children aged 3–10
13. Bhubaneswar, India (State of Orissa)	Susan Seymour 1965–67	36 households; 103 children aged 0–10

actor to change the behavior of another. It classifies mands on the basis of the inferred intention of the actor. *Nurturant mands* are of two types. Of the first type are those that are judged to have the intention of *offering material goods* such as food, physical care and/or privilege. Of the second type are those that have the intention of *offering emotional comfort,* including attention and praise to those perceived by the actor to be in a state of need. *Prosocial dominance* includes mands judged to have the intention of changing the behavior of another so that it acts for the benefit of the welfare of the group and conforms to group norms. These mands may be the assignment of tasks expected of the children, mands requiring proper hygiene, proper social behavior, and/or other mands that are judged to have the intention of influencing the alter to behave in a responsible manner. Our code includes two types of egoistic mands: those that have been traditionally called *dependent* and those that have been labeled *dominant*. The *egoistic-dependent mands* include those that are judged to have the intention of gaining material goods, food, privileges or emotional comfort, attention, and praise. *Egoistic-dominance* includes behavior that is judged to have the intention of hurting another symbolically or physically. We do not include rough-and-tumble play or verbal teasing in this category. We have kept these types of behavior for separate analysis or combined them with sociability. *Sociable mands* are those judged to have the intention of eliciting friendly interaction. Some sociability cannot be coded as mands as the observer is unable to judge who is the elicitor of the interaction. The exchange of information is also often difficult to classify as a mand and has been analyzed separately or combined with sociability. Information exchange that was judged to have the intention of transmitting knowledge was coded as *training mands*. Interaction was recorded in running sequences of mands and responses to mands.

Our analysis is on a cultural rather than individual level. Dyad types are compared across the cultures. Within each sample we have pooled interactions that take place between mothers and sons and between mothers and daughters of specific ages. We have pooled the behavior between same-sex male and female siblings and pooled the behavior of cross-sex siblings, categorizing the dyads according to age groups and the relative age of actors and alters. We have a small sample of dyads consisting of children who are not kin. Most of our analyses are based on the comparison of the rank order of the proportion of macro-categories of behavior.

The samples in most of our culture types are small. Statistical analysis was only practicable in the subSaharan sample. For this reason we have most often relied on the consistency of the direction of relationships rather than formal tests of significance.

FREQUENCY OF DYAD TYPES

In some of the communities (Table 4.2) the researchers made random spot observations during the daylight hours, noting the persons present and the activities in progress when the observer caught the first glimpse of the sample child. In these communities we can estimate the percent of time spent with different categories of individuals. In the societies where we have

Table 4.2

Spot Observations Randomly Collected during Daylight Hours

Location	Field Researcher	Subjects
1. Santa Domingo and Concaste, Guatemala	Sara Nerlove 1971	28 girls, 25 boys
2. Nyansongo (Gusii), Western Province, Kenya	Sara Nerlove 1968	10 girls, 12 boys
3. Ngeca, (Kikuyu), Central Province, Kenya	Ruth Munroe R. L. Munroe 1970–71	12 girls, 9 boys
4. Vihiga, (Logoli), Western Province, Kenya	Ruth Munroe R. L. Munroe 1971	8 girls, 8 boys
5. Santa Barbara, (Canchitos), Peru	Charlene Bolton Ralph Bolton 1974	5 girls, 6 boys
6. Claremont, California	Amy Koel Carol Michelson 1975	7 girls, 10 boys
7. San Pedro, Guatemala	Barbara Rogoff 1975–76	10 girls, 12 boys

observations of social behavior we have data on the relative frequency of dyadic interaction with different categories of alters. On the basis of these two types of data we can estimate how much practice the sample children have in the behaviors that characterizes the interaction of the most frequently occuring dyads.

Patterns of Dyadic Interaction Practiced in Early Childhood

MOTHER–CHILD DYADS

Mothers are the primary caretakers and socializers of young children. They model styles of interpersonal behavior that their children imitate. The mother, by assigning children to various settings, regulates the amount of time a child is in her presence. By assigning tasks such as sibling care, she encourages her children to imitate her style of interaction.

The culture types of mother–child interaction are associated with three variables that program the settings in which they interact: the workload of the mother, the number of female adults present in the household, and the value the families place on schooling. The workload rating is based on an assessment of (1) the amount of work a mother does outside the home; (2)

the amount of help she receives from other adults, including her husband; (3) the number of children in the family; and (4) the facilities that make the daily household maintenance relatively easy or labor intensive.

Ranked on the workload dimension our communities may be divided into three major types. The mothers of our rural Kenyan samples who work in the fields for a minimum of 4 or 5 hours a day, 5 days a week, are rated at one extreme. These women are responsible for raising the food for their children. At the other extreme are the New England mothers of Orchard Town (Fischer & Fischer, 1966), most of whom, at the time the observations were made, did not work.

Table 4.3 presents the sample communities that represent the three major culture types. Type A includes the sub-Saharan communities where the women are involved in the production of the family food supply, have few household conveniences and little help from their husbands or other adults Kpelle men of Liberia do more agricultural work than the Kenya men in our sample (Erchak, 1977). All type A cultures, on the average, have large families. Type B cultures include those societies where the women work outside the home but are joined in their work by their husbands. Many of these families have other adult females living close by who share in the work. In Juxtlahuaca (Oaxaca, Mexico), the men are responsible for the major agricultural work, with the women helping at planting and harvesting, taking care of small kitchen gardens near the house, and selling cooked

Table 4.3

Culture Types as Defined by the Mother's Workload and Presence
of Female Companions in Household

Mother's workload	Culture	
High (Type A)	Nyansongo (Kenya)	
	Ngeca (Kenya)	
	Kisa-Kariobangi (Kenya)	
	Kokwet (Kenya)	
	Kien-taa (Liberia)	
Medium (Type B)	Tarong (Phillipines)	
	Juxtlahuaca (Mexico)	
	Taira (Okinawa)	
	Lower-class Bhubaneswar (India)	
	Female companions in households	
	Present (Type C1)	Absent (Type C2)
Low (Type C)	Khalpur (India)	Orchard Town (USA)
	Middle-class Bhu-baneswar (India)	Tennessee

food and other products in the market. Parents of the husband or wife often shared the same courtyard (Romney & Romney, 1966). Lower-class Bhubaneswar (India) women (Seymour, 1971) work at wage-earning jobs like their husbands. They have adult women helpers, grandparents, sisters-in-law or other relatives. Type C includes the women of Khalpur in India, (Minturn & Hitchcock, 1966) the middle-class families in Bhubaneswar, (Seymour, 1971) and in the Orchard Town (U.S.) sample (Fischer & Fischer, 1966). We were also able to include mothers observed by the Schoggens in Tennessee (Schoggens & Schoggens, n.d.). Type C is divided into two types: those mothers who have female companions living with them, C_1, and those who live in isolated nuclear households, C_2.

Styles of mother–child dyadic interaction differ in these culture types. Type A mothers emphasize the training aspect of the maternal role. The mothers of Ngeca (Kenya) that I studied belong to this group. They believe that a child from two years of age on should be assigned chores that increase in complexity and arduousness with age. Children should be punished for failure to perform these tasks responsibly, or for refusing to do what their elders request of them. Praise is not considered necessary as the reward for the correct performance of the type of chores assigned. It is intrinsic, and the learning of the necessary skills is primarily by imitation. A child can tell when he or she has successfully carried water, cut firewood, dug potatoes, or tended to fire under the daily pot of maize and beans. His or her competence as a child nurse is measured by the infant's or toddler's state when the mother returns from her gardening.

If one rank orders four types of initiated maternal behavior in all Type A cultures, all of whom live in rural subSaharan Africa, prosocial mands (mands advising regrading etiquette and proper behavior and mands regarding the assignment of chores and child care) rank first in the percent of a mother's observed initiated behavior. Controlling behavior ranks second, including the proportion of the mother's reprimands and the proportion of commands that are judged to be arbitrary and not related to training, that is, egoistic-dominance. The sum of training mands and controlling mands account for 69% of a mother's behavior to sons and daughters. The remaining 31% of maternal behavior in Type A is accounted for by initiated nurturance and sociability. It should be noted that our analysis is of initiated nurturance. These Type A mothers are in fact compliant to their children's dependency demands. Mothers, on the average, comply immediately in a little less than half the time to requests made by children as recorded by the observer. If one includes delayed compliance, the average is nearer two-thirds of the time. The picture of nurturance that emerges is that of a compliantly nurturant mother, responsive to overt seeking mands of her child.

To an American observer, one of the most salient characteristics of Type A mothers is their tendency not to intervene in the squabbles of their children. In most of the homesteads where we made observations, there was little or no adult supervision of sibling interaction. In spite of this, there was a low frequency of agonistic behavior. In part, this can be attributed to culturally prescribed rules of dominance that are learned early. Older siblings may dominate younger siblings, and boys may dominate girls.

It is interesting to note however, that in these Type A cultures, as children mature, comparatively speaking, they do not initiate interaction with their mothers as frequently as in the other societies in our sample, In fact, in two of the eight samples of Type A families, there are no observations of boys initiating interaction with their mothers more than six times overall in the sessions when they were observed. There is only one sample in which there were no girls who initiated at least six interactions with their mothers. It is our hypothesis that in Type A societies, where children are expected to begin working as early as 4-years of age, running errands or performing other simple chores, they avoid their mothers. They learn that they avoid being assigned tasks if they are not around the mother. Many of the chores require the child to remain in the house and yard. Since boys are assigned fewer chores they are freer to avoid the mother.

It is often difficult for individuals raised in Type A societies to understand the continuing interdependence and frequency of interaction of children older than 4 or 5 with their parents. African students in the United States have commented with surprise on the young child's choice of the mother's companionship in preference to a sibling's.

Type C_1 cultures are high in control mands (eogistic-dominance). Mothers were observed attempting to control their children proportionally more than training them. Initiated nurturance ranks second in Type C_1 cultures. Sociable interaction between mothers and children is comparatively low. It is our hypothesis that the increase in control and the low proportion of mother–child social interaction is associated with the presence of other adults as residents in the households. There is continuous social interaction between the women of the courtyard. In comparison to the Type A and B cultures, there are few tasks that the mother performs that she can delegate, or wants to delegate, to her young children. Since the adults are interacting with each other, they are less responsive to sociable overtures from their children and often attempt to control them so they will not interrupt adult interaction. The children, with less to do, are more apt to get underfoot and are reprimanded for doing so.

In Type C_2 cultures, sociability is second to control mands. As in Type C_1 cultures, mothers have few tasks to assign to their children. Unlike Type C_1 cultures, however, the mothers do not have adult companions and enjoy social interaction with their children. There is constant seeking and offering of information and friendly exchanges. The children of these mothers are high on seeking behaviors, seeking information, friendly interaction, attention, and praise. Isolated nuclear families foster children with this profile. The Orchard Town mothers, especially in the cooler months, when it is difficult to bundle up two preschoolers and take them on visits to neighboring houses, spend many hours during the day without adult companionship.

INTERACTING WITH INFANTS AND YOUNGER SIBLINGS

In Type A and Type B cultures, children are assigned the care of young siblings and learn maternal behaviors. The mother serves as the model, and the child nurses, anxious not to have unhappy, crying or complaining charges, are motivated to monitor and imitate the mother. It is also apparent that infants elicit a high proportion of nurturance and sociability from all children. Konrad Lorenz has hypothesized that the physical characteristics of an infant, including its large head size in proportion to its body, elicit nurturant responses from other human beings. Most children respond in a positive way—smiling and laughing and imitating the infant— and frequently try to guess the wants of the preverbal child. (For review articles see Lorenz, 1971; Whiting, B., 1982; Berman, Agplanalf, Cooper, Mansfield, & Schields, 1975; Berman, 1980; Radke-Yarrow et al., 1983). Our observations across the cultures confirm Lorenz's observations: children are positively responsive to the overtures of infants.

Toddlers elicit a high proportion of prosocial dominance and training mands. Children who have just learned to walk like to explore. They also like to tag along after their older siblings. Since they are too young to perceive dangers in the environment, their older sibling caretakers constantly attempt to restrain them to warn them of dangers. Modeling their mothers' behavior, they also attempt to teach the rules of appropriate behavior that they have so recently learned themselves (Whiting, B., 1982).

It is our hypothesis that styles of interaction learned in the child–infant dyad and the child–toddler dyad generalize to child–older sibling, child–mother, and child–peer dyads. The child's first experience in social interaction is with the mother. Assigned the care of siblings, the child's caretaking style is influenced by the mother's treatment of infants and toddlers and by the way the child itself has been treated by the mother (reciprocal role learning). The nature of infants and toddlers elicits nurturance and prosocial dominance, as well as training mands, behaviors that are required of caretakers in all societies essential for keeping the infant and toddler alive and essential for socializing a child into the norms of a society (Whiting, B., 1980, 1982; Whiting & Edwards, in preparation).

Our spot observations and ethnographic data on setting occupancy affirm that girls are more frequently involved in the care of infants and toddlers than boys. Across the samples, with the possible exception of the United States, girls are with infants and toddlers more frequently (Edwards & Whiting, 1980; Whiting, B., 1980; Whiting, B., 1982). That the experience of caring for infants and toddlers teaches the child maternal behavior is demonstrated by the social behavior of boys who are assigned the care of young children. In the societies where boys serve as child nurses, they have styles of interaction with children other than their charges that are similar to that of girls. They develop a high proportion of nurturance and prosocial dominance, although it never reaches the same level as that of girls. In contrast, boys in the same communities who have not taken care of infants are proportionately lower in these behaviors (Ember, 1973; Whiting & Whiting, 1983; Whiting, B., 1980; Whiting & Edwards, in preparation).

Our spot observations also indicate that girls are more frequently in the presence of adult females. The girls who spend time as child nurses perceive themselves to be of the same gender as the mother–caretaker role model. This increases the probability that they will behave more like their mothers than will the boys who are assigned the role of sibling–caretaker, a role not assigned to older boys or fathers. It is not surprising, therefore, that girls are more responsive, nurturant, and more prosocially dominant than boys. Behavior learned and practiced in caring for siblings generalizes to other categories of individuals.

INFLUENCE OF PLAY VERSUS WORK
ON SOCIAL INTERACTION

We have speculated on the effect of free time on the development of competitiveness, styles of dominance and techniques of conflict resolution. Boys in all our samples spent more time than girls in activities classed as play. Girls more frequently were found working in settings where the adults set the goals for children and the expected behavior is detailed by instruction and modeling. In play, the child is allowed, within specified limits, to set his or her own goals. Since individual children's goals may differ at any time during play, there is need for conflict resolution and negotiation in order that the play continue (Gottman, 1982; Lubin & Whiting, 1976; Forbes, Lubin, Schmidt, & Van der Laan, 1982; see also Forbes, Katz, & Paul, Chapter 10, this volume).

Thus, boys across our samples have more opportunity to learn strategies of influencing their playmates, usually children close in age. Playmates may be siblings and housemates. Our data indicate, however, that these children establish a pecking order determined by the cultural rules of gender and age relationships. Relationships with peers must be negotiated so that they are rewarding to both members of the dyad, or one or another of the children will prefer to find another more rewarding playmate.

Since boys are in play settings more frequently than girls, they will have more experience in dominance struggles than girls, more experience in trying to persuade peers to join them in their chosen activity. We would also expect these struggles to be more conflictful when the interactors are equal in power, measured by physical, cognitive, and social skills. A recent study by Judith David reports that children who have had the experience of interacting with many different peers in preschool show a higher proportion of egoistic dominance than children who have spent their preschool years with the same group of children (David, 1983). These children who have learned to be successful in their egoistic dominance often become the leaders of the group.

Girls, in contrast, working frequently with their mothers, learn to cooperate in reaching a given goal. They develop skill at working with others, synchronizing their activities, often without the necessity of verbal communication. They have training in helping others to reach their goals. Since the majority of our observations are of family member dyads (mother–child, child–mother, and child–sibling), we cannot test the effect of generalization of behavior styles to child–peer dyads. We can, however, explore the effect of frequency of dyadic interaction with mothers, infants, and toddlers on the interaction between older siblings. As mentioned above, we have found that children growing up in Type A and Type B cultures are on an average more nurturant and more prosocially dominant to each other than children who grow up in Type C cultures. In all the societies, girls on an average are more nurturant and prosocially dominant than boys (Edwards & Whiting, 1980; Whiting, B., 1980; Whiting, & Edwards, et al., in preparation; see also Berndt's findings, Chapter 5, this volume).

Conclusion

In sum, it is our hypothesis that setting variables influence styles of interpersonal behavior. The interpersonal behavior learned in the primary relationship with the mother, in relationships with infants and toddlers, and with sibling playmates close in age will influence peer relationships. The amount of time spent with these different types of family dyads and the activities performed while associating with them will increase the proportion of certain types of social behavior that are characteristic of social interaction in these dyads. The amount of time spent in these different dyads is determined by the culture. Children who spend more time interacting with a mother who does not work outside the home will develop styles with a high proportion of seeking behaviors (seeking sociability, attention, etc.) habits that will influence their style of interaction with peers. Children who spend time with infants will develop habits of nurturance and responsiveness that will influence their style of interaction with peers. Children who spend time with toddlers, and in the presence of their mothers, will develop habits of prosocial dominance that will influence their style of interaction with peers. Children who spend time with peers and nonkin children close of an age will develop styles of dominance and techniques of persuasion for avoiding conflict but reaching egoistic goals.

Inasmuch as there are similarities across cultures in the different amounts of time girls and boys spend in these settings in which they interact with these types of dyads, we will expect similarities across cultures of gender differences in the behavior styles of girls and boys.

These setting variables that have proved fruitful in explaining differences between cultures and universal gender differences also predict individual differences within cultures. In studying the development of children, knowledge of the people with whom they live and their daily companions and activities will enhance our understanding of their behavior at home, in school, on the playground or in the laboratories where they are observed.

References

Baltes, P. B., & Schaie, K. W. (Eds.). (1973). *Life-span developmental psychology: Personality and socialization.* New York: Academic Press.

Barker, R. G., & Gump, P. V. (1964). *Big school, small school: High school size and student behavior.* California: Stanford University Press.

Barker, R. G., & Wright, F. (1955). *Midwest and its children.* Illinois: Row, Peterson.

Belle, D. (Ed.). (1982). *Lives in stress: Women and depression.* Beverly Hills: Sage Publications.

Berman, P. W., Agplanalf, J., Cooper, P., Mansfield, P., & Schields, S. (1975). Sex differences in attraction to infants: Do they occur? *Sex Roles, 1,* 311–318.

Berman, P. W. (1980). Are women predisposed to parenting? Developmental and situational determinants to sex differences in responsiveness to the young. *Psychology Bulletin, 88,* 668–695.

David, J. (1983). *Preschoolers' social competence in relation to peer experience: A study in a naturalistic setting.* Doctoral dissertation, Harvard University, Cambridge, MA.

Draper, P. (1972). *Kung Bushman childhood.* Doctoral dissertation, Harvard University, Cambridge, MA.

Draper, P. (1973). Crowding among hunter–gathers: The Kung Bushmen. *Science, 182,* 301–303.

Edwards, C. P., & Whiting, B. B. (1980). Differential socialization of girls and boys in the light of cross-cultural research. In *New Directions for Child Development: Anthropological Perspectives on Child Development, 8,* 45–57.

Elder, G. H. (1974). *Children of the great depression.* Chicago: University of Chicago Press.

Elder, G. H. (1979). Historical change in life patterns and personality. In P. G. Baltes & U. G. Brim, Jr. (Eds.), *Life-span development and behavior* (Vol. 2). New York: Academic Press.

Ember, C. (1973). Female task assignment and the social behavior of boys. *Ethos, 1,* 424–439.

Erchak, G. (1977). *Full respect: Kpelle children in adaptation.* New Haven: Human Relations Area Files.

Fischer, J. L., & Fischer, A. (1966)*The New Englanders of Orchard Town U.S.A.* New York: Wiley.

Forbes, D., Lubin, D., Schmidt, M., & Van der Laan, P. (1982). *Verbal social reasoning and observed persuasion strategies in children's peer interactions.* Unpublished paper, Harvard University.

Gottman, J. (1982). How children become friends. Paper presented at Social Science Research Conference on Social Relationships, Harwichport, MA.

Hollos, M. (1974). *Growing up in Flathill.* Oslo: Universitets ForLaget.

Kohn, M. L. (1969). *Class and conformity: A study in values.* Illinois: Dorsey Press.

Konner, M. (1972). Aspects of developmental ethology of foraging people. In N. G. Burton Jones (Ed.), *Ethological studies of child behavior.* Cambridge: Cambridge University Press.

LeVine, R. (1974). Parental goals: A cross-cultural view. *Teacher's College Record, 76,* 2.

LeVine, R., & LeVine, B. (1966). *Nyansongo: A Gusii community in Kenya.* New York: Wiley. (Republished by Robert E. Krieger Publishing Co., Huntington, New York, 1977).

Loo, C. M. (1972). The effects of spacial density on the social behavior of children. *Journal of Applied Social Psychology, 2,* 372–381.

Lorenz, K. (1971). *Studies in human and animal behavior* (Vol. 2). Cambridge: Harvard University Press.

Lubin, D., & Whiting, B. (1976, March). *Learning techniques of persuasion: An analysis of interactional sequences.* Paper presented at a biennial meeting of the Society for Research in Child Development, New Orleans, LA.

Maretzki, T. W., & Maretzki, H. (1966). *Taira: An Okinawan village.* New York: Wiley.

Minturn, L., & Hitchcock, J. (1966). *The Rajputs of Khalapur, India.* New York: Wiley.

Munroe, R. L., & Munroe, R. (1971). Household density and infant care in an East African society. *Journal of Social Psychology, 83,* 3–13.

Radke-Yarrow, M., Zahn-Waxler, C., & Chapman, M. (1983). Children's prosocial dispositions and behavior. In P. Mussen & E. M. Hetherington (Eds.), *Handbook of Child Psychology* (Vol. 4, pp. 469–546).

Rogoff, B. (1978). Spot observations. *Quarterly Newsletter of the Institute for Comparative Human Development, 2,* 2.

Romney, A. K., & Romney, R. (1966). *The Mixtecans of Juxtlahuaca, Mexico.* New York: Wiley.

Rossi, P. H., Sampson, W. A., Bose, C. E., Jasso, G., & Passel, J. (1974). Measuring household social standing. *Social Science Research, 8,* 169–190.

Schoggens, M., & Schoggens, P. (n.d.). The behavior and home environments of three-year-old children from low- and middle-income homes. Darcee Demonstration and Research Center for Early Education, Nashville, Tennessee.

Seymour, S. (1971). *Patterns of child-rearing in a changing Indian town: Sources and expressions of dependence and independence.* Doctoral dissertation, Harvard University, Cambridge, MA.

Swanson, G. E. (1958). *The changing American parent: A study in the Detroit area*. New York: Wiley.

Warner, W. L., Meeker, M., & Eels, K. (1949). *Social class in America: A manual for the measurement of social status*. Chicago: Science Research Associates.

Weisner, T. (1979). Urban–rural differences in sociable and disruptive behavior in Kenya children. *Ethnology, 18,* 153–172.

Weisner, T., Bansana, M., & Kornfein, M. (in press). Putting family ideals into practice: Pronaturalism in conventional and nonconventional California families. *Ethos*.

Weisner, T., & Martin, J. (1979). Learning environments for infants: Communes and conventionally married families in California. *Alternative Lifestyles, 12,* 201–242.

Weisner, T., & Weibel, J. C. (1981). Home environments and family lifestyles in California. *Environment and Behavior, 13,* 417–460.

Whiting, B. (1950). *Paiute Sorcery*. New York: Viking Fund.

Whiting, B., & Edwards, C. (in preparation). *The company they keep: The effect of culture on social behavior*.

Whiting, B. B. (Ed.). *Six cultures: Studies of child rearing*. New York: Wiley.

Whiting, B. B. (1968). Transcultural code for the study of social interaction. Laboratory of Human Development, Harvard University.

Whiting, B. B. (1980). Culture and social behavior: A model for the development of social behavior. *Ethos, 8,* 2.

Whiting, B. B. (1982). The genesis of prosocial behavior. In D. Bridgeman (Ed.), *The nature of prosocial development*. New York: Academic Press.

Whiting, B. B., & Whiting, J. W. M. (1975). *Children of six cultures: A psychocultural analysis*. Cambridge: Harvard University Press.

Whiting, J. W. M. & Whiting, B. (1973). Altruistic and egoistic behavior in six cultures. In I. Nader & T. W. Maretzki (Eds.), *Cultural illness and health: Essays in human adaptation* 56–66. Washington, D.C.: American Anthropological Society.

Whiting, J. W. M., & Whiting, B. B. (1975). Aloofness and intimacy between husbands and wives: A cross-cultural study. *Ethos, 3,* 2.

PART III

PROCESS IN FRIENDSHIPS

Current research on children's relationships with peers has progressed beyond tallying the number of children desigated as friends or nonfriends. The nature and function of what transpires within these relationships are now key topics of investigation. Although friends are considered to have a special role in the development of mutuality and intimacy, children learn a great deal with nonfriends as well. Social scientists are expanding their focus to include these relationships in studying patterns of reciprocal influence in children's peer experiences.

In "Sharing between Friends: Contexts and Consequences," (Chapter 5, this volume) Berndt examines factors that influence altruistic behavior among friends, including the nature of their activity, the instructions, and the rewards and costs of prosocial behavior. In general, children's preference for equality over competition increases with age. As Berndt considers the consequences of friends' altruistic behavior for relationships with nonfriends, he draws on the work of Sullivan and Piaget, who hypothesized that preferences for equality and reciprocity generalize from friends to nonfriends. To account for the considerable lack of generalization he observes, Berndt draws upon the work of social psychologists such as Bem, who emphasize that generalization of attributions of the self learned within a friendship depends upon their specificity. Berndt's work exemplifies the increasing interest of peer researchers in children's attributions regarding their interpersonal behavior.

In "Friendship Selection: Development and Environmental Influences," (Chapter 6, this volume) Epstein analyzes the selection process at three levels: patterns of selection and nonselection, the ascribed features or "surface characteristics" of friends, and the qualities of the relationships themselves in terms of stability and reciprocity of choice. Epstein traces patterns of developmental change in these areas from preschool through adulthood, providing an unusual lifespan perspective on the development of friendship. With increasing age, friendships become selective, reciprocal, and stable, and friends grow more similar in personal characteristics. These qualities emerge as children become increasingly aware of themselves and others in relationships and more able to deal with stresses and disruptions in friendships. Changes also occur as other people in the child's world respond to these developmental changes. Important environmental factors such as the age, sex, and racial composition of classrooms and schools, affect mixed-age, cross-race, and cross-sex choices of friends. Epstein argues that school and classroom environments can alter patterns of friendship selection and thus the process of influence within which social and intellectual development proceed.

As is often noted, emotionally troubled children lack friends; almost invariably, their peer relations are marked by anger, aggression, or withdrawal. In "Peer Therapies and the Little Latency: a Clinical Perspective," (Chapter 7, this volume) Mueller and Cohen consider the role of peer relations in therapeutic interventions for emotionally troubled children. They outline reasons why peer therapies have been applied mostly to elementary school children. This is a period of development many clinical psychologists call latency because of a hypothesized lull in emotional readjustments during these years. They propose a second period of latency much earlier in development and present case material from very young children who were too emotionally troubled to attend to the mastery goals of this pe-

riod. Whereas toddler peer interaction is very difficult for
emotionally disturbed children, thereby offering a context
for diagnosis, peer relations can be the setting for the development of autonomy and play skills among normal children.

CHAPTER 5

Sharing between Friends: Contexts and Consequences

Thomas J. Berndt

Introduction

When children are asked to explain why another child is their friend, they often say that the other child shares with them, helps them, or shows other types of altruistic behavior toward them (Berndt, 1981c; Bigelow & La Gaipa, 1980; Youniss, 1980). These responses could be viewed as support for the common sense notion that altruistic interactions have a major impact on the formation and maintenance of friendships. The responses could be viewed less directly as support for hypotheses about the consequences of friendships for children's social and personality development (e.g., Sullivan, 1953). Children whose friends share with them, and who share in return, may begin to act in the same way toward other people as well. In short, the amount of sharing between two friends could indicate both how close their friendship is and how much of a positive influence that friendship has on their social behavior in general.

There are good reasons, however, for a more detailed and more critical analysis of sharing and other altruistic behaviors between friends. First, recent research has shown that the frequency of these behavior is greatly influenced by the situational context. The context is defined by the task on which friends are working when their behavior is observed, by the instructions for doing the task, and by the rewards and costs associated with behaving altruistically. Taken together, these features of the situational context

105

affect the motives that govern sharing and not sharing. For example, in contexts where competitive motivation is aroused, close friends may compete more and share less with each other than do children who are not close friends. In contexts where the motive for equality is dominant, close friends are likely to share more than nonfriends. Moreover, the situational context has a strong effect on whether or not age changes in friends' altruistic behavior are found. In the first section of this chapter, entitled "Sharing in Context," current evidence regarding context effects on altruistic behavior between friends is examined.

Second, most hypotheses about the consequences of friendships for children's development are based on the assumption that interaction patterns established in one important relationship generalize to other social relationships. In other words, the procedures developed in interactions with friends are taken as the basis for principles of behavior toward all people (e.g., Youniss, 1980). Although this assumption is plausible, there are alternative hypotheses that need to be considered. In the second section of the chapter, entitled "Consequences of Friends' Altruistic Behavior," the ambiguities in existing hypotheses about the consequences of behavior toward friends are explored. The transition from procedures to principles is shown to be only one of several processes by which generalization could occur. Other processes that involve self-perceptions or perceptions of other people are discussed. In addition, methods for testing these hypotheses are reviewed.

Sharing in Context

The amount of research and writing on children's friendships has increased dramatically in a short time (e.g., Asher & Gottman, 1981; Duck & Gilmour, 1981; Foot, Chapman, & Smith, 1980; Rubin, 1980). Nevertheless, there are still relatively few studies of friends' altruistic behavior. Although the recent research does not provide an exhaustive sampling of the contexts for altruistic behavior, it vividly illustrates the effects of variations in the situational context. In this review, the effects of context on the motives for sharing or refusing to share with a friend are emphasized.

SHARING VERSUS COMPETITION BETWEEN FRIENDS

Some of the most surprising findings concerning friends' behavior were obtained in a recent study of kindergarten, second-, and fourth-grade children (Berndt, 1981b). The children were asked first to name their best friends. Then they were asked to indicate how much they liked each of their same-sex classmates by selecting one point on a 5-point scale ranging from *don't like* (1) to *like very much, as much as a best friend* (5). Pairs of children were considered close friends if either one or both of them named the other as a best friend and they had a high degree of mutual liking (i.e., the mean rating for the pair was 4.0 or higher). Children who did not name each other as best friends and who had moderate liking for each other were considered merely as classmates rather than close friends. Children were never paired with someone whom they disliked or who disliked them.

The assignment of children to the friend and classmate conditions was done randomly, with one constraint. To avoid confounding the friend–classmate contrast with differences between children who did and who did not have friends, only children with at least one close friend in the sample were included in the study. Out of a total sample of more than 100 children, 2 children were excluded for this reason.

The crayon-sharing task

Shortly after the pairings were made, children were observed as they worked on tasks that provided them with opportunities to share with each other. The children were shown a colored geometric design made up of circles, squares, or diamonds, and asked to color a design like the model. Each child was given a separate design to color, but they were told that they had to share a single set of crayons. In addition, they were told that they could use only one crayon at a time, so they would need to share it. One child in the pair, selected randomly, was given the crayon at the beginning of each trial for the first half of the trask. For the second half of the task, the other child received the crayon first.

The children were also told that they would get a prize for how well they did on their own design. To show them how well they were doing, the experimenter distributed rewards after each trial. Nickels were used as rewards because they appeared to be highly motivating to the children. The child who colored more on a trial received two nickels and the other child received one nickel. During each trial, the experimenter recorded how long the child who initially had the crayon shared it with his or her partner, how often each child requested the crayon, how often requests were unsuccessful because they were ignored or refused, and how much each child actually colored.

Results

The pattern of results was unexpected. Girls shared the crayons fairly equally with their partners, regardless of whether the partner was a close friend or another classmate. Girls also colored about the same amount as their partners. Their responses seem to reflect the preference for equality that frequently has been observed in previous research with girls and women (e.g., Kahn, Nelson, & Gaeddert, 1980).

In contrast, boys shared less with friends than with other classmates, especially at second and fourth grade. Across all grades, boys tended to comply with a friend's requests for the crayons less often than with another classmate's requests. In addition, the amounts actually colored by the two children in a pair were more discrepant for boys paired with friends than for boys paired with other classmates. Apparently, boys reduced their sharing with friends so that they could get more done on their own design and so get more rewards or avoid getting fewer rewards than their friend. In other words, they chose to compete with friends rather than share equally. The reasons for boys' greater competition with friends are not clear. In previous research, sex differences in competitive motivation were inconsistent (cf. Knight & Kagan, 1981; Lever, 1978). The later studies provide more evidence on this issue.

Discussion and Interpretation

To many people, evidence of competition between friends is counter-intuitive. Friends are expected to share with each other more than children who are not close friends. If this result is not obtained in research with laboratory-type tasks, questions about the validity of the data are likely. That is, people are likely to assume that the study was flawed in some way. Several types of flaws may be suggested.

First, the data may be unreliable. If so, comparable data should not be obtained in other studies. Evidence suggestive of competition between friends has been obtained in other research, however. In a recent study with third- and fourth-grade boys (Staub & Noerenberg, 1981), friends shared less with each other as they were drawing pictures than nonfriends did, if the boys had not already had a disagreement with their partner. In another study (Tesser & Smith, 1980), male college students helped a close friend less than another student, if they believed helping might allow the friend to obtain a higher score than their own on an important test. In both these cases, the investigators stated that the results could be explained by the intensity of competition between friends. The studies indicate that the data on friends' competition are replicable, at least for males.

Second, even if findings can be replicated on laboratory-type tasks, they may be due to experimental artifacts or demand characteristics of the experimental setting. It is worth noting that the studies of friends' behavior were seldom conducted in a psychological laboratory. Most often, children were observed as they worked on tasks in an empty classroom in their own school. Furthermore, if the results were due to experimental artifacts, measures of behavior on the tasks should show little relation to other types of measures. Strong relations of task behavior to other types of measures have been demonstrated, however. In one study (Berndt, 1981a), the amount that children shared crayons with a friend was compared to the children's responses in a separate interview regarding how much they would help or share with their friend in several hypothetical situations. Some of the situations were similar in their essential features to the tasks for measuring actual behavior (i.e., they involved sharing things at school when children were working for individual prizes), but they differed from the tasks in their details. The children's interview responses correlated between .34 and .61 with their actual behavior. The correlations suggest that behavior on the tasks was not greatly influenced by experimental artifacts. They are also evidence for the convergent validity of the measure of sharing.

At this point, it is also worth noting that the crayon-sharing task is a more naturalistic measure of altruistic behavior than the tasks often used in other research. In many studies, children have been asked to donate money, toys, or other rewards to another child with whom they have not interacted and will never meet (e.g., Grusec & Redler, 1980). In still other studies, the strength of altruistic, competitive, and egalitarian motives has been assessed by children's responses to a series of choice cards (e.g., Avellar & Kagan, 1976). Despite the apparent artificiality of these measures, there is evidence for their construct validity and their relation to behavior outside the experimental setting (e.g., Eisenberg, 1982; Knight, 1981). Nevertheless, the tasks used in research on friendship probably are preferable because they involve observations of actual interactions between friends.

On the other hand, a focus on the details of these tasks could lead to a third type of question about the data on boys' competition with friends. The tasks are designed so that there is a definite cost to sharing with one's partner. On the crayon-sharing task, sharing is disadvantageous because it reduces the amount of time that children can color on their own picture. Children who share for a long time are likely to get less done on their own design and get fewer rewards than their partner. In this respect, the tasks for measuring friends' altruistic behavior are similar to virtually all measures of altruistic behavior in childhood, adolescence, or adulthood. Researchers have tried to ensure that this behavior has costs, not only because self-sacrifice is part of the definition of altruism, but also because otherwise altruistic behavior cannot be distinguished from self-interested behavior.

It would still be possible to argue that the crayon-sharing task measures altruistic behavior in a context that rarely occurs or is of little importance in children's own lives. This criticism cannot be countered by evidence that similar results are obtained with tasks or measures that involve similar contexts. The issue ultimately concerns the representativeness of the data obtained in such contexts.

Although Sullivan (1953) did not systematically observe children's behavior toward their friends, his clinical observations led him to emphasize the intensity of competition between friends during middle childhood. In a recent series of experiments, Tesser (1984) indirectly examined academic competition between friends in school settings. He also presented an explanation for friends' competition. The explanation is based on assumptions about similarity and social comparison. Children and adults view themselves as more similar to their friends than to other people. Therefore, they more often compare their own performance with that of a friend than with that of a nonfriend. If they believe that helping or sharing with a friend would result in the friend's outperforming them on a task that is important for their self-esteem, they will prevent this outcome by refusing to help or share. In other words, children and adults care more about the results of a contest with a friend than with a nonfriend, so they are less likely to behave altruistically when this behavior increases their chances of losing the contest.

Tesser's theory suggests that boys were especially likely to view the crayon-sharing task as an important contest. Because the only alternatives were to "win" on each trial by getting two nickels or to "lose" by getting one nickel, boys were forced to compete with friends or risk seeming inferior to them.

There is another possible interpretation of the boys' behavior. Friends may not feel forced to compete with each other; they may compete because it is pleasant or enjoyable. Although the data from the first study do not clearly discredit this hypothesis, less systematic observations of the children's interactions cast doubt on it. Rather than enjoying the competition, both friends and nonfriends seemed upset and angry when their partner did not share the crayon equally with them. Moreover, even the children who "won" by getting more nickels seemed to recognize that they should have shared equally with their partners. In one striking example, a kindergarten boy never shared the crayons with his friend after he received them from the experimenter, despite his friend's repeated requests. At the conclusion of the task, however, he apologized to his partner for not sharing with him. These data are not consistent with the hypothesis that competition was enjoyable for the children. Stronger evidence against this hypothesis was obtained in subsequent studies.

THE PREFERENCE FOR EQUALITY BETWEEN FRIENDS

Although Sullivan (1953) commented on the competition between friends and nonfriends during middle childhood, the relatively equal sharing displayed by the girls in the first study is more significant in developmental theory. Piaget (1932/1965) argued that children gradually develop a special set of procedures for egalitarian interactions with their peers. Within a group of peers, no child can claim the authority to tell the others where to go or what to do. Instead, each child must be allowed to participate in making decisions that affect the group. If the children initially disagree with each other, they must listen to the others' reasons for their opinions and try to find a position that is acceptable to all. In Piaget's terms, these procedures illustrate the general norm of reciprocity: If I want to be able to express my own views and be treated fairly, I must extend the same rights to you. Piaget also defined these procedures as creating an atmosphere of mutual respect.

Piaget argued that the adoption of procedures based on reciprocity and mutual respect leads inevitably to certain principles for behavior. Just as other children deserve to be treated as equals in discussions and decision-making, they deserve to be treated equally when rewards or other resources are distributed. According to Piaget, the general principle of equality also obligates children to behave altruistically toward peers under certain conditions. In particular, a child who is in need of help should be helped by other children so that they can create or restore equality among themselves. Piaget assumed that these principles for behavior develop gradually during middle childhood and early adolescence, as children begin to follow the procedures that are required by reciprocity and mutual respect.

Youniss (1980) suggested that the procedures identified by Piaget may be most characteristic of children's interactions with friends. Consequently, the preference for equality and the sharing and helping that lead to equality may be most apparent in friends' interactions. Youniss also suggested that the growing preference for equality identified by Piaget was consistent with Sullivan's hypothesis that friends increasingly try for mutually satisfying outcomes, because equality is likely to be mutually satisfying. These hypotheses about equality in friendship were tested in a study with first and fourth graders (Berndt, 1981a).

Methods

In the fall of the school year, all children in the study were paired with a close friend. At that time, the pairs of friends were observed as they worked on the crayon-sharing task and a second task in which children had opportunities to help each other. On both tasks, children received more rewards if they spent less time helping or sharing with their partner. In other words, altruistic behavior had costs or was in conflict with self-interest. If

hared fairly equally and helped their partners for some of the
, they received an equal number of rewards on each trial. The
̇ ucture was changed from that in the first study to provide a more
direct test of the hypotheses about preferences for equality.

The new reward structure also allowed a comparison of the alternative
interpretations of competition between friends. If friends enjoy competition, they should compete even when they could obtain equality on each
trial. If friends compete only when they feel they might lose by not doing
so, they should share more and compete less than nonfriends when placed
in the new context where equality can be easily achieved.

Although all children were paired with friends in the fall, the same pairs
of children were observed again during the following spring, whether or
not they were still close friends with each other. With this design, the effects
of changes in friendship on children's sharing and helping could be examined.

Results and Discussion

In both the fall and the spring, fourth graders helped their partners more
often than first-graders did. In addition, the number of rewards received
by the two children in a pair was more similar for fourth-graders than first-
graders. That is, the greater helping of fourth-graders led to greater equality
in outcomes. These data are consistent with the hypothesis that the preference for equality between friends increases with age.

Fourth-graders also shared more than first-graders, but the difference
was significant only in the spring. The difference emerged because first-
graders shared less with their partners in the spring than in the fall. Other
data suggested that the decline in sharing was due to the weakening or end-
ing of many first-graders' friendships. Apparently, first-graders shared more
with their partners when they had remained close friends than when they
had not.

Finally, neither helping or sharing varied with sex. The contrast between
these findings and those in the previous study can be attributed to the change
in the context for the behavioral observations. As already indicated, the
most important change was in the reward structure for the tasks. Because
the children in this study could attain an equal number of rewards on each
trial, they did not risk losing to their partners by helping or sharing equally
with them. Therefore, there was less pressure to compete with the partner
and, in particular, less pressure to compete with friends. The findings do
not support the hypothesis that the boys in the first study were engaged in
a "friendly" competition with their friend because, if so, they should have
competed as much in the second study.

AGE CHANGES IN FRIENDS' ALTRUISTIC BEHAVIOR

The major purpose of the next two studies was to further test the hypothesis that friends show a stronger preference for equality as they grow older. The studies also tested Sullivan's (1953) hypothesis that children begin to act in an especially positive way toward friends during early adolescence. According to Sullivan, at this age children show special sensitivity to a friend's needs and requests. They act more positively toward a close friend than toward other classmates.

Study 1

In the first of these studies (Berndt, in press), fourth-, sixth-, and eighth-graders were paired either with a close friend or with another classmate. The pairs of children were asked to work on two tasks that provided them with opportunities to behave generously or helpfully toward each other. One task was an adaptation of the card-choice task used extensively by Kagan (e.g., Avellar & Kagan, 1976). Children were shown a series of cards and, on each one, asked to choose between two alternatives that provided different numbers of rewards for themselves and their partner. Equality was one alternative on each card. The children were given different decks of cards and they made their choices with no knowledge of the partner's choices.

For the second task, the children were asked to make a flag together by pasting small colored triangles on a large cardboard sheet. One child was placed at a disadvantage, however. To get the same number of rewards as the partner, this child had to paste more triangles than the partner. The partner was allowed to help the child with the disadvantage. Although children could achieve rough equality in rewards by helping, exact equality was unlikely because the amount that they could complete during a trial was difficult to estimate.

After both tasks were completed, the children individually answered questionnaires that asked for reports on their own motives and attributions about their partner's motives for behavior on each task. Four motives were specified: (1) try for equality ("get the same number of rewards"); (2) maximize their own gain ("get as much for myself as I could"); (3) compete ("try to get more than my partner"); or (4) act altruistically ("let my partner get as much as I could"). The wording of the alternatives was changed appropriately when the questions referred to attributions about the partner's motives.

As Sullivan's (1953) hypothesis suggested, differences in the altruistic behavior of friends and other classmates increased with age. Eighth-graders were more generous and more helpful toward friends than toward other classmates. Fourth and sixth-graders behaved similarly toward friends and toward other classmates. In addition, eighth-graders who were paired with close friends usually assumed that their partners tried for equality in rewards; eighth-graders paired with other classmates usually assumed that their partners were commpeting with them. Attributions about the motives of friends and other classmates did not differ at fourth or sixth grade.

The results suggest that eighth-graders were more generous and helpful to their friends than to other classmates because they more strongly preferred equality over competition when paired with friends. Yet it is puzzling that friend–classmate differences were nonsignificant at fourth and sixth grade. In retrospect, one might argue that the tasks used in this study occupied an intermediate position between those used in the first two studies. For example, although equality was an option on the Kagan choice cards, the children chose independently and they could not be sure that their partner was trying for equality. Similarly, when making the flag, children could not completely control whether they got an equal number of rewards on each trial. Under these conditions, fourth-graders interacting with friends apparently showed a mixture of competitive and egalitarian motives that was not distinguishable from that for other classmates.

Study 2

The next study (Berndt, Hawkins, & Hoyle, 1984) was conducted partly to clarify the age changes in preferences for equality and competition between fourth and eighth grade. The study included fourth-graders and eighth-graders who were paired with a close friend in the fall of the school year. Each pair was observed as they worked on a variant of the crayon-sharing task used in previous studies with younger children. The child who completed more of the task on each trial received more rewards than his or her partner. Equality in rewards was not provided as an option. In other words, the reward structure was identical to that in the earlier study with kindergarten through fourth grade.

Unlike the earlier study, this one did not include a separate group of children who initially were paired with nonfriends. Instead, the same pairs of children were observed again in the spring of the school year, when some of them were still close friends and some were no longer close friends. In both the fall and the spring, children were asked to describe their own motives and make attributions about their partner's motives for behavior after they completed the task.

In the fall, eighth-graders shared more equally with their partners than fourth-graders did. In reporting their motives, eighth-graders said that they tried for equality more often than fourth-graders did. These data confirm that the preference for equality between friends continues to increase between fourth and eighth grade.

The amount that children shared in the spring was affected by whether or not they had remained close friends with their partners. At eighth grade, children who were still close friends shared more equally than those who were not. In contrast, at fourth grade, children who had remained close friends shared *less* than those who had not. Sex differences in sharing were not found in the fall or in the spring. In the spring, however, fourth-grade girls reported that their partners competed more and tried for equality less when they were still friends than when they were no longer close friends. The reverse was true at eighth grade. Comparable differences were found for self-reported motives, but the differences were nonsignificant for boys. The sex difference in reported motives cannot be easily explained, but along with the absence of sex differences in behavior, it demonstrates that both girls and boys are likely to compete with friends in certain circumstances. Taken together, the findings illustrate that the preference for equality over competition between friends increases between middle childhood and early adolescence.

Finally, the questionnaires about motives also included a series of questions about the children's reactions to their own and their partner's behavior. For example, children were asked if they or their partner should have shared more than they did, and if they or their partner took advantage of the other. Responses to these questions were negatively correlated with sharing. That is, children who shared less reported more dissatisfaction with their own and their partner's behavior. Moreover, the correlations did not vary significantly with grade. Although fourth-graders competed more and shared less with friends, they were less satisfied with their interactions when they shared less. These data do not support the hypothesis that competition is accepted or enjoyed by friends during middle childhood, at least not in contexts where equality in outcomes can be achieved only by equal sharing.

Summary and Implications

Three major conclusions can be drawn from this review of research. First, in contexts where sharing conflicts with self-interest but equality in outcomes can be easily achieved, children share more equally with close friends than with other classmates. Second, in contexts where sharing increases the risk of losing in an important contest, elementary school children share less and compete more with close friends than with other classmates. Third, with increasing age, friends more regularly choose equality in outcomes over self-interest or competition. Helping and sharing between friends is most likely when these behaviors promote equality in outcomes.

It is important to emphasize that these conclusions are based on observations of friends' behavior in a restricted range of contexts. In all studies, children were observed as they worked on projects for prizes or rewards. Other researchers have observed friends' behavior not as they worked on a task but as they explored an interesting "puzzle box" (Newcomb & Brady, 1982; Newcomb, Brady, & Hartup, 1979). In these studies, friends were more cooperative with each other than nonfriends, and friend–nonfriend differences changed little between first and sixth grade. Unlike the studies reviewed earlier, the costs of cooperation seem not to have been very obvious as children explored the box. Therefore, the friends' history of positive interactions with each other may have encouraged cooperation. Conversely, the relative unfamiliarity of nonfriends may have made them less comfortable with each other and so less able to develop a cooperative interaction pattern.

The variety of contexts in which sharing between friends might be investigated is great. What rationale could be given for focusing on any specific context? Although many answers to this question are reasonable, a strong argument could be made for focusing on friends' behavior in contexts that have a major impact on children's development. To identify such contexts, an analysis of the potential consequences of friendship is needed.

Consequences of Friends' Altruistic Behavior

Does sharing between friends lead to altruistic behavior toward other people? Both affirmative and negative answers to this question could be justified by reference to theory. Relevant empirical research is scarce. Therefore, it is necessary to approach the question indirectly. Specific hypotheses about the conditions in which altruistic behavior will generalize from friends to other people can be derived from joint consideration of the processes that lead to sharing between friends and the processes that govern the generalization of behavior patterns. One hypothesis about these processes was presented by Piaget (1932/1965) and Youniss (1980). This hypothesis is examined first. Then alternative hypotheses suggested by social-psychological theories and research are discussed.

FROM PROCEDURES TO PRINCIPLES

As indicated earlier, Piaget (1932/1965) believed that children develop procedures for peer interaction based on reciprocity, mutual respect, and a preference for equality. Piaget argued that these procedures become the foundation for principles of behavior that extend the preference for equality to all other people. In its most general form, the preference for equality is synonymous with the Golden Rule: do unto others as you would have them do unto you. This principle becomes part of children's morality and one source of their altruistic behavior.

Youniss (1980) agreed with Piaget about the gradual transformation of procedures into principles. He suggested further that experiences with friends may be most important for this transformation. Finally, along with Piaget and Sullivan (1953), he assumed that once these principles have emerged, they affect other social relationships as well. For example, they transform children's relationships with their parents and provide a model for relationships with colleagues during adulthood.

These hypotheses about the consequences of friendship raise a number of issues, of which four seem especially important.

Context Specificity

First, the hypotheses are stated very generally, as if they applied in all situational contexts. Yet as indicated in the first section of this paper, age changes in altruistic behavior between friends have been found only in contexts where this behavior had an obvious impact on the rewards that individual children received for their performance (Berndt, 1981a, 1982a, 1982b). When the impact of altruistic behavior on individual children's rewards was not emphasized, age changes in friends' behavior were absent (Newcomb & Brady, 1982). Piaget (1932/1965) also found effects of the situational context on children's judgments of other children's behavior. Age changes in judgments about the fairness of an equal allocation of privileges or responsibilities were found for situations that included older children or adults. When situations involved only groups of peers, children at all ages judged equal allocations as most fair (see Berndt, 1982). The effects of context seem to be due largely to variations in the reasons or motives that lead to unequal treatment of other people. Just as these variations affect friends' behavior, they should affect the generalization of behavior from friends to nonfriends.

Does Generalization Occur?

Second, few writers on children's friendships seem to have carefully considered the possibility that behavior toward friends would not generalize to other people. This is a serious error, because strong arguments against the hypothesis of generalization could be presented. For example, social learning theorists emphasize the situational specificity of behavior or, as Mischel (1973) phrased it, the ability of individuals to discriminate between different settings. From this perspective, the generalization of behavior patterns acquired during interactions with friends is not inevitable and may not even be likely.

In addition, most recent studies of friendship have established that altruistic interactions between friends differ in frequency or in patterning from those between nonfriends. These differences could be viewed as evidence that there is no generalization from friends to nonfriends. The absence of generalization could be explained in several ways.

To begin with, the procedures adopted for interactions with friends may be different from those for interactions with nonfriends (cf. Bronfenbrenner, 1979). Nonfriends may not have the mutual respect that encourages frank discussion, consideration of others' views, and attempts to achieve outcomes that are equally satisfying to all. The procedures that adults use for making decisions are affected by the type of relationships that they have with the other individuals concerned (Scholar & Clark, 1981). When they anticipate forming close friendships with these other individuals, they try to reach a consensus position. When they do not expect to have a continuing relationship with them, they base their decisions on majority rule. Comparable differences may be found in the procedures that children adopt for interactions with friends and nonfriends.

The principles for acceptable behavior also may differ for friends and nonfriends. Children may assume that friends should be treated as equals and helped when they are in need, and may regard nonfriends as less entitled to such treatment. A substantial amount of research with children and adults suggests that there are different principles of behavior for different types of social relationships. For example, when children act as supervisors for other children who ostensibly are working on a task, they usually give each worker the same number of rewards if they believe the workers are on the same team. If they believe the two workers are not part of a team, they usually distribute rewards in rough proportion to how much each one actually accomplished (Berndt, 1982; Lerner & Whitehead, 1980). These findings are consistent with the recent evidence (e.g., Berndt, 1981a) that equality is more often chosen as a goal by friends than nonfriends, as long as competitive motivation is relatively weak.

Finally, even when children assume that the same principles apply to interactions with friends and nonfriends, they may more frequently act in accordance with those principles when interacting with friends. Youniss (1980) suggested this hypothesis when summarizing the responses of a group of 14-year-olds. He suggested that these children "held that peers in general, *and friends especially,* deserved to be treated fairly" (p. 245, italics added). Friends might have this advantage over nonfriends because of the value children place on a friend's praise and approval.

Of course, experiences with friends could affect children's behavior toward other people even if children never behaved in exactly the same way toward friends and nonfriends. In support of this claim, Mannarino (1976,

1979) reported that sixth-graders with an intimate, mutually responsive, and relatively stable and exclusive friendship gave more altruistic responses on a self-report measure and showed more cooperative behavior in a modified Prisoner's Dilemma game than sixth-graders who did not have such a friendship. (In the Prisoner's Dilemma game, children did not interact directly with other children, and they assumed their partner was a stranger to them.) Thus the features of the children's friendships were related to their altruistic behavior toward nonfriends. Before drawing the definite conclusion that this relation indicates an effect of friendships, two additional issues must be considered.

Effects of Friendship, or Effects on Friendship?

The first of these issues concerns the assumed direction of effects. Although Mannarino's findings could illustrate that children with closer friendships become more cooperative and generous toward other people, they are also consistent with the argument that helpful and generous children are preferred as friends and, therefore, more often have close and stable friendships. Research on the social behavior of popular children— children who have many friends—is consistent with this conclusion (Hartup, 1983; Masters & Furman, 1981). Because Mannarino's studies were purely correlational, they cannot establish which factor was the cause and which the effect.

Mediators of Friendship Effects

Finally, in most writings on the consequences of friendship there is little attempt to specify the processes that would lead to generalized effects of friendship. Speculations about these processes can be presented in terms of Piaget's and Youniss' hypotheses. From this perspective, the generalization of behavior patterns established during interactions with friends should be mediated by the generalization of interaction procedures or principles for behavior.

Examples of the former can be found in previous research. In one study (Goldberg & Maccoby, 1965), groups of children developed a procedure for building towers of blocks which ensured that each child in the group was able to place roughly the same number of blocks on the tower during each trial. The number of blocks that children placed was important because it determined how many rewards they received. Children who developed this procedure for completing the task often continued to use it when they moved to a new group. They apparently convinced the other members of their new group to adopt the procedure because it was both fair and efficient.

Other studies provide less direct information about the procedures that are transferred to new settings and social partners, but they provide more evidence that the transfer is not task-specific. In their general form, these studies are experimental interventions (see Strain, 1981). Through a series of interactions with one or more peers, attempts are made to change children's behavior toward all their classmates. In one prominent example (Furman, Rahe, & Hartup, 1979), preschool children who engaged in little social behavior in their regular classroom were asked to participate in a series of special play sessions with a single other peer who either was roughly the same age or roughly a year younger than they were. Participation in these sessions increased children's social behavior in the regular classroom. The investigators suggested that the special sessions allowed the isolated children to initiate behavior with a peer and demonstrate social leadership. The children then were more able to act as social leaders with a variety of partners.

Unfortunately, the effects of peer interactions on the development of general principles for behavior have seldom been investigated (but see Berkowitz, Gibbs, & Broughton, 1980). Moreover, no study to date has shown a specific effect of interactions with friends.

Summary and Implications

Interactions with friends may contribute to the development of procedures and principles that subsequently affect behavior toward other people, but this hypothesis has not yet been adequately supported. The evidence that children behave differently toward friends than toward nonfriends is not directly contradictory to the hypothesis, but it seems more compatible with the alternative hypothesis that children develop a distinctive set of procedures and principles for interactions with friends. Moreover, children's social behavior toward their classmates could affect their ability to form and maintain mutually responsive friendships rather than vice versa.

There are examples in previous research of the generalization of behavior patterns to settings and social partners different from those with whom the patterns originally were learned. Experimental research of this type, with friends' interactions as the focus of investigation, is needed. Experimental interventions might be designed to change the interaction procedures or principles for behavior that normally are adopted by children who have few friendships or unsatisfying friendships. Then the effects of the interventions on the children's popularity, reputation with classmates, and actual behavior toward other classmates could be evaluated.

In addition, longitudinal studies could be employed to determine whether and how strongly changes in children's behavior toward their friends are related to changes in behavior toward other classmates. One advantage of longitudinal studies is that they assess the generalization of behavior in the real world. Consequently, they can provide information not only about whether statistically significant effects are obtained, but also about the strength of these effects.

EFFECTS OF FRIENDSHIP ON PERCEPTIONS
OF SELF AND OTHER PEOPLE

The impact of children's friendships on their altruistic behavior toward other people may be mediated by processes different from those emphasized in developmental theories of friendship. The literature on altruistic behavior among children and adults contains many possible explanations for the generalization of this behavior (see Eisenberg, 1982; Staub, 1978, 1979). Rather than reviewing all of these explanations here, a few theories that emphasize the processes of social perception and attribution are described.

Self-Perception Theory

The attributions that children make about themselves when they share with a friend may greatly influence whether or not they subsequently share with other people. In self-perception theory (Bem, 1972), people are assumed to judge themselves by observing how they have behaved. According to the theory, children who have behaved generously toward another person begin to think of themselves as generous and helpful. In order to maintain this perception of themselves, they may continue to share in the future. Evidence for these processes has been obtained in recent research with children (Grusec & Redler, 1980). In this research, the influence of altruistic behavior on children's self-perceptions was enhanced by having an adult tell them that they seemed to be "nice and helpful" children. It seems likely, however, that the same processes operate when children make their own judgments about their traits or dispositions.

There may also be general effects of receiving altruistic behavior from friends. Having friends who are interested in their welfare may convince children of their own worth and increase their self-esteem (Sullivan, 1953). Children with a positive sense of self are likely to be more empathic toward others and to feel more competent to help others in need (Hoffman, 1975; Staub, 1978).

Because children interact more frequently with close friends than with other classmates, friendships may have especially strong effects on children's self-perceptions. It is important to state explicitly, however, that these effects need not be positive ones. If children shared little with their friends, or their friends shared little with them, they might conclude that they are not very generous persons and that other people neither like nor value them.

Friendships of this type probably are not very stable, but their prevalence and stability remain to be determined.

Perceptions of Other People

Experiences of sharing with friends may also affect children's perceptions of their social environment and the people in it. Having a friend share with them, or sharing and receiving the friend's thanks in return, may put children in a good mood that is not linked directly to those specific interactions. The children may feel good about their world and about people in general. In such a mood, children are more likely to be generous and helpful toward others (see Isen, Clark, & Schwartz, 1976).

The studies reviewed earlier have demonstrated that children do not always act altruistically toward their friends. Sometimes they compete with friends. Competition with friends may also influence children's perceptions of other people. In one social-psychological theory (Kelley & Stahelski, 1970), competitive people are assumed to believe that all other people are as competitive as they are. A competitive individual can elicit competitive responses from other people by acting competitively toward them. In this way, individuals may determine their social environment and repeatedly confirm their beliefs about it.

On the other hand, the ability of a person to create his or her own environment is limited. Individuals with different perceptions of other people often interact. During these interactions, they must accommodate to each other. Even competitive individuals are influenced by their partners, and they can recognize when other people want to cooperate rather than compete with them (Bixenstine, Lowenfeld, & Englehardt, 1981). In other words, perceptions of other people are flexible and are modified by experience. This flexibility limits the extent to which experiences in any relationship, such as friendship, can permanently affect perceptions and behavior toward other people.

Summary and Implications

Prosocial interactions with friends may affect children's self-perceptions and perceptions of other people in positive or negative ways. When they share with friends, children may make the attribution that they have a generous disposition. When friends share with them, they may feel good about themselves and good about their environment. These feelings may foster altruistic behavior toward other people. In contrast, when children refuse to share with friends or they compete with friends, the resulting self-perceptions and perceptions of other people may reduce the likelihood of altruistic behavior in the future. The balance of positive and negative effects depends on the experiences of each child with his or her own friends.

The most attractive feature of these hypotheses is that they clearly indicate when and why experiences with friends affect behavior toward others. Interactions with friends will have general effects on children's behavior if the attributions made after these interactions are not relationship-specific. For example, after they share with a friend, children are assumed to make the attribution that "I am a generous person." If children instead made the attribution that "I share with my friends," no generalization of altruistic behavior would be expected. Similarly, children who compete with friends may conclude that "you have to compete because everyone else does," or they may conclude that "my friends always compete with me." Thus knowledge of children's attributions about their behavior toward friends could be used to judge the degree to which this behavior will generalize to nonfriends.

Finally, the effects of self-perceptions and perceptions of other people have been extensively investigated. In most studies, experimental designs were used, so there is little ambiguity about the direction of causality. The greatest need for the future is research that focuses on friendship specifically, and on the development of self- and social-perceptions and their relations to behavior.

Conclusions

The major purpose of this paper is to raise certain questions that thus far have received little attention in the literature on friendship. In a broad view, the questions illustrate the need for more precise hypotheses about the nature and consequences of altruistic behavior between friends. The hypotheses discussed in this paper neither exhaust the possibilities nor fully achieve the level of precision that is desirable, but they clarify the types of research designs and measures that are likely to be heuristically valuable.

In one sense, the central conclusions drawn about altruistic behavior between friends are negative ones. Recent research suggests that children do not help and share with their friends simply because they like them. The research also suggests that children's altruistic behavior toward friends cannot be understood without an appreciation of the situational context.

The positive versions of these conclusions are more difficult to state concisely. In many contexts, friends help and share with each other because they want to maintain a state of equality between themselves. Equality not only is likely to be mutually satisfying; it also is consistent with the mutual respect between friends. In some contexts, however, friends are especially likely to compete rather than share with each other. A child competes most with a friend when he or she feels in danger of losing to the friend in an important contest. Competition between friends is more likely in middle childhood than in early adolescence. Even when the situational context encourages comparisons of relative performance, adolescents are more likely to try for equality than are young children. When comparisons of relative performance are of little importance, age changes in friends' behavior usually are absent.

A formal theory of contextual variations in friends' behavior cannot be presented as yet, because the current evidence is too limited. Nevertheless, the recent research demonstrates that the development of altruistic behavior between friends cannot be adequately explained by general hypotheses which ignore the effects of context. A knowledge of the meaning and functions of friends' altruistic behavior is most likely to be achieved by further exploration of specific contexts and the processes that govern behavior in them.

The central conclusion drawn about the consequences of friends' altruistic behavior also might be stated negatively: Interactions with friends do not necessarily have a strong influence on behavior toward other people. During social contacts with friends, children may develop procedures for social interactions and principles for social behavior that are applied to nonfriends as well. On the other hand, children may acquire a distinctive set of procedures and principles for interactions with friends. Theoretical arguments for and against the generalization of behavior patterns from friends to nonfriends are available. Research designed to test these theories is almost nonexistent.

In nearly all cases, hypotheses about the consequences of friends' altruistic behavior have been derived from developmental theories of friendship and peer relations. Hypotheses could also be derived from general theories of altruistic behavior in children and adults. Theories that emphasize the effects of self-perceptions and perceptions of other people on an individual's altruistic behavior were discussed earlier. These theories are particularly useful because they specify the processes that mediate the generalization of behavior. Through the direct examination of these processes, for these theories or any other theories, it should be possible to determine the extent to which friendships do and do not have general effects on children's social behavior.

Finally, negative conclusions about the current state of knowledge and theorizing in any research area are helpful only when they are designed (and interpreted) as constructive criticism. Criticism is most likely to be constructive if it suggests new techniques or ideas for research. Specific suggestions for future research were given in the course of the paper. At this point, only brief comments about possible approaches are appropriate. Comparisons between the altruistic behavior of friends and nonfriends provide information about the development and the dynamics of friendships. These comparisons are less useful for testing hypotheses about the consequences of friendships. The most direct way to investigate the consequences of friendship is by experimental studies of the transfer of interaction procedures or principles from friends to nonfriends. In addition, intervention programs for children lacking in close friendships might be implemented and evaluated. Longitudinal studies that are conducted in natural settings also would be valuable.

The diversity in research designs should be matched by diversity in measures. Further studies of friends' actual behavior are obviously necessary. For certain purposes, however, information about children's social cognition may be more useful. For example, the relations between the features of children's friendships and their reasoning about altruistic behavior could be explored. The influence of friendships on children's self-concepts also could be examined. Still other types of measures would be valuable for testing certain hypotheses. For example, the effects of friendships on moods or affective states could be assessed. The systematic use of a variety of research designs and measures probably will lead most quickly to an understanding of why friends share with each other, and how much sharing between friends contributes to children's social development.

References

Asher, S. R., & Gottman, J. M. (Eds.). (1981). *The development of children's friendships.* Cambridge, England: Cambridge University Press.

Avellar, J., & Kagan, S. (1976). Development of competitive behaviors in Anglo-American and Mexican-American children. *Psychological Reports, 39,* 191–198.

Bem, D. J. Self-perception theory. (1972). In L. Berkowitz (Ed.), *Advances in experimental social psychology* (Vol. 6). New York: Academic Press.

Berkowitz, M. W., Gibbs, J. C., & Broughton, J. M. (1980). The relation of moral judgment stage disparity to developmental effects of peer dialogues. *Merrill–Palmer Quarterly, 25,* 341–358.

Berndt, T. J. (1981a). Age changes and changes over time in prosocial intentions and behavior between friends. *Developmental Psychology, 17,* 408–416.

Berndt, T. J. (1981b). The effects of friendship on prosocial intentions and behavior. *Child Development, 52,* 636–643.

Berndt, T. J. (1981c). Relations between social cognition, nonsocial cognition, and social behavior: The case of friendship. In J. H. Flavell and L. D. Ross (Eds.), *Social cognitive development: Frontiers and possible futures.* Cambridge, England: Cambridge University Press.

Berndt, T. J. (in press). Prosocial behavior between friends in middle childhood and early adolescence, *Journal of Early Adolescence.*

Berndt, T. J., Hawkins, J. A., & Hoyle, S. G. (1984b). *Stability and change in childhood and adolescent friendships.* Unpublished manuscript, University of Oklahoma.

Berndt, T. J. (1982). Fairness and friendship. In K. H. Rubin & H. S. Ross (Eds.), *Peer relationships and social skills in childhood.* New York: Springer–Verlag.

Bigelow, B. J., & La Gaipa, J. J. (1980). The development of friendship values and choice. In H. C. Foot, A. J. Chapman, & J. R. Smith (Eds.), *Friendship and social relations in children.* New York: Wiley.

Bixenstine, V. E., Lowenfeld, B., & Englehardt, C. E. (1981). Role enactment versus typology: Another test of the triangle hypothesis. *Journal of Personality and Social Psychology, 41,* 776–788.

Bronfenbrenner, U. (1979). *The ecology of human development.* Cambridge, MA: Harvard University Press.

Duck, S., & Gilmour, R. (Eds.). (1981). *Personal relationships. 2. Developing personal relationships.* New York: Academic.

Eisenberg, N. (Ed.). (1982). *The development of prosocial behavior.* New York: Academic Press.

Foot, H. C., Chapman, A. J., & Smith, J. R. (Eds.). (1980). *Friendship and social relations in children.* New York: Wiley.

Furman, W., Rahe, D. F., & Hartup, W. W. (1979). Rehabilitation of socially-withdrawn preschool children through mixed-age and same-age socialization. *Child Development, 50,* 915–922.

Goldberg, M. H., & Maccoby, E. E. (1965). Children's acquisition of skill in performing a group task under two conditions of group formation. *Journal of Personality and Social Psychology, 2,* 898–902.

Grusec, J. E., & Redler, E. (1980). Attribution, reinforcement, and altruism: A developmental analysis. *Developmental Psychology, 16,* 525–534.

Hartup, W. W. Peer relations. (1983). In P. H. Mussen (Ed.), *Handbook of child psychology* (4th ed.). New York: Wiley.

Hoffman, M. L. (1975). Developmental synthesis of affect and cognition and its implications for altruistic motivation. *Developmental Psychology, 11,* 607–622.

Isen, A. M., Clark, M., & Schwartz, M. R. (1976). Duration of the effect of good mood on helping: "Footprints on the sands of time." *Journal of Personality and Social Psychology, 34,* 385–393.

Kahn, A., Nelson, R. E., & Gaeddert, W. R. (1980). Sex of subject and sex composition of the group as determinants of reward allocations. *Journal of Personality and Social Psychology, 38,* 737–750.

Kelley, H. H., & Stahelski, A. J. (1970). Social interaction basis of cooperators' and competitors' beliefs about others. *Journal of Personality and Social Psychology, 16,* 66–91.

Knight, G. P. (1981). Behavioral and sociometric methods of identifying cooperators, competitors, and individualists: Support for the validity of the social orientation construct. *Developmental Psychology, 17,* 430–433.

Knight, G. P., & Kagan, S. (1981). Apparent sex differences in cooperation-competition: A function of individualism. *Developmental Psychology, 17,* 783–790.

Lerner, M. J., & Whitehead, L. A. (1980). Procedural justice viewed in the context of justice motive theory. In G. Mikula (Ed.), *Justice and social interaction.* New York: Springer–Verlag.

Lever, J. (1978). Sex differences in the complexity of children's play and games. *American Sociological Review, 43,* 471–483.

Mannarino, A. P. (1976). Friendship patterns and altruistic behavior in pre-adolescent males. *Developmental Psychology, 12,* 555–556.

Mannarino, A. P. (1979). The relationship between friendship and altruism in pre-adolescent girls. *Psychiatry, 42,* 280–284.

Masters, J. C., & Furman, W. (1981). Popularity, individual friendship selection, and specific peer interaction among children. *Developmental Psychology, 17,* 344–350.

Mischel, W. (1973). Toward a cognitive social learning reconceptualization of personality. *Psychological Review, 80,* 252–283.

Newcomb, A. F., & Brady, J. E. (1982). Mutuality in boys' friendship relations. *Child Development, 53,* 392–395.

Newcomb, A. F., Brady, J. E., & Hartup, W. W. (1979). Friendship and incentive condition as determinants of children's task-oriented social behavior. *Child Development, 50,* 878–881.

Piaget, J. (1965).*The moral judgment of the child.* New York: Free Press. (Original work published, 1932).

Rubin, Z. (1980). *Children's friendships.* Cambridge, MA: Harvard University Press.

Sholar, W. A., & Clark, M. S. (1981). *Deciding in communal and exchange relationships: By consensus or should majority rule?* Unpublished manuscript, Carnegie–Mellon University.

Staub, E. (1978). *Positive social behavior and morality. Vol. 1. Social and personal determinants.* New York: Academic.

Staub, E. (1979). *Positive social behavior and morality. Vol. 2. Socialization and development.* New York: Academic.

Staub, E., & Noerenberg, H. (1981). Property rights, deservingness, reciprocity, friendship: The transactional character of children's sharing behavior. *Journal of Personality and Social Psychology, 40,* 271–289.

Strain, P. S. (Ed.). (1981). *The utilization of classroom peers as behavior change agents.* New York: Plenum.

Sullivan, H. S. (1953). *The interpersonal theory of psychiatry.* New York: Norton.

Tesser, A. (1984). *Self-evaluation maintenance processes: Implications for relationships and for development.* In J. C. Masters & K. Yarkin-Levin (Eds.), *Boundary areas in social and developmental psychology.* New York: Academic Press.

Tesser, A., & Smith, J. (1980). Some effects of task relevance and friendship on helping: You don't always help the one you like. *Journal of Experimental Social Psychology, 16,* 582–590.

Youniss, J. (1980). *Parents and peers in social development.* Chicago: University of Chicago Press.

CHAPTER 6

Friendship Selection: Developmental and Environmental Influences

Joyce L. Epstein

Introduction

Friends are not selected at random. Nor are they selected on the basis of one individual's preferences and decisions. Friends are not selected the same way or for the same reasons by young children and adults in every social setting. Research is often presented, however, as if the selection of friends were random, ironically asocial, similar over the life course, and generalizable across environments. One reason that friendship choice has been poorly understood is that research has not focused on how the selection process changes with age or in differently organized environments.

This paper discusses research on three aspects of friendship selection. First, we consider *the facts of selection:* the presence or absence of friends. The number of friends chosen and the number of isolated students are two facts about selection that establish the existence of friends and permit more detailed analyses of the selection process. Second, we review results of research on *the surface of selection:* the visible features of friends. Sex and race are two primary characteristics on which students base their selections of friends. We look at the extent of same- or cross-sex choices and same- or cross-race choices of friends from preschool through adulthood. Third, we examine *the depth of selection:* the characteristics of friendships. The reciprocity and stability of choices are two characteristics of selection that determine the quality and longevity of friendships. These are variables that link the selection and influence processes.

Research on the facts, surface, and depth of selection is discussed in terms of the *developmental patterns* and the *environmental conditions* that affect the choice of friends. In this paper, *development* refers to normative patterns of selection that change with age and years in school from preschool to adulthood. *Environment* refers to the organizational structures of schools and classrooms or to the organization of environments in which adults live and work. This paper integrates developmental and environmental issues for the study of friendship selection and influence. It offers a framework for new studies of friendship choice, peer group interactions, and the effects of social exchange on behavior.

The synthesis is offered with circumspection. The studies differed widely in methodological style and sophistication. Few were rigorously empirical. Few used comparable measures to study the same age groups, different age groups, or comparable subgroups. Terms differed, so that the definition of a friend in one study was the definition of a best friend in another. Time frames in studies differed, so that the intervals of stability of friendship choices ranged from two weeks to a year or more. Few studies were both longitudinal and developmental, and most that included several grade levels treated the students as one group. Thus, students from grades 9 through 12 were treated often as a single group of high school students and not as separate groups of freshmen in a transition year or as sophomores, juniors, and seniors in a different year of transition. Very few studies measured or compared the environments in which the friendship choices were made.

A synthesis of results from diverse studies cannot take the place of coherent, longitudinal studies of friendship selection, maintenance, dissolution, and reselection. Nevertheless, patterns emerge from the disparate studies that illustrate how developmental and environmental conditions affect the selection of friends.

The Facts of Selection

NUMBER OF SELECTIONS

The number of friends and the absence of friends are basic data required for the study of selection. Numbers establish that choices are made and provide information on the breadth of students' social networks. Not all students choose friends or are chosen by friends. Some may be isolated, rejected or ignored by other students; others may elect to remain separate from the available group. Measures of isolation are important because they indicate the cohesiveness of groups, and because they may be used to identify students who have portentous social problems and who may require special training in social skills (Asher, Oden, & Gottman, 1977; Asher & Renshaw, 1981; Putallaz & Gottman, 1981). Developmental and environmental conditions affect the number of friends selected and the prevalence of isolates.

Developmental Patterns

Number of selections. Across the grades, students select, on the average, about 4 to 6 best friends. Elementary school students had an average of 5 best friends, with a range from 2 to 8 best friends (Hallinan, 1976, 1980). About 6 best friends were selected by Australian students in grades 4 through 6 (Dunphy, 1963). At the high school level, an average of 4 to 5 same-sex, best friends were selected (Cohen, 1977; Hansell, 1981; Weiss & Lowenthal, 1975), with only about 9% of the students choosing more than 6 close friends (Cohen, 1977).

There is some indication that the number of close friends selected is curvilinear over the school grades. Leinhardt (1972) compared selections of children from pre-kindergarten to grade 6 and found that very young children made fewer selections of close friends than did the children in upper elementary grades. Epstein (1983b) reported that significantly more best friends were chosen by sixth graders than by twelfth graders. Lerman (1967) showed that the size of close friendship groups increased among 14- to 16-year-olds in urban areas but then decreased to pairs after age 16. This dramatic decrease is not evident in most other studies. For example, adults selected 3 to 7 close friends (Booth, 1972; Caldwell & Peplau, 1982; Laumann, 1973; Reisman, 1981; Weiss & Lowenthal, 1975). Across the years of adulthood, young adults chose slightly more friends and met them more frequently than did older adults (Reisman & Shorr, 1978; Steuve & Gerson, 1977).

The curvilinear pattern in numbers of friends selected—fewer close friends for very young students and for older adolescents and adults, with more friends selected by preadolescents—is explained in part by cognitive changes in concepts of friendships, perceptual skills, and accumulated experiences with friends, including the recognition of increased demands of mutual friendships. Children in the middle years stress the importance of activities they enjoy with any friends, whereas adolescents stress the importance of the loyalty and commitment of particular friends and the quality of their friendships (Bigelow & La Gaipa, 1980).

In addition to best friends, students have other friends who are members of cliques and groups. A clique includes from 3 to 9 friends who select each other in an interlocking network of choices. A crowd is an association of cliques, with up to about 30 members. Student cliques are likely to meet and interact in school daily, whereas crowds interact mainly outside of school and on weekends (Dunphy, 1963). The little information available suggests that older students are more likely to be members of cliques than are younger students (Cohen, 1977). Being in a clique may increase the number of friends among clique members or may limit friendships because of boundaries built between cliques and nonclique members.

Isolates. The number of *different* students who are selected as friends increases over the school years. More and different students were chosen as best friends in grade 3 than in grade 1, as students spread their choices more realistically (Rardin & Moan, 1971). Over time there should be fewer "stars" and fewer unchosen "isolates" if students learn to share close friendship with one or two others.

The proportion of isolates reported in studies is a function of the type of measure used. The percentage of isolates is low when the measure of isolation is *not choosing* friends (i.e., naming no friends). About 2% of young children and 3% of adolescents and adults made no choice of friends (Reisman & Shorr, 1978). The percentage of isolates is higher when the measure of isolation is *not being chosen* as a friend (i.e., being named by no one as a friend). Between 6% and 11% of elementary students received no choices as friends (Gronlund, 1959). The rate of no choice of best friends was higher than no choice of friends. Epstein (1983b) reported that about 15% of secondary students made no choice of *best* friends in school.

There is greater isolation from cliques than from friendship dyads. Hallinan (1976) found few cliques in most elementary classrooms, but, when they did exist, many more students were excluded from cliques than from dyadic friendships. Cliques were more frequent in high schools (Cohen, 1977), but even among older students, youngsters are more likely to be friends with one other student than to be members of cliques characterized by mutual choice among three or four friends.

There is no clear developmental trend in isolation across the school years because of the absence of comparable measures in studies across the grades. Among adults, however, fewer young adults are isolates than older adults (Fischer & Phillips, 1981; Laumann, 1973). Young adults tend to participate more than older adults in work environments, clubs, schools, and other community settings. The number of isolates among adults ranged from 3% to 4% among young adults (Reisman & Shorr, 1978; Rosow, 1967), to about 9% among older adults (Pfeiffer, 1977). Adults over 65 years old who retired or who had limited mobility in the community had fewer opportunities than young adults for social contacts (Chown, 1981).

Children who do not choose friends or are not chosen by other students may not be "true" isolates. They may be temporarily in a period of reselection, after losing or dropping a best friend; or, they may be members of a large group of friends in which none are considered "best"; or, they may not yet be sure of the qualities that define a best friend; or, they may have friends outside of school who cannot be listed when the instructions of a sociometric measure require the names of friends in a school or classroom. On the other hand, there are some true isolates. Gottman's (1977) study of preschoolers revealed that children who had frequent negative interactions with the teacher, and children who were daydreamers or "tuned out," tended to be rejected by and isolated from other children. Horrocks and Benimoff (1966) showed how the timing of measures of selection made a difference in the prevalence of isolates. They reported that 25% of the students in grades 7 through 12 were unchosen as best friends, but only 5% were unchosen over a 2-year-period. The number of true isolates may be relatively small because, over time, most students without a friend seek and find one.

Other distinctions are made between students who are satisfied with one or few friends versus those who are dissatisfied and wish for more friends. The former may not be isolated, and the latter may feel more isolated than they are. Reisman (1981) and Rosow (1967) made similar distinctions in identifying isolated adults. Hartup (1983) reminded us that solitary play is a healthy, accepted behavior among preschoolers. Although total reclusion is unhealthy, solitary activities and few commitments to best friends may be preferred by some older children and some adults who appear isolated or unchosen by their peers. Studies are needed to document clear trends in numbers of isolates.

From the information available, we would estimate that very young children—with limited networks of friends, limited geographic boundaries, and undeveloped concepts of close friendship—probably choose relatively few close friends. Older adolescents who understand and practice the intense and time-consuming commitments of close friendship probably choose relatively few close friends. There may be fewer isolates among older students who have opportunities to seek and find at least one compatible companion from their expanding social boundaries. Children in the middle years of preadolescence select and reselect friends as they pursue active play and group games and activities. These children probably make more choices of best friends than either the younger or more mature students. There may be fewest isolates during the middle years because of the generally inclusive nature of friendship choices, and because environmental characteristics of upper elementary and middle school classrooms often dictate and require social interaction among all children. At the same time, the isolated students in the middle years may feel their exclusion especially keenly. They may be candidates for special coaching to assist the development of social skills. And, students at this age may respond well to changes in school and classroom environments that create opportunities for contact and interaction among students on academic tasks.

Environmental Conditions

Number of selections. Students in differently organized environments have different numbers of friends. A few studies conducted at the nursery, elementary, and secondary school levels, and also with adults show how organizations can affect social ties. Charlesworth and Hartup (1967) reported that participatory activities (e.g., dramatic play) increased positive social exchange among nursery school children. In contrast, individualized activities (e.g., quiet work at tables) reduced social exchange. Rubin (1980) observed that a less-structured, child-centered nursery school organization created many small groups of friends with frequent changes in group membership. In contrast, a highly-structured, teacher-centered organization created a single, large group of students who focused a major amount of attention on the teacher.

Differently organized school environments promote or discourage the formation of cliques. Hallinan (1980) found fewer cliques in open elementary classrooms than in traditional classrooms. She suggested that less exclusive, more fluid friendships among many students were made in open elementary classrooms. At the high school level, significantly more students were chosen as best friends in high-participatory secondary schools in three of the four grade levels studied (Epstein, 1983b). College-bound high school students, who tend to participate in more school activities, had more extensive networks of friends than non-college-bound students, even though their numbers of close friends were similar (Hansell & Karweit, 1983). Students who participated in extracurricular activities at school chose and were chosen by more friends (Karweit, 1983). Thus, several studies at all educational levels found that more participatory environments promoted more inclusive friendship choices.

Schmuck (1978) distinguished between student relations in classrooms with diffusely versus centrally structured groups. He concluded that in diffusely structured classrooms—where many students receive some choices rather than few students receive many choices—more students had high self-esteem and positive attitudes toward learning. Differently organized classrooms create conditions that promote diffuse or centralized social structures which assist or hinder students from developing positive attitudes and success in learning in school.

Adults are, over the years, in a variety of environments that affect the number of friends they make and the frequency of interactions with friends. Blau (1961) discussed how events in adulthood such as marriage, parenthood, retirement, and widowhood alter the environments from which friends are selected. Other researchers have reported how the numbers of adult friends change with age, personal circumstance, and settings (Feld, 1982; Laumann, 1973; Reisman & Shorr, 1978; Steuve & Gerson, 1977; Verbrugge, 1977; Weiss & Lowenthal, 1975).

Isolates. The organization of classroom and school environments reduces or increases the number of students isolated from others. Fewer students were isolated in open elementary classrooms (Hallinan, 1976) or in high-participatory secondary schools and classrooms (Epstein, 1983b; McClelland & Ratliff, 1947). When students participate frequently in activities with peers and are rewarded for doing so, they may be more apt to find at least one friend, and may be more able to replace lost friends. In contrast, there were more isolates in secondary school classes that were characterized by low cooperation or low cohesiveness (Muldoon, 1955). When students are assigned permanent seats, work individually, or are rewarded for passive or noninteractive behavior, they may be more restricted in finding or changing friends. If interaction on academic activities is not part of the classroom organization, more students may be excluded from the informal social networks that students build in schools.

The discussion of numbers of friends and isolated students raises the ancient question of how many friends is a good number. The answer, unclear to Aristotle, remains unclear today. One good friend may be enough to promote feelings of security or self-confidence; many friends and acquaintances may be needed to develop skills in communicating, negotiating, and problem solving. Epstein (1983c) found that students who selected no best friends were better off one year later on measures of self-reliance and college plans than students with stable, low-scoring friends. However, students with no best friends at school were worse off on most measures than students with stable, high-scoring friends. The importance of no friends or a number of friends depended on *which friends* were made and kept.

With age, students become more selective in their choice of friends as they learn more about themselves, about others, and about what they can expect from and give to a friendship. But environments, as well as age, affect the number of friends students have. Figure 6.1 shows estimated curves across the school years and into adulthood of the number of friends chosen as a function of grade level and environmental opportunities and restrictions. The x's reflect research findings and the dotted lines represent potential effects due to environments that restrict or increase options for meeting and choosing friends. The curves portray the developmental pattern that fewer close friends are maintained when full responsibilities for friendship are practiced. A set of curves for other friends or acquaintances would predict greater environmental effects and a more linear relationship between age and number of selections.

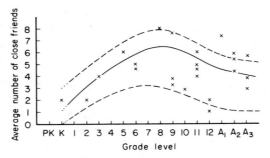

Figure 6.1. Estimated curve of number of close friends. × denotes number of close friends reported in research: ——— signifies estimated patterns due to environmental opportunities (top) and restrictions (bottom); A_{1-3} refers to early, mid-, and late adulthood.

Older students participate in wider, more varied contexts, and meet and interact with many more students than do young children (Epstein, 1983a, b). Greater selectivity and wider circles of friends affect the selection process, restricting the number of best friends and extending the number of other friends and acquaintances. The number of best friends may decrease as older students become closer to a few special friends; at the same time, the number of friends and acquaintances may increase as older students make social contacts in wider boundaries. The structure of activities in environments influences the number of friends made, with some activities offering more opportunities for participation and interaction with others who may become friends. In order to understand differences in numbers of friends or isolates in different environments, researchers must clearly measure organizational procedures and practices that affect interpersonal contact and interaction in school, work, and other settings where friendships are studied.

The Surface of Selection

SAME AND CROSS-SEX CHOICES

Developmental and environmental factors influence the selection of same- and opposite-sex friends.

Developmental patterns

Same-sex choices. The most important surface feature of selection is the gender of the chooser and the chosen. Research conducted on students at all educational levels and on adults reports the predominance of same-sex choices, with same-sex more important than race or age for the selection of friends (Campbell, 1964; Gottman & Parkhurst, 1980; Kandel, 1978; Moreno, 1934; Pitts, 1968; St. John, 1975; Schofield, 1981; Singleton & Asher, 1979; Tuma & Hallinan, 1979; Verbrugge, 1979; Wheeler & Nezlek, 1977).

There are many informative reports on the size of friendship groups, patterns of reciprocation, ease of making friends, and patterns of informal interaction of males and females. Preschool females made more choices of friends than preschool males (Clark, Wyon, & Richards, 1969), but after about age 7, males had more extensive, large-group associations than females (Maccoby & Jacklin, 1974; Savin–Williams, 1980; Waldrop & Halverson, 1975). This pattern continued in reports of 9- to 11-year-olds (Eder & Hallinan, 1978), but was not so clear or consistent in later adolescence. Montemayor and Van Komen (1982) found that among 13- to 19-year-olds, males and females were members of similarly-sized groups in and out of school, and Caldwell and Peplau (1982) found no significant differences in the numbers of intimate, good, or casual friends of college men and women. Some studies found that females made more reciprocated choices in the middle and high school grades and in adulthood (Epstein, 1983b; Karweit & Hansell, 1983; Hansell, 1981; Reisman, 1981; Weiss & Lowenthal, 1975).

An interesting difference has been noted in the ease with which males and females make new, same-sex friends in new settings, or add new friends to existing friendship groups (cf. Eder & Hallinan, 1978; Epstein, 1983a; Feshback & Sones, 1971). The studies suggest that males make new friends or add friends to existing groups easier than do females. Little is known about the processes that might explain these differences, or how experiences in different school environments affect the readiness with which new friends are made by males or females.

Observers of school behavior report that most informal interaction is between same-sex students. For example, in a middle school lunchroom, fewer than 5% of the freely-chosen, side-by-side seats were selected by opposite sex peers (Schofield, 1981). Choosing a lunch partner may be a more exclusive selection than acknowledging the friendliness of male and female classmates on a checklist of names. Particular selections (e.g., choosing a seat partner, working on a joint project, or sending a party invitation) have different meanings from general sociometric measures.

Cross-sex choices. In contrast to the relatively high rate of same-sex choices of best friends across ages and grade levels, the literature suggests a curvilinear, developmental pattern of cross-sex choices of friends. Very young children made frequent cross-sex choices (Damon, 1977; Gottman & Parkhurst, 1980); children in the elementary and middle school grades made almost no cross-sex choices (Bossert, 1979; Eder & Hallinan, 1978); and adolescents increased their cross-sex choices of friends (Douvan & Adelson,

1966; Duck, 1973b; Epstein, 1983a; Montemayor & Van Komen, 1982). In written comments, older students discussed the importance of cross-sex friendships more than did younger students (La Gaipa, 1981). The students' justifications help to explain how the observed increase in cross-sex choices among adolescents becomes an accepted social pattern, even at the expense of same-sex choices of friends.

More cross-sex choices of friends are made than cross-sex choices of best friends. For example, Hallinan (1978) reported up to 35% cross-sex choices of friends among students who chose only same-sex best friends. There were more cross-sex choices of friends than cross-sex memberships in cliques (Hallinan, 1980). It is more likely that a dyadic cross-sex choice will be made than that a clique of three or four friends will all make the same cross-sex choices. Cross-sex cliques increase in the later years in high school (Dunphy, 1963; Hansell, 1981). Different rates of cross-sex choices result from different measures of selection. When respondents are asked to report their friendly feelings towards all classmates or school mates, not just their closest friends, the extent of cross-sex choices will be higher than when they can list only their best friends.

Before age 13, males and females do not differ in their selection of opposite-sex friends (Maccoby & Jacklin, 1974). In adolescence, however, girls made more heterosexual choices than did boys (Epstein, 1983a,b; Kon & Losenkov, 1978), and girls' choices were often of older boys (Dunphy, 1963). Measure of friends in a students' own grade or classroom, artificially minimize the extent of cross-sex choices, especially in adolescence when the heterosexual choices are often mixed-age (e.g., younger girls and older males) and out-of-school friends. In adolescence, males and females increase their heterosexual choices of best friends, but females increase their choices of males earlier and with greater frequency than do males (Kon, 1981). Girls' status with same-sex friends may depend on their relations with boys at an earlier time than boys' status with same-sex friends depends on their cross-sex friendships (Schofield, 1981). From the few studies that examined details of cross-sex choices, we get some insight into the subtlties of sex as a status variable. Sex of student may be an equal status variable for same-sex choices of friends, but an unequal status characteristic for cross-sex choices, with males more often chosen (and perhaps more highly valued) by females than females are by males. This hypothesis requires specific studies of same- and cross-sex choices and valuations.

Environmental Conditions

Same-sex choices. The organization of classroom instruction influences the rate and acceptance of same-sex choices of friends. Eder and Hallinan (1978) found that in traditional classrooms boys had less exclusive, more transitive triadic friendships than do girls. In open elementary classrooms, males and females had more similarly structured friendships that emphasized dyadic relationships. It may be that in more open classrooms, males (and females) have numerous opportunities to work together and to select a close friend during academic activities; in traditional settings, males may make numerous friends (but not necessarily close friends) in their non-academic contacts with other boys in large group games. This interpretation of Eder and Hallinan's results connects the school or classroom organization with the influential play-group structures. In traditional secondary schools, females made and received more best-friend choices than did males, but males were more equally included in friendship choices in high-participatory environments (Epstein, 1983b). The opportunities for contact and participation may change the typical patterns of interaction and selection, especially among male students.

Cross-sex choices. Two features of environments that have been found to influence cross-sex choices of friends and patterns of interactions are numbers of males and females in a group, and the reward structures for cross-sex choices of friends. Cross-sex choices were more common in small preschool classes than in large ones (Smith & Connolly, 1981). Hallinan (1979) also recognized that size of the classroom population affected cross-sex choices. Students in larger classes made fewer cross-sex choices than did students in smaller classes. It may be that students have more opportunities to choose among a large number of same-sex friends, or that the large number of students causes the teacher to use management strategies that emphasize the separation of boys and girls in classroom activities.

When cross-sex interactions were rewarded in classrooms (e.g., when teams or games required cooperation among male and female team members), more cross-sex helping behavior and friendships occurred (DeVries & Edwards, 1974; Serbin, Tonick, & Sternglanz, 1977). If the task and reward systems of the school or classroom provide official, structural support for cross-sex choices, then opposite-sex friends would be among the normative patterns of selection. Without institutional support, the individual's cross-sex choices would be based on personal decisions, and would not necessarily be understood or accepted by same-sex peers. Elementary school children's cross-sex choices were more unstable than their same-sex friendships (Gronlund, 1959). This instability could be due to many factors, including the lack of peer and institutional support for cross-sex choices. Students may more quickly drop or dissolve opposite-sex friendships if there is no positive support from others for their continuation.

A combination of personality and environmental characteristics may affect the rate of cross-sex choices of friends. In Maas' (1968) study "warm" boys made more cross-sex choices of friends than did "aloof" boys, who tended to avoid cross-sex interactions. "Warm" girls had larger groups of playmates than did "aloof" girls. Environments that encourage warm and close relationships may change the way heterosexual relations and friendship choices are structured. Whiting (Chapter 4, this volume) reports that boys who were given opportunities to take care of younger children were more nurturing in their dyadic relations than boys whose environments did not require or encourage child care. The early responsibility for nurtural behavior may indirectly increase cross-sex friendships. Opportunities for nurtural behavior may promote warmth, acceptance of opposite-sex friends, and the earlier development of reciprocated friendships. The activities children are asked to perform in their social and educational environments influence their interpersonal relationships, including the pattern of cross-sex selections of friends.

The research suggests that variables such as class size, proportions of male and female students, authority and reward structures in school, and responsibilities for child care at home can alter the expected patterns of same-sex and cross-sex choices of friends. Environmental factors, not just biological ones, help to determine how boys and girls form same- and cross-sex friendships. New research is needed on the developmental and environmental factors in schools and classrooms that encourage friendships earlier than adolescence. Schools that support the separation of the sexes and reward (overtly or subtly) same-sex choices of friends should have students who, on the average, have different attitudes and behaviors than do students in schools that support and reward cross-sex interaction. We lack information on the long-term effects of school and classroom practices that support cross-sex interaction. For example, does official support for cross-sex interaction lead male and female students toward greater understanding, trust, and appreciation of the opposite sex?

SAME- AND CROSS-RACE CHOICES

Like sex, race is an ascribed, visible, surface characteristic that may influence students' choices of friends. Although there is considerable discussion about the benefits in coeducational schools of exclusively same-sex friends for learning sex-appropriate behavior (Fine, 1981; Hartup, 1983; Maccoby & Jacklin, 1974), there is no analogous discussion of the benefits in desegregated schools of exclusively same-race friends. Accepted goals of integrated education are cross-race acceptance and friends (St. John, 1975). Research documents developmental and environmental effects on same-race and cross-race choices of friends.

Developmental Patterns

The importance of race as a criterion for choice changes across the school years. Very young children placed less emphasis on race in their choices of friends than did older children (Asher, Singleton, & Taylor, 1982). Soon after school begins, however, same-race choices dominated students' selections (Bartel, Bartel, & Grill, 1973; Blanchard, Weigel, & Cook, 1975; Criswell, 1939; Hauserman, Walen, & Behling, 1973; Schofield, 1981; Tuma & Hallinan, 1979). Carter, DeTine, Spero, and Benson (1975), and Carter, Detine-Carter, and Benson (1980) determined that 5- to 8-year-olds made few racial distinctions in selecting friends, but 9- to 13-year-olds selected friends of their own race to obtain recognition and support in social and academic activities.

Most studies report that fewer cross-race choices of friends are made by high school students than by elementary students. There was a decline in cross-race choices across the elementary grades (Hallinan, 1982; Singleton & Asher, 1979) and over the secondary grades (Asher, Oden, & Gottman, 1977; Epstein, 1983a). Hartup (1983) discussed a British study that showed a large decrease in cross-race choices of friends at the time of transition to the secondary school level.

Figure 6.2 compares estimated curves of cross-sex and cross-race choices of best friends. The curvilinear pattern of cross-sex choices of friends across the school years illustrates the typical increase in heterosexual relationships in adolescence. In contrast, the linear pattern of cross-race friendships reflects the increasing exclusions of out-group members from the intimacies of best friendships in adolescence. An increase in cross-sex best friends may

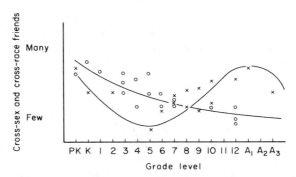

Figure 6.2. Estimated curves of proportions of cross-sex and cross-race friendship choices. × denotes cross-sex choices reported in research; o signifies cross-race choices reported in research; metric not defined for few or many friends because of different measures used across studies.

be made at the expense of cross-race friendships. Environmental factors have been shown to alter these patterns in several ways. For example, classroom structures may reward the development of cross-sex friendships earlier in elementary grades or encourage the maintenance of cross-race best friendships longer than would usually be the case.

Reports of students' dominant choices of friends may hide the facts about cross-race acceptance. There was considerable cross-race acceptance of friends, teammates, and workmates, even though *best* friends were most often the same race (Asher et al., 1977; Asher et al., 1982; Kandel, 1978; Singleton & Asher, 1979). In one study, about 50% of black and white students reported that they participated in out-of-school activities with students of a different race, with about 10% in frequent participation (Patchen, 1982). About one third of each racial group visited the homes of friends of a different race (compared to one-half for visits to homes of same-race friends).

The prevalence of same-race choices may be overestimated and misinterpreted because of a lack of other important variables in the measurement models. Same-race choices are often explained solely by race, but the selection process is not unidimensional. Some studies have tried to determine whether race or other characteristics are the key facts for selecting friends. Achievement may be more important than race in determining students' acceptance or friendships in desegregated settings (Blanchard et al., 1975; Carter et al., 1975; and Miller, 1983). Race may be important for some selections (e.g., social activities) but not others (e.g., academic work groups).

Research on adult friendships suggests that race neither determines all friendship choices nor does its importance disappear when other characteristics are considered (Laumann, 1973; Mayhew, 1970). Rather, the interplay of age, race (and other ascribed, surface characteristics), achievement (and other achieved, or profound characteristics), and environmental factors affect friendship selection.

Environmental Conditions

School and classroom environments can be organized to maximize or minimize the importance of race as a basis for selecting and accepting other students as friends. Environmental effects on cross-race selections have been more widely studied than other environmental effects on friendship choice because of the changes resulting from the court-ordered or voluntary desegregation of schools and classrooms. Studies of school and classroom organizations suggest that the task and reward structures, participation structures, demography of the school population, and the organization of transitions to new educational levels affect students' cross-race choices of friends from kindergarten through high school.

At the elementary school level, cross-race choices increased when the teacher rewarded this social behavior and decreased when the rewards for cross-race interactions were withdrawn (Cooper, Johnson, Johnson, & Wilderson, 1980; Hauserman et al., 1973). At the secondary level, cross-race choices increased when students worked as members of integrated teams in which group progress was rewarded by the teacher (DeVries, Edwards, & Slavin, 1978). Some cross-race choices that developed in cooperative learning settings were strong (best friends) and others weak (just friends) depending on the sociometric measures used (Slavin & Hansell, 1983). Cross-race acceptance by older students may be more lasting. For example, cross-race acceptance was maintained nine months after a 12-week intervention that rewarded cooperation by junior high school students on biracial learning teams (Slavin, 1979). Ziegler (1981) found similar, long-term acceptance of cross-ethnic group friends after a cooperative learning program in Grade 6. Some integrated teams in triethnic classrooms (especially Hispanic–white teams), resulted in more friendships than other cross-race combinations (Weigel, Wiser, & Cook, 1975).

Other structural arrangements encouraged cross-race choices in kindergarten through Grade 4, including the organization of open classrooms, mixed grade levels, high interaction of students on school tasks, and slightly more blacks than whites in the classrooms (Bartel et al., 1973). Students in high-participatory secondary schools made more cross-race choices than did students in low-participatory schools (Epstein, 1983b; Patchen, Davidson, Hoffman, & Brown, 1977).

Other environmental conditions may affect the number of cross-race choices. The history of the students' experiences in desegregated schools and classrooms (Carter et al., 1980); whether the school was predominately black or white prior to desegregation; the percent of majority and minority students in the school and in classrooms; opportunities for participation in class and extracurricular activities; and racial attitudes of the family at home have been shown to influence cross-race choices of friends (McPartland & York, 1967; Patchen, 1982; St. John, 1975). Clearly, if a school is segregated, cross-race choices of friends in school will not occur. If a desegregated school is resegregated, with black students in one classroom or instructional group and white students in another, cross-race choices of friends are unlikely to occur unless other well-planned activities create cohesive, integrated groups of students.

The level of desegregation is a basic environmental condition that affects the extent of contact, interaction and cross-race choices of friends. For example, in a 20% black elementary school, Shaw (1973) found 6% cross-race choices by whites and 33% cross-race choices by blacks. Blacks tend to make proportionately more cross-race choices than whites in most desegregated settings (St. John, 1975). In a 40% black elementary school, there were about 18% cross-race choices by whites and 44% cross-race choices by blacks (Asher et al., 1977). But, cross-race choices of best friends are only part of the story. In a 21% black third-grade classroom, between 94% and 100% of all cross-race interactions were positive (SIngleton & Asher, 1977). Thus, in-class cross-race acceptance can be uniformly positive, even if close friendship choices do not predominate.

An increase in the proportion of the minority racial group may lead to more cross-race choices by members of the majority group. For example, when the number of black students in a school or class increased, more cross-race choices were made by whites (Patchen, 1982). The patterns are neither simple nor predictable, however. In one study in which black students were in a 90% majority, white students were at a significant social disadvantage, receiving relatively few friendship choices (Tuma & Hallinan, 1979); in another study in which white students were in a 90% majority, blacks and white students received about equal numbers of choices and reciprocations (Epstein, 1983b). White students' choices were less stable in predominately black elementary schools (Tuma & Hallinan, 1979); black students' choices were less stable in predominately white secondary schools (Epstein, 1983b). In minority black schools, black students increased same-race choices from the beginning to the end of the year (Hallinan, 1980).

The patterns get especially complicated when choices of students in sex-by-race subgroups are examined separately. For example, in one study black males but not black females made more same-race choices when the proportion of their own race increased (St. John, 1975), but in another study it was the females who made more same-race choices than males (Singleton & Asher, 1979). Miller (1983) reported more positive choices by black and white males in elementary school classrooms and play yards than by black and white females in the same settings. Schofield and Sagar (1977) observed remarkably few cross-race adjacent seating choices at the middle school level. The differences in expected patterns cannot always be explained, in part because the studies do not document the school or classroom structures, rewards or punishments, teachers' practices or prejudices, or other environmental factors that influence cross-race contact and acceptance. The length of time in newly desegregated settings is also an important factor. If sociometric measures are taken too soon after desegregation, cross-race choices will be low due to the lack of time needed to develop positive feelings of acceptance and to work through the selection process from shallow to deep friendships (Carter et al., 1975).

Transitions to new classrooms and larger schools often instigate the regrouping of students. In many elementary schools, students are grouped by ability in ways that separate many black and white students. In later transitions (e.g., to middle school, or to high school), tracking and grouping practices often result in even greater separation of black and white students. The reorganization of groups into college, vocational, and general curricula, may contribute to the dramatic increase in same-race choices of best friends when students move to high schools (Epstein, 1983a,b). In high schools, tracking and grouping practices place students in programs that are located in separate classrooms and even in separate areas of the school building. New pressures to select same-race friends for dating and social activities are often experienced by adolescents that were not of concern to students in the earlier grades. Students' choices of friends may be greatly affected by coincidental environmental and developmental factors.

Despite over two decades of interest in race relations and sociometric choice, comparable studies have not been conducted that clarify the selection process in desegregated settings at different grade levels and under different environmental conditions. The opportunities structured by the school for contact, interaction, shared rewards, and purposeful cooperation on school activities help to define the nature of inter-racial experiences. New research will be useful that shows how different organizational structures in desegregated schools emphasize or minimize the importance of race and affect students' interactions and choices of friends. Longitudinal studies that permit students to distinguish between tolerance, acceptance, friendship, and best friendship are needed for better estimates of how cross-race choices change over time in different school, classroom, and work environments.

The Depth of Selection

RECIPROCATION OF CHOICES

This section discusses research on developmental patterns of reciprocated choices and the features of school and classroom environments that increase or decrease the prevalence of reciprocated friendships.

Developmental Patterns

There is a general increase in reciprocation from prekindergarten to Grade 3 or 4 (Rardin & Moan, 1971), and then a general leveling off, with between 40% to 55% of best friends reciprocating choices. Cross-sectional studies report little difference in rates of reciprocation across grade levels (Busk, Ford, & Schulman, 1973). Recent longitudinal analyses of the choices of friends by middle and high school students showed small but consistent increases in reciprocations from one year to the next (Epstein, 1983a). Females made more reciprocated choices than did males in middle school, high school, and adulthood (Epstein, 1983a,b; Hansell, 1981; Reisman, 1981).

Reciprocated friends are more similar (Alexander & Campbell, 1964; Cohen, 1977; Epstein, 1983c; Kandel, 1978). Reciprocated choices of friends are more stable than unreciprocated choices. At the elementary (Hallinan, 1978), secondary (Epstein, 1983b; Kandel, 1978), and post-secondary or adult levels (Allan, 1979; Verbrugge, 1977), friends who reciprocated choices at one time were more likely to remain friends than were those who did not reciprocate choices. Reciprocated friends liked each other more (Newcomb, 1961) and may stay friends longer.

Youniss (1980) discussed Piaget's and Sullivan's concepts of reciprocity between friends from 6 to 14 years old. Young children are believed to share symmetrical reciprocity in their exchanges of ideas and in their growing recognition of others. For them, reciprocation refers to responses returned in sequence or to the simple recognition that friends are people who have their own ideas (Youniss, 1980). Older children are thought to enter *cooperative reciprocity* in which they increase the depth of their social exchange, consider each other's ideas, and discuss and resolve their differences.

The theoretical and empirical studies suggest that reciprocation of time spent together in activities may be more important than reciprocation of labels of best friend until children develop an understanding of the concept of commitment between friends. From preschool to adolescence, youngsters increase communication, task-related behavior, cooperation, collaboration, problem-solving, and concern for equity among friends (Berndt, 1981; Hartup, 1983; Hartup, Brady, & Newcomb, 1982; Selman, 1976, 1981; Selman & Jacquette, 1978). These social skills should affect the quality of students' friendships and the rate of reciprocated choices.

The lack of clear trends and rates of reciprocation across the years may be due, in part, to measurement problems. For example, different estimates will result if the measure refers to friends or best friends. More friends can be reciprocated than can best friends. The number of reciprocated friendships will differ if the respondent is given a check list of names or is asked to write out the full names of friends. The former is easier to complete, should result in more choices recorded, and, therefore, more reciprocations. Rates may differ, too, if the respondents were asked to list or check only those friends who would surely reciprocate the choice, or who would reciprocate a friendly behavior such as an invitation to a birthday party or dinner. Very few studies have compared the rates of reciprocation that result from different measures of reciprocation. We know little about the links between the measures used, the underlying concept of reciprocity, the age of the respondent, and the environmental conditions that affect reciprocation.

Environmental Conditions

> Three aspects of school environments affect rates of reciprocation. First, studies of the effects of cooperative versus competitive instruction in classrooms showed that students who are given opportunities and rewarded for cooperative activities with their peers made more reciprocated friendship choices (Hertz–Lazarowitz, Sharan, & Steinberg, 1980). In one study, significantly more reciprocated, cross-race choices were made in cooperative learning versus control classes after a ten-week instructional treatment (Hansell & Slavin, 1981). If students help and reward each other on academic tasks, the benefits they share may lead to mutual acceptance and liking.

> Second, open or participatory educational methods increased reciprocated choices between friends. Intransitive friendships became transitive sooner in open than in traditional elementary school classrooms in Grades 4 to 6 (Hallinan, 1976). Students in high-participatory secondary schools made more reciprocated choices than students in low-participatory schools (Epstein, 1983b). Students in open or high-participatory schools have more opportunities than other students to interact on academic work and are rewarded by the school for doing so. Students who are actively involved with other students should get to know more about the skills, talents, and personalities of more classmates and so may make more mutually satisfying choices of friends.

> Third, transitions from one educational level to another (e.g., the transition from elementary to middle school, or from middle to high school), may affect rates of reciprocation (Epstein, 1983a). When students change schools, they are organized by new grading and grouping procedures. The middle and high school students join populations that may be larger and demographically different from their previous schools, and there may be many opportunities to meet new students is curricular and extracurricular activities. A period of selecting new friends and learning the social skills demanded by new school organizations may lower rates of reciprocation for a short time after the transitions. Newcomers to schools at any grade level are individually affected by the disruption of their friendships in their former schools.

Cooperation, equal exchange, purposeful academic interactions, and increased understanding may result from the organization of school and work environments. Few studies have examined how differently organized environments encourage or discourage the behaviors and attitudes that promote reciprocity among friends.

STABILITY OF CHOICES

One of the most complex topics on children's friendships is the stability of relationships. Research suggests that stability of friendships increases as youngsters mature, but stability is also influenced by the time between the measures of selection, the types of measures used, and by school and classroom organizations.

Developmental Patterns

Most research that includes students from several grade levels shows that older students have more stable friendships. This was reported in studies that compared preschool to kindergarten children (Hartup, 1975); kindergarten to Grade 3 (Rardin & Moan, 1971); kindergarten to Grade 5 (Horrocks & Buker, 1951); kindergarten to Grade 6 (Duck, Miell, & Gaebler, 1980); Grade 4 to Grade 6 (Hallinan, 1980); Grade 4 to Grade 8 (Busk et al., 1973); Grades 6 through 10 to Grades 11 through 12 (Thompson & Horrocks, 1943); and Grades 6 to 12 (Horrocks & Benimoff, 1966). Figure 6.3 depicts an estimated curve of increasingly stable friendship choices based on research results from several studies. The regularity of the trend of increasing stability of friendships is impressive, but the consistency is partly a function of the short time between measures of choices (Busk et al., 1973). Most of the findings of more stable friendships of older students compared to younger ones were based on relatively short periods of two weeks or a

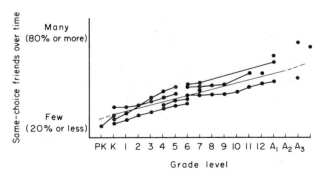

Figure 6.3. Estimated curve of stability of friendship choices. •—• denotes change in stability of choices estimated from research; metric not defined because of different measures used across studies.

few months. When one full year elapsed between measures, only students in grade 12 had significantly more stable friendships than students in Grades 6, 7, or 9 (Epstein, 1983a,b). Although older students tend to have more stable friendships than younger students, even older students' relationships are not very stable.

The consistent trend toward greater stability in older students' friendships is elaborated by some related findings. The classification "friend" was more stable over a six week period than the classification of "best friend" or "nonfriend" (Tuma & Hallinan, 1979). Best friends who reciprocated choices had more stable friendships (Epstein, 1983b,c; Hallinan, 1979; Kandel, 1978). People have relatively few "genuine" friendships even in late adolescence and adulthood (Kon & Losenkov, 1978; La Gaipa, 1981), but the few true friends may last longer.

Because students belong to several dyads and groups of friends, it is not surprising that some of their relationships are characterized by change and instability, realignments, and reordering of best friends. A few studies have been conducted of the characteristics of groups of friends. Sorenson and Hallinan (1976) found that, over time, intransitive triads move toward stability of relationships among the three friends. The features of group memberships change with age. Hrybyk and Farnham-Diggory (1981) concluded that time and experience in social relations led to more stable group memberships at around the seventh grade. More stable group memberships should support more stable choices of friends, because friends tend to be chosen among group members. At the elementary school level, 6 out of 34 cliques, or about 18%, remained stable from fall to spring (Hallinan, 1976). At the high school level, 55% of the cliques that existed in the fall remained stable, while the others disintegrated by the spring (Cohen, 1977). Although there was greater stability in older students' groups, group relations were not very stable even at the high school level.

It is necessary to differentiate between the *relative rates* of stability of older and younger students' friendships, and the *absolute rates* of stability. In Grades 3 to 8, only 25% of the students had the same best friends after one month (Seagoe, 1933). In Grade 6, about 38% of the students made at least one change in three best friends over two weeks (Austin & Thompson, 1948). Most research finds a high rate of change in students' choices of best friends over time. In a study of students from Grades 4 to 6, 25% of their choices of best-liked friends were predictable after one year, and 16% were predictable after three years (Roff, Sells, & Golden, 1972). Among secondary school students, the predictability of students' choices ranged from 8% (Horrocks & Benimoff, 1966) to 33% (Epstein, 1983a,b). The differences in reports may be due to many factors including a variety of school organizational conditions in elementary and secondary schools.

Another aspect of stability is measured by asking individuals how long they have known each other, and whether they ever previously classified each other as best friend or as friend (Montemeyer & Van Komen, 1982; Steuve & Gerson, 1977). Using this type of measure, Weiss and Lowenthal (1975) found that 73% of school friends (vs. 30% of adult friends) had known each other for at least 5 years. By collecting only the names of friends, researchers overlook the longevity of contact and familiarity among school children, and underestimate one aspect of stability of relationships. The *preselection* process of gathering and storing information about potential friends is part of the history of selection of friends.

A different kind of stability is the maintenance of social positions in student populations. Some students receive choices as friends or are nominated for positive or negative social characteristics, even though they are not always chosen by the same people. For example, the choices received over an 8 week period were more stable than the choices made over the same time (Busk et al., 1973). Popularity is relatively stable even though individual choices of best friends are relatively unstable. Lippitt and Gold (1959) reported high correlations from the beginning to the end of the school year for most-liked and least-liked students, with the correlations ranging from .6 in Grades 1 to 3 to .8 in Grades 4 to 6. Continued sociability and acceptance may be more important than the stability of particular friendships for the development of some positive attitudes and behaviors.

Youniss (1980) attributes the lack of stable friends among children under 9-years-old to their lack of understanding of the concept of reciprocity. Others place the critical stage for the development of concepts of reciprocity at age 12 or older (Piaget, 1932). The concept of loyalty, developed at about age 11, adds expectations for constancy and dependability in relationships (La Gaipa, 1979; Youniss, 1980). Rules for inclusion and exclusion develop between the ages of 8 and 11 (Douvan & Gold, 1966) and may help to stabilize interactions and selections of friends. From preadolescence, youngsters increase problem solving and conflict resolution skills that help them stabilize group relations. The physical, psychological, and cognitive changes that occur in preadolescence and adolescence seem to intensify students' needs for close and intimate friends with whom ideas, goals, and feelings can be shared (Douvan & Adelson, 1966; Duck, 1973a; Selman, 1976, 1981).

The development of expectations about friendships, the translation of concepts of loyalty to behavior, and the improvement of problem-solving skills are long, slow processes during which children test, evaluate, reject, and reselect friends. Even with the development of advanced social reasoning skills, the probability of instability of best friends continues to be high through adulthood (Allan, 1979; Hauser, 1982; Kerckhoff & Davis, 1962;

Laumann, 1973; Verbrugge, 1977). Stability is neither typical nor required for best friendships across the life span.

A basic question is whether increased stability early in the school years has positive or negative effects on social and academic development. Although many assume that stability is a good quality of friendship, Epstein (1983c) showed that this is not necessarily the case. Students with initially low-scoring friends who kept those friends over one year had lower self-reliance, less ambitious plans for college, and lower report card grades than students who selected no friends in school. Thus, stability of some friendships may be detrimental to development, especially for outcomes that are expected to change with age.

Environmental Conditions

Several environmental factors may affect the stability of children's friendships. Grouping procedures that put similar students together in classrooms may increase the likelihood of stable choices of friends. Bossert (1979) suggested that homogeneous grouping increased the stability of elementary students' friendships. Tuma and Hallinan (1979) documented that children who are similar in achievement (whether or not they are homogeneously grouped for instruction) had more stable best friendships. Schools' grouping practices may hasten the development of stable group memberships if the students remain in the same groups for most of the school day. One important question for new research is: What is the price paid in breadth of associations, tolerance of others, awareness and understanding of different strengths and weaknesses when group memberships are fixed early in students' school years?

Another environmental condition that affects the stability of students' friendships is the organization of transitions from elementary to middle or junior high school, or from junior high to senior high school (Elder, 1969) when students and their friends change to different schools with larger populations. Epstein (1983a,b) found that stability of friendships increased from one year to the next when the students and their friends remained in the same school. In that study, students in Grade 12 were in the same school for at least two years, but this was not the case for students in Grade 6 and for some in Grade 7 who were moving to new middle schools, or for students in Grade 9 who were entering new high schools.

Outside of school, children's games create social environments that may influence the stability of friendships. Lever (1976) suggested that boys' larger groups for games lead to more stable group relations. Even when best friends change, they may change among the same group members. Best friends may not be as easily exchanged or replaced by girls whose play groups are smaller, often dyadic.

Social, cognitive and environmental factors work for or against stability in friendships. There is some evidence that older students have more advanced concepts of friendship and more stable friends, and that environmental factors—especially grouping practices—may affect stability of friendships. The stability of children's and adults' friendships is affected by the development in each friend of concepts of friendship and of social skills that can be used to resolve conflicts so that friendships can continue. Stability is also affected by the structured, natural upheavals that are part of the life course, such as transitions to new levels of education or new locations of school or work. Day to day factors that determine the regularity or disruptions in patterns of contact and exchange may also affect stability of friendships. The less the environmental disruption, (e.g., students remaining in the same school over the time when selections are measured), the more friendships will be stable. The shorter the time between measures, the more friendships will be stable. The broader the measure (e.g., friends vs. best friends), the more friendships will appear stable. Studies are needed on how disruptions affect friendships at different ages, or how friendships are buffered or intensitifed by differently organized schools, classrooms, and other environments. Little is known about the stability of students' memberships in multiple groups of friends, or about the benefits and disadvantages that result from stable or unstable friendships.

Summary and Discussion

Three aspects of selection were examined—facts of selection, surface characteristics of selection, and deep characteristics of selection. The three aspects were arranged heuristically, not temporally, in order to allow the discussion to flow from spare facts to more elaborate conditions of selection. Information on the number or lack of friends and isolates tells *whether* students are connected to other students. Surface or ascriptive characteristics such as sex and race tell *which* students are attracted by others' visible features that match or differ from their own. Information about who is selected leads to questions about *how* students develop the quality of their friendships, and how they keep or change the friends they select. The facts, surface characteristics and deeper qualities of selection were studied to learn whether patterns of selection changed with age and under different environmental conditions. We can draw several conclusions:

1. There are important developmental patterns in the selection of friends. The patterns of selection of older students are significantly different from those of younger students, and selections by young adults are different from those of older adults. On the average, older students

choose fewer best friends, but more friends and acquaintances; increase their cross-sex choices, but decrease their cross-race choices; reciprocate more choices and make more stable choices. The facts, importance of surface characteristics, and deeper qualities of selections change with age and with the advancement of cognitive and social skills. Selections reflect students' increasing abilities to make more accurate estimates of their own and others' personalities and the demands of friendship. They become better able to deal with stresses and disruptions in friendship. Youngsters move from self-interested choices and limited commitments to many friends, to awareness of themselves as members of groups and deeper commitments to particular friends. Among adults, developmental patterns are linked to the demands and opportunities of different life stages.

2. There are important environmental patterns in the selection of friends.

   a. The basic characteristics of environments affect the selection of friends. For example, one -room schools, black or white neighborhood schools, or single-sex schools or colleges, create predictable patterns of same- or cross-race, same- or cross-sex choices of friends, respectively. Of course, the basic characteristics of environments may change. One-room schools may be expanded, segregated schools may be integrated, single-sex schools may be made coeducational. The patterns of selection that were all but guaranteed under an earlier scheme can change.

   b. The natural changes in environments affect friendship choices. For example, high schools are typically larger than elementary or junior high schools, and so students come into contact with more students who may become new friends. Compared to elementary schools, high schools typically require more self-direction and permit more self-selection into courses, classes, and extracurricular activities. When students make these choices, they join others who are similar in achievements, goals, or interests, and they increase the likelihood of selecting friends who are similar on important characteristics. High schools establish structures such as extracurricular activities, dances, and rallies that encourage heterosexual interaction and support the development of more cross-sex friendship choices by older students.

   The natural changes in school organizations often occur simultaneously with the cognitive, social and physical development in youngsters. Because the developmental and environmental changes may be concurrent, it is necessary to conduct research on the selection of friends across the age range in differently organized schools and classes. In much the same way, the basic characteristics and natural changes in settings where adults work, reside, and spend leisure time affect adult friendships.

c. The purposeful changes in environments affect friendship choices. School and classroom environments can be revised or redesigned in ways that change the expected patterns of selection. They can be changed in how they (i) distribute demographically diverse populations of students to schools and, within schools, to classrooms; (ii) set grouping or tracking policies in schools and in classrooms; (iii) establish curricular and extracurricular offerings and prerequisites; or (iv) design the task, reward and authority structures of the instructional program. These factors affect which students come in contact, why they interact, which interactions are rewarded, and who becomes friends. For example, selections of friends were affected by demographic characteristics in schools and classrooms (e.g., the percentage minority and majority students affected cross-race choices); tracking and grouping practices (e.g., students selected friends mainly from the same curricular tracks; students had more stable friendships with others from the same ability groups); extracurricular activities (e.g., students selected friends from the same clubs, teams, or activities); cooperative tasks and rewards (e.g., students reciprocated more friendship choices if they worked cooperatively on learning tasks; students made more friends if they were rewarded for cooperative behavior); and participatory organization (students made more friends and reciprocated more choices, selected friends from wider contexts, and selected friends with more diverse status characteristics if they were in high-participatory classrooms).

In general, participatory structures—whether in cooperative learning, open education, project-oriented, child-oriented, multi-ability, or other classrooms—enable students to work together without continuous, direct supervision from the teacher, ask each other questions, give assistance, and gain shared rewards. These conditions help students learn more about other students, increase the number of students who are accepted as friends, and reduce the number of students who are isolated or unselected. Studies are needed on how selection processes in contrasting environments affect outcomes such as tolerance, helpfulness, leadership, problem-solving, sportsmanship, and empathy—outcomes that, in turn, affect how students make friends.

Environments encourage wide or narrow contacts. Differently organized schools and classrooms reward, ignore, ridicule or punish cross-sex or cross-race choices; school and work environments can influence the number of friends, number of isolates, and the reciprocity and stability of friendships.

The patterns of environmental effects begin to explain why children of the same ages differ in their rates and directions of social development, and why children and adults differ in their friendship behaviors. The findings reported here support Blau's (1977) general theory that social structure influences interpersonal contact, associations, and friendships. Nevertheless, most of the research findings summarized in this paper are inconclusive or unconfirmed. Vast gaps in our knowledge about even the most popular, well-covered topics of friendship selection can be filled only with rigorous examinations of developmental and environmental effects on the selection and influence of friends. A life-course approach in research on the selection and influence of friends must attend to environmental factors that occur naturally in the course of development or that are imposed by design.

References

Alexander, C. N., & Campbell, E. Q. (1964). Peer influences on adolescent aspirations and attainments. *American Sociological Review, 29,* 568–575.

Allan, G. A. (1979). *A sociology of friendship and kinship.* Boston: Allen & Unwin.

Asher, S. R., Oden, S. L., & Gottman, J. M. (1977). Children's friendships in school settings. In L. G. Katz (Ed.), *Current topics in early childhood education.* Norwood, NJ: Ablex Co.

Asher, S. R., & Renshaw, P. D. (1981). Children without friends: Social knowledge and social skill training. In S. R. Asher & J. M. Gottman (Eds.), *The development of children's friendships.* New York: Cambridge University Press.

Asher, S. R., Singleton, L. C., & Taylor, A. R. (1982). Acceptance versus friendship: A longitudinal study of social integration. Paper presented at the annual meeting of the American Educational Research Association.

Austin, M. C., & Thompson, G. G. (1948). Children's friendships: A study of the basis on which children select and reject their best friends. *Journal of Educational Psychology, 39,* 101–116.

Bartel, H., Bartel, N. R., & Grill, J. (1973). A sociometric view of some integrated open classrooms. *Journal of Social Issues, 29,* 159–173.

Berndt, T. J. (1981). Relations between social cognition, nonsocial cognition, and social behavior: The case of friendship. In L. Ross & J. H. Flavell (Eds.), *Social cognitive development: Frontiers and possible futures.* New York: Cambridge University Press.

Bigelow, B. J., & La Gaipa, J. L. (1980). The development of friendship values and choice. In H. C. Foot, A. J. Chapman, & J. Smith (Eds.), *Friendship and social relations in children.* New York: Wiley.

Blanchard, F. A., Weigel, R. H., & Cook, S. W. (1975). The effect of relative competence of group members upon interpersonal attraction in cooperating interacial groups. *Journal of Personality and Social Psychology, 32,* 519–530.

Blau, P. M. (1977). *Inequality and heterogeneity: A primitive theory of social structure.* New York: The Free Press.

Blau, Z. S. (1961). Structural constraints on friendships in old age. *American Sociological Review, 26,* 429–439.

Booth, A. (1972). Sex and social participation. *American Sociological Review, 37,* 183–192.

Bossert, S. T. (1979). *Tasks and social relationships in classrooms.* New York: Cambridge University Press.

Busk, P. L., Ford, K. C., & Schulman, J. L. (1973). Stability of sociometric responses in classrooms. *Journal of Genetic Psychology, 123,* 69–84.

Caldwell, M. A., & Peplau, L. A. (1982). Sex differences in same-sex friendships. *Sex Roles, 8,* 721–732.

Campbell, J. D. (1964). Peer relations in childhood. In M. L. Hoffman & L. W. Hoffman (Eds.), *Review of child development research* (Vol. 1). New York: Russell Sage.

Carter, D. E., DeTine–Carter, S., & Benson, F. W. (1980). Interracial acceptance in the classroom. In H. C. Foot, A. J. Chapman, & J. R. Smith (Eds.), *Friendship and social relations in children.* New York: Wiley.

Carter, D. E., DeTine, S., Spero, J., & Benson, F. W. (1975). Peer acceptance and school-related variables in an integrated junior high. *Journal of Educational Psychology, 67,* 267–273.

Charlesworth, R., & Hartup, W. W. (1967). Positive social reinforcement in the nursery school peer group. *Child Development, 38,* 933–1003.

Chown, S. M. (1981). Friendship in old age. In S. Duck & R. Gilmour (Eds.), *Personal relationships 2: Developing personal relationships.* New York: Academic Press.

Clark, A. H., Wyon, S. M., & Richards, M. P. (1969). Free play in nursery school children. *Journal of Child Psychology and Psychiatry, 10,* 205–216.

Cohen, J. (1977). Sources of peer homogeneity. *Sociology of Education, 50,* 227–241.

Cooper, L., Johnson, D. W., Johnson, R., & Wilderson, F. (1980). Effects of cooperative, competitive, and individualistic experiences on interpersonal attraction among heterogeneous peers. *Journal of Social Psychology, 111,* 243–252.

Criswell, J. H. (1939). A sociometric study of race cleavage in the classroom. *Archives of Psychology,* No. 235a.

Damon, W. (1977). *The social world of the child.* San Francisco: Jossey–Bass.

DeVries, D. L., & Edwards, K. J. (1974). Student teams and learning games: Their effects on cross-race and cross-sex interaction. *Journal of Educational Psychology, 66,* 741–749.

DeVries, D. L., Edwards, K. J., & Slavin, R. E. (1978). Biracial learning teams and race relations in the classroom: Four field experiments on Teams-Games-Tournament. *Journal of Educational Psychology, 70,* 356–362.

Douvan, E., & Adelson, J. (1966). *The adolescent experience.* New York: Wiley.

Douvan, E., & Gold, M. (1966). Modal patterns in American adolescence. In L. Hoffman & M. Hoffman (Eds.), *Review of child development research* (Vol. 2). New York: Russell Sage Foundation.

Duck, S. (1973a). *Personal relationships and personal constructs: A study of friendship formation.* New York: Wiley.

Duck, S. (1973b). Personality, similarity, and friendship choices: Similarity of what, when? *Journal of Personality, 41,* 543–558.

Duck, S., Miell, D. K., & Gaebler, H. C. (1980). Attraction and communication in children's interactions. In H. C. Foot, A. J. Chapman, & J. R. Smith (Eds.), *Friendship and social relations in children.* New York: Wiley.

Dunphy, D. C. (1963). The social structure of urban adolescent peer groups. *Sociometry, 26,* 230–246.

Eder, D., & Hallinan, M. (1978). Sex differences in children's friendships. *American Sociological Review, 43,* 237–250.

Elder, G. H., Jr. (1969). Peer socialization in an educational context. *Educational Leadership, 26,* 465–473.

Epstein, J. L. (1983a). Examining theories of adolescent friendship (Chapter 3). In J. L. Epstein & N. Karweit (Eds.), *Friends in school.* New York: Academic Press.

Epstein, J. L. (1983b). Selection of friends in differently organized schools and classrooms

(Chapter 5). In J. L. Epstein & N. Karweit (Eds.), *Friends in school*. New York: Academic Press.

Epstein, J. L. (1983c). The influence of friends in achievement and affective outcomes (Chapter 11). In J. L. Epstein & N. Karweit (Eds.), *Friends in school*. New York: Academic Press.

Feld, S. L. (1982). Social structural determinants of similarity among adolescents. *American Sociological Review, 47,* 797–801.

Feshbach, N. D., & Sones, G. (1971). Sex differences in adolescent reactions to newcomers. *Developmental Psychology, 4,* 381–386.

Fine, G. A. (1981). Friends, impression management, and preadolescent behavior. In S. R. Asher & J. M. Gottman (Eds.), *The development of children's friendships*. New York: Cambridge University Press.

Fischer, C. S., & Phillips, S. L. (1981). Who is alone? Social characteristics of people with small networks. In L. A. Peplau & D. Perlman (Eds.), *Loneliness: A sourcebook of current theory, research and therapy*. New York: Wiley.

Gottman, J. M. (1977). Toward a definition of social isolation in children. *Child Development, 48,* 513–517.

Gottman, J. M., & Parkhurst, J. (1980). A developmental theory of friendship and acquaintanceship processes. In W. A. Collins (Ed.), *Minnesota symposia on child psychology* (Vol. 13). Hillsdale, NJ: Erlbaum.

Gronlund, N. (1959). *Sociometry in the classroom*. New York: Harper.

Hallinan, M. T. (1976). Friendship patterns in open and traditional classrooms. *Sociology of Education, 49,* 254–264.

Hallinan, M. T. (1978). The process of friendship formation. *Social Networks, 1,* 193–210.

Hallinan, M. T. (1979). Structural effects on children's friendships and cliques. *Social Psychology Quarterly, 42,* 43–54.

Hallinan, M. T. (1980). Patterns of cliquing among youth. In H. C. Foot, A. J. Chapman & J. R. Smith, (Eds.), *Friendship and social relations in children*. New York: Wiley.

Hallinan, M. T. (1982). Classroom racial composition and children's friendships. *Social Forces, 61,* 56–72.

Hansell, S. (1981). Ego development and peer friendship networks. *Sociology of Education, 54,* 51–63.

Hansell, S., & Karweit, N. (1983). Curricular placement, friendship networks and status attachment. In J. L. Epstein & N. Karweit (Eds.), *Friends in school*. New York: Academic Press.

Hansell, S., & Slavin, R. E. (1981). Cooperative learning and the structure of interracial friendships. *Sociology of Education, 54,* 98–106.

Hartrup, W. W. (1975). The origins of friendships. In M. Lewis & L. A. Rosenblum (Eds.), *Friendship and peer relations*. New York: Wiley.

Hartup, W. W. (1983). Peer relations. In P. Mussen (Ed.), *Handbook of child psychology*. New York: Wiley.

Hartup, W. W., Brady, J. E., & Newcomb, A. F. (1982). Social cognition and social interaction in childhood. In E. T. Higgens, D. N. Ruble, & W. W. Hartup (Eds.), *Social cognition and social behavior: Developmental issues*. New York: Cambridge University Press.

Hauser, R. M. (1982). The structure of social relationships, cross-classifications of mobility, kinship, and friendship. In R. M. Hauser, A. O. Haller, D. Mechanic, & T. S. Hauser (Eds.), *Social structure and behavior*. New York: Academic Press.

Hauserman, N., Walen, S. R., & Behling, M. (1973). Reinforced racial integration in the first grade: A study in generalization. *Journal of Applied Behavioral Analysis, 6,* 193–200.

Hertz-Lazarowitz, R., Sharan, S., & Steinberg, R. (1980). Classroom learning style and co-

operative behavior of elementary school children. *Journal of Educational Psychology,*
72, 99–106.

Horrocks, J. E., & Benimoff, M. (1966). Stability of adolescent's nominee status, over a one-
year period, as a friend by their peers. *Adolescents, 1,* 224–229.

Horrocks, J. E., & Buker, M. E. (1951). A study of friendship fluctuations of preadolescents.
Journal of Genetic Psychology, 78, 131–144.

Hrybyk, M., & Farnham-Diggory, S. (1981). Children's groups in school: A developmental
case study. Unpublished manuscript.

Kandel, D. (1978). Homophily, selection and socialization in adolescent friendships. *American*
Journal of Sociology, 84, 427–436.

Karweit, N. (1983). Extra-curricular activities and friendship selection. In J. Epstein & N.
Karweit (Eds.), *Friends in school.* New York: Academic Press.

Karweit, N., & Hansell, S. (1983). Sex differences in adolescent relationships: Friendship and
status. In J. L. Epstein & N. Karweit (Eds.), *Friends in School.* New York: Academic
Press.

Kerckhoff, A., & Davis, K. (1962). Value consensus and need complementarity in mate selection. *American Sociological Review, 20,* 317–325.

Kon, I. S. (1981). Adolescent friendship: Some unanswered questions for future research. In
S. Duck & R. Gilmore (Eds.), *Personal relations 2: Developing personal relations.* New
York: Academic Press.

Kon, I. S., & Losenkov, V. A. (1978). Friendship in adolescence: Values and behavior. *Journal*
of Marriage and the Family, 40, 143–155.

La Gaipa, J. L. (1979). A developmental study of the meaning of friendship in adolescence.
Journal of Adolescence, 2, 201–213.

La Gaipa, J. L. (1981). Children's friendship. In S. Duck & R. Gilmore (Eds.), *Personal*
relations 2: Developing personal relations. New York: Academic Press.

Laumann, E. O. (1973). *Bonds of pluralism: The form and structure of urban social networks.*
New York: Wiley.

Leinhardt, S. (1972). Developmental change in the sentiment structure of children's groups.
American Sociological Review, 37, 202–212.

Lerman, P. (1967). Groups, networks, and subcultural delinquency. *American Journal of So-*
ciology, 73, 631–672.

Lever, J. (1976). Sex differences in the games children play. *Social Problems, 23,* 478–487.

Lippitt, R., & Gold, M. (1959). Classroom social structure as a mental health problem. *Journal*
of Social Issues, 15, 40–49.

Maas, H. S. (1968). Preadolescent peer relations and adult intimacy. *Psychiatry, 3,* 161–172.

Maccoby, E., & Jacklin, C. (1974). *The psychology of sex differences.* Stanford, CA: Stanford
University Press.

Mayhew, L. (1970). Ascription in modern societies. In E. O. Laumann, P. M. Siegel, &
R. W. Hodge (Eds.), *The logic of social hierarchies.* Chicago: Markham.

McClelland, F. M. & Ratliff, J. A. (1947). The use of sociometry as an aid in promoting social
adjustment in ninth grade homeroom. *Sociometry, 19,* 147–153.

McPartland, J. M., & York, R. L. (1967). Further analysis of equality of educational opportunity survey. *Racial isolation in the public schools.* U.S. Commission on Civil Rights.

Miller, N. (1983). Peer relations in desegregated schools. In J. L. Epstein & N. Karweit (Eds.),
Friends in school. New York: Academic Press.

Montemayor, R., & Van Komen, R. (1982). The development of sex differences in friendships
and peer group structure during adolescence. Unpublished manuscript.

Moreno, J. L. (1953). *Who shall survive: Foundations of sociometry, group psychiatry and*
sociodrama (rev. ed.). Beacon, NY: Beacon House.

Muldoon, J. F. (1955). The concentration of liked and disliked members in groups and the relationship of the concentration to group cohesiveness. *Sociometry, 18,* 73–81.

Newcomb, T. (1961). *The acquaintance process.* New York: Holt, Rinehart & Winston.

Patchen, M. (1982). *Black-white contact in schools: Its social and academic effects.* West Lafayette, Indiana: Purdue University Press.

Patchen, M., Davidson, J. D., Hoffman, G., & Brown, W. R. (1977). Determinants of students' interracial behavior and opinion change. *Sociology of Education, 50,* 55–75.

Pfeiffer, E. (1977). Psychopathology and social pathology. In J. E. Birren & K. W. Schaie (Eds.), *Handbook of the Psychology of Aging.* New York: Van Nostrand.

Piaget, J. (1932). *The moral judgement of the child.* London: Routledge & Kegan Paul.

Pitts, J. (1968). The family and the peer group. In N. W. Bell & E. F. Vogel (Eds.), *A modern introduction to the family.* New York: Free Press.

Putallaz, M., & Gottman, J. M. (1981). Social skills and group acceptance. In S. R. Asher & J. M. Gottman (Eds.), *The development of children's friendships.* New York: Cambridge University Press.

Rardin, D. R., & Moan, C. E. (1971). Peer interaction and cognitive development. *Child Development, 42,* 1685–1699.

Reisman, J. (1981). Adult friendships. In S. Duck & R. Gilmour (Eds.), *Personal relationships 2: Developing personal relationships.* New York: Academic Press.

Reisman, J., & Shorr, H. (1978). Friendship claims and expectations among children and adults. *Child Development, 49,* 913–916.

Roff, M., Sells, S. B., & Golden, M. M. (1972). *Social adjustment and personality development in children.* Minneapolis: University of Minnesota Press.

Rosow, T. (1967). *Social integration of the aged.* New York: Free Press.

Rubin, Z. (1980). *Children's friendships.* Cambridge, MA: Harvard University Press.

St. John, N. H. (1975). *School desegregation: Outcomes for children.* New York: Wiley.

Savin-Williams, R. C. (1980). Social interaction of adolescent females in natural groups. In H. C. Foot, A. J. Chapman & J. R. Smith (Eds.), *Friendship and social relations in children.* New York : Wiley.

Schmuck, R. A. (1978). Application of social psychology to classroom life. In D. Bar-Tal & L. Saxe (Eds.), *Social psychology of education.* New York: Wiley.

Schofield, J. W. (1981). Complementary and conflicting identities: Images and interaction in an interracial school. In S. Asher & J. Gottman (Eds.), *The development of children's friendships.* New York: Cambridge University Press.

Schofield, J. W., & Sagar, H. A. (1977). Peer interaction patterns in an integrated middle school. *Sociometry, 40,* 130–138.

Seagoe, M. V. (1933). Factors influencing the selection of associates. *Journal of Educational Research, 27,* 32–40.

Selman, R. L. (1976). Toward a structural analysis of developing interpersonal relations concepts: Research with normal and disturbed adolescents. In A. D. Pick (Ed.), *Minnesota symposia on child psychology* (Vol. 10). Minneapolis: University of Minnesota Press.

Selman, R. L. (1981). The child as a friendship philosopher. In S. R. Asher & J. M. Gottman (Eds.), *The development of children's friendships.* New York: Cambridge University Press.

Selman, R. L., & Jacquette, D. (1978). Stability and oscillation in interpersonal awareness: A clinical developmental analysis. In C. B. Keasey (Ed.), *Nebraska symposium on motivation* (Vol. 25). Lincoln: University of Nebraska Press.

Serbin, L., Tonick, I., & Sternglanz, S. (1977). Shaping cooperative cross-sex play. *Child Development, 48,* 924–929.

Shaw, M. E. (1973). Changes in sociometric choices following forced integration of an elementary school. *Journal of Social Issues, 29,* (4), 143–157.

Singleton, L., & Asher, S. R. (1977). Peer preferences and social interaction among third grade children in an integrated school district. *Journal of Educational Psychology, 69,* 330–336.

Singleton, L., & Asher, S. R. (1979). Racial integration and children's peer preferences: An investigation of developmental and cohort differences. *Child Development, 50,* 936–941.

Slavin, R. E. (1979). Effects of biracial learning teams on cross-racial friendships. *Journal of Educational Psychology, 71,* 381–387.

Slavin, R. E., & Hansell, S. (1983). Cooperative learning and intergroup relations: Contact theory in the classroom. In J. L. Epstein & N. Karweit (Eds.), *Friends in school.* New York: Academic Press.

Smith, P. K., & Connolly, K. J. (1981). *The ecology of preschool behavior.* New York: Cambridge University Press.

Sorenson, A. B., & Hallinan, M. T. (1976). A stochastic model for change in group structure. *Social Science Research, 5,* 43–61.

Steuve, C. A., & Gerson, K. (1977). Personal relationships across the life cycle. In C. S. Fischer (Ed.), *Network and places: Social relations in the urban setting.* New York: Free Press.

Thompson, G. G., & Horrocks, J. E. (1943). A study of the friendship fluctuations of urban boys and girls. *Journal of Genetic Psychology, 70,* 53–63.

Tuma, N. B., & Hallinan, M. T. (1979). The effects of sex, race, and achievement in school children's friendships. *Social Forces, 57,* 1265–1285.

Verbrugge, L. M. (1977). The structure of adult friendship choices. *Social Forces, 56,* 576–597.

Verbrugge, L. M. (1979). Multiplexity in adult friendships. *Social Forces, 57,* 1286–1309.

Waldrop, M. F., & Halverson Jr., C. F. (1975). Intensive and extensive peer behavior: Longitudinal and cross-sectional analysis. *Child Development, 46,* 19–26.

Weigel, R., Wiser, P., & Cook, S. (1975). The impact of cooperative learning experiences on cross-ethnic relations and attitudes. *Journal of Social Issues, 31,* 219–243.

Weiss, L., & Lowenthal, M. F. (1975). Life course perspectives on friendship. In M. F. Lowenthal, M. Turner, & D. Chiriboga et al. (Eds.), *Four stages of life.* San Francisco: Jossey–Bass.

Wheeler, L. & Nezlek, J. (1977). Sex differences in social participation. *Journal of Personality and Social Psychology, 35,* 742–754.

Youniss, J. (1980). *Parents and peers in social development.* Chicago: University of Chicago Press.

Ziegler, S. (1981). The effectiveness of cooperative learning teams for increasing cross-ethnic friendship: Additional evidence. *Human Organization, 40,* 264–268.

CHAPTER 7

Peer Therapies and the Little Latency: A Clinical Perspective

Edward C. Mueller and Deborah Cohen

Introduction

In this chapter, we explore how clinical psychology perceives the development and role of peer relations in children's lives. Because this is a different view than is represented in the predominant cognitive-learning orientation of much academic psychology, it may help broaden the conception of peer relations presented in this volume. It also seems appropriate to include the views of child clinicians in a volume focused on the process and outcome features of peer relations. Surely the clinical hour is one of the fundamental methods in use today for observing the interpersonal functioning of the child. Clinicians are trained in the communication process: in accurately hearing the meaning of children's communications and in ensuring that children accurately understand adults. When practiced well, this process always involves a profound respect for the subtlty and complexity of children's communications at every age.

As therapists, we naturally are concerned with outcomes. Any child therapy is valuable only if it in some way assists in the child's mental and emotional growth—two features, incidentally, which clinicians tend to view as inextricably related. There is currently a small body of clinical literature which suggests that peer relations may be of therapeutic value for children. In the section called "Peer Therapies," we examine this suggestion by exploring some approaches to psychotherapy with children which entail the

PROCESS AND OUTCOME
IN PEER RELATIONSHIPS

use of peer relations. We limit this brief review to work pairing agemates with an adult therapist in attendance. This excludes related and important work, for example, on the role of younger children in the social rehabilitation of withdrawn children (Furman, Rahe, & Hartup, 1979) and in the sibling subsystem in family therapy (Bank & Kahn, 1975). Beyond describing these peer therapies, our goal in the first section is to spell out the theoretical basis of the existing techniques. This is a new area of clinical practice and the conceptual foundations have never been considered.

In the section, entitled "Theories of Emotional Development in Latency," we address the fact that the present peer therapies have focused on the latency-aged child, that is, 6 to 12 years old. We explore the reasons in theory why this is so and then offer a reformulation of the concept of latency. This view will lead us to suggest a second period, much earlier in development, with many latency-like features, a *little latency*.

If peer relations are important during the latency stage, then they may also be important during the little latency. In the last section, denoted "Theories of Emotional Development in Latency," we pursue this hypothesis with case material, showing how troubled emotional development translates itself into troubled peer relations in the second year of life. We conclude with some speculations about early interventions for troubled toddlers.

Peer Therapies

The technique of peer therapy involves treating two children together with one adult therapist. While there are variations in the theoretical basis and practical application of this technique, one commonality is that latency-aged children are often singled out as primary candidates for peer therapy. We will examine two examples of this technique referred to as duo therapy and pairs therapy.

Duo therapy was first instituted in 1972 by Jennie S. Fuller of the Framingham (Massachusetts) Youth Guidance Center. In duo therapy, two unrelated children are selected to participate in long-term treatment with one therapist, the main criterion being that each child has a viable personality to share with the other (i.e., not autistic). The child pairs are matched on both sex and age (or relative maturity), as well as on the basis of some shared problem or concern. For example, two 8-year-old boys who are both experiencing parental divorce might be selected as duo partners. In addition to these commonalities, the pairs are matched on perceived compatible differences in personality style or symptomatology, such that a child who acts out might be paired with a withdrawn one. This is apparently done in order to help the children see that there are numerous ways of responding to their pain and distress.

The technique of duo therapy is based in part on psychodynamic thought, and as such, one of its goals is to provide an environment in which the client can re-experience and resolve those conflicts which occurred in his or her early relationships with significant others (e.g., mother, father, siblings). This is achieved through the development of the transference relationship, where the client projects family-related feelings, memories, and wishes onto the therapist. The therapist's role in the establishment of the transference involves the maintenance of a sufficient neutrality so as to enable the client to perceive the therapist as one or another of these conflict figures. In this sense, the therapist is a source of frustration to the client in much the same way as the early significant others were: Wishes or needs that were not met by the parents are also not met by the therapist. However, through the transference of feelings onto the therapist, the client can re-experience past wishes and frustrations in the present and thus bring to them his or her current level of insight and understanding.

Fuller (1977) suggests that duo therapy establishes a more intensive transference situation than individual therapy, with the presence of an agemate contributing to the re-creation of a small family unit. We can see this at work through her description of one aspect of the process of duo therapy. In its initial stages, the duo partners are wary of each other and engage in competition for the therapist's attention in much the same way as siblings are presumed to vie for parental affection. By maintaining a certain amount of neutrality and refusing to "take sides," the therapist frustrates the children in their attempts to be in the number one position. In essence, the therapist removes one of the main reasons for competition between the duo partners, and they are joined together in their frustration over being unable to win the therapist's affections. An alliance between the duo partners is thus formed, and the therapist fosters this alliance so that the two children can come to make use of and help one another. One question to be raised here, which will be explored further in this chapter, is why this approach to the development and treatment of the transference relationship is seen as particularly viable with latency-aged children.

In addition to its psychodynamic orientation, duo therapy has also been influenced by group theory. Fuller (1977) discussed the manner in which the process of duo therapy reflects the five stages of group treatment outlined by Garland, Jones, and Kolodny (1973). In the first stage of *preaffiliation,* the duo partners engage in mutual approach–avoidance maneuvers and attempt to interact with the therapist alone. As the therapist encourages interaction between the children and frustrates their attempts to form a strictly child–adult alliance, the therapy moves into the second stage of *power and control.* This is the period when transference issues are at the forefront.

The third stage of duo therapy, *intimacy*, is characterized by a growing alliance between the duo partners and a gradual decrease in their dependence on the therapist. Fuller (1977) notes that this period involves a focusing on the commonalities between the two children, through which a sense of closeness and sharing develops. In the fourth or *differentiation* stage, the duo partners come to accept their own uniqueness even as it highlights their differences. *Separation,* the final stage of duo therapy, concerns the process of termination.

Mitchell (1976) points out that the opportunities for interpersonal growth in duo therapy are similar to those in group therapy. She contends that the duo situation offers its participants the chance to improve both peer relations and social skills, to share common problems and their solutions, and to experience the benefits of modeling and of vicarious reinforcement. Fuller (1977) suggests that at least some of these group-like benefits are made available to the duo client because the presence of a peer enhances both the quantity and quality of play in the therapeutic situation. She argues that since latency-aged children are "characteristically involved in play with other children," play in duo therapy may be more reflective of problems in peer relations than play in individual therapy. Such problems in peer interactions as arise within the duo treatment hour can presumably be recognized and addressed as they occur.

Much of the work in duo therapy appears to be aimed at this facilitation of appropriate peer interaction. The therapeutic situation is viewed as providing an environment in which involvement with a peer can develop, and in which problems in interaction can be addressed and resolved. Just as the psychodynamic basis of duo therapy is expressed through the establishment and treatment of the transference, its basis in group theory is expressed through the fostering of healthy peer interactions. A question we will ask ourselves in regard to this group orientation is why latency-aged children are seen as primary candidates for the facilitation of peer relations.

A second form of peer therapy is being conducted by Robert Selman and his associates at Judge Baker Guidance Center, Boston. His *pairs therapy* is part of a clinic school program for emotionally troubled and learning disabled children. To date, the program is limited to the younger children in the school, all of whom fall into the period of latency. Each child is assigned a pairs partner with whom he or she meets one hour per week with a specially assigned adult pairs therapist. The therapist seeks to help the children learn how to negotiate their own needs more effectively with their agemates. For example, one child may want to go have a snack at a local store while the agemate wants to play kickball. The therapist would try to get each child to understand that the other child's need is different from their own and then say something like "How could we work it out so you could both get to do what you want?'' The therapist tries to get the children to negotiate directly with each other rather than appealing to the adult to solve the dilemma. Emotionally troubled children are seen as being immature in their understanding of how to negotiate their own wishes with each other. Rather than being seen only in psychoanalytic terms as defensively restricted from thinking about other people, they are seen as lacking the social developmental progress that affords the skills of negotiating their wishes with each other. Therapy teaches higher level ways of reaching their own ends.

Selman's pairs therapy has theoretical links to the cognitive-developmental theory based on the work of George Herbert Mead and of Jean Piaget. Social-cognitive views of social development presently dominate the thinking of many American developmental psychologists (e.g., Damon, 1977; Kohlberg, 1969). Selman starts with Mead's (1934) postulate that social intelligence emerges through a human's capacity to coordinate roles. It is the child's growing ability to take the role of the other that permits interpersonal understanding of self, friendship, peer group, and parent–child relations. For each of these domains, understanding moves through a series of levels based on the child's basic perspective-taking ability. For example, at Level 1 (ages 5–9 years), the child recognizes that each person has a unique and covert psychological life. The child can appreciate that the subjective perspectives of self and other are different. The understanding of another's perspective, however, is still seen in rather ''one-way'' terms. Thus, a child of this age expects that a gift will automatically make someone else happy. At Level 2 (ages 7–12 years) children can step mentally outside themselves and take a somewhat reflective perspective on their own thoughts; they realize that others can do so as well. They see that others will try to analyze what they are thinking and not merely what they are doing. By the same token, however, they can practice their first deceits on others by utilizing a new understanding about their own inner realities.

Selman (1981) has extended the stage theory of social understanding to a more direct analysis of actual interchange among children. For each of his levels, he finds that children employ more than one actual negotiaton strategy. Thus, at Level 1 the recognition of each individual's separate ''will'' leads to feeling either more powerful and stronger or more helpless and threatened by the mental control of others. In negotiation, the only choices for achieving consensus are to bully or submit. At Level 2, consideration of others' thoughts leads to influence and manipulation or to compliance, ''shying away from'' and ''presenting a false front.''

Pairs therapy is centrally concerned with the negotiation strategies employed by troubled children. The goal is not only to help them advance to higher levels of social understanding but also to enable children to be more flexible in their negotiation style at a given level. The children are encouraged to drop rigid adherence to either dominating-controlling or submissive-withdrawn styles. In this sense, pairs therapy is not so much concerned with peer friendship formation as with developing the ability to meet one's own needs through the instrumentality of agemates.

One of the authors, Edward Mueller, is also at the Judge Baker Clinic school and is an individual therapist for several of the latency-aged boys participating in pairs therapy. From the observations of these children in the individual setting, it appears that pairs therapy affects not only the growth of communication skills but results in actual friendship formation as well. At present, it is not possible to distinguish the processes of the development of negotiation skills from the formation of friendship. Clearly they are interrelated; yet the emphasis in negotiation is on assisting in developing individual skill or competence while friendship is a social relationship, a form of peer relationship. Negotiation enables each child to do what he or she wants some of the time in peer relations. Friendship is an emotional attachment dependent on a history of shared activities and feelings (Howes & Mueller, 1979).

The sharing of intense emotional expression may play a special role in the creation of these feelings of mutual liking among very troubled children. For example, one case involved the pairing of a submissive child who had retreated into a private fantasy world with a dominating, aggressive child given to frequent temper tantrums. One day this pair of 10-year-old boys was given musical instruments and asked to prepare a musical performance for the other children to hear. During their practice session, the assertive child beat violently on an inverted trash can drum and his partner attached bells to his ankles, jumped around, and occasionally let out deep, gutteral screams. This session was tape-recorded and, subsequently, the assertive boy brought the tape to his individual therapy sessions. During his therapy, after discussing his emotional issues, he used the tape to calm himself down. He especially liked the part when his partner screamed; when he heard this he often smiled and closed his eyes. Although he could not articulate the reasons for this pleasure, his therapist interpreted it as the reliving of a shared emotional release with an agemate. In his partner's scream, he recognized a feeling of both the intensity and tone of what he himself felt. He discovered that someone who seemed on the outside so different was fundamentally like him. Based on such sharing, it was not surprising that each of these children began to express liking for the other and each requested to be paired with the same partner again the next year.

In the other case with which we had first hand experience, there was less progress toward friendship formation. Given the differences in the two cases, it could be argued that progress in pairs therapy is related to the developmental sources of the emotional difficulties. The assertive child just discussed underwent traumatic family experiences chiefly between the ages of 4 and 6. For him, in psychodynamic terms, entry into latency was but a step away. In contrast, the child to be considered next was neglected and abused by his mother from birth to age two. His level of interpersonal trust began at a very low level in individual therapy; psychodynamically, he was not at all near to being a latency child. Although he made progress in negotiating with his pairs partner during the year, there was no emergent friendship and the pair did not continue the next year. The individual work with this 11-year-old involved considerable accommodation by the therapist to comprehend and accept the private, pseudo-social world of this boy's creation. As the first trust in the therapist emerged, it was expressed physically by holding onto the therapist's leg or gently mouthing the therapist's arm. Emotionally, this boy remained an infant and the therapeutic accommodations were perhaps as great as to an actual infant.

In addition, we should note that this child had a very difficult peer partner to adjust to; thus, we do not mean to attribute the problems with this pairs group only to his central emotional problems. At the same time, we are trying to make clear that a peer cannot always be expected to accommodate to the emotional disabilities present in some forms of disturbance in another child. Although the pairs experience seemed to help this boy learn some adaptive peer behaviors, the building of basic trust in such a child requires caring and understanding difficult even for adults.

Theories of Emotional Development in Latency

The peer therapy work just reviewed focuses on latency-aged children, conventionally of the ages 6 to 12 years. What are the features of latency within psychodynamic thought that make the latency-aged child a primary candidate for peer therapy? In reviewing the ideas of Sigmund Freud, Anna Freud, Erik Erikson, Paul Kay, and others, we will pave the way for an extension of the latency idea to an earlier age.

Sigmund Freud was always ambivalent, if not unclear and ambiguous (Kay, 1972, p. 62), about the source of the latency phase of growth. Freud proposed both biological and psychological hypotheses about the origins of latency. The biological hypothesis was that sexual physiology waxed and waned across development. In 1935, he stated that "the period of latency is a physiological phenomenon" (1935, p. 37). The psychological hypothesis was that latency was characterized by a set of defenses, specifically sublimations and reaction formations, by which children came to suppress sexual impulses which continued unabated throughout *all* of childhood.

Modern physiological evidence does not support Freud; there is no evidence for a reduction in estrogen or androgen secretion across these years (Shapiro & Perry, 1976). In addition, there is no evidence that latency is a purely defensive strategy against sexual impulses. Kay (1972) summarizes the current situation in theory this way: "The available data [do] not decisively support latency as defenses or latency as a biologically-determined drive inhibition. [They do] clearly support latency as a period in which there is drive modification by the ego" (p. 63). In other words, while continuing to stress the role of sexual and aggressive impulses throughout childhood, modern psychodynamic theory has broadened its view of latency to include ego maturation, self-theory, and object relations. Shapiro and Perry (1976) argue that Freud was correct in stressing a biological time clock but incorrect in placing it in the drive area. What is maturing at about age seven, they assert, are aspects of brain function, including perceptual, spatiotemporal and cognitive changes. These, they submit, permit the major advances in adaptive functioning seen during latency:

> The normal child of 7 + 1 has reached a level of maturation and development that permits autonomy. He is emotionally less dependent on his family, has at his disposal a neuromuscular apparatus that is ready for the challenge of environmental mastery; and he has a new set of cognitive strategies to outwit and control his environment. (p. 97)

Surely Erikson's (1950/1963) conception of the latency-aged child was among the central pillars in this reconstructed view of strengthened ego processes at this time. The psychosocial stage of Industry versus Inferiority, which corresponds to latency, is described by Erikson as the time of a child's entrance into life. This stage is characterized by the development of a sense of mastery and inclination toward industry, but Erikson is quick to note that this must involve a new awareness of others "since industry involves doing things beside and with others" (p. 260).

The beginning of the stage of Industry versus Inferiority corresponds to entrance into school; at this time the child becomes an active member of a nonfamilial group, a group in which "he now learns to win recognition by producing things" (p. 259). Erickson's focus here is on the child's emerging industrial association, which he views as the first real social connection the child experiences outside the family. What we see in the psychosocial conception of the latency-aged child is the development of both a social awareness and an awareness of one's own capabilities. For Erikson, these two aspects of the personality in latency are inseparable: an awareness of one's role in relation to others must involve a sense of what one can and cannot do.

Traditional psychodynamic theory has held that during latency, energy which is no longer directed toward infantile impulses and defending them from the outside world can be directed *to* the outside world, to the acquisition of knowledge and to new social experiences. Anna Freud (1968) discusses this outer/other orientation which begins during latency. She writes that group life for *prelatency* children has no therapeutic value per se (except for children who have experienced a complete deprivation of family life); rather it is the relationship with the primary caretaker of the group which proves therapeutic. For *latency-aged* children, however, she notes that group life itself can be a therapeutic factor.

In a discussion of the challenges presented by child analysis, Anna Freud (1936/1966) raises a number of issues which we might consider in relation to peer therapy with latency-aged children. She notes that while analysis with adults is centered around the flows and interruptions of free association, this is not the case in the analysis of children, since the child analysand is unable to engage in and make use of free association in the same manner as the adult patient. Although this does not present a problem for the analysis of unconscious or id material, which is accessible through dreams, drawings, and fantasy play, it does present a problem for the analysis of ego functioning.

In adult analysis, interruptions in the flow of free associations are understood to be the result of defensive resistance, and as such they provide the opportunity for both analyst and patient to observe the ego at work. Due to the absence of free association in the analysis of the child—and therefore the absence of such interruptions—alternate means of assessing ego functioning must be made available. Without such alternate means, child analysis is limited to an analysis of id material alone.

Anna Freud (1966) offers what she calls the analysis of "transformations of affect" as one means of making accessible the ego functioning of the child patient:

> A child sees more attention paid to another than to himself; now, we say, he will inevitably feel jealousy and mortification. . . . But, contrary to expectation, observation may show us a very different picture. For instance, a child may exhibit indifference when we should have looked for disappointment . . . excessive tenderness instead of jealousy. In these cases something has happened to disturb the normal process; the ego has intervened and has caused the affect to be transformed. (pp. 38–39)

The presence of a peer in the therapeutic situation enhances the opportunity for such transformations of affect to occur and be observed, since the type of interaction is more varied in the conjoint experience. At the most simplistic level, we can see that the child patient in peer therapy experiences the following: (1) interactions between him or herself and the therapist; (2) interactions between the other child patient and the therapist; and (3) interactions between him or herself and the other child patient. Each

situation may give rise to a different set of emotional responses and subsequent transformations.

One can argue that the peer experience provides for greater clarity with
respect to the analysis of these transformations of affect, since the various
dyadic interactions described above represent different relationships in the
child's life. For example, when two children are engaged in interaction and
an unexpected response is observed in one of the children, it is most likely
reflective of the child's conflicts around sibling or peer relations. Addi-
tionally, when interaction between the therapist and one of the children
gives rise to an unexpected response in the other child, we can understand
the response to be reflective of issues around jealousy or sibling rivalry.

It is not immediately clear whether this facet of peer therapy contributes
to its usefulness with latency-aged children per se, or children in general.
However, given our understanding of the latency-aged child as particularly
outer- and other-oriented, we might expect him or her to be highly attuned
and responsive to the variety of interactions available through the conjoint
experience.

Alongside the increases in ego adaptibility, changes in object relations
constitute the second main feature of the modern psychoanalytic view of
latency. Latency, in this view, is an emotional peace treaty in the family, a
product of the child's resolving his or her oedipal jealousy toward the same-
sexed parent and giving up the incestuous attraction to the opposite-sexed
parent.

It is with this continuing effort to diffuse these intense family ties that
we come at last to the role of the latency peer group: it is the peer group
that acts as a transitional experience for the child between the family and
the outside world (Kay, 1972, p. 77). This is a double transition, from a
protected and fantasized position within the family to adapted thought necessary in the broader world of school, and a change in object ties from
parents to peers. Kay (1972) emphasizes the role of the peer group in this
transition of the latency period. First, it supports the child's strivings for
independence from the family. In other words, it provides a "welcome shel-
ter" (p. 77) at the point where the child is first breaking away from home
physically and emotionally. Second, the new identifications provided by the
peer group allow the child to deal with separation anxieties and with resid-
ual guilt over oedipal wishes. The peer group provides physical independence from the family. Third, participation with the peer group furthers
the growth of "social consciousness" in the child with manifestations in
empathy, compassion, and altruism. The group offers some moral independence from the family as well.

Given these conceptualizations of latency, it is understandable that peer
therapies have focused on the latency-aged child. However, to more fully

understand the role of peers during latency, it must be noted that modern theorists have broken the latency period into two phases. The first lasts from 6 to 10 years (the juvenile period) and the second from 10 to 12 years (preadolescence.). In this scheme, deriving from Sullivan (1953), the juvenile cooperates merely to preserve his or her own prestige or feeling of superiority and merit. The juvenile is thought to prefer the group with strong parental-like leaders as providing a smaller shift in identification objects from those represented by the parents (Redl, 1942). In preadolescence, the child collaborates rather than merely cooperates with peers. In collaboration, children adjust their actions "to the expressed needs of the other person in the pursuit of increasingly identical—that is, more and more nearly mutual—satisfaction . . . " (Sullivan, 1953, p. 245). For Sullivan, collaboration is the process involved in the formation of the first truly emotionally *close* peer relationship. At these ages, and not earlier, the child tries to contribute to the happiness of the friend, "to support the prestige and feeling of worthwhileness of my chum" (p. 245).

To summarize, we have shown why the peer therapies have focused on the latency period. It is the earliest age at which children need to form emotional ties outside the family. Only at these ages do ego processes become sufficiently well-developed to keep aggressive impulses in check. In addition, the latency period itself is no longer seen as uniform. Early in the period the therapist should provide a strong leadership model for the child's initial extra-familial identifications. Later on, the therapist should stand back to allow true peer friendships to emerge.

A PARTIAL REFORMULATION OF LATENCY WITH AN EYE TOWARD ITS EXTENSION TO TODDLERS

Theory both guides and blinds. Our views of early childhood have been so much under the sway of constructs like "impulse-ridden" (from Freud) and "egocentric" (from Piaget) that a latency period hidden within the early years of development would seem impossible. Yet we shall develop precisely this thesis, showing that it is not as incompatible with theorists like Freud or Piaget as it might first appear.

Freud's theory, like Piaget's, evolved and changed a great deal over the years. It was his first description of latency, circa 1905, that is compatible with the expanded view of the concept to be proposed. In the first edition of *Three Essays on the Theory of Sexuality* (1905), he equated latency with *all* of childhood prior to puberty, a fact which is overlooked today. Latency was the long period after early infancy when the child built up the mental forces which could restrict the flow of the sexual instinct (p. 177). Besides the sexual instinct, Freud proposed an instinct for mastery which he later expanded into the self-preservative instincts, including aggression. Yet the instinct for mastery was never seen as autonomous; instead it depended for its expression on the sexual instinct. Mastery efforts for Freud, in other words, always took on a defensive character. They were ego-based ways of coping with sexual impulses. In *Three Essays,* Freud stressed the child's efforts to sublimate sexual impulses that could not reach his or her sexual aim given maturational immaturity. He also stressed reaction formation— in the forms of disgust, shame and morality—as a defensive means by which the child tries to cope with sexual impulses.

While proposing the latency concept in *Three Essays,* Freud's emphasis was not on latency so much as it was on the childhood expression of sexual impulse itself. He particularly stressed infantile orality and the pre-schooler's genitality. Thus in 1905, Freud saw the oral and oedipal phases as times of merely "partial latency" (p. 177), in other words, as "inter-ruptions" (p. 176) of the long latency period. In the first edition of *Three Essays* (1905), there were but two interruptions of latency prior to puberty. The first occurred in early infancy and was gratified largely through non-nutritive sucking. The second occurred between ages three and five when "the sexual excitation of early infancy returns" (p. 190). At this age, how-ever, its expression was primarily genital rather than oral.

From the theory of 1905, it follows that if the sexual excitation of infancy returns at around age 4, it must have been absent or successfully defended against in the period after infancy. Thus, it does not exaggerate our case to say that an early latency period was proposed by Freud himself. Also, in the 1915 edition of *Three Essays,* Freud's stress on the "instinct for mas-tery" (p. 198) at the same age period also meshes well with the present view.

After 1905, however, as Freud's thought continued to develop, he in-serted another impulse-ridden psycho-sexual stage between orality and gen-itality; he called this stage "sadistic-anal" (p. 198). It was seen as a period of intense ambivalence between the active and passive aspects of sexuality. The active side of sexual instinct was put into operation by the "instinct for mastery through the agency of the somatic musculature" (p. 198). At the same time, the passive side of sexuality was experienced erotogenically through the agency of the anus. In this direct experience of erotogenic plea-sure, Freud was directly contradicting his earlier idea of a lull in impulse experience between the oral and phallic-genital stages.

Freud's notion of anality, and not his earlier view of an early latency, has been carried forward in the growth of ego psychology. For example, Erikson describes the toddler's "sudden violent wish to have a choice, to appropriate demandingly, to eliminate stubbornly" (1950/1962, p. 252).

Notice that the anal period differs from the oral and phallic-genital pe-riods with respect to the role of object relations. In the oral stage, gratification of oral impulses is impossible outside of a satisfactory attachment to a caregiver. Similarly, in the phallic-genital stage, the oedipal situation, with its new identifications with the same-sexed parent, insures a central role for object relations. By contrast, the focus on activity and passivity of the anal stage is purely autoerotic; there is no major reformulation of object relations during the sadistic-anal period.

Instead, anal period children resist bringing their bodily functions under control (Erikson, 1950/1963) and we can understand this as an attempt to prolong a pleasurable impulse expression from infancy. The parent–child conflict which arises around this wish is experienced within the attachment bond that has already been formed during infancy. It is not a conflict about the bond itself but instead concerns children's reluctance to harness their impulses.

For those of us who stress object relations as being at the heart of successful emotional development, the presence of relative interpersonal safety, love, peace, and stability becomes a central feature defining any period of latency. In the anal stage, anxiety is lower because there is greater security than during either the attachment (oral) or reattachment (oedipal) stages. This is because the oral and oedipal periods involve attachment in *process* which can never feel as safe as attachment *established*. It is not that anxiety is absent in the toddler but rather that the fears generated around "body control and body integrity" (Mehlman, 1980, p. 409) can be dealt with in the context of "felt security," (Sroufe & Waters, 1977) which itself is the all-important product of successful bonding with caregivers.

In other words, in this view, latency periods are neither solely the result of defenses nor of diminutions in biological drive pressures. Instead, latencies occur because of sustained drive gratification in successfully developed attachment relations. Good object relations are not easily achieved and some of the complexity of the process is well-described by Mehlman (1980). It involves the interaction between drive pressures, cognitive abilities, narcissism, ego defenses, and the achieved state of personal identity. Yet in all this complexity, the core relation is between gratification in a secure relationship and the attendant reduction in anxiety, with its accompanying reduction in defensive processes. Freed from distracting anxiety around bonding, the latency child's adaptive goals come to dominate everyday functioning, and the product is major bursts in cognitive communication skills (i.e., representation and language, reading and writing), in broadening emotional bonds outside the family (peer relations, peer friendships), and in motor competencies (walking, participation in sports).

Each of these achievements in the two latency periods is in agreement with Freud's emphasis on the building up of "mental forces" (1905, p. 71) during these times. Yet such early Freudian insights were forgotten both in the later positions taken by Sigmund Freud himself and also in the writing of Anna Freud: "In periods of calm in the instinctual life, when there is no danger, the individual can permit himself a certain degree of stupidity . . . objective security and superfluity tend to make [men] comfortably stupid" (1936/1966, pp. 163–164). Anna Freud, to attempt a more balanced overview, seemed ambivalent about this proposition herself, noting a few pages later that the intellectual work performed during latency is more reliable and solid than that performed during periods of high drive intensity. The present view of latency is in agreement with this latter remark but in total disagreement with the idea that the emotional turmoils of infancy and the oedipal stages are spurs to intellectual gain, while latencies are times of laziness.

In the interest of clarity, given this discussion, we must reiterate one point. We do not see latency as a time of low-drive intensity, but rather of high-drive gratification. In the 6- to 10-year-old period, the oedipal resolution has not resulted in the loss of the opposite-sexed parent. Instead the oedipal adjustment has broadened object cathexes to include the same-sexed parent. Drive gratification with the opposite-sexed parent resumes and felt security increases when the child sees that continuing oedipal ties do not preclude same-sex identifications. The double sense of felt security from this new arrangement is one central basis for the second latency period of the school years.

PROPOSAL FOR A "LITTLE LATENCY"

In summary, clinical work with children supports the belief that bonding or object ties is the central achievement in successful emotional development. Yet as early as 1905, Freud proposed that bonding occurs in spite of intense upheaval—the first in infancy, the second around age 4, and the third in adolescence. Between these upheavals were periods of relative calm that Freud called latency. The long latency beginning around age 6 is remembered, but the short one just after infancy has been forgotten.

We propose to consider these toddler years, ages 1 to 3, as a *little latency*. The term "little" is intended as a play on the fact that the period involves little children and is of short duration in comparison to the latency of school age.

Table 7.1 summarizes both similarities and differences between these two periods in development. The basic similarity, of course, is the relative emotional stability of the parent–child bond established prior to little latency and re-established prior to latency. The stability of this bonding or rebonding is necessary for entrance into either period of latency; as the resolution of the oral stage (i.e., attachment) is a prerequisite for entrance into

Table 7.1
Comparison of the Toddler and Latency Periods in Normal Development

Characteristics of the period	Little latency 1–2 years	Latency 6–11 years
Bonding issues surrounding and limiting this period		
1. resolved for onset	initial attachment	oedipal redefinition
2. signaling end of period	oedipal onset	puberty redefinition
Characterized by autonomy striving	yes (Erikson)	yes (Kay)
Mastery achievements in communication	language	literacy
Primary peer attachment possible	no	yes
Superego functions (e.g., controls on aggression, morality)	absent	present
Identification with groups	absent	present

little latency, so the resolution of the oedipal situation (i.e., reattachment) is a prerequisite for entrance into latency. Children who have not achieved secure attachments with adult caregivers are not free emotionally to concentrate on the formation of peer relations that normally occurs in both latency periods.

The importance of this bond stability to adults can be understood in light of a second similarity between these two developmental periods. Both toddlerhood and latency involve active strivings for autonomy. The toddler is often characterized as a challenger of authority, and indeed Erikson (1950/1963) described this stage in terms of "Autonomy versus Shame." As we have seen, the latency-aged child also engages in autonomy struggles as he or she begins to relate and identify with people outside the family. Such strivings for independence as occur during toddlerhood and latency could not be tolerated by the child in the absence of a secure bond to the parents. Without this security, the child would be overwhelmed by the fear that his or her willful independence might result in loss of the parents' love.[1] Jacobson, Tianen, Wille, and Aytch (Chapter 3, this volume) summarize the growing evidence that only those children who are securely attached to their parents are capable of early autonomous peer relations during the little latency.

Besides departing from Freud's later views, we recognize that viewing toddlerhood as a period of emotional calm is not compatible with some current psychoanalytic theory; for example, it is incompatible with the prominant work of Mahler, Pine, & Bergman (1975). Mahler views the first

---

[1]In extreme cases of parental rejection, children may also go to the opposite extreme, pretending they are the strong rejecting adult-figure. It can take months or even years for the therapist to dissolve this defense.

8 months after birth as a period of fusion and lack of differentiation between the infant and its mother. Given this slow start, the basic problems
of infant individuation and reapproachment (i.e., attachment) are not encountered and resolved until the toddler period itself. However, the research
literature, both on the competencies of the early infant and on the timing
of the attachment process has led Stern (in press) to challenge Mahler's
view. Stern, Brazelton, and others have shown that the infant is highly in-
dividuated at birth and begins forming attachment relationships virtually
from birth. Summaries of the attachment literature (e.g., Bee, 1981) indicate that the most intense *single* attachments are fully in place by the 6–
12 month period. The toddler period consists of considerable expansion of
meaningful bonds to other people.

Under what conditions these extensions include peer attachments at this
early age is still a subject of contention. Some studies exist which are compatible with this view that early peer attachments are possible. For example,
Rubenstein and Howes (cited in Howes & Mueller, 1979) interviewed mothers about the emotional functioning of children who had begun daycare as
infants. Mothers sometimes responded in this fashion:

> If I have enough time to wait for Jerry to settle into a game with Kathy, then there
> is no trouble leaving. They have been together since he started and are really friends.
> I just put him down beside her and then I can easily leave. (1979, p. 11)

Small (1977) observed two groups of children, one 15- to 24-months-old
and one 33- to 42-months-old, in an unfamiliar playroom. Each child went
through two counterbalanced sessions in which the mother played in the
room, left the room, and returned. In one condition, the friend was present;
in the other, the child was alone. In both groups, the presence of peer friends
served to reduce distress in the mothers' absence. Mueller and Lucas (1975)
observed a durable friendship between boys aged 13 and 15 months, respectively. In true attachments, there should be an enduring sense of loss
when the relationship ends. And indeed, when one family moved away, one
of the children (now almost 3 years of age) continued to ask about his partner for nearly a year. These studies further support the analogy that toddlerhood is a little latency, since we understand latency to be a time of true
friendships.

In the earliest psychoanalytic thought, latency periods were viewed as
fostering growing mastery. If toddlerhood and latency in fact are two periods when mastery is at the forefront, then we would expect that the child
in conjunction with the culture insure major advances in competencies at
these times. At least in the important area of communication skills, this is
precisely what happens (see Table 7.1). During the toddler period the child
acquires the whole system of representational communication both with

gestures and words. In the latency period, many cultures expect the child to acquire reading and writing skills, the second basic system of communication. The role of peer relations in fostering these basic areas of mastery is a topic treated in detail elsewhere in this volume (Cooper, Marquis, & Edward [Chapter 11]; Epstein [Chapter 6]; and Ellis & Rogoff [Chapter 12]).

It has been argued elsewhere (Howes & Mueller, 1979) that an adequate understanding of the mastery functions of peer relations must await a fuller understanding of the role of play in development. The child works in school but plays with peers. In the United States, latency-aged children spend more time playing with peers than watching television (Roberts & Baird, 1971). Thus, in coming to an understanding of the importance of peer relations, one is confronted with understanding the importance of play. As Baldwin (1911) proposed, the "as if" quality of play allows the freedom to consider new combinations; it may allow the development of new ways of understanding things. If Baldwin is correct we will ultimately attribute the mastery potential of peer relations to its play potential. For now, we can only cite the supportive work of Sylva (1976) and Rubenstein and Howes (1976), and hope that many studies in the same vein will be forthcoming.

We have looked at the similarities between the two proposed periods of latency in terms of the secure attachment necessary for entrance into both, as well as the resulting emotional calm that frees the child in several respects. In both periods, the child uses his or her freedom to establish some autonomy and work toward mastery. But there are also differences between toddlerhood and latency.

The most striking difference, in a psychodynamic sense, is the presence of the superego at latency and its absence in toddlerhood. In the resolution of the previous oedipal stage, the child identifies with the same-sexed parent and internalizes his or her values and morals. During latency the child does not only have a sense of right and wrong; the superego also acts as an overseer, checking ego activity for adherence to these internalized standards. Latency children share cookies with their agemates, inhibit aggressive impulses, and avoid arguments. It is not that they lack selfish and aggressive feelings, but rather that they suppress them in adherence to their new standards. In contrast, the lack of a superego in toddlerhood results in the unfettered expression of these same impulses. When toddlers are frustrated, they yell and hit. When they want an object, they take it. This difference does not preclude toddler peer relations (e.g., Brenner & Mueller, 1982), but it surely determines their character.

A second difference between the periods concerns the latency-aged child's cognitive ability to identify with groups and the toddler's inability to do so. Latency-aged children see themselves as members of the third-grade class, the Y camp, and the gymnastics class at the community center. In contrast, toddlers do not understand group membership and cannot even direct behavior to several other children at once (Mueller & Vandell, 1979).

Despite these differences, in our judgment, the similarities discussed still warrant the proposed analogy between toddlerhood and latency. It alters the impulse-dominated view of toddlerhood, seeing toddlers instead as more effective in their world. They are emotionally ready for expanded social relationships and are experimenting with autonomy. Peer friendships are possible but must assume a somewhat different character than those of the older latency period.

Peer Relations in Toddlers Who Have Not Yet Achieved the Little Latency

For 12 years, we have conducted a series of observational, videotape studies on social communication and peer relations among normal children of little latency age. The screening criteria were designed to locate normal children from intact families. However, reviews of the videotapes subsequent to the completion of the studies revealed that some of the children had clear emotional difficulties. Of the 24–30 children participating in four to five different playgroups, three showed psychiatrically significant signs (such as head banging, social withdrawal, and failure to attach to substitute adult figures). Of these three, we were sufficiently concerned about one to make a referral at the time to a clinical child psychologist. In all three instances, we provided practical advice to the parents about the day-to-day aspects of relating to their children and to their children's behavioral problems.

Looking back now, however, we tended to discount the negative emotional expressions from these few children, trusting that they were merely "surface" expressions of problems that would soon correct themselves. For example, an extremely aggressive boy in one group, we hypothesized, pulled other children's hair because he had siblings who perhaps pulled his hair. We tended to stay away from clinical inferences such as "this is an angry child" or "this is an emotionally isolated child in need of firm, secure attachments." In retrospect, and with the intervening benefit of considerable clinical training, such majors inferences, with all they imply, seem fully warranted by our videotape analyses of these children's behavior and by the quality of their peer relations.

It so happened that two of these three children were in a single playgroup. We cannot describe their problems in much detail here because we must protect the confidentiality of the families involved. Suffice it to say that both were boys: one was insecure socially and the other produced more than twice as many aggressive actions as any other child in his playgroup. On the basis of these emotional difficulties, we now view both children as not having achieved the emotional peace necessary to enter the little latency.

It was our procedure to pair all six boys in a playgroup with each other child for dyadic free play sessions each day. Each pair met several times across the playgroups' 7–8 month duration. In the course of this procedure, the withdrawn child, of course, was paired with the aggressive child.

When we were making the videotapes, we understood that the one boy was aggressive, but we failed to see how actively his companion assumed the role of helpless victim. Our ability to look at the aggressive sequences on video tapes many times has improved our vision. In the fifth month of the playgroup, for example, we recorded the following sequence:

> One first sees toddler A (for "aggressive") pounding on radiator grating with cylindrical block. He then approaches child W (for "withdrawn") holding the block up against his own head as he walks. Child W is sitting, playing with a toy and does not notice A's approach.
>
> A strikes W on the arm with the block. W cries out, looks at his arm, but does not seek the teacher's support.
>
> A returns to the radiator and hits it again. This time W stands up, joins A, copying A's action with the block he has found. A game of mutual copying ensues for several rounds. But then A walks to the teacher, making hitting gestures with the block, and then strikes the teacher lightly with the block. He then returns to W, hugging him, but turning immediately back to the teacher, and giving a broad smile as if seeking the teacher's approval for his "friendly" act. A also points at W's face or nose while vocalizing, and looks again at the teacher, seemingly in some sort of referential gesture. W is poked slightly by A in this process and walks away.
>
> A goes immediately to W, swinging his block lightly against his own hand as he approaches, and raising it up when he arrives. W shuts his eyes and tilts his head away as if to anticipate a blow on the head, but A merely rubs the block against W's hair. W again walks away but A follows and pushes him hard from behind right into the teacher's arms.
>
> A resumes pounding with the block against a wall and W again copies him; they continue to copy each other back and forth, three more times.
>
> W next walks, almost runs, to the middle of the room and A runs after him making a humming sound, his block not raised.
>
> W again anticipates being hit, again by shutting his eyes and angling his shoulders away from A. This time A grabs W's shirt partly from behind, reveals a facial grimace (teeth clenched, mouth open), and shoves W toward a nearby wall.

A, in yet another rapid shift of affect, then tries to get W to join
him in climbing a special toddler ladder in the playroom (sequence duration: 3 minutes 47 seconds).

This sequence reveals many typical features of toddler peer communication: rapid changes in both emotional time and play topic, the often unsuccessful search for themes that can be understood in common, the focus
on motoric imitation in play. Yet this sequence is also atypical of most toddler peer communication in the intensity and duration of A's aggression
and in the helplessness of W's reaction. A even strikes his teacher, an event
never seen elsewhere in our records. W's behavior is also atypical, in that
he never seeks support from the teacher after being struck, even when he
walks toward the teacher, his approach is not marked by crying or other
social signaling.

At the same time, these children signal clearly enough to each other. A
gives "war cries" as he attacks, waving his block about like a weapon, and
W clearly signals his abject submission, shutting his eyes and turning from
anticipated blows. The fact that these blows only sometimes materialize
does not indicate a miscommunication between A and W. Rather A sometimes displaces his aggressive impulses at the last moment, only rubbing the
block against W's hair.

From watching tapes like this one, we have come to hypothesize that
toddlers are ideal subjects for clinical intervention because their emotional
states are so transparent, so unfettered by later developed inhibitions. Adults
supervising children such as these are in a unique position for recognizing
early emotional problems and for intervening toward the resolution of these
problems. At this point, aggressiveness or social withdrawal are less likely
to be so deeply ingrained in personality as they will become later on if not
attended to.

Yet one must raise the question of how such interventions are to be conducted. The goal in working with the emotionally troubled toddler is to
achieve improved attachment with primary caregivers, not peer bonding.
The latency child, with his or her longing for broadened emotional ties,
increased superego restraints, and intellectual abilities for relating to many
people, remains a better candidate for peer therapy than the toddler.

In working with the troubled toddler, the therapist should set up sessions
where the caregiver–toddler relationship can be directly observed and aided.
In the case where the parent is psychotic or there is no caregiver in the
child's life, the therapist must either find a substitute figure or be prepared
to become that figure. In working with a child deprived of any significant
bond except a therapeutic one, it is a mistake for the therapist to view this
bond with the child only in terms of transference relations. Rather than

offering the toddler a chance to rework some other relationship, the therapist may be giving the child his or her first adequate attachment. When therapy ends, its termination can only be experienced by the child as something akin to parental abandonment, unless the child has been continued to the point of having other safe, ongoing relations beyond that of the therapist.

While not stressing the role of peers in intervention during the little latency, we should remember that early participation with other children can be an important mechanism for the *identification* of troubled children, as was illustrated in the cases of "A" and "W." Furthermore, early peer relations are of considerable direct importance to the normal child whose emotional development in infancy has been satisfactory. However, the troubled child is not ready for the peer challenges of the little latency because such a child is still trying to accomplish the emotional tasks of infancy. In contrast, for the healthy child whose temperament and social milieu combine to form secure attachments, the little latency becomes an opportunity for all forms of learning, including the first broadening of social relationships to include peers. It is in this area that recent knowledge about toddler peer relations reveals aspects of latency that apply to the little latency as well. For example, as we have discussed, Erikson stressed the industrial connections that occur among peers when latency-aged children work together to produce things. Yet these same industrial connections can be observed as toddlers work side by side mastering the toys in the playroom (e.g., Mueller & Lucas, 1975). As we have seen, Sullivan stressed the mutuality of friendships that become possible during latency. Yet the same mutuality can be observed in some of the peer play of toddlers. However, at this early age, the sharing is temporary and discontinuous. It is not yet a property of an ongoing friendship so much as it is a necessary component in the construction of successful play themes among toddlers (Brenner & Mueller, 1982).

We can now see the importance of peer relations for healthy toddlers. Such relations allow them to develop some autonomy from their parents, as well as a sense of being able to relate with persons unrelated to their family. They thus begin to master the skills of peer play that will form the basis of friendship; the latter will remain important throughout life as peer bonds must inevitably replace initial attachments.

It is striking how the importance of this aspect of the little latency has been overlooked by psychodynamic theory, too much under the sway of only a part of Freud's ideas about the early years of life. We have proposed that, through the concept of the little latency, one sees an early period of peacefulness in social–emotional growth, a time when achievements usually ascribed to the latency stage in fact have their developmental roots. While the achievements of this little latency include the well-known "walking and talking," they also include the initial autonomy-seeking and peer play skills that will form the basis for the inevitable shift to peer relations that must accompany normal emotional growth. Within early peer play, we see the reciprocity, cooperation, and sharing that form a basis for friendship—a basis of lifelong importance.

Acknowledgments

The authors express thanks to Jennie Fuller Norman, Robert Selman, Steven Brian-Meisels, and Ellen Berger for materials on peer therapies and the theory of latency. We also thank Russell Lyman and Stephen Shirk, peer therapists at the Judge Baker Guidance Center, for their assistance.

References

Baldwin, J. M. (1911). *Thought and things: Interest and art, or genetic epistemology* (Vol. 3). New York: Macmillan.
Bank, S., & Kahn, M. D. (1975). Sisterhood–brotherhood is powerful: sibling sub-systems and family therapy. *Family Process, 14,* 311–337.
Bee, H. (1981). *The developing child* (3rd ed.). New York: Harper and Row.
Brenner, J., & Mueller, E. (1982). Shared meaning in boy toddlers' peer relations. *Child Development, 53,* 380–391.
Damon, W. (1977). *The social world of the child.* San Francisco: Jessey–Bass.
Erikson, E. H. (1963). *Childhood and society* (2nd ed.). New York: Norton. (Original work published 1950).
Freud, A. (1966). *The ego and the mechanisms of defense* (Revised ed.). New York: International Universities Press. (Original work published 1936).
Freud, A. (1968). Nursery school education: Its uses and dangers (1949). *The writings of Anna Freud* (Vol. 4, 1945–1956). New York: International Universities Press.
Freud, S. (1905). Three essays on the theory of sexuality. In J. Strachey (Ed. and Trans.) *The standard edition of the complete psychological works of Sigmund Freud* (Vol. 7). London: Hogarth Press.
Freud, S. (1935). Autobiographical study. In J. Strachey (Ed. and Trans.) *The standard edition of the complete psychological works of Sigmund Freud* (Vol. 20). London: Hogarth Press.
Fuller, J. S. (1977). Duo therapy: a potential treatment of choice for latency children. *Journal of the American Academic of Child Psychiatry, 16,* 469–477.
Furman, W., Rahe, D. F., & Hartup, W. W. (1979). Rehabilitation of socially withdrawn preschool children through mixed-age and same-age socialization. *Child Development, 50,* 915–922.
Garland, J. A., Jones, H. E., & Kolodny, R. L. (1973). A model for the stages of development in social work groups. In S. Bernstein (Ed.), *Explorations in group work.* Boston: Milford House.
Howes, C., & Mueller, E. (1979). Early peer friendships: Their significance for development. In W. Spiel (Ed. and Trans.), *The psychology of the twentieth century.* Zurich: Kindler.

Kay, P. (1972). Psychoanalytic theory of development in childhood and preadolescence. In B. B. Wolman (Ed.), *Handbook of child psychoanalysis*. New York: Van Nostrand Reinhold.

Kohlberg, L. (1969). Stage and sequence: The cognitive developmental approach to socialization. In D. Goslin (Ed.), *Handbook of socialization theory and research*. Chicago: Rand McNally.

Mahler, M. S., Pine, F., & Bergman, A. (1975). *The psychological birth of the human infant: Symbiosis and individuation*. New York: Basic Books.

Mead, G. H. (1934). *Mind, self, and society*. Chicago: University of Chicago Press.

Mehlman, R. D. (1980). A conceptual model for the assessment of developmental normality. In J. R. Bemporad (Ed.), *Child development in normality and psychopathology*. New York: Brunner/Mazel.

Mitchell, C. A. (1976). Duo therapy: An innovative approach to the treatment of children. *Smith College Studies in Social Work, 45,* 236–247.

Mueller, E., & Lucas, T. (1975). A developmental analysis of peer interaction among toddlers. In M. Lewis & L. A. Rosenblum (Eds.), *Friendship and peer relations*. New York: Wiley.

Mueller, E., & Vandell, D. (1979). Infant–infant interaction. In J. Osofsky (Ed.), *Handbook of infant development*. New York: Wiley Interscience.

Redl, F. (1942). Group emotion and leadership. *Psychiatry, 5,* 573–595.

Roberts, J., & Baird, J. L. (1971). *Parent ratings of behavioral patterns of children*. Vital and Health Statistics. Data from the National Health Survey (Ser. 11, No. 108). Washington, D.C.: U.S. Government Printing Office.

Rubenstein, J., & Howes, C. (1976). The effect of peers on toddler interaction with mother and toys. *Child Development, 47,* 597–605.

Selman, R. L. (1981). The development of interpersonal competence: The role of understanding in conduct. *Developmental Review, 1,* 401–422.

Shapiro, T., & Perry, R. (1976). Latency revisited: The age 7 plus or minus 1. *Psychoanalytic Study of the Child, 31,* 79–105.

Small, M. (1977). Peer attachments. *Dissertation Abstracts, 37,* 4707.

Sroufe, L. A., & Waters, E. (1977). Attachment as an organizational construct. *Child Development, 48,* 1185–1199.

Stern, D. (in press). The early development of schemas of self, of other, and of various experience of "self with other." In S. Kaplan and J. D. Lichtenberg (Eds.), *Reflections on self psychology*. New York: International Universities Press.

Sullivan, H. S. (1953). *The interpersonal theory of psychiatry*. New York: Norton.

Sylva, K. (1976). The role of play in the problem solving of children 3–5 years old. In J. S. Bruner, A. Jolly, & K. Sylva (Eds.), *Play*. New York: Basic Books.

PART IV

PROCESS IN PLAY

The common theme of Chapters 8–10 is a view of play as a spontaneous, mutually constructed interaction that includes both literal elements, such as the allocation of space, and fantasy content. In this section, reports from three research teams address the process of peer play by emphasizing the importance of children's creation of the shared context of play.

For Shugar and Bokus, in "Children's Discourse and Children's Activity in the Peer Situation," (Chapter 8, this volume) the child's *agency,* which involves the capacity to set goals for independent or socially coordinated activity, can be fruitfully examined in peer discourse during play. Play is not seen as different from work but, instead, as a prototype of future serious activity. Children's discourse, then, can be viewed as a medium in which agentiveness is expressed in the organization, regulation, and reporting of activities and events. In a dyadic free-play situation, 3-year-olds typically used language to involve their partner in their own activity, whereas 4-year-olds more frequently discussed joint activities. Temporal and spatial indicators revealed developmental differences in the ways children reconciled conflicting requirements of their individual and social activity. Four-year-olds spent somewhat more time interacting

PROCESS AND OUTCOME
IN PEER RELATIONSHIPS

with a partner but also spent longer times in separate activities than did 3-year-olds. When asked where a third child might play, children designated common areas for themselves and their original partners when allowed less space but more distinct areas when given more. This work suggests that peer interaction may provide a key context for the development of a child's sense and capacity for agency, both in its individual and social aspects.

In Chapter 9 (this volume), "Organization of Social Play among Toddlers: an Ecological Approach," Stamback and Verba consider how the context influences our estimation of the social skills of young children. Context includes not only the physical environment but also (and of greater importance, in their view) the nature of the relationships among children, teachers, and staff in the crèches, the public day-care centers in France. In their work, children from 13 to 18 months of age were observed in order to analyze the organization of social play in spontaneous interaction. Sequences were examined for the means by which toddlers initiated and elaborated the themes of their play. Toddlers' negotiation of shared meanings was accomplished with preverbal and nonverbal behaviors that changed when a third child entered or as sources of disagreement appeared. The readjustments seen in these patterns are contrasted with those required for object-oriented play. The authors emphasize how competence in social play among toddlers varies with the context in which they are observed.

In " 'Frame Talk': A Dramatistic Analysis of Children's Fantasy Play," (Chapter 10, this volume) Forbes, Katz, and Paul argue that a core developmental attainment of middle childhood is the ability to negotiate the context or frame of fantasy play in explicit terms. In their analysis of fantasy play episodes among 5- to 7-year-olds, three phases were examined, each with different communicative demands: setting up, enacting, and transition. Because of the nonliteral nature of play and the need for meanings to be shared with the partner, the continued negotiation and renegotiation of themes with the partner were crucial to the continuity of the shared fantasy. *Setting up* required discussion and persuasion about the proposed themes, *enactment* involved maintenance of the frame of the fantasy and clarification of the roles being played, and *transition* involved tying themes from a past episode to a new one by creating cohesive devices. Forbes and his colleagues apply concepts of dramatistic analysis to describe the skills of children in constructing the contexts of their play.

The investigation of play appears to be a crucial means of understanding the meaning of context for children. Although developmental changes in children's ability to negotiate context are striking, very early signs of skilled behavior are apparent. Play experiences may contribute both to children's sense of agency as well as to their capacity for fantasy and spontaneity.

CHAPTER 8

Children's Discourse and Children's Activity in the Peer Situation*

Grace Wales Shugar and Barbara Bokus

Introduction

Peer relations are nowadays often seen as interaction processes of functional importance in some period of childhood. It has been suggested in this book that what is needed is a better integration of the functional significances attributed to peer relations. This raises the problem of envisioning a developmental end product that is appropriate to the process of peer interaction. What is implied is that we look at the process under study selectively, through the prism of the outcome for which we hold it responsible. Clearly researchers bring different schemes of thinking to such a task, and a broad range of orientations is to be anticipated. Each researcher, however, is required to be conceptually clear about what is understood by peer process and outcome. Therefore, we propose the following as the process-outcome relation that is central to an understanding of our perspective: "To be accounted an autonomous individual in social life, we must be solely responsible for our own actions" (Shotter, 1974, p. 198). We could add: "and to be thought by others to be responsible for our own actions."

*This project has been funded by Grants K-17 from the Ministry of Education and W-266 from the Institute of Philosophy and Sociology, Polish Academy of Sciences. The data collection and analysis owe a great deal to Alicja Kawalec, Grazyna Kozlowska, Teresa Terlecka, Elzbieta Samojluk, Jolanta Zamecka, and others. Ida Kurcz provided valuable criticism of the draft.

This sums up the notion of *agency* at work in a social world and the notion of agentive methodology, that is, the diversity and choices of ways of functioning which can be selected at will by agents oriented to their goals—goals which are themselves embedded in social interaction. We believe that the processes relevant to such an outcome lie before our eyes in the natural activity and discourse of preschool children. But we may only perceive them by looking for them. This is what we have undertaken to initiate.

Research Issues and the Problem of Approach

The large and ever-growing literature on preschool children's play activities in social settings has been, and continues to be, motivated by numerous research concerns that are mainly developmentally oriented. Prominent among these concerns are social competence, social-cognitive abilities and personality formation. Only in recent years has the study of social interaction proper come to the fore, and questions are being raised about how these interactions come into existence, how they are sustained, how they evolve, and about the skills and abilities of children that account for these achievements as well as the origins of these skills. It has become increasingly clear that the formation of social interaction follows a child-specific course from infancy through toddlerhood into the preschool years (Mueller & Vandell, 1979). Given the opportunities for experience in social interaction, children enter their preschool years with knowledge and abilities necessary for the further development of interactional competence.

Little, if any, serious attention has been given in the research on children's behavior in peer settings to the extent and character of "self-activity" manifested in social conditions. The term itself is usually encountered in interchangeable use with "solitary activity," distinguishing it from participation in social activity. This has apparently been a considerable oversight, as some recent research has revealed.

TWO DIMENSIONS OF RESEARCH
ON PRESCHOOL CHILDREN'S PLAY

Half a century ago, a study on preschool children's behavior in a peer setting was conducted that subsequently had a strong impact upon the conceptions held by researchers and educators about preschoolers' typical social activity. This study (Parten, 1932) produced a social–developmental-stage conception of how a child passes from isolated play and onlooking to increasing social participation as a function of age. Parten's findings, replicated several times in varying circumstances, (e.g., Barnes, 1971; Hurtig, Hurtig, & Paillard, 1971; Rubin, Maioni, & Hornung, 1976) have not in themselves been refuted.

Not long ago, another study was published which produced an altered picture of children's individual and social activities in the nursery school setting (Roper & Hinde, 1978). Using more detailed observations and more sophisticated analytical techniques than prior researchers, these authors found two relevant components, one involving self play and the other ranging from parallel to group and interactive play. How much children play on their own and how much they interact with other children when playing with them turned out to be separate issues. Referring to this study, Hinde (1979) comments on the fact that theories adults hold can blind them to the way in which individuals actually behave.

> The older views that children mature through stages of predominantly self-play and parallel play to showing predominantly group and interactive play, and that a given group of children can be ranged along a dimension of social maturity according to how much of each type they show, was not borne out by a principal components analysis of the observational data. Yet in answering a questionnaire containing items concerned with the children's social behaviour, not only the teachers but also the observers (who had not yet analyzed their data) answered as though the children could be arranged along such a dimension. For instance, children who were noticed often to engage in group or interactive play were scored as seldom showing self-play, when later examination of the observational data showed that that had not necessarily been the case. (p. 120)

The negative assessment of independent play, treated as the least mature form of social play (Parten, 1932) and the least cognitively developed (Piaget, 1962; Smilansky, 1968) has also come into question. Self-activity in the peer situation, shown to be often cognitively rich and task-oriented (Moore, Evertson, & Brophy, 1974), may have been misrepresented in the early peer research literature (Rubin et al., 1976).

The evidence that self (solitary) play does not necessarily mean immaturity or lack of social ability (Roper & Hinde, 1978), taken together with the general view of the importance of peer interactive play for social-cognitive development (Mueller & Lucas, 1975; Piaget, 1932; Rubin & Pepler, 1980), suggest that there are intersections of these two dimensions. If there are two relevant dimensions of independent status describing social participation in play (how much a child is involved with other children when playing alongside them, and how much he or she plays totally independently of other children [see Roper & Hinde, 1978, pp. 575–576]), their interrelationships in the concrete peer setting must be sought. Neither, apparently, can be disregarded if one wishes to understand how and why children link their play, or take separate ways, in their ongoing activities. No adequate picture of preschool children's social organization can be gained without accounting for both dimensions.

THE PEER SITUATION: POTENTIAL FOR BOTH
SELF- AND SOCIAL ACTIVITY

The peer situation of young children has been mainly researched for the development of social activity. Yet the peer situation also contains processes pertaining to the development of self-activity (understood as activity pursued independently by the child). In fact, the situation may be considered one in which either form of activity can occur, with each affecting the other. Perhaps we can use the existing research on infancy and toddlerhood to clarify the nature of the developmental change in the relative importance of social interaction with peers and nonsocial interaction with objects across the early years of life.

In studies of the formative process of social interaction, Mueller and Vandell (1979) distinguish three stages differing organizationally. In the first, peer contacts arise in play with the same objects or materials and are referred to as "parasocial," since actions may be peer-focused or object-focused; the situation is likened to that known as "parallel play." In the next stage, social interaction emerges out of peer contacts as the outcome of contingent responses to social behaviors, which in the third stage takes on structure with role reversability and complementarity as displayed in the giving and taking of objects. In this account, presented in detail in Mueller & Lucas (1975), objects are treated as a component in the toddler-specific system of social interaction (Mueller, 1979), and their presence is viewed as a central factor for the occurrence of contacts (Eckerman, Whatley, & Kutz, 1975), as well as a primary force of attraction for the clustering of children (Mueller & Rich, 1976).

But while there is general agreement over the importance of objects in the research on early peer relations, there is apparent confusion over functions of objects and the character of object-oriented actions. Mueller and Vandell (1979) point to the unstable role of objects in social contacts. Lewis & Feiring (1979) do not support the conclusion as to their necessary role in early peer contacts. Maudry and Nekula (1939) suggest an early priority of object-interest in itself over object-interest as a social device. Yet, later in development, peer conflict over object-access suggests a melding of the two interests (Flament, 1982; Lichtenberger, 1965). Another factor observed is the accretion of the value of an object for a child who observes it being used by another child, as shown in heightened exertions to gain access to that object. Also, the action of another child upon an object renders the action itself a focus of interest and of imitative behavior (Nadel–Brulfert & Baudonniere, 1982) and encourages children to witness and imitate the novel event (Eckerman et al., 1975; Mueller & Rich, 1976). Pairs of 2-year-olds, observed over time, were found to increase the frequency both of play with the same materials and of play involving them in the other child's activity, yet at the same time maintaining a high level of independent play. Thus objects have an organizing function. When objects are deliberately selected for experimentation, as in Flament's (1982) study of infant pairs in a task-oriented situation, they almost inevitably call forth reciprocal and complementary activity. Coordinations of actions by two children take place through objects but, as the study by Eckerman et al. (1975) shows, objects also have an organizing function for individual play.

Inherent in the peer situation featuring the presence of objects at the free disposal of its participants are clearly two kinds of utilizations: use of objects as central foci for social interaction and use of objects as the substantive base for the pursuance of independent activity. Clarification of these differentiations may not be available until research is addressed more directly to the question of what children do with objects, in terms not only of their momentary activities but also of their developing skills and capacities. The skills acquired early in the mastery of objects (Connolly & Bruner, 1974; Piaget, 1952) continue to require access to new, more complex material for their exercise and growth. The classic term "functional play" (Buhler, 1931) does not mesh well with the growing constructive and creative uses of objects displayed by active preschoolers observed in the peer situation. His or her independent play displays goal-directed and constructive character (Moore et al., 1974), expansive expression of imagination and fantasy (Dyner, 1971; Herron & Sutton–Smith, 1971), and is well illustrated in monologic speech (Shields, 1979). If one considers what children do and strive to do with objects in terms of their developing skills and capacities, as suggested above, it would seem helpful to recognize the *agentive* character of these performances. The child is becoming the organizing center of his or her own activities. Children can deliberately select their forms of activity, independent or interactive, according to the privileges of the agentive role. This appears to be demonstrated in the study by Roper and Hinde (1978): The same children who at one time are noted as engaged solely in their own activities are those who, at another time, are noted as taking active part in social play.

This discussion has brought us to the following conclusion. The peer situation at the preschool age retains the potential, as in toddlerhood, for both self- and social activity. But there may be an important difference, instead of being object-focused in character, the preschool peer situation may be agentive in character. The best evidence for this conclusion is seen not only in what children do, but in what they say. As able users of language, they are able to explicate their activity through speech.

PRESENT APPROACH

Let us examine more closely the notion of agency as applied within the context of preschool peer relations. Distinguishing between the activity of things and the activity of persons (Ingleby, 1974, p. 296), we refer to the latter as the type of activity that characterizes the human agent. The characteristics of such activity include a forward orientation and choices among ways of functioning that may be selected freely by agents oriented to their yet-to-be-achieved goals. Activity originates in and is organized by the agent. The origination of activity is never abstract, always situated in space and time. Any situation presents an array of possibilities, and the agent selects among them according to their relative value for him or her (Tomaszewski, 1975). Just as situations change and transform, so does the range of possibilities and, accordingly, the value hierarchy for the agent.

In the peer situation, the notion of agency contains both individual and social aspects. It may possibly be the basic category by which young children perceive each other and understand each other's behavior and language. From the early stages of acquisition of language, children have used in common the basic semantic relations—agent, action, object, receiver of action, possession, attribution, time, place (Brown, 1973; Bruner, 1975)— to exchange meanings with others. As some evidence suggests, children recognize each other's needs for space and objects, as well as their priority rights to them (Corsaro, 1979), and they may exact rational accounts for requests for action (Garvey, 1975). It is the social situation that assists children in achieving agentive status in their own eyes and those of others.

In this chapter, we focus on an approach that views the peer situation in the manner just described. Our conception of play encompasses the belief that children's activity is central and the proper point of departure for research on play and that play belongs within this framework. Children's activity is assumed to be essentially social in character, and comprises the source of children's active participation in the world of human relations (Tomaszewski, 1967; Vygotsky, 1966). At the same time, children's play is a well-recognized source of cognitive development (Piaget, 1952; Szuman, 1955), leading to the development of awareness by the child of his or her own activity and of the individual self (Elkonin, 1948). Play, emerging from the child's free initiative, can be thought of as a prototype of future "serious" activity. And so we cast the child early in the role of "agent," in line with Shotter's reasoning that the primitive natural agent takes on features of autonomy and responsibility for his or her actions and for their rationalization through his or her participation in the social world (Shotter, 1974, 1978).

The basic methodological principle adopted here is that the child's continuous behavior produces an ongoing stream of events that contain the phenomena of interest to us, activity originating in the child and enmeshed in that of others in the course of social interactions. To disentangle these events, we depend principally upon interpretation of the relations between children's speech and their activity.

Discourse in the Peer Situation

The research task outlined in the foregoing section, that of investigating two independent yet related dimensions of preschool children's activities, self and social, in the peer situation, might well be facilitated through the study of their language. Analysis of the procedures children employ for the conduct of both individual and concerted activities could be based on their discourse. The main reference domain of children's utterances is unquestionably the events occurring to them that concern them and in which they actively participate. The relations of children's language to their activity might reveal the particular uses of language that are specific to the child as well as those they adopt from the surrounding world of adults. Yet again one encounters conceptual obstacles to approaching such a study.

On the face of it, it would seem impossible to consider the investigation of children's activities, individually and socially coordinated, without the explicit treatment of children's speech practices. As argued by Speier (1970), the building of talk as well as the building of practical activity require methods worked out by participants in a common social scene. At the same time children are also creating speech as they work out the lengthening perspectives of their individual courses of action. A key issue in the organization of childhood activity is how talking and acting are linked together in the service both of coordinating activities or different participant agents and of advancing the activity of a single and independent agent in the common social setting.

CHILDREN'S SPEECH: DEFICIENT OR DIFFERENT?

Of late, developmental psychologists and sociologists have expressed concern over the prevailing tendency for underestimating the preschool child's verbal skills mirrored in the traditional formulations (e.g., Donaldson, 1978; Flavell, 1977; Gelman, 1978; Mackay, 1973). One of the strongest arguments for this position has been provided by methods devised for the study of children's communicative competence in natural situations that have yielded a considerably increased estimate of children's abilities to communicate (Flavell, 1977, pp. 172–183). There is evidence of mounting reluctance to accept the classical characterization of young children's speech as primarily to and for self and as undergoing socialization. The old paradigm that treats children as deficient communicators, unable to adapt their language to an interlocutor, is apparently being replaced by a new paradigm which treats children as different *communicators,* in the sense of being different from the adult in terms of what is communicated, in what manner, under what circumstances, to what end. The essentials of these differences seem yet to be clarified. One place to look for their manifestations is in the social world of the preschool child, admitting a priori that mutual understandings among children may exist about what utterances are for. Utterances comprise procedures children work out to organize, regulate, and report on the organization of activities and events, originating in themselves or happening to and around them, hypothetically or in fact. Children can be assumed to have basic competences in interpreting the social world (Mackay, 1973; Shields, 1978), particularly the immediate world of their peers.

In treating children's language practices, we shall not employ the dichotomy based on addresseeship, a criterion which is not always functional (Shugar, 1978c, in press-a). Instead we shall consider speech as an integral part of the behavior of the speaker, the prime means of relating to other children and to their activities. We shall contrast this avenue of approach to the prevailing one in the literature, referred to most often as *conversational,* one that is principally concerned with the relations between utterances. The latter approach to children's speech focuses on the social effects of utterances themselves.

SOCIAL SPEECH AND SOCIAL PLAY

Over the last decade, positive evidence has accummulated about the extent and nature of the mutual social effects of toddler and preschooler speech. The facts about the strong social effects of children's utterances have been disclosed through observations conducted in naturalistic but *purified* conditions, that is, in minimal social units or child pairs (Garvey & Hogan, 1973; Mueller, 1972). Controlling factors have been found to be both utterance properties and the listener's state of engagement with the speaker. When conditions were optimal, a response seemed virtually inevitable (Mueller, Bleier, Krakow, Hegedus, & Cournoyer, 1977). The same tendencies can be discerned in 2-year-olds, the best predictor of a response being the listener's prior behavior, either that of attending to the speaker, or to his or her utterance (Mueller et al., 1977). Another important factor of social effect appears also to be a single visual behavior by the preschool speaker, a scan serving to locate the listener prior to speaking and affecting subsequent utterance content that invariably referred to the speaker's activity (Bokus, 1981, 1982; see also the section entitled "How Children Perceive Their Action Fields in the Dyadic Situation"). This is contrary to Mueller's (1972) finding that preschoolers' utterances referring to the listener's rather than to the speaker's interests has a higher probability of evoking a response.

While the above studies demonstrate that the elementary and basic skills in verbal interaction pertain to elicitation-response control, they are alone insufficient to grasp the essentials of children's verbal interaction as a mutual system of engagement (Mueller & Vandell, 1979). A more detailed account of what could be called a shared code of conduct has been provided by Keenan (1974), from longitudinal observations of twins starting in the fourth quarter of the third year. Conducted in highly purified conditions (situations conducive to interactive talk, and adult-free), this study provides evidence of the acquisition of mutual speaker–hearer expectations for sustained and coherent exchanges. By the end of the third year, in favorable conditions, children are apparently able to work out on their own conventions for patterning their discourse, for which the prerequisites are reliable anticipations about given social effects of their utterances.

In view of such findings pertaining to children under 3 years of age, it is no surprise to observe further developments of the same type of conversational skills in preschool children, skills operating now upon a certainly richer content drawn from accumulated experience and knowledge of the world. For example, the social play formats extracted from the ongoing play of preschoolers in a dyadic situation (Garvey, 1974) are apparently governed by the basic principles of turn-taking applying to both verbal and nonverbal behaviors, each child modifying successive behaviors as a result of the other's acts, such that neither child alone determined the course of the episode. Besides their ritualizing influence, these formats provide conditions for the mutual creation of novelty. Format-constructing skills are supplemented by other abilities to jointly develop a pretend play theme. Such constructions develop best when children's abilities operate upon a shared base of organized knowledge, as argued and illustrated by Nelson and Gruendel (1979). But while the integration and mutual intelligibility of preschoolers' play conversation are ensured by the inferences children make about what the other knows that pertains to the underlying content theme, such conversation must also resolve the differences of underlying content, as Shields (1976) emphasizes. To resolve dissimilar interpretations in realizing a content theme, children need dialogic skills to arrive at a common meaning. Such skills, serving to resolve cognitive discrepancies in the interpretation of a given reality, can be detected at an early preschool age (Shugar, 1978c).

Numerous recent studies of social play and conversation (e.g., Garvey & Berninger, in press; McTear, 1978) reveal more advanced discourse and dialogue skills emerging in the preschool period than hitherto supposed. These include abilities to make substantive links across utterances remote from each other and to create common topical domains (Keenan & Schieffelin, 1976). Such studies follow the approach used to study the development of adult conversation and the adult mode of verbal conduct of social affairs.

DISCOURSE AND THE ORGANIZATION OF ACTIVITY— SELF AND SOCIAL

Whereas children's discourse, analyzed by observing the direct social effects of utterances and viewed as mutual systems of verbal engagement, reveals how children learn to build coherent and topically-oriented discourse, large areas pertinent to children's speech usage are still untouched. It is not apparent how the above approach can reveal the speech practices of children in terms of self-activity and their implications for the formation of social activity, discourse that cannot logically be controlled by turn-taking principles. In a different approach to the analysis of children's discourse, utterances are assumed to have other types of effects than direct listener response. If one grants that a child's speech forms an integral part of his or her ongoing behavior, then one readily finds connections between much of that speech and its referents in ongoing activity. The effect of a child's utterance can be identified in his or her own activity and indirectly, in the activity of co-present children. Consequently, a factor mediating the social effects of an utterance lies in its reference field, since it is this field that both speaker and listener focus attention upon.

Action Discourse and Topical Discourse

To clarify this conception, we refer to a distinction drawn between the notions of *action discourse* and *topical discourse* (Shugar, in press-a, -b). The former refers to the engagement of speech among other forms of action in a general category of activity called "working on things," as opposed to the latter, which refers to the engagement of speech in the verbal activity of "talking about things." The notion of action discourse rests on a differentiation of *activity field* and *reference field*. Activity field designates the spatial–temporal domain in which the child is actually functioning, whereas reference field designates the ensemble of elements and relations to which the speech refers. In action discourse, the child gives priority to mapping his or her utterances upon some state of the activity field, in which case the reference field and activity field are to some degree matched. Coherence is to be sought not so much across utterances, which may occur intermittently, as between utterances and states of activity referred to. The effect of the utterance upon participant hearers (which includes, in the first place, the speaker) is to bring the actual state of the action field into line with the propositional content of the utterance. In topical discourse, on the other hand, it is the topic of utterances rather than the action field that is manipulated. In this case, the referential role of the activity field changes: The child extracts the topic of discourse directly from that field for linguistic manipulation. While the topic attains some autonomy in relation to that field, the activity field remains always a potential resource influencing the course of topical flow. The ongoing changes effected by speakers and listeners in the activity field determine the shifts from topical discourse to action discourse, or the reverse. The description and explication of actions specify the requirement priorities for such shifts. The present, past, and future states of the activity field dictate the occurrences and uses of utterances.

The distinction made here (which obviously does not hold only for children) is considered crucial for grasping the child-specific ways of using language that externalize ongoing cognitive processes. This conception is derived from empirical studies of the child's linguistic functioning in the interactional context with adults during language acquisition (Shugar, 1976, 1978a, 1978b) and in the early preschool years (Shugar, 1978c, 1980). These studies were concerned with the natural formation of continuous behavior in the social world.

The Social Effects of Action Discourse

In the situation of a minimal social unit, that is, a dyadic situation in which two children spend time together, the social effects of action discourse become apparent to the observer. Each child may seem to be producing a speech referring to his or her ongoing activity, each child has auditory access (by ear) to the speech produced by the other and may also have visual access to the activity referred to. Hence each child can, in addition to confronting his or her own speech with the state of his or her activity field, do likewise in respect to that of the co-present child: He or she can match what is spoken by the other child with the state of the latter's activity. These ongoing processes have social effects leading to the intersection of activities.

In our dyadic situational observations, a mutual tendency has been noted in children to monitor each other's ongoing activities and to be particularly alert to the changes occurring in that activity as signaled by utterances referring to it. The social effect of utterances are thus indirectly obtained. What concerns the listener is the correspondence between the actual state of the speaker's activity field and the utterance content referring to that field. Thus the listener, as well as the speaker, becomes attentive to the potential changes occurring in the activity of the speaking child.

Discourse Analysis

In analyses of early adult–child discourse, it has been noted that the 2-year-old tends to represent ongoing activity in speech, thus matching reference field to activity field, according to the conception outlined above (Shugar, 1978a). This study also found that 2-year-olds tend to participate actively in situations described in their speech, a tendency noted in 3-year-olds' discourse with an adult (Bokus & Shugar, 1979) and in preschoolers' peer discourse, as observed in the dyadic situation. We have noted that the reference field of utterances is predominantly that of the activity field, whether in a child–child situation or a child–adult one (Shugar, in press-a). In the peer situation, to which the remainder of this chapter is devoted, children's discourse effected changes upon the activity fields of each other. Interactional analysis showed high levels of interactivity, which spoke for a prevailing tendency to intertwine activities of co-present children. The goal of discourse analysis is to describe how this happens.

In devising a method of discourse analysis, our observations lead us to posit two relevant components: the linguistic and the proxemic. The latter component, termed "display," functioned in a way that rendered perceptually accessible the speaker's activity field by opening, as it were, the activity field to the inspection and eventual participation of the listener. The former component contained both propositional content and a directive element, explicit or implicit, indicating what is to be done, or what information is needed. The directive element, it was noted, did not necessarily distinguish between self or other child as addressee. Both components of discourse were important for the conduct of action discourse, as defined above, while the proxemic component might lose importance in topical discourse situations.

This view of discourse provides a framework or filter through which it is possible to interpret the events registered in discourse, anticipated in discourse, and created by discourse. Adopting the point of view of the "I" who is speaking casts an illuminating beam upon the social scene. This perspective permits certain inferences about how children interpret speech procedures used similarly by each other—not only as ways of referring to the speaker's activity but as ways of opening that activity to the participation of another.

In the rest of this chapter our purpose is not to present the direct application of the method of discourse analysis but to present what its application discloses about the organization of self and social activity.

How Children Participate in the Dyadic Situation: Basic Data

The investigations that the discussion in this chapter is based upon were addressed, in the initial stage, to an open question: How do children spend their time in a minimal social situation, that is, together with a same-age peer? We expected that they would interact considerably with each other, as found by Garvey and Hogan (1973) in their dyadic study that served as a design model for us. However, we also thought that they would devote time to activities on their own. The dyadic session might turn out to be a mosaic of interactive and noninteractive events involving two children. Our subjects were introduced into a situation characterized by novelty: They had had no previous experience with each other nor with the play setting and its contents. We expected them to contribute their activity interests, discourse practices, and stores of interactional knowledge and skills. The object of analysis became the dyadic session.

The basic data of our research are derived from analyses of dyadic sessions. These data provide a stock of material to which various research problems can be addressed. In the remainder of this chapter we shall present two such research problems. First, the basic data are presented.

SUBJECTS, PROCEDURES, AND RECORDS

Twenty-four dyadic sessions were observed in which 24 children from different neighborhood nursery schools participated. Unacquainted children, aged 3 to 5, were paired in half-year age brackets and each participated in two dyadic peer sessions, once in a same-sex pair, once in a cross-sex pair. (The observational base has since been expanded by an additional 48 dyadic sessions with children aged 3 to 7 years). Three sessions took place on a single day, involving 3 pairs of children, each session lasting about 15 minutes. The laboratory playroom measured 2.8 by 5.6 m², and contained a variety of nursery school type toys without large play equipment. Children met outside the playroom and were invited to come in and play for a while. Sessions were adult-free and monitored through television circuits.

Videotaped recordings of the sessions were transcribed in detail by two analyzers, each following one child's continuous behavior. Speech, visual behaviors, and proxemic information were recorded separately. Synchronized records provided the basis for further analyses. Details are reported elsewhere (Shugar, 1982). A more detailed coding and recording procedure has been elaborated by Bokus (1982).

Data Selection

The basic data presented here concern 12 dyadic sessions, of which 6 comprise the set for the youngest age bracket studied (36 to 42 months) and 6 the set for the oldest (54 to 60 months). In selecting these sets for detailed exploratory analyses of the processes involved in the dyadic sessions, we were able to concentrate on the similarities and differences from the perspective of the two clearly distinguished age groups (mean age difference 18 months). The two groups will henceforth be referred to as *3-year-olds* and *4-year-olds*.

THE DYADIC SESSION

The dyadic session was considered a natural whole event comprising the activity and speech of the members of the pair. The event was conceived of as having inherent dynamic properties, moving from a starting point to a break-off point (fixed arbitrarily). Developments over time would evolve, successive happenings affected by preceding ones. Prospectively, for its members, the dyadic session at the entry point was a future event; what could happen was determined by the available objects and materials of play and by the presence of another similar child. Retrospectively the dyadic session was characterized by the realization, by each member separately and together, of the potentialities of the dyadic session.

Segmentation of the Dyadic Session

The session was first marked off into its naturally formed parts based on the criteria of interactive activity and noninteractive activity. Junctures were identified by employing such sources of information as flow of talk and pauses, changes in direction of gaze, mutual body orientations, distancing and approaching, actions focused on objects and on the other child. Interactive stretches were unitized on the general principle of directionality, using as junctures the change of mutual focus, that is, the object or action of the mutual engagement, or the topic of discourse. The portion of talk that occurred within any of the segments was treated as a discourse entity. Silence over several seconds, occurring during an interaction unit, was also marked; this permitted the distinction between inactive states of ongoing interaction (silent) and active states, when speech flowed almost continuously.

The Temporal Structure of the Dyadic Session

Segmentation of the dyadic session provided a temporal dimension on which to measure the different parts comprising the event. This is illustrated by the data in Table 8.1 that contrasts the average picture of the dyadic sessions of the 3-year-olds and the 4-year-olds as well as presenting the overall picture for the two age brackets. Excluded from the analysis was one session in each age bracket in which no interaction occurred.

The temporal shape of the dyadic session shows a general profile since, with one exception, no differences were established across age brackets. The 4-year-olds spent significantly longer stretches of time in separate activity than the 3-year-olds. Otherwise segments, either interactive or noninteractive, tended to last about half a minute before a change of focus occurred, either to another center of mutual interest (interaction unit) or to separate centers of interest (noninteractive segment). Of the two segment types, the interactive was overwhelmingly more frequent than the noninteractive. Active parts of interaction units (i.e., nearly continuous talk), as compared to whole units, were virtually indistinguishable in mean duration.

In short, the dyadic sessions we observed were composed of many interactive events and minor, but recurrent, foci on activities of separate interest. Interactive segments were filled with ongoing talk; very little silent time occurred during states of interaction.

MANNER AND STRUCTURES OF DYADIC INTERACTION

The procedure adopted for tracing individual children's behavior courses allowed for locating points of intersection of these courses. The main criterion for identifying a mutual focus of attention and action was a "crossing" of one child's course of behavior with that of the other. The observed behaviors were interdependent; typically, they were utterance exchanges, or visual or physical actions accompanied by such exchanges. An utterance followed by a response, both having a common reference to some element in one or the other child's field of activity, or some related topic, served as a marker of interaction initiation. (More detailed analyses on the interaction initiation process, conducted by Bokus [1982], confirmed the predominant function of the utterance as activizing the potential state of dyadic initiation).

By locating these points of behavior stream interactions, we could conclude on what terms children initiated interactions, what they proposed to each other, and how they structured interactions initiated by themselves. Thus the initiating child was found to use his or her own ongoing activity

Table 8.1

Temporal Segment Composition of Dyadic Sessions

	Dyadic sessions of		
Segment types	3-year-olds[a]	4-year-olds[a]	Both
Interaction units			
Mean frequency	24.6	20.4	22.5
Mean duration (secs)	30.9	34.2	32.5
Mean duration of active part (secs)	30.6	33.1	31.9
Noninteractive segments			
Mean frequency	5.2	3.0	4.1
Mean duration (secs)	25.3*	40.0	32.6

[a]Number of sessions = 5; number of children = 10.
*Significant cross-age differences, $p < .001$.

as the terms on which to involve the partner, or alternately to use the partner's activity as focal center. On the other hand, the initiating child might propose a new line of action which required the accord of the other for a concerted action to be initiated. A fourth basis for interaction was on the purely verbal plane of exchange; a topical focus was either introduced by an initiating speaker or was picked up from a previous utterance. Pursuance of topical discourse comprised a separate basis for interaction (see the section on "Discourse in the Peer Situation"), and was ranked on equal terms with the other three, which differed in that they oriented interaction to the plane of practical activity with objects.

The manner in which interactions were initiated determined their structure. The four distinctive manners in which children initiated interaction are defined as follows:

OWN ACTIVITY (OA)—in which the coordination of partners' behavior comprising the interaction occurs around the action line of the initiator. In this case, the initiator draws the partner into his or her action line. Typical initiating behaviors consist of verbal calls to attend (Look; Come), and/or verbal information about the initiator's action or object of action (I'm doing X; This is X).

OTHER CHILD'S ACTIVITY (OCA)—in which the coordination of partners' behaviors comprising the interaction occurs around the action line of the noninitiating child. In this case, the initiator leaves his or her own action line and enters the partner's line, which dominates. Typical initiating behaviors consist of verbal inquiries or comments about the partner's activity (You're doing X, right? You're doing X well or wrong), and/or action upon the partner's objects.

JOINT ACTIVITY(JA)—in which the coordination of partners' behaviors comprising the interaction occurs around a newly forming action line which starts from an initiating proposal or act instituting a common activity. In this case, both initiator and partner leave their current action line to focus upon a joint line, which dominates. Typical initiating behaviors consist of verbal proposals or instructions (C'mon let's do X; I'll do X and you do Y).

TOPICAL CONVERSATION (TC)—in which verbal interaction, focused on a topic, occurs simultaneously with noncoordinated or coordinated action lines reduced to secondary importance. In this case, the initiator introduces a topic related, or not related, to current activity which becomes a mutual main focus. Typical initiating behaviors consist of verbal comments or inquiries (We have X at home; X is like Y; Did you do X before? What is X?).

Commenting on the above set of patterns, it will be noted that a category of parallel activity does not appear. In using as criterion whose activity (or topic) constituted the axis of the interaction, we discarded earlier attempts to apply the parallel activity category (Shugar, 1979), since it was not obvious to us that children actually initiated this type of coordinated activity. (This does not mean that parallel activity did not occur, but that aspect will not be dealt with here).

The above set of patterns indicates the crucial role of discourse in initiating as well as sustaining interactions. Starts of interaction units could be located at utterance points. The threshold at which any interaction began in our 3- and 4-year old sessions was always synchronous with the beginning of a verbal exchange—an utterance and its response. Noninteracting children did not cross this threshold. Once the threshold was crossed, our subjects spent a minimum of half the dyadic session in active interaction and a maximum of the entire session. The mean ratio for interacting children was .81 of the total time. No significant differences were found across sex and age groups for interaction time ratios.

The distribution of the structural patterns initiated by the children in ten dyadic sessions is shown in Table 8.2.

The structural pattern which stands out clearly as that most frequently used in the dyadic sessions analyzed is the one referred to as Own activity where children initiate interaction by effective engagement of the partner in his or her own line of action. This pattern prevails overwhelmingly in the 3-year-olds, its frequency being responsible for the significant differences found between groups, despite the fact that the 4-year-olds did not use this pattern significantly more often than they used any of the other three. It is to be noted that some of the older children increased their use of two other patterns: the Joint action and the Topical conversation. No

Table 8.2

Structural Patterns of Interactions in Dyadic Sessions:
Absolute Frequencies and Mean Percentages for Dyads in Two Age Groups

Dyad number	Interaction patterns			
	Own activity (OA)	Other child's activity (OCA)	Joint activity (JA)	Topical conversation (TC)
3-year-olds[a,c]	(60.2)	(14.6)	(13.0)	(11.4)
1	12	6	1	0
2	20	2	5	2
3	10	4	0	6
4	23	2	8	3
5	9	4	2	3
4-year-olds[b,c]	(34.3)	(16.7)	(26.5)	(22.5)
1	9	2	7	2
2	3	3	0	3
3	6	4	5	14
4	4	3	4	3
5	13	5	11	1
Both groups[a]	(48.4)	(15.6)	(19.1)	(16.5)

[a]OA > (OCA = JA = TC) by Friedman tests; 3-year-olds $S = 9.24$, $p < .05$; combined groups, $S = 13.89$, $p < .01$.

[b]OA = OCA = JA = TC by Friedman tests, ns.

[c]Cross age comparison: 3-year-old OA > 4-year-old OA by Mann-Whitney tests, $U = 3.5$, $p < .05$. All other comparisons = ns.

increase was observed for the Other child's action pattern. These shifts, however, do not constitute significant changes in pattern distribution (see Table 8.2).

The general picture obtained from this analysis is that, for younger and older children alike, the majority of interactions are structured around activities focused on actions with objects and around discourse that initiates and sustains these activities as compared to verbal interactions that comprise topical conversations.

CHARACTERIZATION OF THE DYADIC SESSION

In the situation in which our children found themselves, their dyadic sessions evolved within a fairly constant format with similar temporal properties. The format consisted of lengthy spans of interactivity interspersed with breaks for individual activity. In general, the children preferred to open their activity for the participation of another child; they also, but to a far lesser degree, entered uninvited into the other's activity. Note that the preferred pattern (Own action), to be successful, required the readiness of the participating child to relinquish momentarily his or her own ongoing activity in favor of turning to that of the initiator. Apparently, another child's activities have strong drawing power, as testified to by the response readiness of the child participant. The less-used pattern, on the other hand, (Other child's action), required the initiator to drop his or her own activity in order to join that of the noninitiating child. The explicit initiating act that characterizes the Own action pattern, by calling upon the other child to participate, marks the opening of the initiator's activity to accommodate that participation.

A major outcome of this process may be a mutual building up of knowledge about each other's actions, ways of acting and talking, by participation in one another's action fields. It is a logical step, then, for children to initiate concerted action (use of the Joint action pattern) once they are informed through experience of interaction with a similar child acquired by use of simpler patterns, such as those referred to as Own action and Other child's action.

How Children Pursue Their Activity in Dyadic Conditions

In the light of the descriptions obtained in the analyses of the dyadic session, the issue was considered of the self- versus social-activity distinction. Does the child, in the pursuance of actions originating in him or herself, seek primarily conditions of separateness, or does the child exploit the social conditions afforded in the dyadic situation by seeking the participation of another child in his or her pursuits? As the question implies, self-activity is not treated as synonymous with solitary activity, as is apparently the case in the literature on preschooler's social participation, (e.g., Smith & Connolly, 1972, p. 80). In line with our conception, the child is envisaged as an agent striving to execute intelligible activity. Thus it is not a matter of indifference for such a young agent to recognize him or herself as the "author" of activities. One might anticipate that a child, as he or she strives towards ends that have yet to come into being, would welcome the participation of a similar agent in a manner analogous to that in which the younger child calls upon the mother to look on, listen, comment, and actively participate (Shugar, 1978). At the same time, the child who seeks to maintain prime control over his or her enterprises requires time for organizing these activities, that is, time to independently focus upon his or her proper activity. The evidence of the foregoing section supports this view. We found that if 3-year-olds engage in interaction in the course of a dyadic session, which is usually the case, they will do so mainly by gaining the social participation of the other child in his or her ongoing activity. Their favorite way of initiating interaction is by establishing self-initiated activity as their dominant base. Yet some time always remains during which they are disengaged from social interaction and occupy themselves with their own enterprises.

With these considerations in mind, we addressed the following questions using the basic data from the analyses of the dyadic session. The first question concerned the extent to which children used the time at their disposal to follow their own activity pursuits, either separately and alone, or socially with a participant. The second question concerned the effects of the pursuit of individual activity upon the interaction in the dyadic session. How did our subjects reconcile the requirements of individual activity with their interactional propensities?

We started by measuring the duration of children's self-originated activities.

DURATION OF ACTION LINES IN ISOLATION
VERSUS SOCIAL CONDITIONS

Treating only the formal properties of the data, leaving aside qualitative aspects of children's activity, we followed the behavior stream of each child through the course of the dyadic session.

Analyses

The procedure was based on identifying the points of origin for any activity commenced and sustained by a single child and measuring its duration. The sum of durations comprised a total for the given child. The behavioral flow fell naturally into the temporal segments already distinguished in the dyadic session of which the given child was a member, segments distinguished as noninteractive and interactive. By definition, self-originated activity excluded unoccupied time, time devoted to joint action (according to the pattern thus labeled in the section on "How Children Participate in the Dyadic Situation: Basic Data.") However, procedures had to be adapted to the behavior stream organization of the child which allows for the co-occurrence of more than one focus of activity (Shugar, 1976). Thus a child might continue an ongoing self-originated activity while also participating in other ongoing activities, such as conversational activity. The phenomenon of overlapping of self-originated activity and of participation in other than self-originated activity is reflected in the results shown in Table 8.3. A "rounded" unit of fifteen seconds (corresponding to the time block used to synchronize behavior streams in the transcription records) was employed as the time measure. The analysis of reliability rests solely

Table 8.3
Duration of Individual and Joint Action Lines

Action Line Types	Proportional duration[a]	
	3-year-olds	4-year-olds
Individual action lines[b]		
Mean	49.2	55.7
Pursued in *isolated* conditions		
Mean	20.6	31.2
Range	0.0 – 91.2	0.0 – 100.0
Pursued in *interactional* conditions		
Mean	28.7	24.5
Range	0.0 – 74.2	0.0 – 44.8
Joint action lines[c]		
Mean	14.0	26.9
Range	0.0 – 30.0	25.6 – 47.8

[a]Durations proportional to total session length ($=100\%$).
[b]Calculated for all dyadic members (i.e., including members of noninteracting dyadic sessions), $N = 12$ at each age.
[c]Calculated for interacting dyadic sessions only (i.e., joint product of interacting dyadic members, $N = 5$ at each age.

upon intra-analyzer consistency in application of the procedures. A margin of error must be assumed due to the complexity of the raw data. Owing to the gross nature of the analysis, the results are orientational.

Findings

Results of analyses are best illustrated by the example of a single dyadic session. Let us take a session in which the dyadic members are mix-sexed 3-year-olds. The boy spent 91% of the total duration of the session in self-originated activity, of which the major part (75%) was spent in social conditions, that is, with the invited participation of the girl. Notice that this form of interaction has been referred to in the foregoing section as the Own action pattern, in which the initiator's line of action dominates, the partner being drawn into that line. Only a minor part of the boy's activity (7%) was spent on his own. The other dyadic member, on the other hand, used only 8% of the total duration of the session in self-originated activity, all spent in social conditions, either with the invited or uninvited participation of the boy. Notice that the latter form of interaction has been referred to earlier as the Other child's action pattern, in which the initiator enters the partner's line of action without being called in. In this session, then, the "prime agent" was mainly the boy, and the "participatory agent" mainly the girl. Furthermore, the two children spent 13% of the total duration of the session in joint activity (according to the pattern so labeled), thus constructing a line for which they were co-agents.

If we sum the durations of the two children's individual (self-originated) action lines, we obtain 89% of total time (about 13 min) spent in their pursuit; the sum of the durations of these action lines pursued in interactional conditions is 82% of total time (about 12 min). Taking into account the 13% (about 2 min) spent in joint action line pursuit, we obtain an overlap (89 + 13) of 2% (about 18 s) of concurrent pursuit of individual action lines and joint lines. To account for all the time for both children, we need only note that, while the boy pursued his action line alone (isolated conditions) for 7% of the total time (about 1 min), the girl's corresponding time was unoccupied.

In transposing these data into the means for dyadic members, as presented in Table 8.3, we take the mean for the two children's percentage values as follows: for individual action lines, 44.5%; pursued in isolated conditions, 3.5%; and pursued in interactional conditions, 41.0%. However, the percentage value for joint action lines (13%) is treated as a single value for the dyadic pair.

The data from the analysis for 12 dyadic sessions are summarized in Table 8.3. Individual action lines refer to the self-originated activity of each of 24 dyadic members. Joint action lines refer to the line of activity constructed together by the 2 dyadic members.

The composite mean values, calculated separately for each age bracket, show the extent of overall similarity across the children. Individual action lines for both age brackets tended to last one-half the total session and were conducted to similar extents in isolated and in interactional conditions. But the 3-year-olds spent somewhat more time in interactional conditions than in isolated ones and, conversely, the 4-year-olds spent somewhat more time in isolated conditions than in interactional ones. Further, on the basis of mean duration values for joint action lines, the 4-year-olds tended to devote more time than the 3-year-olds to this pattern of interaction, averaging twice as much time. Comparing the mean durations for individual and joint action lines across age brackets, we note a greater temporal overlap for the 4-year-olds. This would reflect the fact that, to a greater extent than for the 3-year-olds, these children conducted simultaneously different lines of activity.

In short, the temporal dimension of children's self-originated action lines turns out to be an important factor in the building of the dyadic session, taking priority and precedence over durations of the joint line of action. The growing importance of the latter for the 4-year-olds is not likely to be irrelevant to the fact that the 3-year-olds conduct much of their own activities in the course of interaction. The strong tendency to draw a participant into the self-originating activity presumably exists mutually in the dyadic situation, at least to some degree. But its realization for both children is, for obvious reasons, mutually exclusive—a situation which is seemingly paradoxical. How do the children resolve the problem of coexistence of two individual action lines displaying this same tendency?

MUTUAL ACCOMMODATION
OF INDIVIDUAL ACTION LINES

As the broad range of mean values indicates (Table 8.3), many possibilities are open for establishing terms of coexistence of individual action lines in the dyadic situation. Basically, these differences relate to the extent to which one child develops the temporal dimension of his or her own activity, and how much he or she limits it in favor of participation in that of the other child. We argue that some accommodation must be worked out in the management of action line duration before children's interactivity can take on the character of joint action.

Such accommodation can be exemplified in the dyadic session described above. In this session of 3-year-olds, the boy developed the durational dimension of his proper activity over the course of the session, while the girl limited hers accordingly, thus rendering herself available to act on call as a participant in the boy's activity. At the same time, the girl, however slightly she developed her own line of activity, maintained interactional conditions mainly by drawing in the other child. Hence both children were once prime agents of their own activities and once participatory agents in those of the other, but to greatly different extents. In this way, they constructed a highly interactive dyadic session, in the course of which they together originated a joint action line of a certain duration. What characterizes this session is the combination of a high-durational line with a low-durational one. Individual action lines with these relational features achieve compatibility by eliminating potentially competing action lines. Two action lines with equally strong durational properties would be incompatible for pursuance in interactional conditions, but would be compatible for pursuance in solitary conditions. This surmise found confirmation in our analyses of the observed dyadic sessions.

An equitable arrangement, permitting a high level of interactivity, would be a modulated action line, making for reciprocation of the interactional roles of prime and participatory agency. This prediction was also confirmed in our analyses, as a type of compatibility found only in the 4-year-old sessions, that is, in the age bracket that also developed the more durable interactions based on joint action (Shugar, 1982).

In summary, so far the answers found to the question posed in this study, using a relatively imprecise methodology, point to the social factor in self-activity, the manifestation of which seems to be incontestable if these analyses are valid. There appears to be a mutual attractiveness about what the other child is doing that rivals the value of self-activity, underlying the greater reciprocity of interactional roles in the children with more experience. In the younger children, a prior stage may provide important experience in which, through the display of their growing agentive powers to peers, children provide each other with fields of observation and participation and sources for learning agentive activity. The social nature of self-activity, as understood here, is revealed in the dyadic session of same-age peers. Results also suggest a dynamic factor operating in the dyadic situation, an impulsive force for pursuing activities through coordinations of agentive roles.

How Children Perceive Their Action Fields
in the Dyadic Situation

The question of how children use space has been related to their manner of conducting discourse (see the section on "How Children Participate in the Dyadic Situation: Basic Data"). Among the verbal procedures employed by the children that we have observed for initiating and sustaining social interaction is the combination of a proxemic component with a linguistic one. The spatial component serves to give the listener perceptual access to the speaker's action field. As our discourse analyses show, the area that is accessed is the field in which the speaker's activity is already located. Spatial relations between children in the dyadic situation may be a factor in the way both proxemic and linguistic components are utilized.

In this section, spatial fields will be investigated and their relation to linguistic components tested. The present topic follows logically from the foregoing one, which considered the durational aspect of activity and its importance for determining forms of social interaction. A site of activity is necessary for that activity to develop temporally, allowing it to follow a planned and organized course. We will present research that demonstrates that the agent of located activity takes a particular attitude to the place of his or her activity, and keeps it for the duration of his or her activity. The research will also show that the same child who appropriates a field for him or herself will attribute a field to the second child as well in the dyadic situation. In certain proxemic conditions, the child will consider both to share a common field, while in other proxemic conditions, the child will consider each to possess a separate field.

This research is presented in two parts, the first dealing with the source of the hypothesis, the second with the experiment and its findings.

UTTERANCES CHILDREN USE TO START SOCIAL
INTERACTIONS: THE PROXEMIC FACTOR

The suspicion that the spatial factor may be playing a more specific and determinative role in how children start social interaction than could be judged from other studies (Mueller, 1972; Mueller et al., 1977; Shugar, 1979) arose in the course of a detailed observational analysis of the initiation process in preschool dyads, based on a portion of the raw data described in the section on "How Children Participate in the Dyadic Situation: Basic Data" (Bokus, 1982). This study, which confirmed the predominance of the pattern of interaction initiation by which the initiator draws the respondent into the former's ongoing activity, undertook to examine this initiation process in finer detail. It has been noted that initiation of any form of social interaction involves an utterance and its response and that, although the initial utterance does not necessarily display direct elicitational properties, it produces the effect of drawing the listener into the speaker's action field. An inspection of the entire list of utterances in this category led to two groupings: utterances of an ostensive character (calling and indicating some element in the action field), hence manifesting elicitational features (e.g., "Look—see this") and utterances of a descriptive or reportative nature, seldom associated with eliciting features (e.g., "I'm gonna be a cowboy, y'know" or "Tracks and wagon for a train, I'm making," [translated from the Polish]). Antecedent behaviors of these utterances were then examined, and it was found that a perceptual act occurred with high frequency just prior to either type of utterance. This was a brief (1–2 s) visual scan terminating at the point of location of the other child. When the distance between the child was small ($\leq$ 65 cm) the descriptive utterance type followed, and when the distance was greater ($\geq$ 95 cm), the ostensive type occurred.

The regularity with which this difference was noted in initiatory utterances caused us to speculate on why children should use different speech procedures to draw a partner into interactive play in accordance with such a minimal proxemic variable, and why listeners should respond reliably to one or the other type of utterance in the two proxemic conditions. To verify the observations, an experiment was conducted (Bokus, 1982; Bokus & Shugar, 1981). The hypothesis will be quoted in full.

> In a dyadic free-play situation children start interaction with a same-age partner by constructing utterances according to two different patterns depending on the proxemic relation of their action fields; short utterances lacking in referential content when the mutual distance is greater, and longer utterances with fuller referential content when the mutual distance is lesser. Further, empirical evidence would be sought for the role of an intervening variable of perceptual assessment, that is, that the children actually gauge the relation holding between their action

fields in terms of separateness or commonality. These perceptual assessments would be strongly linked to proxemic relations between the action fields. (Bokus & Shugar, 1981, p. 6.)

The experiment yielded results in support of the hypothesis, as stated above. In this report, we shall be more interested in the evidence obtained from the subjects to the effect that they understood play spaces in the category of "action field" belonging either to both or solely to themselves.

HOW CHILDREN APPROPRIATE SPACE AS ACTION FIELD

The experiment will be sketched briefly (reported in detail in Bokus & Shugar, 1981). The technique used employed a "third child" in the situation. The latter was introduced to ascertain what effects the child would exert on an already existing dyadic situation (Nadel–Brulfert & Baudonnière, 1982). In this case, interest centered on the events prior to the entry of the third child.

Subjects

The subjects were 24 unacquainted same-age pairs of children, 6 pairs in each of 4 half-year age brackets, from 3 to 5 years. Twelve pairs were mixed, 6 girls and 6 boys. All 48 children attended nursery school.

Setting

The experiment took place in a natural nursery school setting. The playroom measuring approximately 3.4 by 6.5 m and containing toys.

Design and Procedure

A structured play session was conducted by a partially participating adult (Bokus), whose interventions in the children's ongoing play were prearranged and systematically controlled, thus ensuring the naturalness and spontaneity of the children's behaviors. A pair of children were introduced into the room "to play." By observing their play through a screen, the experimenter was able to select a moment to enter the room when the children had begun social interaction under the design requirements of a given spatial condition. The experimenter informed the children that a third child would be coming in and inquired where that child might play. The responses were invariably of the type: "over there," with a vague hand wave. The experimenter then conducted a structured interview with each child separately in order to obtain exact information as to where the newcomer could be located. (During the dialogue with one child, the other child was given a task to perform blindfolded as part of the game). Any speech overheard would be noninformative. The interview was framed so that the child verbally and nonverbally defined his or her own play area as well as that of the other child, using chalk or small objects to mark the boundaries of the areas. Tape recordings were made with a concealed microphone. The independent variable was inter-child distance. In one condition (close), the inter-child distance was $\leq$ 65 cm, and in the other (far), $\geq$ 95 cm. Each subject was questioned in both conditions with questions alternating between subjects. The session lasted about 20 min.

Results

The data obtained from the children's responses to the experimenter's queries and requests were both nonverbal and verbal and will be discussed separately.

In general, all subjects attributed a delineated area to self in both inter-child spatial conditions. The self-appropriated area was always excluded from space declared available to the newcomer on the grounds that it belonged to the present speaker. All subjects also attributed a delineated area to the other child in both spatial conditions, which was also always excluded from space declared available to the newcomer on the grounds that it belonged to that other child. However, the relationship between the areas attributed to self and to the other differed significantly in the two spatial conditions. In the *closer* situation, the majority of the 48 children (73%) perceived their own and their partner's action fields as one shared field, while in the *farther* situation, the majority again (77%) perceived their own and their partner's fields as two separate areas. Response distributions are given in Table 8.4, where detailed data are included to show how the same

Table 8.4

Child Patterns of Action Field Assessment under Varied Proxemic Conditions[a]

	Close proximity*		
	Isolated	Shared	Total
Far proximity			
Isolated	11	26	37
Shared	2	9	11
Total	13	35	48

[a]For example, eleven subjects who judged their action field as isolated in the far proxemic condition (> 95 cm) also judged their field as isolated in the close proxemic condition (< 65 cm), $N = 48$.

*$p < .001$, $X^2 = 20.6$, McNemar's test for dependent pairs.

children made the assessment in the two spatial conditions. As it turned out, there were as many as 26 children (54% of the total) who assessed the two situations in the same differentiated manner. Thus, in the *closer* situation, they ascribed to themselves a field of action in common with the partner, while in the *farther* situation, they ascribed separate fields for themselves and for their partners. The significance of the differences in field arrangement assessments according to the inter-child distance factors, as given in Table 8.4, holds as well for each age group of 24 children taken separately (McNemar's test = 10.285, $p < .01$).

A check was made to ascertain whether the factors of object content of the action fields, or type of actions with objects, occurring simultaneously with perceptual assessment, affected the results. It turned out that, when fields were perceived as separate, object contents of these fields were in one case similar and in 48 cases dissimilar (98% dissimilarity), and when perceived as shared, object contents were in 4 cases similar and in 42 cases dissimilar (91% dissimilarity). As concerns the type of action pursued by the children on the objects in the field, it turned out that, when fields were perceived as separate, children's actions were similar only in 4 cases (92% dissimilarity), and when fields were perceived as shared, their actions were similar only in 9 cases (80% dissimilarity). Clearly these factors did not control the perceptual assessment of separateness or sharedness of action fields.

Nonverbal Presentation of the Action Field

During the interview, after the child had indicated an area declared as his or her own or that of the other child or that of both, the experimenter requested the child to "show me where, exactly, with this chalk" (or blocks). The relevant dimensions were noted (measurements could conveniently be estimated by counting parquet floor boards). Typical shapes of the delineated areas are presented schematically in Figures 8.1 and 8.2.

The shapes produced by our subjects differed systematically for isolated and shared field perceptions. When fields were perceived as isolated (Figure 8.1), the shapes were typically circular for both self and partner. For the subject's own field, the circumference was more or less traced at arm's length, while for the other child, the circumference was somewhat smaller. Location of the children's bodies within these areas differed according to the inter-child distance. When the distance was greater than 125 cm (Fig. 8.1a), the subject located both children, self and other, at the hub of the circles (33% of all cases). When the distance was between 95 and 125 cm (Fig. 8.1b and 8.1c), child-to-circumference distance was shortened on the side of each partner, thus allowing more space behind each of the children and less space between them (31% of all cases) (Fig. 8.1b). In fewer cases

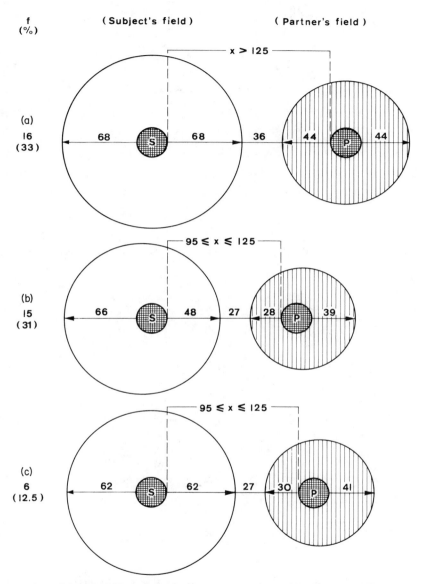

Figure 8.1. Typical shapes of isolated action fields. Distance is in centimeters.

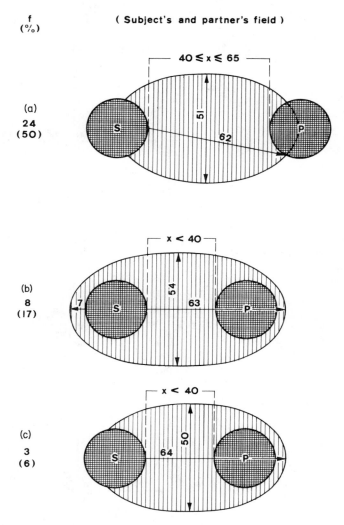

Figure 8.2. Typical shapes of shared action fields. Distance is in centimeters.

(12%), however, the subject maintained his or her own location at the hub of the circle (Fig. 8.1c). The remaining cases of isolated action field perception (24%) did not assume the described shapes. The main point is that invariably the children concretized lines distinguishing unequivocally between that space seen as belonging to self and that belonging to the other child.

In the case of shared field perception (Fig. 8.2), one single area was demarcated, the shape of which was typically elliptical, with both children's bodies located on the border or inside the ellipse. When the inter-child distance was between 40 and 65 cm (Fig. 8.2a), the subject allowed for no play space to the rear of either: all space in common lay between the two. This occurred in half of the cases of shared field perception. When the children were even closer (less than 40 cm) (Fig. 8.2b and 8.2c), the size and shape of the ellipse were not altered, but common space was included to the rear of both the subject and the other child (17% of all cases) (Fig. 8.2b), or to the rear only of the partner (6%) (Fig. 8.2c). The demarcations of the remainder of shared field perceptions were not so clearcut (27%).

The regularity with which these shapes were produced by our subjects came as a surprise; nothing we knew about children's voluntary play space arrangements was suggestive of such patterning in the allocation of action fields. Presumably some principles must have guided the children in differentiating their spatial configurations, and we interpret these as principles of control and accessibility. The arm's reach radius of the circular fields speaks for direct physical control over the field, as well as access to its contents. The same applies for the elliptically shaped fields but with a reduction of the area in mutual arm's reach to the narrowed portion lying vis-a-vis, on which both children are presumably mainly focused. But the rear areas also taken into account in the elliptical configuration are not so easily explained. The evidence that rear space was deliberately attributed to both as part of the shared areas was established by the experimenter's additional queries at the moment when the child was in the act of marking them out. In answer to the direct queries: "Is he (she) playing here too?" (experimenter pointing to the space to the rear of the subject just marked out) and "Are you playing here too?" (experimenter pointing to the space to the rear of the other child just marked out by the subject), the responses were typically affirmative, thus confirming verbally the state of commonness established by the nonverbal act of delineation.

The striking aspect of the phenomenon is that the child, in demarcating a common field, is acting as if he or she were taking into account the perspective of the other child as well as his or her own perspective. This perspective refers to direct physical control and content accessibility for the other child as well as for self.

The Verbal Presentation of the Action Field

Three verbal modes were noted whereby children presented the action fields (own, partner's, and shared). These were by deictic indication only, by definition in terms of place, and by description with reference to an actual location in the real world. The last mentioned mode produced descriptions differing in the degree of specificity with which they related to the activity occurring in the action field. Some were nonspecific, that is, a setting for various activities, for example, backyard, playground, park, plot (approximate translation of terms of Polish nursery school talk), while others were quite specific in terms of the activity pursued by the speaking child, for example, garage, theatre, railway station, airport.

The three verbal modes were employed with different frequency. In presenting any of the fields, the most common modes were deictic indication only and description; it was rare for the child to use a mere identifying term, such as "place" (maximum 6% for isolated fields and 11% for shared fields). Further discussion will concern only the two more frequent modes.

Deictic indications were employed most often in only two cases: in presenting the partner's field as isolated (62%) and in presenting the shared field (52%). Much less frequently were descriptions used in these cases (32% and 37%, respectively), and when they were presented in this mode, nonspecific names were mainly used (22% for both fields). It was noted that, when specific descriptions were employed (5 cases, or 10%, for the partner's field, and 7 cases, or 15% for the shared field), both children were using similar objects and were conducting similar activity. In other words, the field which concerned the other child was defined as an actual place in the real world; it underlined the meaning of the activity only in the case when the speaker's activity was similar to that of the partner.

The latter point is of interest in view of the fact that the speaker, in presenting his or her own action field, used primarily the descriptive mode (70%); of which in 15 cases (30%) descriptions were nonspecific and in 20 cases (40%) specific. In only 12 cases (24%) the child's own action field was presented by deictic indication.

In presenting *the child's own field and that of the partner as isolated,* the child displayed two ways of delineating and presenting verbally: (1) by marking the boundaries of the child's own field, and immediately contrasting it with that of the partner (spontaneously, without the experimenter's query); and (2) by marking the boundaries of the child's own field, and presenting it noncontrastively, after which the boundaries of the partner's field were marked and presented (in response to the experimenter's queries in sequential order). Examples of the *contrastive* presentation are the following:

1. "My yard is here and she's got hers there."
2. "This is just for me and that boy's place is over there."
3. "Here's my place to play, not the boy's, it's mine, he's playing on his place."

Examples of the *noncontrastive* presentation include:

4. Own field: "I'm working here. My store takes all this room."
   Partner's field: "That boy is playing over there."
5. Own field: "I'm a garage man. My garages . . . one, two, two, and one, and three, (pointing to places around cars) and here too."
   Partner's field: "That girl is playing here."
6. Own field: "See! My park is this big, with a swing."
   Partner's field: "He's playing trains over there, he's got a station."

In presenting the *shared field,* delineated by elliptical configuration, the commonness was underlined, often redundantly, as in the following examples:

Examples of *deictic* indication

7. "I'm playing here and she's playing here. We're playing together here and here."
8. "Johnny is playing here with me."
9. "Here and here we're playing, Kasia (self) and that little boy."

Examples of *definition*

10. "We've got a big place to play, me and her."
11. "Together we've got this much, me and her, we're playing here."
12. "We've got lots of place to play, I'm playing here and she can play here too."

Examples of *description*

13. "That's our school, where we're playing. Together. It's a school."
14. "Here's our work (factory), it's here."
15. "We've got a big palace full of fairy tales."
    (Translations from the Polish are close approximations—G. W. S.)

ASPECTS OF IMPORTANCE

There are a number of aspects which seem to be important about the reported experiment. It underlines a different approach to research on children's spatial organization than, for instance, the ethological (McGrew, 1974; Strayer, 1978, 1980), by foregrounding the issue of the meaning of space for the persons who are organizing it (Corsaro, 1979; Shugar, 1979). Space, like time, is treated as an integral part of the structure of activity, which is a spatio–temporal organization, as stressed by some action theories (Tomaszewski, 1967). Preschool children have been shown in this study to use space and to transform it as a basic component of their actions over time, and, furthermore, to be aware of doing so.

The study is also an example of the approach we have advocated to children's discourse analysis, in which two components, linguistic and proxemic, are posited. Children have been shown here to use their own action accompaniments not only for themselves but for the other child as well. Thus they obtain in this fashion social interest in their activity and this leads to social interaction. Furthermore, the result is in line with the argument presented in the section called "Discourse in the Peer Situation." Children seem to know what these utterances are for, as the expression of agentive thinking and endeavor, and they display a tacit understanding about the availability of utterance content for use by both expressions. Thus children control the proxemic factor for discourse purposes while maintaining the autonomy of their own activities.

A third aspect, consequent to the foregoing two, is the evidence obtained for the psychological reality of the notions of action field, agents and their attributes, and actions and their necessary dimensions. The reality of these notions, as well as the awareness of them manifested in preschoolers, cannot have crystallized in a social vacuum, since they are communicated both verbally and nonverbally in social-evaluative terms, such as in prerogatives and privileges over the physical aspects of activity. The evidence is that these social-evaluative aspects are recognized by children with respect to themselves and to others and govern their mutual relations. This suggests that they are products of social processes in the peer world of preschoolers that we have as yet hardly begun to grasp.

Conclusion

This chapter has attempted to develop a fresh approach to children's language and activity whereby children are treated as agents of activity and are perceived as treating one another in the same manner. Evidence is based on the interpretations of children's language as it is related to their activity. In concluding this chapter, discussion will center on some implications for a better understanding of preschool peer relationships.

RELEVANCE TO THE LITERATURE
OF SOCIAL PARTICIPATION

What light, if any, does the study of children in dyadic situations shed upon the multi-child situation typical of preschoolers' life in playgroups and nursery schools, where these school children's social formations are usually observed? It is evident that the social formations found in the dyadic situation do not correspond directly to those apparent in the multi-child setting. The processes revealed in the minimal social unit may not occur in the same way in the differing conditions of a more complex social unit. However, certain extrapolations may be ventured.

On the grounds of process analyses of toddlers' interactions in the play group, it has been suggested that *parallel play* is the birthplace of peer social interaction (Mueller, 1979; Mueller & Vandell, 1979). Likewise, from our process analyses of preschoolers' interactions in the dyadic group, it might be suggested that *associative play* is the origin of the primary structures of interactions of children *as* activity organizers. From these structures are derived the concerted actions characteristic of jointly coordinated play in the group. The primary structures of interactions evolve through different kinds and degrees of social participation, which correspond to qualitatively different engagements in the social situation governed by privileges of agency. Thus, in selecting *onlooking,* the child focuses on gaining information about how other children pursue their activity, while holding his or her own in abeyance. In preferring *parallel play,* the child maintains the separation of his or her action line, ensuring its autonomy but gaining the advantage of access, perceptual and physical, to the actions and objects of others which he or she then can reproduce in variation. In selecting *associative play,* interpenetration of one another's action lines occurs with division into *prime and participatory agency roles.* Children who form neighborhoods create conditions of close proximity for alternating the dominance of one or another's action line and modulating the dominance of one over another. In evolving *cooperative play,* children negotiate the terms of joint participation in a common program of action, to which the activity of all is ordered.

Verification as to whether these or other speculations have a basis in reality would require new methods that overcome the static feature of direct observation based on time sampling. The momentary state of affairs, as Roper and Hinde (1978) have shown, tells us little about abilities. It tells us nothing about plans and planfulness; rather it portrays the cross-section of many children's momentary choices.

SOCIAL INTERACTION AND SOCIAL RELATIONSHIPS OF PRESCHOOLERS

According to Hinde (1979), research on short-term interactions takes us only part way toward understanding relationships. In drawing the distinction between the concepts of interaction and relationship, Hinde considers that relationships have properties that depend on patterning in time—in terms of their absolute and relative frequencies of interactions—but these properties are not present in the interactions themselves. What, then, is there in the single events of interactions that contribute to forming relationships? Hinde's answer is that "the proper initial assumption about any interaction . . . is that the nature of the interaction is a product of both partners" (1979, p. 16). The meaning of actions by acting individuals can become mutual. A relationship can be referred to when the participants "do not merely behave to each other in accordance with how each perceives the other now, but in accordance with what they expect each other to do next, next week, or at some indefinite time in the future" (1979, p. 26). We cite Hinde's formulations since they elucidate certain qualitative changes occurring in young children's interactions. Gathering experience in participation in peer interactions, children may be said to be forming peer relationships, in which the meaning of actions take precedence over actual behaviors. If one accepts that children interpret each other's behaviors in terms of shared meanings, as is becoming evident from various descriptive analyses (Brenner & Mueller, 1982), inferences must be made about children's own inferences if we wish to extend our understanding about the essential underlying nature of their relationships. Grounds for our inferences about children's inferences can be found only in the clarity and consistency with which accounts can be made of children's interactions. This appears to us to be an important methodological principle.

THE DEVELOPMENTAL VISTA

Prominence has been given in the present account to the notion of *agency* as an aspect of children's development, the aspect that has an originating and organizing function, and which permeates their language and governs its uses. A developmental vista that embraces both individual and social aspects of agency could be that offered by Shotter (1978):

> Men develop from beings able only at first to essay short sequences of action with vague and elementary meanings, into beings able to essay longer and longer sequences of activity involving more and more people, with greater and greater precision of meaning. (p. 56)

We advance this formulation as the developmental issue in the light of which to elucidate the process of constructing meaningful peer relations. Peer interactions may be those events that contribute essentially to the development of agency in both its aspects.

References

Barnes, K. (1971). Preschool play norms: A replication. *Developmental Psychology, 5,* 99–103.

Bokus, B. (1981). Initiating social interactions at the preschool age. A method of analysis and some results. *Polish Psychological Bulletin, 12,* 321–332.

Bokus, B. (1982). *Nawiazywanie interakeji spolecznch przez dzieci w mkodszym wieku przedszkolnym* [Initiation of social interaction by children in the early preschool years]. Unpublished doctoral dissertation, University of Warsaw.

Bokus, B., & Shugar, G. W. (1979). What will a three-year-kid say: An experimental study of situational variation. In O. K. Garnica & M. L. King (Eds.), *Language, children and society.* Oxford: Pergamon Press.

Bokus, B., & Shugar, G. W. (1981). What do young children say to start peer interaction? Some discourse processes at preschool age in the child–child dyadic relation. In C. Thew & C. Johnson (Eds.), *Proceedings of the Second International Congress for the Study of Child Language* (Vol. 2). Lanham, Maryland: University Press of America.

Brenner, J., & Mueller, E. (1982). Shared meaning in boy toddlers' peer relations. *Child Development, 53,* 380–391.

Brown, R. (1973). *A First language: the early stages.* Cambridge, MA: Harvard University Press.

Bruner, J. S. (1975). The ontogenesis of speech acts. *Journal of Child Language, 2,* 1–19.

Buhler, C. (1931). The social behavior of the child. In C. Murchison (Ed.), *A handbook of child psychology.* Worcester, MA: Clark University Press.

Connolly, K., & Bruner, J. (Eds.). (1974). *The growth of competence.* New York: Academic Press.

Corsaro, W. A. (1979). "We're friends, right?" Children's use of access ritual in a nursery school. *Language and Society, 8,* 315–336.

Donaldson, M. (1978). *Children's minds.* Glasgow: William Collins.

Dyner, W. J. (1971). *Zabawy tematyczne dzioci w domu i przodszkolu* [Children's thematic play at home and in nursery school], Wroclaw: Ossolinoum.

Eckerman, E. O., Whatley, J. L., & Kutz, S. L. (1975). Growth of social play with peers during second year of life. *Developmental Psychology, 11,* 42–45.

Elkonin, D. B. (1948). Psychological problems of play in the preschool years. In A. N. Leontiew & A. W. Zaporozec (Eds.), *Voprosy psichologii riebionka* [Problems of child psychology]. Moscow: APN SSSR.

Flament, F. (1982). Du système d'interactions sociales entre jeunes enfants: Dynamique et signification. *Bulletin d'Audiophonologie,* in press.

Flavell, J. (1977). *Cognitive development.* Englewood Cliffs: Prentice–Hall.

Garvey, C. (1974). Some properties of social play. *Merrill–Palmer Quarterly, 20* (3), 163–180.

Garvey, C. (1975). Requests and responses in children's speech. *Journal of Child Language, 2,* 41–63.

Garvey, C., & Berninger, G. (in press). Timing and turn taking in children's conversations. *Discourse Processes.*

Garvey, C., & Hogan, R. (1973). Social speech and social interaction: Egocentrism revisited. *Child Development, 44,* 562–568.

Gelman, R. (1978). Cognitive development. *Annual Review of Psychology, 29,* 297–332.

Herron, R., & Sutton-Smith, B. (Eds.). (1971). *Child's play,* New York: Wiley.

Hinde, R. A. (1979). *Towards understanding relationships.* London: Academic Press.

Hollander, M., & Wolfe, D. A. (1973). *Nonparametric statistical methods.* New York: Wiley.

Hurtig, M.- C., Hurtig, M., & Paillard, M. (1971). Jeux et activities des enfants de 4 a 6 ans dans la cour de recreation. *Enfance, 1–2,* 79–142.

Ingleby, D. (1974). The psychology of child psychology. In M. F. Richards (Ed.), *The integration of a child into a social world.* London: Cambridge University Press.

Keenan, E. O. (1974). Conversational competence in children. *Journal of Child Language, 1,* 163–185.

Keenan, E. O., & Schieffelin, B. B. (1976). Topic as a discourse notion: A study of topic in the conversations of children and adults. In C. Li (Ed.), *Subject and topic* (pp. 337–385). New York: Academic Press.

Lewis, M., & Feiring, C. (1979). The child's social network: social object, social function, and their relationship. In M. Lewis & L. A. Rosenblum (Eds.), *The child and its family*. New York: Plenum.

Lichtenberger, W. (1965). *Mitmenschlishes Verhalten eines Zwillingspaares in seinen ersten Lebensjahren.* (Social behavior of a pair of twins in the first year of life.) Munchen: Ernst Reinhardt.

Mackay, R. W. (1973). Conceptions of children and models of socialization. In H. P. Dreitzel (Ed.), *Recent sociology* (Vol. 5). London: Macmillan.

Maudry, M., & Nekula, N. (1939). Social relations between children of the same age during the first two years of life. *Journal of Genetic Psychology, 54,* 193–215.

McGrew, W. C. (1974). Interpersonal spacing of preschool children. In K. Connolly & J. Bruner (Eds.), *The Growth of competence.* London: Academic Press.

McTear, M. F. (1978, August). "Hey! I've got something to tell you": A study of the initiation of conversational exchanges by preschool children. Paper presented at 5th International Congress of Applied Linguistics, Montreal.

Moore, N. V., Evertson, C. M., & Brophy, J. E. (1974). Solitary play: Some functional reconsiderations. *Developmental Psychology, 10,* 830–834.

Mueller, E. (1972). The maintenance of verbal exchanges between young children. *Child Development, 43,* 930–938.

Mueller, E. (1979). (Toddlers + toys) = (an autonomous social system). In M. Lewis & L. A. Rosenblum (Eds.), *The child and its family,* New York: Plenum.

Mueller, E., & Lucas, T. (1975). A developmental analysis of peer interaction. In M. Lewis & L. A. Rosenblum (Eds.), *Friendship and peer relations,* New York: Wiley.

Mueller, E., & Rich, A. (1976). Clustering and socially-directed behaviors in a playgroup of one-year-olds. *Journal of Child Psychology and Psychiatry, 17,* 315–322.

Mueller, E., & Brenner, J. (1977). The origins of social skills and interaction among playgroup toddlers. *Child Development, 48,* 854–861.

Mueller, E., Bleier, M., Krakow, J., Hegedus, K., & Cournoyer, P. (1977). The development of peer verbal interaction among two-year-old boys. *Child Development, 48,* 284–287.

Mueller, E., & Vandell, D. (1979). Infant–infant interaction: A review. In J. D. Osofsky (Ed.), *Handbook of infant development* (pp. 591–622). New York: Wiley–Interscience.

Nadel-Brulfert, J., & Baudonniere, P. M. (1982). The social function of reciprocal imitation in two-year-old peers. *International Journal of Behavioral Development, 5,* 95–109.

Nelson, K., & Gruendel, J. M. (1979). At morning it's lunchtime: A scriptal view of children's dialogues. *Discourse Processes, 2,* 73–94.

Parten, M. B. (1932). Social participation among preschool children. *Journal of Abnormal and Social Psychology, 27,* 243–269.

Piaget, J. (1932). *The language and thought of the child.* New York: Harcourt.

Piaget, J. (1952). *The origins of intelligence in children.* New York: International Universities Press.

Piaget, J. (1962). *Play, dreams and imitation in childhood.* New York: Norton.

Roper, R., & Hinde, R. A. (1978). Social behavior in a play group: Consistency and complexity. *Child Development, 49,* 570–579.

Rose, S. A., Blank, M., & Spalter, I. (1975). Situational specificity of behavior in young children. *Child Development, 46,* 464–469.

Rubin, K. H., Maioni, T. L., & Hornung, M. (1976). Free play behaviors in middle- and lower-class preschoolers: Parten and Piaget revisited. *Child Development, 47,* 414–419.

Rubin, K. H., & Pepler, D. J. (1980). The relationship of child's play to social-cognitive growth and development. In H. C. Foot, A. J. Chapman, & J. R. Smith (Eds.), *Friendship and social relations in children*. Chichester: Wiley.

Shields, M. (1976). Some communicational skills of young children—a study of dialogue in the nursery school. Paper presented at the Psychology of Language Conference, Stirling.

Shields, M. (1978). The child as psychologist: Construing the social world. In A. Lock (Ed.), *Action, gesture and symbol: The emergence of language*. London: Academic Press.

Shields, M. (1979). Dialogue, Monologue and egocentric speech by children in nursery schools. In O. K. Garnica & M. L. King (Eds.), *Language, children and society*. Oxford: Pergamon Press.

Shotter, J. (1974). The development of personal powers. In M. P. Richards (Ed.), *The integration of a child into a social world*. London: Cambridge University Press.

Shotter, J. (1978). The cultural context of communication studies: Theoretical and methodological issues. In A. Lock (Ed.), *Action, gesture and symbol: The emergence of language*. London: Academic Press.

Shugar, G. W. (1976). Behavior stream organization during early language acquisition. *Polish Psychological Bulletin, 7,* 27–36.

Shugar, G. W. (1978a). Text analysis as an approach to the study of early linguistic operations. In N. Waterson & C. Snow (Eds.), *The development of communication*. Chichester: Wiley.

Shugar, G. W. (1978b). Child's intent: Functional development of early utterances. In G. Nickel (Ed.), *Proceedings of 4th International Congress of Applied Linguistics*. Stuttgart: HochschulVerlag.

Shugar, G. W. (1978c). A discourse analysis system applied to talk of children at age three to five. Paper presented at 5th International Congress of Applied Linguistics, Montreal.

Shugar, G. W. (1979). Peer face-to-face interactions at ages three to five. *International Journal of Psycholinguistics, 5-4,* 17–37.

Shugar, G. W. (1982). *Interakcja, Koordynacja linii dzialania i funkcjonowanie jezvkowe* (Interaction, coordination of action lines and functional language). Monografie psychologiczne *36.* Wroclaw: Ossolineum.

Shugar, G. W. (in press a). Early child discourse analyzed in the dyadic interaction unit. (Revised version of paper presented at the 22nd International Congress of Psychology, Leipzig, 1980.) *International Journal of Psycholinguistics.*

Shugar, G. W. (in press b). Action discourse and topical discourse in learning to use language. *Grazer Linguistische Studien.*

Smilansky, S. (1968). *The effects of sociodramatic play on disadvantaged children*. New York: Wiley.

Smith, P. K., & Connolly, K. (1972). Patterns of play and social interaction in preschool children. In H. Blurton Jones (Ed.), *Ethological Studies of Child Behaviour*. Cambridge: Cambridge University Press.

Speier, M. (1970). The everyday world of the child. In J. Douglas (Ed.), *Understanding everyday life*. Chicago: Aldine.

Strayer, F. F. (1978). L'organisation sociale chez des enfants d'âge préscolaire. *Sociologie et societés, 10,* 43–64.

Strayer, F. F. (1980). Child ethology and the study of preschool social relations. In H. C. Foot, A. J. Chapman, & J. R. Smith (Eds.), *Friendship and social relations in children*. Chichester: Wiley.

Szuman, S. (1955). *Rola dzialania w rozwoju umysłowym małego dziecka* [The Role of action in the mental development of the young child]. Wrocław: Ossolineum.

Tomaszewski, T. (1967). Aktywność czlowieka [Human activity]. In M. Maruszewski, J. Reykowski, & T. Tomaszewski (Eds.), *Psycholigia jako nauka o czlowieku* [Psychology as a science of man]. Warsaw: Kiazka i Wiedza.

Tomaszewski, T. (1975). Czlowiek i otoczenie [Man and environment]. In T. Tomaszewski (Ed.), *Psychologia* (3rd ed.,) pp. 13–36. Warszawa: PWN.

Vygotsky, L. S. (1966). Play and its role in the mental development of the child. *Soviet Psychology, 12* (6), 62–76.

CHAPTER 9

Organization of Social Play among Toddlers: An Ecological Approach

Mira Stambak and Mina Verba

Introduction

CRESAS (Centre de Recherches de l'Education Specialisée et de l'Adaptation Scolaire [Center for Research in Specialized Education and Educational Adaptation]) is a research center concerned with the ways and means of overcoming the difficulties encountered by children in crèches, kindergartens, and schools. (Crèches are public institutions in which children from 3 months to 3 years old regularly spend the day. The centers are open weekdays from 7 A.M. to 7 P.M.) This research focuses on the improvement of conditions of life in the educational set-up rather than on efforts to determine what in the individual child may create behavioral problems, since we assume that it is precisely this set-up which is the principal source of the difficulties. Several studies (CRESAS, 1978, 1981) have shown that the same children who in one context are nonparticipant, passive and unresponsive, are curious, inventive, active and communicative in another context. Children who do poorly in school, and who are often labeled "mentally defective" by psychologists can, in certain contexts, prove to have similar learning and reasoning abilities as good students.

The term "context" has to be taken in a wide sense: it does not refer only to the material environment (e.g., buildings, classrooms, toys, books) and educational methods, but also, and mainly, to the nature of the interindividual relationships that develop between all the persons present in the educational set-up (children, teachers and other staff). The children's be-havior varies according to these relationships, particularly those between the children and the adults, and among the children themselves.

These results encouraged us to choose an ecological orientation for our studies, and to create different environmental contexts in order to under-stand their influences on children's behavior. This ecological approach is also prominent in our studies of young children's peer relations which are of interest for us because in our first contacts with the crèches, we observed that children under two years old spontaneously form small groups of two or three, that they could often communicate successfully, and that they could carry out activities together harmoniously. This finding goes against current opinion in France, according to which peer relations at an early age tend to be rare, short-lived, and often aggressive.

This opinion, frequently and forcibly expressed, has influenced educa-tional practice in crèches: Adult–child relations are stressed rather than child–child relations, and staff are encouraged to follow a mother-infant model in dealing with children. Since, however, for many staff members such a model is not readily attainable, this recommendation may create feelings of uneasiness. In these circumstances, it is not surprising that peer relations among very young children have hardly been studied, and that they have not been taken into account in the organization of crèches. If, however, our observations of sustained and harmonious interactions among very young children can be systematized and their ecological parameters ana-lyzed through research, it should be possible for crèches to be organized in such a way as to be conducive to the development of peer relations that will enhance the children's social, cognitive, and communicative compe-tence.

ENVIRONMENTAL FACTORS IN PEER INTERACTIONS AMONG YOUNG CHILDREN

From earlier research, and, more generally, from our observations in crèches and kindergartens, two conditions stand out as being particularly important in influencing peer interaction:

1. The attitude of the adults present (educational staff and researchers)
2. The number of children in the group (Stambak, Bonica, Maisonnet, Rayna, & Verba, 1979)

Harmonious and varied interactions were observed when:

1. The adults present adopt an attitude that may be qualified as "non-directive but interested"; without intervening directly in the children's activities, and the adults manifest interest in what is going on.

2. Three to eight children are together; groups of this size appear to favor dynamic interactions extending to all members of the group.

These conditions of adult attitude and size of group were kept constant in all our studies of peer relations among young children, since they appeared to be optimal for the observation of numerous interactions. What was varied was the type of objects placed at the children's disposal, since previous research (Sinclair, Stambak, Lezine, Rayna, & Verba, 1982) showed that particular collections of objects incited children to particular activities. In that research, children were observed singly and it appeared that when they were presented with certain familiar small objects and toys, their activities were often imitative, developing into "pretend" or "symbolic" play; collections of several identical objects led to prelogical activities such as collecting, seriating and establishing one-to-one correspondences, whereas several unfamiliar small objects (tubes, strings, cotton wool, etc.) led to the exploration of physical properties and to the construction of new objects.

In our first study of peer relations (Stambak, et al., 1979), the latter collection of small objects was presented to groups of four children between the ages of 18 and 24 months, seated together at a small table. In a subsequent study, different objects were used, e.g., big cardboard cases that were easily pushed by the children and were roomy enough for two of them to get inside, and cylindrical containers that could be used as drums and were light enough to be lifted by the children. These big objects led to many varied activities, and, especially, incited the children to organize different kinds of social play in which the presence of playmates was more important than the presence of the objects themselves.

SOME GENERAL FINDINGS DERIVED FROM THE FIRST TWO STUDIES CHILDREN OF 18–24 MONTHS

The modes of interaction are strikingly different according to whether the children interact in object-centered activities or in social play where their attention is mainly focused on their partners (Musatti, 1979; Stambak et al., 1979; Verba, Stambak, & Sinclair, 1982). In the first study (Stambak et al., 1979), with the collection of small objects mentioned above, the same activities were observed as when the children played alone. They explored the properties of the different objects, "experimented" (e.g., they inserted small sticks into the tubes, varying the angle at which they held the tube and observing how the stick slid out of it) and constructed "new objects" (e.g., a stick with a piece of cotton wool at one of its extremities). However, the presence of the other children led to frequent interactions. Intricate sequences of related activities were observed, during which the ideas of one member of the group were taken up by one or several others. The children looked at one another, each individual pursued an activity similar to the others with an object he or she had chosen, and their related activities were a continuous source of reciprocal inspiration.

For example, Child A takes a small rod and slips a bead into it (action a1), then slips the bead off and on again several times (action a2). Child B watches Child A, takes a ball of modelling clay and a rod, and proceeds to push it into the clay (action b1). A adds a second, and then a third bead to the first one (actions a3 and a4). B observes A, takes a bead from him or her and adds it to the ball of clay on the rod (action b2). The two children achieve, one after the other, similar results with different objects.

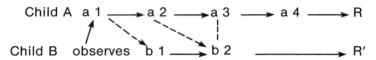

Thus, parallel activities of exploration and construction are organized in a process of imitative actions leading to similar results (Verba et al., 1982).

In the second study (with large cardboard boxes and cylindrical containers), the kinds of activities noted were different (Verba et al., 1979). We observed, in particular, children engaged in social play such as peek-a-boo games, object exchanges, etc. The themes of these shared activities often corresponded to those observed by other researchers (Bruner, 1975; Mueller & Brenner, 1977). In these games, each participant's responses to the proposals and demands of the other(s) are necessary for the continuation of the shared activities; the interactions are organized as in a dialogue, with one child responding to the initiations of another, and each partner having a different role.

In this paper, only episodes of social play are presented. In earlier work, we have been impressed by the fact that such young children can "invent" a game using spatial features of the room (the space under a bed) or of the objects (the flap of a cardboard box) as organizational elements in their play, and find ways of making their intentions clear to others with whom they wanted to share their "idea." Therefore, we decided to observe even younger children (13–18 months) in order to capture, if possible, an earlier stage in organizing social play.

SOCIAL PLAY AMONG 13–18-MONTH-OLD TODDLERS

Our principal aim is to study two aspects of the children's interactions in social play. First, like several other authors (Brenner & Mueller, 1982; Bruner, 1975; Bullowa, 1979; Garvey, 1974; Schaffer, 1975), we try to understand how meanings are shared before language, analyzing the different nonverbal means children use to construct social play. Moreover, we have been impressed by the way children manage their interpersonal relationships, being attentive to their playmates, either waiting patiently or taking the initiative, by directly accepting proposals or modifying them. So we also analyzed these interpersonal negotiations, trying to understand how the children succeed in coordinating their intentions and in adjusting their roles during these episodes of social play (Forbes, Katz, & Paul, Chapter 10, this volume; Garvey & Berndt, 1977; Schwartzman, 1978).

Method

We presented to the young toddlers (13–18 months old) the second situation described above. As in our other studies, these observations were made in a crèche where we are often present and where the children are used to us and have been well acquainted with one another for at least three months. Our attitude was the one described above: without intervening, we (and the educators present) manifested our interest in the children's activities; whenever the children wanted to communicate with us, we responded naturally, with smiles and gestural and verbal expressions. All the toddlers were observed in the room where they always spent their time. The usual toys had been taken away, and replaced by a number of empty cardboard boxes and detergent containers. Nine observation sessions of thirty minutes each were videotaped with three different groups of children, each group being observed three times a week. All the children belonging to this section of the day care center were included, but not all were present at every session. The number of children observed varied from five to seven.

Results

Numerous social interactions and shared activities were observed in the situation described above. We discovered children attentive to one another, desirous of doing things together. Sometimes playful, sometimes serious, they succeeded in carrying out various games together and in solving the problems that sometimes arose. In all our observations, each child took part, at some time or other, in a shared activity; not one of them remained isolated throughout the total observation period.

The record of each observation session showed several shared activity sequences or episodes of different length. Sometimes there were difficulties in determining exactly what made up a sequence. The main criteria we adopted are the following: a sequence is considered to start when after a first contact two or more children begin to interact, the initiatives of some combining with those of others; a sequence is considered to be over when the children separate again.

The sequences thus delimited vary in both duration and theme. They also vary in the way they are organized. The same two types of shared activities observed in the older children, object-centered activities and social play, were also found with these much younger ones, some of whom could not yet walk. With the younger children, a third type of social episode was also observed: a simple getting-together in a small circumscribed space, without any particular activity.

The sequences develop generally into dyadic interactions (76%). Some are organized among three children (17%) and on rare occasions (7%) four or more children interact together. Only once did we observe the whole group engaged in the same activity. The above percentages vary from one session to the next and are but a rough indication of the kinds of groups that were formed. The number of participants in social play seems to be mainly determined by the nature of the activity. Episodes of role complementarity develop between two partners only. Sometimes a third child joins in, but this frequently creates difficulties. Sequences based on imitative interaction can take place in a larger group. Imitative play can, indeed, develop among three or more children without a disruption of the activity or a threat to the interpersonal relations within the group. Several "drumming sessions" were observed in which four children took part, some "choir practice" with three children, and one particularly interesting episode during which six cylindrical containers were collected and put upon a cardboard case by all five children present working together.

Figure 9.1 shows in a schematic way the interactions occurring in the same group of familiar children over three different observation sessions. Seven children were in the group: A,B,S,R,M,E,H; their ages ranged from 13 to 15 months. Child H was the youngest, B and R were the oldest. E and M could not yet walk but crawled easily.

The lines linking the names of the children represent one or more associations in sequences of interactions (whatever the length of the sequence). All the children were together in the third session; only five were present in the first and second sessions.

As the diagrams show, each child associated with at least two other children during a play sequence; no child remained isolated. Some children had more contacts than others, but the pattern varied from one session to the next. An analysis of the duration of shared activities and their content suggests that even at this early age there is some peer preference. A study on this aspect of the interactions is in progress.

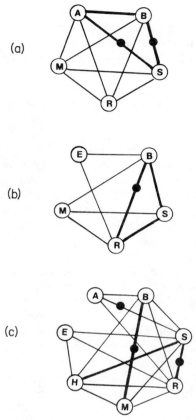

Figure 9.1. Exchanges of toddlers in Group B, for 3 successive sessions: (a) first session (child E and child H are absent), (b) second session (child A and child H are absent), (c) third session (all children are present). ——, denotes one shared activity at least between partners; ——, denotes high frequency of shared activities, ●, denotes high total length of shared activities.

ANALYSIS OF SOCIAL PLAY EPISODES

Many of the interactive sequences observed can be defined as social play episodes. Whenever the children engaged in activities which depend on interaction with others, such as object exchange, peek-a-boo, or follow-the-leader, we considered the sequence to be an episode of social play. When one child wishes to start such a play theme, the need for sharing the idea with one or more others obviously arises. With children as young as those taking part in this study, it is not always easy to understand how the episode develops. All the children's behaviors (actions, gestures, gazes, vocalizations) are coded within the episode. Then, in order to analyze the processes of interactive construction, the underlying meanings of children's behaviors are deduced through inferences and comparisons. It is often necessary to go back and forth between a global apprehension of the episode's meaning and microanalysis of its component parts.

The themes of the social play eposides observed with our very young children often correspond to those observed by other researchers (peek-a-boo, object exchange, etc.). However, our interest is not primarily to discover what themes or meanings the children share (Brenner & Mueller, 1982), but rather how they come to share meanings and to organize their social interactions (Stambak et al., 1983; Stambak & Verba, 1982). Our aim is to analyze the processes of interactive construction of social play, its gradual elaboration and organization. To this end, two related aspects that appear to determine the organization of social interaction need to be considered simultaneously. First, in order to understand the themes proposed by the children and the way they came to exchange meanings, the different means used to make their proposals and intentions clear to their partners need to be analyzed. Second, in order to understand how the intentions of some children fit in with those of others, the succession of proposals, acceptances or refusals, and agreements or disagreements needs to be analyzed.

The analyses of these various features cannot be done separately: each one helps in understanding the others. When the children come to share meanings in dynamic social interaction, they do so by a process of inference; shared meanings, as other researchers have also pointed out, are inferential social constructs. The final description and interpretation of a sequence is based on our understanding of the meanings shared by the partners. In our view, the inferential processes that lead to socially shared meanings and that are present, to a greater or lesser degree, in all interactive sequences, constitute an important contribution to both cognitive and social development.

Within this general framework, the analysis of an episode cannot proceed in a linear manner. The general meaning of the interaction has to be constantly compared with the detailed interpretation of each of its parts. To understand how an episode evolves and how it comes to a close, several points have to be clarified.

Before analyzing a sequence, we try to decide whether the children who take part in it often play together, whether they are friends. We also note if they have already played together earlier in the observation period. It appears that interactive dynamics vary according to whether the partners are used to playing with one another or not.

Within the sequence itself, we first need to understand how the initial encounter of the partners came about. We try to answer the following questions:

1. Did the interaction start with a fortuitous encounter of two children, or did one child actively search for a partner?
2. How did the first proposal originate? How did the theme that will generate the whole sequence arise? Was it already observed during the same day or does it appear for the first time in the observation record?
3. Was the proposal immediately understood by the partner(s), or did it need further explication?

Subsequently, other questions will have to be answered in order to understand the gradual organization of the sequence:

1. After the initial agreement, did the partners elaborate the same theme? Were other themes proposed, and if so, were they linked to the first? Were several themes combined?
2. How easily did the intentions of one child fit in with those of an other? If a third child wanted to join, what changes took place? Did tensions or conflicts arise? If so, how were they overcome?

The progressive organization of episodes of social play will be illustrated by two examples. We chose two rather complex episodes, each consisting of a large number of interactions (at least 20). Each episode is divided into its component parts; the different interactions and the successive phases of the episodes are indicated. The first example illustrates the organization of an episode in which several themes and meanings are shared and combined by two partners. The second example shows the progressive organization of a very long episode (14 minutes) in which a third child joins in a dyadic interaction. In this example, the interpersonal relations are more "dramatic", with the desires of each child coming into conflict with those of the others.

Example 1

This sequence of interaction (Session 1) illustrates the organization of an object exchange game between two toddlers, involving transformation of the game's rules: Two children, Aurelien and Sylvie, both 14 months old and well-acquainted, are standing by a large cardboard box which is lying on the floor with its flaps open on either side, forming a house (see Figure 9.2). The game initiated by Sylvie takes place in three phases, each of which corresponds to a variation of the rules of play. To facilitate the understanding of our analyses, we have listed the children's behaviors during the episode, each designated by a number. A diagram of these significant

Figure 9.2.   The situation in the paper-licking game (Example 1).

behaviors clarifies the whole dynamic of the episode, both in the temporal order of the actions and in the relations between the actions of the two partners (see Figure 9.3).

The initial encounter. From the beginning of the observation, the two children manifested many socially-directed behaviors toward each other. Moreover, for short periods of time, they also shared some activities focusing on the box, such as tapping on it and exploring its flaps. They also appeared to appreciate each other's company. The episode begins as Sylvie shows an interest in the piece of paper held by Aurelien and snatches it out of his hand (1). (Reference numbers of described behaviors in Figure 9.3 are indicated in parentheses.)

Phase A: The paper-licking game. After this direct contact, which does not provoke any negative reaction from Aurelien (2), Sylvie licks the piece of paper and makes clear her intention of having him do the same (3). Aurelien takes the hint and shares in the game straight away (4). Both of them, in turn, repeat the action of licking the piece of paper at Sylvie's initiative (5,6,7). As a result of these repetitions, Aurelien introduces the idea of offering the piece of paper directly to Sylvie without licking it himself (8). However, his partner does not approve of this idea either, because her interest in the game has been exhausted or because she does not accept

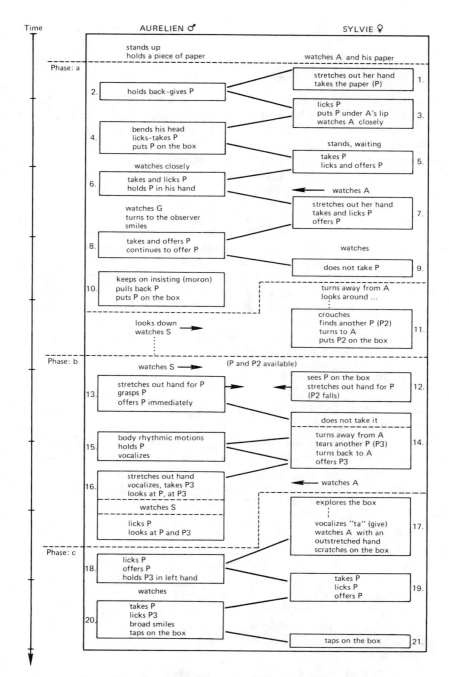

Figure 9.3. Dynamics of the paper-licking game (Example 1).

her partner's taking the initiative. Sylvie turns away from him (9). Although Aurelien seems to want to continue the game, he gives up as well (10).

Phase B: Offering and receiving the paper. In this phase, Aurelien stays with the idea of offering his own piece of paper to Sylvie, whereas she takes an interest in other pieces of paper (11–14). Yet Aurelien keeps insisting and shows her that he wants to continue (13–15). At last, Sylvie understands his intention and offers him another piece of paper. In this phase of shared activities, the paper-licking game turns into a mutual offering game initiated by Aurelien.

Phase C: Combination of paper-licking and offering games. After the short game of offering and receiving pieces of paper, Aurelien compares the two papers now in his hand, as though he wants to make sure they are alike (16). Then he continues, combining the two previous rules of the initial paper-licking game and the reciprocal offering game (18). Sylvie agrees to share in this game (19). Each child in turn takes and licks, then offers the piece of paper. The game comes to an end and the two children separate. We should like to point out that this relatively complex rule game, involving two partners, takes place harmoniously. Each of the children appears to try to understand and adapt to the other's wishes.

Example 2

This second sequence illustrates the organization of a peek-a-boo game. Three toddlers are interacting: Celine (17 months), Leila (14 months), and Marie (17 months). The sequence takes place around a big cardboard box that is open on one side. The two flaps on the open side can be opened or closed (see Figure 9.4).

Celine, who is sitting in a big cardboard box, proposed a peek-a-boo game. Leila, who is strolling in front of the box, notices Celine and accepts. Immediately afterwards, Marie enters the box and sits down next to Celine. The peek-a-boo game continues. Marie interrupts the game by blocking the flaps of the box. She then lets Leila know that she must go away. Leila first refuses, but then leaves. Marie and Celine then become involved in a cheerful game inside the box. During this time Leila plays unhappily by herself.

Some time later, Leila comes back to the box. This time, the two friends accept her presence, and the peek-a-boo game is begun again. After a moment, Leila leaves them, finds two pieces of paper, and returns. Marie then comes out of the box and goes toward her. Leila offers her one of the pieces of paper, and the two go off together.

For the analysis of the first part of the sequence, it is advisable to follow the detailed behavior record in Figure 9.5.

Figure 9.4.   The situation in the peekaboo game (Example 2).

The initial encounter. The interaction begins with Celine's proposal for a peek-a-boo game. She does not seem to be searching for a particular partner, but just "calling" for somebody. Using very subtle means (leaning her body against the wall of the box, then sticking her head out of the box), it appears that she is trying to indicate that this box could be used to play at not being seen (not seeing)/being seen (seeing). She repeats these two actions twice, persisting in her attempt to find a partner.

By chance, Leila is passing and notices Celine. She approaches her and appears willing to play with her, but does not understand that a game has been proposed. She goes away. Celine then modifies her behavior in order to show Leila what she wants: she closes the flaps from the inside. This time the message is clear; Leila agrees to play peek-a-boo. From the outside she opens and closes the flaps.

The interruption of the game. The arrival of a third toddler interrupts the game between the first two partners. Marie arrives from the opposite side of the room, where she could not see the game going on between Celine and Leila. Without hesitation, she sits down next to Celine inside the box. A few seconds later, Marie interrupts the peek-a-boo game by closing the flaps from the inside, indicating her intention is otherwise. Leila, who is outside of the box, wants to continue playing with the other two. She tries

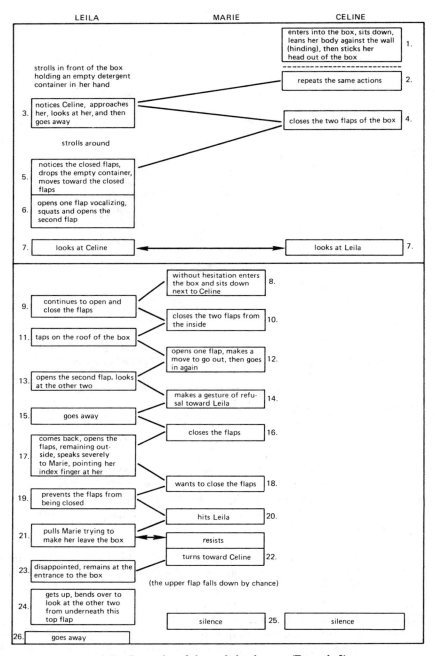

Figure 9.5. Dynamics of the peekabook game (Example 2).

to get Marie to come out; she taps on the roof of the box, but in vain. Marie wants to stay and play with Celine, but excluding Leila. Since Leila persists, Marie makes her intention clearer: in the end, she hits her (see interventions 13–26, Figure 9.5). Marie thus manages to impose her will, and Leila goes away.

In this part of the sequence, we see one of the most dramatic moments in our observations. The conflict between Marie and Leila is quite violent, leading to the exclusion of one of the partners. It is interesting that Celine does not involve herself in this conflict; she remains neutral. It was Celine, however, who initiated the game, but Leila was only her partner by chance. On the other hand, Marie is a good friend of Celine's; they often play together.

The separation phase (summary). After Leila's departure, Marie realizes her aim to play alone with Celine. For quite a while, they engage in many sorts of play, laughing together. During this time, Leila is alone in a crouched position, appearing hurt.

The reconciliation. Leila is the one who, without any apparent resentment, takes the first steps. She gets up, walks around the room, picks up a piece of paper, and moves toward the box. The two friends, Marie and Celine, have noticed her, but do not pay her any attention. Leila walks around the room again and once more approaches the box. This time, Marie and Celine agree to play with her; the three play peek-a-boo briefly. Then Leila goes away again, picks up a second piece of paper, and moves toward the box. This time, Marie leaves the box and approaches Leila, who in turn offers Marie one of the pieces of paper, perhaps as a present. The two go off together to play with the paper.

All's well that ends well. It is important to stress that Marie who, at first, had strongly rejected Leila, subsequently respected Leila's desire to play with her. She not only accepted the peek-a-boo game, but was also willing to abandon her friend, Celine, to play with Leila. After this reconciliation, Leila and Marie separate, and the sequence ends.

Discussion

As the two examples show, these very young children are able to construct social play together. Each partner succeeds in understanding the underlying meanings of the overt behaviors of the other(s): using a continuous process of successive inferences, they often achieve very harmonious episodes.

The processes of the construction of an episode show great similarity (1). After a first contact between partners, one of them proposed an idea whose content is made more or less explicit. The partner understands totally or partially, and acts in response. This response in turn elicits a response from the other child, and so on. A first meaning is shared, and a theme is elaborated. Each partner adjusts and modifies his or her activities according to the particular interest of each step in the proceedings, and according to the responses of the other child. Similar processes have been found to exist in other shared activities among toddlers (Verba, 1982b).

The variety and efficacy of the ways and means invented by these very young children to make their intentions and expectations clear to their partners is truly surprising. When calling for somebody to join them, when appealing to a partner to do something, in moments of agreement or of conflict, the children interact with one another in well-adapted and often subtle ways. Thus, in the first example, Sylvie proposes to Aurelien to play "licking a piece of paper." She makes her intention clear by holding the piece of paper against Aurelien's mouth. Aurelien understands, and licks the paper, and Sylvie wants a repeat performance. This time, she just holds out the piece of paper to him; no need to be as explicit as the first time—he knows! Later in the sequence, Aurelien uses the movement of his arm to attract Sylvie's attention when she does not respond to his invitation; later, when Sylvie once again ignores him, he makes bouncing movements and accompanies them with vocalizations.

Similar instances of successful communicative devices occur in our second example. Celine signals her desire to play peek-a-boo: she gets into one of the cardboard boxes, sticks out her head, vocalizes, pulls back inside, turns to the back of the box, and sticks out her head again. This call for a partner is not addressed to anybody in particular, but Leila, who passes by, responds. In the same example, we observe Marie and Leila using various means to make clear their disagreements; before scuffling, they express their intentions through a variety of facial and body gestures with progressively increasing intensity.

Despite similarities, the overall organization of the different episodes of social play also show substantial differences. We noted that the strategies of the child's first approach, the possibilities of developing the initial proposal (the theme), and the nature of interpersonal relations vary considerably from one episode to the next. The number of children taking part in the episode seems to be an important factor in these variations.

The two examples we analyzed illustrate these differences. In the first example, one of the children proposes to another child an activity to be shared; he chooses his partner. The second child agrees immediately in sharing the initial proposal. Throughout the episode, these two children remain together and no other child joins in, so they can elaborate a complex game with "rules," clear up their misunderstandings, and manage to combine two ideas, each child contributing one idea to the final game. Thus, in this first example, the reciprocal adjustments get organized without any conflict or great difficulties, so children can achieve surprising cognitive performances.

In the second example, one child indicates that she would like to play peek-a-boo, but she does not address herself to anyone in particular. A chance encounter brings another child into this play. Though this second child is a fortuitous partner, they together develop the theme the first child proposed, but only for a short while. Another child, a "friend" of the first, elbows in on the act, and a conflict develops. The "intruder" wins, and the first partner is left out. However, in the end, some clever strategical moves permit harmony and peace to be restored.

In this second episode, where three children are interacting, the reciprocal adjustments are achieved in a more dramatic way, the intentions and the desires of each child coming into conflict with those of the others. Under these circumstances, the theme one of them proposed cannot be developed quite thoroughly. But in this case we note the children's surprising capacities to take into account the intentions of the partners, thus showing strong social competence.

The study of these different kinds of organization must be conducted by detailed analysis of social play among children from 12- to 24-months old.

SOCIAL PLAY AS AN EXPERIENCE WHICH FOSTERS COGNITIVE, COMMUNICATIVE AND SOCIAL COMPETENCE

Though we do not like to speak in terms of "outcome" in peer interactions, since the type of research we carry out does not lend itself to any evaluation of its effects on development in general (especially in view of its ecological character), we think that peer relations among very young children foster their cognitive, communicative, and social competence. In our opinion, these contributions have to be investigated in terms of the process and organization of interactive episodes. The contribution is probably best conveyed in communication terms; even without the use of verbalizations, the sequences show a dialogue-like pattern, with messages linked together through a sustained theme (Verba, 1982a,b). Suggestions ("peek-a-boo, anybody?"), explicit information on what to do ("you're supposed to *lick* the paper"), and exhortations ("come on, I'm waiting") seem to be conveyed and understood. Such proto-dialogues have both form and content, and it is difficult to imagine that they would not contribute to the development of the future mother tongue of these children and to their capacity to discuss, to argue, and to elaborate projects.

Discussing and planning are, of course, as much communicative as social and cognitive activities. In previous research, we have already analyzed the cognitive aspects of peer interactions in object-centered activities (Stambak et al., 1979; Verba et al., 1982). However, in social play, which becomes constructed into the kind of episode of which we have given two examples, each partner's contributions to the shared meaning of the activities also depend on his or her cognitive capacities for inference making, adjustment, and coordination. The first example illustrates particularly clearly such cognitive activities which underlie the constructive process. In the first two phases of the sequence, two activities are shared by the partners (licking a piece of paper and object exchange). In the third phase, these are combined into a new game with two "rules." In general, it appears that the construction processes in social play among peers have a strong cognitive component.

The more directly social aspects of these sequences, that is, the interpersonal relations, are equally striking. Many of the social play sequences have a strong "dramatic" ingredient, since the intentions and desires of the partners may not be identical. The reciprocal readjustments necessary in interactions with living beings are far more complex than those occurring when one child plays with inanimate objects. The latter may not always lend themselves to the activity the child has in mind, but their reactions are regular and far less varied than those of living beings. Despite this difficulty, the children's interactions are, on the whole, surprisingly harmonious, as if the partners put all their ingenuity to work in order to satisfy their shared desire to act together; the subtlety of their interactive procedures is evidence of the strength of their desire.

Clashes do occur, as we have seen. However, these are only momentary phases in the "drama" that unfolds, and they have a very positive influence: children face up to contradictions and organize strategies for resolving them (Barriere, Bonica, Ferreira-Whitaker, 1979). As our second example showed, children are capable of elaborating highly successful strategies to deal with most problems that arise.

In short, in the context we designed, open conflict and aggressive behavior were extremely rare; thus their oft-reported frequency in other instances cannot be attributed only to internal characteristics of the children themselves, but must also be considered as a result of the environmental situation.

References

Barriere, M., Bonica, L., Ferreira—Whitaker, S., & Goma, E. (1979). A propos de conflits chez les jeunes enfants. (Concerning the conflicts of young children) *Travaux de CRESAS, 19*, 105–140.

Brenner, J., & Mueller, E. (1982). Shared meaning in boy toddlers' peer relations. *Child Development, 53*, 380–391.

Bruner, J. S. (1975). From communication to language: A psychological perspective. *Cognition, 3,* 255–87.

Bullowa, M. (1979). *Before speech—the beginning of interpersonal communication,* Cambridge: Cambridge University Press.

CRESAS (ouvrage collectif). (1978). *Le handicap socio-culturel en question* (Socio-cultural handicaps in question), Paris: Editions Sociales Francaises.

CRESAS (ouvrage collectif). (1981). *L'echec scolair n'est pas une fatalite* (The scholarly defeat is not a fatality). Paris: Editions Sociales Francaises.

Garvey, C. (1974). Some properties of social play, *Merrill–Palmer Quarterly, 20,* 163–180.

Garvey, C., & Berndt, R. (1977). Organization of pretend play. *Catalogue of selected documents in psychology, 7,* 15–89.

Mueller, E., & Brenner, J. (1977). The origins of social skills and interaction among play group toddlers. *Child Development, 48,* 854–861.

Musatti, T. Modalités d'echanges et organisation des actions de "faire semblant," (Types of exchanges and organization of action in "pretend play"), *Travaux du CRESAS, 19,* 165–208.

Schaffer, H. R. (1975). *Studies in mother–infant interaction.* New York: Academic Press.

Schwartzman, M. B. (1978). *Transformations: The anthropology of children's play.* New York: Plenum.

Sinclair, H., Stambak, M., Lezine, I., Rayna, S., & Verba, M. (1982). *Les bébés et les choses: La creativité du developpement cognitif* (Infants and their activities: The creativity of cognitive development). Paris: Presses Universitaires de France.

Stambak, M., Barriere, M., Bonica, L., Maisonnet, R., Musatti, T., Rayna, S., & Verba, M. (1983). *Les bébés entre eux: inventer, decouvrir, jouer ensemble* (Infants with one another: Invention, discovery, and joint play). Paris: P.U.F.

Stambak, M., Bonica, L., Maisonnet, R., Rayna, S., & Verba, M. (1979). Modalités d'echanges entre enfants de moins de deux ans (Modes of interaction among children younger than two years). *Travaux de CRESAS, 19,* 3–103.

Stambak, M., & Verba, M. (1982). Organisation des jeux sociaux chez des enfants de 12 à 15 mois observes en crèche (Organization of social games among infants from 12 to 15 months observed in day care). *Etudes de Linguistique Appliquée, 46.*

Verba, M., Stambak, M., & Sinclair, H. (1982). Physical knowledge and social interaction in children from 18 to 24 months of age. In G. Forman (Ed.), *Action and thought.* New York: Academic Press.

Verba, M. (1982a). Contribution à l'étude de la communication preverbale entre enfants (The contribution of the study of preverbal communication among children). *Revue d'Audiophonologie, 2–3.*

Verba, M. (1982b). Dialogue preverbal et organisation de jeux entre bébés (Preverbal dialogue and the organization of play among infants). *Actes du Colloque organisée par l'Institut Piaget,* Lisbonne.

CHAPTER 10

"Frame Talk": A Dramatistic Analysis of Children's Fantasy Play

David Forbes, Mary Maxwell Katz, and Barry Paul

Introduction

The study of children at play is an old one in child psychology. Because play occupies so much of a child's time, developmental psychologists have tended to view it as the "work" of childhood, and have expended much effort to determine just what kind of work the child at play is doing, and what kinds of developmental accomplishments it may bring about. In this paper, we present an analysis of children's "sociodramatic" or social pretend play, and a new perspective for understanding this activity as work that promotes psychological development.

Play has been viewed as an important socializing medium for the child in that it provides a "practice field" of playful pretense which, unlike the real world, can be shaped to meet the child's needs, interests, and levels of ability. Indeed, past studies have documented how, for example, play can involve literal social practice, as in playing "house" or playing "policeman." Our perspective on play extends the notion of practice beyond this literal sense, and considers how play provides an opportunity for creation and manipulation of meaning frameworks within which fantasy action, whatever its specific content, may be understood by the players. Combining the perspectives of Bateson (1955, 1956) and Goffman (1974) on "social

PROCESS AND OUTCOME
IN PEER RELATIONSHIPS

frames," the literary criticism theory of Burke (1969, 1950), and the recent empirical work on the construction of shared knowledge (Franklin, 1981; Garvey, 1974, 1979, 1982; Garvey & Berndt, 1977; Schwartzman, 1976, 1978), we present an analytical scheme and several play dialogues that are discussed as dramas that children create with one another. These examples show that fantasy play, viewed from a "dramatistic perspective" can be seen to promote social-cognitive development, particularly the development of structurally integrated representations of social interaction.

Background

Earliest attempts at understanding children's play as an activity involving psychological "work" tended to focus on how the activities of playing might serve the needs and interests of the individual child. These scholars viewed play as a means for disposing of surplus energy (Spencer, 1896); a chance to exercise behaviors that would become important in adult life (Groos, 1901); an ego expanding mechanism, whereby the psyche of the child elaborates its mastery over the world, both emotionally and cognitively (Claparede, 1911); or an exercising of the cognitive process of assimilation beyond that which is strictly necessary for adaptation (Piaget, 1962; for a review, see Rubin, 1982).

More recently, some students of play have turned their interest toward an understanding of the interactive nature of play and the ways in which playful interactions of children might serve to promote social development. These researchers have viewed social interaction during play as an important context for learning about the perspectives of others and about social negotiation. In the introduction to *Play and Learning,* Sutton-Smith (1979) refers to this orientation as a "secondary paradigm" for the study of play. According to this vision, play is a process for "organizing collective behavior" whose primary function is enculturation into social mores. Sutton-Smith notes that this vision of play predominates in anthropology, folklore, and sociolinguistics. This paradigm also underlies the present study.

G. H. Mead (1934) was a pioneer of the interactive approach in his analysis of levels of coordination between perspectives or roles of individual children. Learning about how others view the world, he suggests, is an important consequence of all children's social interactions. His analysis of play structure into "preparatory," "play," and "game" phases elaborates how play in particular serves as a context for development of skill in constructing systems of meaning which are shared by involved partners. Similarly, Vygotsky (1978) viewed development as guided by socially constructed representational systems, which emerge, principally, through interpersonal experience. Vygotsky stressed the importance, therefore, of concepts such as "negotiated meaning," "shared knowledge," and "interpersonal exchange."

Some researchers who adopt the interactive perspective have focused on how play provides an opportunity to learn about shared norms or rules for interaction. Phenomena recently studied by these workers include ownership (Newman, 1978), sequencing and turntaking (Corsaro & Tomlinson, 1980; Garvey, 1974), establishing and maintaining in conversation (Keenan & Klein, 1975; Keenan & Schieffelin, 1976; Pelligrini, 1982), signaling of pretense versus serious interaction (Franklin, 1981; Garvey & Berndt, 1977), and development of jointly understood "scripts" for fantasy (Nelson & Gruendel, 1979).

Other students interested in play as a social interactive phenomenon have attempted to investigate how children create a shared understanding of what will go on in their play. The work of Bateson (1955, 1956) and Goffman (1961, 1974) has been instrumental in guiding this effort. Bateson's basic proposition is that communication between persons takes place within "frames," or meaning contexts, which allow for agreement about the sense of individual actions. Bateson (1956) points out that play in particular cannot occur without explicit attention to its frame, since the nonliteral meaning in play must be stipulated by agreement. Goffman (1974) notes that play is an especially interesting phenomenon for the study of framing, since the nonliteral meanings of objects and actions in play must be created through explicit "keying," which stipulates the transformation from literal meaning to nonliteral, playful meaning.

To document the emergence of children's ability to work toward shared meanings, Brenner and Mueller (1982) have looked at the play of very young children for evidence of shared meaning systems. They observe that most social interaction of preschoolers is lacking in a shared social agenda on meaning but reveals a striving for shared meaning in some children as young as 18 months. Wolf (1981) also has researched children's talk about the meaning of their play. She finds that children younger than 4 years lack a "zone" of conversation which is about the play without being a part of it. In children of age 4, Matthews (1977) and Garvey (1974, 1979, 1982; Garvey & Hogan, 1973; Garvey & Berndt, 1977) have discerned the appearance of active conversation about play ideas, including the nature of fantasy roles and the form of fantasy object transformations.

Garvey's work shows that 3- and 4-year-olds actively coordinate fantasy frames with a great deal of explicit communication whose apparent intention is the mutual coordination of meaning elements. Garvey & Berndt (1977) note a variety of types of communication in fantasy play that include general introduction of pretense, preparatory and procedural comments, explicit references to pretend transformations, and negation of pretense.

Their analysis of the interrelation among the elements of play suggests that a central role is played by action plans or "schemata." They observe that the nature of fantasy object transformations and role stipulations are largely determined by these plans. They distinguish, for example, four different types of roles—functional, stereotypic, relational, and peripheral and relate the occurrence of each to the action schemata from which it arises (e.g., the "dining" schemata requires two functional roles—one who eats and one who serves).

Franklin (1981) delineates a set of communicative activities in which children must engage to establish, specify, and maintain shared, coordinated fantasy drama. Her observations of 2- to 4-year-old children also suggest active involvement of coordinating shared fantasy meanings. Franklin focuses on three types of communication: planning, describing, and narrating. Planning statements occur before the onset of the play episode and focus agreement on the nature of the action and characters. Description statements are similar, but typically take place within the dramatic action and maintain coordinated understanding. Narrating statements resemble description statements but are part of the fantasy enactment rather than peripheral to it. Franklin found that each type of communication integrated aspects of the drama and promoted consensus among the players concerning its nature.

Schwartzman (1976, 1978) interprets children's interactions during sociodramatic play in the larger context of their on-going social relationships. She notes that fantasy dramas concern issues of control, dominance, and manipulation, which also apply to the real world of the play group and the classroom. Her analysis suggests that children work together to develop joint play themes that embody one of several possible "play genres," and identifies each play genre with a particular type of social relationship structure among the characters within it. For example, she identifies the "asymmetrical dyad" genre with relation structures such as "parent–child" that might occur during playing house. Schwartzman suggests in fantasy play children can interpret and comment upon their actual relationships to one another and can thus also develop new possibilities for social relations.

The present research continues and extends the interest in the interactive construction of meanings during fantasy play by focusing on the thematic content created by children during fantasy play and how thematic elements are integrated by them. This effort includes the interest in role structure, action schemata, and object transformations found in past work, but it seeks a means for examining these as parts of an integrated whole. To do so, we have chosen to look at fantasy play as a drama and have examined how the principle components of the drama are integrated by children during play. The work of Burke (1950, 1969) and Kaplan (1983) has provided the basis for our analytic method. Burke proposes five "key dramatic terms" for denoting the different conceptual dimensions of drama: *act* (what was done), *scene* (where or when it was done), *agent* (who did it), *agency* (how it was done), and *purpose* (why it was done) (1950, p. xv). Burke stresses the interdependence and overlapping of these categories and notes how relationships among them may form the basis of common psychological dimensions of human action:

> Certain formal interrelationships prevail among these terms, by reason of their role as attributes of a common ground . . . At every point where the field covered by any one of these terms overlaps upon the field covered by any other, there is an alchemic opportunity . . . From the central moltenness there are thrown forth . . . such distinctions as between freedom and necessity, activity and passiveness, cooperation and competition, cause and effect, mechanism and teleology. (1950, p. xix)

Using the concept of "dramatic ratios," Burke points out that the relationship between two elements of drama has direct impact on the nature and meaning of the drama. For example, the "scene–act" ratio of someone falling on an icy sidewalk is constructed so that the action is seen as a consequence of constraints inherent in the scene. On the other hand, the scene may be viewed as "set" by the nature of the action as in the case of illegal gambling in a secret back room. Burke refers to the construction of these dramatic ratios as "alchemic opportunities," the central act of dramatic creation.

Kaplan has proposed an extension of Burke's concepts into developmental psychology, proposing that Burke's dramatic terms may be useful dimensions for describing development of both action in, and understanding of, the human social world. Kaplan's work suggests that the structure of children's understanding of the social world would be discerned in the nature of connections that they make between dramatic terms. Our method of analysis is intended to facilitate future description of such structures.

Methods

Child subjects were 5-year-olds from Cambridge, Massachusetts who attended playgroup sessions at a laboratory at the Harvard Graduate School of Education. Each playgroup consisted of 3 boys and 3 girls of the same age, who were unfamiliar with one another at the start of the study. The playgroups met for 12 one-hour sessions over a period of 3 weeks and all sessions were recorded on videotape. The playroom was equipped with age-typical toys, games, art supplies, and a sand-play table.

In order to examine the social construction of meaning in pretend play, the first, second, and sixth day of play were reviewed in entirety for two groups (thus including 12 children viewed for 3 hours of play) and all episodes of fantasy play were transcribed. The dialogues were then analyzed for the presence of related dramatic elements, defined as follows: Dramatic elements are related when one element is presumed or proposed as the given or consensually established aspect of the play, and the second is commented upon or evaluated in terms of its coordination or consistency with the first (cf. Burke's "dramatic ratios," 1969). The following codes were used, comprising all possible relations between the five basic elements:

Act-based relationships underlie statements which presume agreement concerning the nature of some act and evaluate proposals of other dramatic dimensions in terms of their appropriateness to it. They include the following:

1. ACT-AGENT. A child comments on the nature of an agent in terms of its degree of fit with an ongoing action pattern (e.g., "You can't be the captain of the ship if you're swabbing the decks").
2. ACT-PURPOSE. A child comments on the relationship between an ongoing action and a purpose evaluated in terms of its fit with the action (e.g., "If you give up now, you can't be the winner").
3. ACT-SCENE. The nature of an ongoing action provides a context for decisions about the kind of scene which might contain such actions (e.g., "We burned down the forest so there can't be any trees").
4. ACT-AGENCY. A child comments on the appropriateness of a particular means to an ongoing action pattern (e.g., "You can't cut the cake with a pencil").

Agent-based relationships presume the nature of the agent is given, and the other dramatistic terms are discussed in terms of how well they fit with the established agent qualities. They include the following:

1. AGENT-ACT. A particular action is commented upon in terms of its fit with the nature of the agent (e.g., "Kids can't drive").
2. AGENT-SCENE. The nature of the agent or dramatic role is used to evaluate the characteristics of a dramatic scene (e.g., "Dinosaurs don't go to restaurants").
3. AGENT-PURPOSE. A proposed goal or purpose is evaluated in terms of its consistency with a dramatic character or agent (e.g., "Dinosaurs don't want to save people").
4. AGENT-AGENCY. Means for action are evaluated in terms of their fit with established roles (e.g., "Dinosaurs don't use knives to eat").

Scene-based relationships take the nature of a scene in which the drama is taking place as a "given" and make comments about the other four dramatistic dimensions. They include the following:

1. SCENE-AGENT. The nature of a character in the drama is examined in light of the established scene (e.g., "They don't have kings in bookstores").
2. SCENE-ACT. The nature of an action is commented upon in terms of its fit with an established scene (e.g., "You can't run under water").
3. SCENE-PURPOSE. The purposes are evaluated in terms of their fit with the scene (e.g., "This is the good restaurant, we want to keep it clean").
4. SCENE-AGENCY. Particular means for accomplishing actions are evaluated in terms of their fit with the scene (e.g., "I have to use the strong soap on this dirty floor").

Purpose-based relationships take the goal of an agent as a "given" element of a fantasy drama, and other aspects of the drama are commented upon or evaluated in terms of their consistency with this goal. They include the following:

1. PURPOSE-AGENT. The nature of the agent is examined in light of a purpose of action that is already established (e.g., "We need a teacher to have a math lesson").
2. PURPOSE-ACT. An action is evaluated in terms of its consistency with an agreed upon purpose (e.g., "You can't make the baby happy by just rocking it").
3. PURPOSE-SCENE. A proposed scene is commented upon in terms of its fit with an established purpose (e.g., "We want to find some gold so we have to look in the mine").
4. PURPOSE-AGENCY. Means for doing an action are commented upon in terms of their relationships with its purpose (e.g., "You can't get out of jail unless you have a ladder").

Agency-based relationships take the means for performing actions as given, and other dramatic dimensions are commented upon in terms of their established means. They include the following:

1. AGENCY-AGENT. The means for performing an action are viewed as constraining the nature of the agent who will perform it (e.g., "We need a soldier to use the cannon").
2. AGENCY-SCENE. The use of certain means is viewed as calling for a certain type of scene (e.g., "We have to have an office to put the computer in").
3. AGENCY-ACT. The nature of a means prescribes the kinds of action that can be performed (e.g., "You can't fly in a car").
4. AGENCY-PURPOSE. An established means is referred to as a basis for deciding the appropriateness of goals (e.g., "The plane is only for taking vacations").

In reviewing the episodes of fantasy play, it became clear that they contained phases that might influence the use of dramatistic elements, namely, a *setup* phase, an *enactment* phase, and *transitions*. We, therefore, chose to examine the integration of dramatistic elements in each phase separately, and have presented them separately, with their more precise definitions.

The general conclusions drawn in the results section are based on analysis of 15 episodes of fantasy play totalling 206 minutes, and include 12 children, 6 boys and 6 girls. Six examples are presented, which were chosen for their clarity in illustrating how integration of dramatic elements is achieved by children. These examples are drawn from the play of 5 boys in two different groups.

Results

INTEGRATION OF ELEMENTS
DURING THE SET-UP PHASE

In the beginning of a play episode, the elements of the fantasy drama are introduced, negotiated, and assembled. In our observations, a "set-up" phase is distinguishable from other portions of the episode by the nature of the talk. The children appear to understand their conversation as about the play frame, rather than within it. This period of interaction is marked by the absence of confusion about who is talking, that is, children's utterances as playmates are not usually confused with their utterances as fantasy characters.

The set-up phase is also marked by a minimum of dramatic constraint. That is, children are just beginning to construct a joint fantasy frame, and constraint upon any given element of the drama increases only gradually as the frame is elaborated by successive propositions in this context. In our observation, framing in the set-up phase often concerns how ideas will be incorporated into a fantasy and how dramatic consistency between a given idea and previously agreed upon demands, used as a basis of decision making, will be developed. Thus, framing in this context is apparently grounded in the mutual recognition that the need for a coherent, integrated dramatic frame is a legitimate basis for evaluating—and including or excluding—any particular idea concerning the play theme.

Our first case of framing activity within the set-up phase involves 3 children who are about to reinitiate a fantasy that they have played on previous days and that they refer to as "devil mountain." The children are discussing whether their activity will include destroying the large sand pile which is devil mountain.

1. N: We're going to wreck devil mountain.
2. K: No! I like devil mountain (grabs toy bulldozer).
3. N: No, remember what we did yesterday; we wrecked it.
4. K: Why?
5. N: Because they didn't like it.
6. R: It's the *good* devil mountain.
7. K: This is the good one (pats sand pile).
8. N: I'm just gonna carve it.
9. K: No!
10. N: Take off all the bad dirt so it will never die (scrapes at sand).
11. K: We have to take off all the bad dirt so it will never die (joins in).

This episode illustrates manipulations of relations between the scene, agents, and action in service of an integrated fantasy frame. N, whose main interest appears to be continuing to play with the toy bulldozer he is holding, proposes an action theme (wrecking the mountain) that would make this possible. In line 2, K, who wants to play with the mountain as it is, resists by proposing a characteristic of the scene (mountain)—its positive qualities in his view—that makes the agent's proposed (bulldoze) action in the scene inconsistent. In line 3, N counters with an appeal to past actions as a basis for imputing attitude to the agent (we wrecked it yesterday and thus don't like it), that is consistent with N's original proposal for action. This is questioned by K in line 4 and elaborated explicitly by N as a statement of agent's attitude in line 5. In line 6, R joins the discussion by reformulating the scene, with the proposal of a "good" devil mountain—a scenic change which could resolve conflict between N's observations about past action and K's desires in the present (i.e., they didn't like the old mountain but do like the new one, because it is a different one). K welcomes support and reiterates it in line 7. N, in line 8, adapts his action proposal to conform to the new scene, that is, "just carving" will not be detrimental to the good mountain. When K still resists this proposal in line 9, N further elaborates his transformed action proposal by relating the action to a purpose that is consistent with the new scene: "Taking off bad dirt." A social conflict is thus resolved through several iterative transformations of thematic elements, in which the transformations are based upon the children's mutual judgments of appropriateness in the relations of the several elements.

The second case of framing activity in the set-up phase involves an episode of play with rubber dinosaurs, which again occurred at the sand table. In this vignette, R attempts to initiate a fantasy involving conflict between the protagonists, while N prefers a more cooperative motif.

R holds a dinosaur in a threatening posture over N's dinosaur.

1. R: He's gonna stab you!
2. N: No one can beat him up (referring to his own dinosaur) because he's the tyrannosaurus.
3. R: He's gonna bite you.
4. N: No—pretend this was a team of dinosaurs.
5. R: All these gray ones are on my team (indicates his own dinosaurs).
6. N: Yeah, we're all on your team.
7. R: You have two, and I have two, and these (indicates N's) are the bad guys.

In this interaction, R begins with a direct leap into enactment, announcing an impending action of his agent in the voice of the agent. In line 2, N counters by characterizing his agent (soon to be "victim" of R's stabbing) in a way inconsistent with the action, that is, you can't succeed in using force on the tyrannosaurus. In line 3, R ignores the essence of N's dramatic objections but responds superficially by reformulating the aggressive action of "stabbing" into "biting," presumably more characteristic of dinosaurs than stabbing. In line 4, N reveals the underlying agenda of opposition to conflict per se, when he proposes a new quality of the agents ("team membership") as a means of excluding conflict from the action: Members of a team do not fight among themselves. In line 5, R accepts the general notion of "teams," but transforms this characteristic to readmit an agonistic theme by stipulating *his* team and thus implying two teams—his and N's—which again could be in conflict. In line 6, N counters with another transformation of R's team idea, proposing that a team may exist, but that all players are on that team. Thus N again attempts to transform the drama so that conflict is not an appropriate action theme. In line 7, R proceeds to a distribution of the dinosaur toys and refers to N's dinosaurs as the "bad guys." Thus, he reinitiates a quality of the agents—good guys and bad guys—that makes the action themes of conflict appropriate. The interaction ends with N resisting R's characterization of his agents as bad.

This case suggests a representational structure relating agent characteristics to action potential. The debate over relationships between the agents—membership in one joint team versus two opposing teams—is a vehicle for supporting two opposing proposals for action—antagonism versus cooperation.

INTEGRATION OF ELEMENTS DURING ENACTMENT

In the enactment phase, children enter the frames which they have constructed and attempt to play out the drama within the dimensions of the frame. As we defined it, the enactment phase is signaled by the onset of talk which is meant to be understood within the fantasy frame—either as actions of a character per se, or as actions of a narrator or director of ongoing drama.

The onset of a dramatic action apparently indicates the opinion of at least one child that a frame exists within which drama may unfold. Discussion of the nature of the frame may continue during enactment but typically concerns promoting clarity in the construals of the frames, which are now seen as having the power of constraining dramatic action. Confusion about who is talking is also more likely in the enactment phase, so signals concerning the identity of the speaker are sometimes required.

Our first case of framing during enactment again involves play at the sand table, this time in a "savior" motif. S and B are involved, with S in charge of the "dragons" and B in the role of "worried mother."

1. S: I hear somebody saying "mama." I don't want the bad guys to get 'em—I get mad. Arrgh—bad guys go away! (Deep voice).
2. B: Baby, baby, I'll save you my poor baby! (High voice).
3. S: Listen, madam, we are good dragons.
4. B: Give me back my baby!
5. S: I was saving him.
6. B: You mean he almost got runned over; oh, my little baby.
7. S: Now you have to kiss the dragons and say, "Thank you, dragon for saving my baby."
8. B: Thank you, dragon, for saving my little baby.
9. S: Now kiss me.
10. B: (Stares aghast at S.)
11. S: He has to kiss me, that's me (indicates dragon doll).
12: (They kiss with the dolls).

In this interaction, S is engaged in the act of "saving the baby" in what we infer is the role of "the friendly dragon." In line 2, he is interrupted by B, who also begins to save the baby in his role as mother. In line 3, S attempts to clarify the relationship of his agent to the action, qualifying his character as a "good dragon" who, one may infer, is not a threat to the baby. When B continues to enact the role of mother saving baby from dragon in line 4, S specifies in line 5 the relationship between his agent and the action—the dragon is a savior, not the source of threat. B, now clear on this matter, contributes a new scenic element in line 6 to the dramatic frame which integrates the action of S's agent: He provides a new source of threat, getting "runned over," which makes saving appropriate but allows the dinosaur to be the savior. Thus repaired, the action can proceed, and B directs S in appropriate giving of thanks. The double-take of B at the close of the scene also illustrates problems in identifying the speaker that can occur in enactment. It appeared to our coders that B felt S might be personally asking for a kiss, a request which left him open-mouthed. S makes the necessary correction in this respect, and the scene draws to a close.

In this dialogue, we see young children working to coordinate relationships among agents and between agents, actions, and the scene of the fantasy. The attention to details of dramatic consistency is especially noteworthy as B proposes a new source of threat—getting runned over—once he recognizes that S's enactment of the dragon is that of savior and not menace.

TRANSITION: COHESION IN CHILDREN'S FANTASIES

A transition phase may be observed in children's sociodramatic play whenever a continuous interaction spans more than one dramatic episode— as when "cowboys at the roundup on the range" becomes "cowboys in town spending their pay." In the transition phase, children may show concern for dramatic consistency by creating cohesion (Halliday & Hasan, 1976) between episodes, tying the drama of a past episode to a new one through creating connections between elements of the two dramatic frames. In choosing to create dramatic continuity across episodes, in effect to "serialize" play frames, children seem to be stretching their capabilities for manipulation of drama, by creating entire new dramas within the constraints of previous ones through a process of careful transformation.

One case of framing in transition involves play with the dinosaurs at the sand table, and is part of the "devil mountain" motif from which our first case was drawn. K and N have been involved in a drama of fighting and killing between opposing camps of dinosaurs, and have succeeded in killing off all the protagonists.

1. N: They're all buried now.
2. K: Mine are buried too.
3. N: Yeah, cause the dinosaurs get buried at the end, right?
4. K: Pretend we're diggers now and we dig for dinosaurs, right?
5. N: Hey look, I found some dinosaurs, some dinosaur skeletons!
6. K: Yeah, I see some more.
7. N: Let's put them in our big cycle and grind them up, make meat.
8. K: There (places excavated dinosaurs in grinder).
9. N: Oh, look! One is alive! I'll knock him.
10. K: Get him! (Holds dinosaur for N to punch).

In this episode, the children have been confronted with a problem in their dinosaur play: A fighting theme has led to the death and burial of all toy figures. N marks the end of the episode explicitly in line 3, checking with K that all the dinosaurs are indeed buried and explicitly marking this state as "the end." In line 4, K proposes a new frame, in which new agents (diggers) are involved in a new action (digging up dinosaurs). K creates this new frame on the foundation of the old one. Since the dinosaurs are buried, one must dig them up to have access to them. In line 5, N begins to enact the new frame, and observes in his digger role that he is finding dinosaur skeletons. Here, N creates cohesion between the new episode and the previous one by characterizing the agents (or "patients" of digging) in a manner consistent with the end of the prior episode, that is, they are now "skeletons." In line 9, N finally brings one of the dinosaurs back to life. In this effort he again creates cohesion by expressing surprise in finding the dinosaur live, an attitude consistent with an agent who expects the dinosaur to be dead.

This case reveals children at work in adapting a new set of agents and actions to the stage that was the terminal state of their previous fantasy. The character of "dragons" allow for reuse of the toy dinosaurs while respecting their status as "dead and buried." The surprised announcement that "one is alive" similarly lets the dinosaurs resume an active role in the fantasy, while remaining consistent with the constraints from the prior play— that is, the dinosaur "should have been dead."

Discussion

Numerous writers have interpreted the specific content of children's fantasies as in part a reflection of their momentary personal needs and interests. Piaget's (1962) discussion of play as predominately of assimilatory cognitive processes embraces that position in so far as it suggests that play content simply provides a forum for children to exercise their established structures of reasoning. Psychoanalytic theorists (e.g., Peller, 1978) emphasize this position when they treat play as a context for resolution of individual psychological conflicts and issues. Schwartzman (1978) also reflects this perspective by tracing structure of role relations in fantasy to the particular social relationships among the children at play.

The method of analysis we have used, however, highlights the accommodative and nonidiosyncratic aspects of social pretend play. We have seen how children work together to create dramas which take account of regularities in the world as children mutually understand them.

The process of integration and connection of ideas is an explicit focus of concern and conversation among these children. In so far as play serves as a medium for psychological development, talk which seeks to connect and integrate play ideas may be most important. The connected networks of ideas that emerge in fantasy play can be seen as model "worlds" created by the players. The talk which creates these connections is thus an exercise in construction and transformation, which both reflects and supports the child's sense of coherence in the wider world.

Our examples show that children have acquired some explicit notions about regularities in the world by age 5 and that they respect a set of principles regarding relationships between elements of content in the course of their sociodramatic play. Indeed, we have shown how children use dramatic constraints as a tool for decision-making about play content in much the same way that norms or rules of everyday contact might be employed for persuasive purposes in nonfantasy contexts. This implies that children construe dramatic frames as having real prescriptive force, that is, that violation of the frame is an important enough charge to support efforts to elicit compliance to a participant's wishes. Since it is clear that the action is not real, the use of framing statements as instrumental persuasive strategies suggests that internal consistency of frames is very important to children.

The use of framing statements to create cohesion during transitions between adjacent episodes of sociodramatic fantasy is an especially interesting phenomenon. One could argue that there is no drama-based need for children to create these links between thematically distinct episodes, since the fantasy transformations which give rise to the dimensions of a given dramatic episode are certainly arbitrary. The use of transition statements that frame new episodes of fantasy so that they cohere with details of previous fantasy frames suggests an active interest in conforming to norms about dramatic relationships, even where discontinuities in overall episode themes make this unnecessary.

Fantasy play, because of its transformational opportunities, may support the development of structured knowledge about the world. It supports such development because it provides the child with an occasion for active representational exercise. As Franklin (1981) notes, fantasy play operates with the "reality creation" paradigm and involves construction by participants of framework for actions. Through active manipulation of representations in the course of original fantasy creation, the child comes to know the nature of the socially accepted world in a much fuller way than might be possible if play were to consist of simply recreations or recapitulations of observed social phenomena.

In addition, because of the nature of fantasy play action, few constraints on the content of the drama are absolutely given a priori. The child is free to create a fantasy world of any sort, to manipulate the various dimensions of human interaction at will, and to learn about interrelationships among them, including cases which may not be in the child's experience of the real world. Schwartzman's (1976) comment that children use fantasy to experiment with social relationships different from those which existed between the players in reality illustrates this second important quality of fantasy play.

These two features of the fantasy play context make it a valuable context for learning about the social world at many levels. Our suggestion is that they make fantasy especially valuable as a context for learning about the constraints and possibilities for relating the dimensions of social representation as an integrated sensible whole. Bateson (1956) supports this view in his early essay on play and frames:

> The child learns or acquires a new view . . . when he realizes that behavior can, in a sense, be set to a logical type or to a style. It is not the learning of the particular style that you are playing at, but the fact of stylistic flexibility and the fact that the choice of style or role is related to the frame and context of behavior. (1956, p. 149)

Our study of children's "framing" during fantasy play has led us to the conviction that "role-taking" may not be the best all-inclusive rhetoric for subsuming the variety of conceptual knowledge that children acquire about the social world, or the array of skills that children apply to regulate social interaction. Mead (1934), coined this term, and indicated that the goal of "taking the role of the other" is the development of the capacity to coordinate action with that other. We accept the general usefulness and scope of the concept as Mead originally formulated it. However, the word *role* in "role-taking" has directed the attention of social cognitive researchers too much toward the "person" aspect of social situations. It has led to neglect of the other "key dramatisms" that make up the structure of human action and that are equally essential for the child to comprehend if coordination of action is to occur. Indeed, what one must know about another in order to have coordinated interaction is not simply the thoughts, feelings, intentions, et cetera of the other. These are intrapsychic epiphenomena that arise from the other's position in the larger dramatic matrix, which includes the scene with its enabling and constraining properties, the "action plot" with its implications for persons involved in it, and the forces of agency and instrumentality with their assets and limitations. It is the other's larger position in, and not only perspective upon, the social interaction that must be comprehended and responded to. This is not to say that appreciating the subjectivity of persons is unimportant, or that the way that one construes his or her position in an interaction is unimportant. The point is that these factors are only one part of the dramatic matrix, only one piece of the picture that must be understood in a nonegocentric fashion in order for a child to coordinate actions with others.

Studies of children's social development have many directions in which to expand in light of the observations that follow from the dramatistic perspective. Development of social–cognitive representation must be studied in terms of the ability to differentiate and integrate the multiple aspects of content in a fantasy drama.

The dramatistic perspective shows promise as a useful system for indicating new areas of research in children's social cognition. The results of investigations that use a dramatistic perspective may be a much richer account of the child's social world view and hopefully an account of social development that respects the creative, synthetic qualities of meaning in social interactions.

References

Bateson, G. (1955). A theory of play and fantasy. *Psychiatric Research Reports, 2,* 39–51.

Bateson, G. (1956). The message "this is play." In O. Schaffner (Ed.), *Group processes: Transactions of the second conference.* New York: Macy Foundation.

Brenner, J., & Mueller, E. (1982). Shared meaning in boy toddlers' peer relations. *Child Development, 53,* 380–391.

Burke, K. (1950). *A rhetoric of motives.* Los Angeles: University of California Press.

Burke, K. (1969). *A grammar of motives.* Berkeley, CA: University of California Press.

Claparède, E. (1911). Psychologie de l'Enfant et Pedagogie Experimentale [Psychology of the child and experimental pedagogy]. New York: Longmars, Green and Co.

Cook–Gumperz, J., & Corsaro, W. (1977). Social ecological constraints on children's communicative strategies. *Sociology, 11,* 411–434.

Corsaro, W., & Tomlinson, G. (1980). Spontaneous play and social learning in the nursery school. In H. Schwartzman (Ed.), *Play and culture.* New York: Leisure Press.

Franklin, M. (June 1981). *Play as the creation of imaginary situations.* Paper presented at the conference on developmental psychology for the 1980's: Werner's influences on theory and practice. Clark University.

Garvey, C. (1974). Some properties of social play. *Merrill–Palmer Quarterly, 20,* 163–180.

Garvey, C. (1979). An approach to the study of children's role play. *Quarterly Newsletter of the Laboratory of Comparative Human Cognition, 1,* 64–73.

Garvey, C. (December 1982). Communication and the development of social role play. In D. Forbes & M. Greenberg (Eds.), *New directions in child development: Children's playfulness.* San Francisco: Jossey–Bass.

Garvey, C., & Berndt, R. (1977). Organization of pretend play. *Catalogue of Selected Documents on Psychology, 7,* 1589.

Garvey, C., & Hogan, R. (1973). Social speech and social interaction: Egocentrism revisited. *Child Development, 44,* 562–568.

Goffman, E. (1961). *Encounters: Two studies in the sociology of interaction.* Indianapolis: Bobbs–Merrill.

Goffman, E. (1974). *Frame analysis: An essay on the organization of experience.* New York: Harper & Row.

Groos, K. (1901). *The play of man.* (E. L. Baldwin, trans.) New York: Appleton. (Original work published 1898).

Halliday, M. A. K., & Hasan, R. (1976). *Cohesion in English.* London: Longman.

Kaplan, B. (1983). Genetic-dramatism. In S. Wapner & B. Kaplan (Eds.), *Toward a holistic developmental psychology.* Hillsdale, NJ: Erlbaum.

Keenan, E., & Klein, E. (1975). Coherence in children's discourse. *Journal of Psycholinguistic Research, 4,* 365–380.

Keenan, E., & Schieffelin, B. (1976). Topic as discourse notion: A study of topic in the conversations of children and adults. In C. Li (Ed.), *Subject and topic.* New York: Academic Press.

Matthews, W. S. (1977). Modes of transformation in the initiation of fantasy play. *Developmental Psychology, 13,* 212–216.

Mead, G. H. (1934). *Mind, self, and society.* Chicago: University of Chicago Press.

Nelson, K., & Gruendel, J. (1979). At morning it's lunchtime: A scriptal view of children's dialogues. *Discourse Processes, 2,* 73–94.

Newman, D. (1978). Ownership and permission among nursery school children. In M. J. Glick & K. A. Clark–Stewart (Eds.), *The development of social understanding.* New York: Gardner.

Pellegrini, A. D. (1982). The construction of cohesive text by preschoolers in two play contexts. *Discourse Processes, 5,* 101–108.

Peller, L. I. (1978). Play and theory of learning. In E. N. Plank (Ed.), *Lili E. Peller: On development and education of young children: Selected papers.* New York: Philosophical Library.

Piaget, J. (1962). *Play, dreams and imitation in childhood.* New York: Norton.

Rubin, K. H., Fein, G. G., & Vanderberg, B. (1982). Play. In B. Wolman (Ed.), *The handbook of developmental psychology.* NJ: Prentice Hall.

Schwartzman, H. B. (1976). Children's play: A sideways glance at make-believe. In D. F. Lancy & B. A. Tindall (Eds.), *The anthropological study of play: Problems and prospects.* New York: Leisure Press.

Schwartzman, H. G. (1978). *Transformations: The anthropology of children's play.* New York: Plenum.

Spencer, H. (1896). *Principles of psychology* (Vol. 2, 3rd ed.). New York: Appleton.

Sutton–Smith, B. (Ed.). (1979). *Play and learning.* New York: Gradner.

Vygotsky, L. S. (1978). *Mind and society.* Cambridge, MA: Harvard University Press.

Wolf, D. (1981). Playing along: The social side of early pretense. A paper presented at the annual meeting of the Eastern Psychological Association, New York.

PART V

PROCESS IN LEARNING

Once considered only as a source of "social" skills, children's peer experiences are increasingly acknowledged as a potential source of cognitive growth as well. Recent work has examined both *collaboration,* in which children who have comparable skills work together, and *didactic interactions,* in which one child guides a less-skilled partner. In studies involving tasks in academic work, experimental problem-solving tasks, and Piagetian tasks, children have benefited from peer interaction experiences.

A corollary of such developmental gains that merits attention concerns the limitations of children's peer interaction skills. During middle childhood, conscious planning and control of behavioral strategies become possible but may not be accessed in all situations. The relational implications of this bear not only on short-term issues such as children's capacity to plan activities, resolve arguments, and renegotiate the terms of future interactions ("let's not do that any more"), but also on their ability to retain relationships across time and distance.

In their study of "Problem Solving in Children's Management of Instruction," (Chapter 12, this volume) Ellis and Rogoff observe how child teachers distribute their limited cognitive resources as they teach complex tasks. In con-

267

trast to adults, 9-year-olds had difficulty coordinating the complex demands of instruction and were less likely to provide orientation to the task, rehearsal for long-term goals, and other metacognitive guidance that the adults usually offered to the 6-year-old learners.

In "Four Perspectives on Peer Learning among Elementary School Children," (Chapter 11, this volume) Cooper, Marquis, and Edward investigate how children help one another learn in the classroom setting and consider issues in the analysis of spontaneous peer learning discourse and its consequences. They consider contextual, social, cognitive, and discourse themes in the study of peer learning and focus on developmental changes during the elementary years. To examine these issues, a case study is reported of an elementary school in which children were encouraged and assisted in peer learning from the age of three. Cooperative and didactic episodes were recorded as they occurred spontaneously.

CHAPTER 11

Four Perspectives on Peer Learning among Elementary School Children*

Catherine R. Cooper, Angela Marquis, and Deborah Edward

Introduction

The contribution of peer experience to children's development has been receiving renewed appreciation, due in part to greatly increased reserach activity by anthropologists, sociolinguists, educational psychologists, and sociologists, as well as developmental psychologists. This chapter is concerned with how children can help one another learn in the classroom, a topic which is receiving increased attention as scholars examine peer relationships beyond early childhood and in contexts involving cognitive as well as social goals. During the past several years, our work with preschool and primary grade children has indicated that children's skills in peer learning change in significant ways with age, and that within any age group, often poignant and consequential individual differences exist (Cooper, 1980; Cooper, Ayers–Lopez, & Marquis, 1982; Cooper, Marquis, & Ayers–Lopez, 1982). In this paper, we focus on developmental patterns in classroom interactions among elementary school children and differences in effectiveness within age groups. We will do so by drawing upon four different approaches to the study of peer interaction: contextual, social, cognitive, and discourse. Within each area, we consider issues that hold promise for

*This research was supported in part by a grant to the senior author from the University Research Institute of the University of Texas at Austin.

269

illuminating key developmental patterns as well as clues to children's effectiveness in peer learning. We develop these themes with findings from our previous experimental and naturalistic observational work with children from the ages of three to twelve, but we will draw especially from preliminary analyses of data collected in an unusual elementary school which encourages peer interaction as a major means of learning for its children.

We will first introduce the four perspectives on the study of peer process in learning. We next describe the observational, experimental, and interview procedures we have used in our work, and then trace developmental patterns in the nature of competence among younger and older elementary children within each of the four perspectives. Finally, we shall consider the implications of our work for understanding the distinctive contributions of peer experience to development.

A Basic Model of Process in Peer Learning

Our previous work in peer learning has focused on two prototypic situations in which children learn together: cooperative and didactic. In *cooperative* learning, or "doer–doer" interactions (Garvey & Baldwin, 1970), children have an equal amount of information concerning a shared problem. In a *didactic* or "knower–doer" situation, one child has information the other needs to solve a problem. We have used this framework in describing peer interaction in terms of a basic sequence of events involved in peer learning. The core of the sequence is derived from work in speech act, conversational act, and speech event analysis (e.g., Dore, 1979; Coulthard, 1977) which maps the patterns of discourse common to teaching, narratives, and other exchanges which depend on the collaboration of the participants for a conversation to succeed. We view the prototypic sequence of events in spontaneous peer learning as follows: within a conducive context, a child selects a learning partner and negotiates mutually acceptable roles for the interaction. Within this exchange, the initiator must focus and retain the attention of the listener, and provide instrumental moves which accomplish the exchange of information, such as questions, commands, or descriptive comments. The listener has the opportunity to respond, argue, or ignore; finally, the exchange may also be evaluated. By examining these component events and their consequences, we are able to assess factors such as attentional support, listener responsiveness, referential specificity, and other variables for their contribution to the effectiveness of peer exchanges.

We should note that in our investigations of the characteristics of effectiveness in peer-assisted learning we do not claim that the behaviors we report are typical of children attending public schools in the United States. As we will discuss later, relatively few children attend schools which allow them to help one another with classroom work on a regular basis. Consequently, our work has involved designing experimental tasks and finding naturally occurring contexts which enable children to display and develop these complex skills. Thus we consider our description of peer-assisted learning as suggesting what might occur, rather than what typically occurs, among children during the elementary years.

Contextual Perspectives

The work of developmental psychologists has been increasingly integrated with the perspectives of those who study larger social systems, including sociolinguists (Wilkinson, 1982), ethnographers (Cook-Gumperz & Corsaro, 1976; Green & Wallat, 1981); and anthropologists (Greenfield & Lave, 1982; Ochs & Schieffelin, 1979). These investigations have emphasized several points. The first is that context is a multidimensional construct, and includes not only physical aspects (for example, what materials are available to children), but also historical/temporal aspects (how successful was the peer tutoring program last year), situational (whether a child's regular work partner is present today), and linguistic features (what has just been said). It is not surprising that a systematic dimensionalization of context has not emerged.

Another obstacle to any simple taxonomy of contexts stems from the increasing recognition, articulated by Cook-Gumperz and Corsaro (1976), that context is composed of a set of variables which continue to fluctuate during the course of social interaction. For example, in the process of a peer collaborative episode, two children may begin to work together, but the arrival of another may alter the context if he or she brings new materials to the work table or reinstates a plan developed the previous day.

A third challenge to the systematic study of contextual effects concerns their often implicit nature. The explication of unstated rules or presuppositions governing interaction in the classroom has been of special interest; some children may be doing poorly in school, not because of academic deficits but because of their lack of knowledge of these implicit communicative rules, such as the need to select an unoccupied channel of teacher attention (Merritt, 1982), or to discriminate what is appropriate to reveal in a show-and-tell narrative (Michaels & Cook-Gumperz, 1979).

Our first question about context concerns the ways that the teacher influences the form and process of peer-assisted learning. Asking this question involves many aspects and levels of context. At the most general level, allowing children to work among themselves is a prerequisite for their doing so at any one time. As obvious as this may sound, we have visited several classrooms described as "open," yet learned this label referred to architectural features of that building—an absence of walls separating classroom groups within a grade level, or, in one case, to the presence of windows in the door from the hall to the classroom. In both sorts of open classrooms, children were not allowed to converse while working.

Investigations of the "goal structure" set by adults (Slavin, 1980) have demonstrated that democratic rules for peer interaction provide conditions for greater participation and in many cases greater productivity than either competitive or autocratic goal structures. Moreover, experiences with cooperative goal structures provide the basis for enduring expectations and skills. In a study comparing children from traditional and open-space schools, in which shared activities were common, Downing and Bothwell (1979) found that children from traditional schools chose their seats in a way that reflected their expectations that they would work without interacting with their peers. In a cooperative game situation, their rate of cooperation was lower than for the open-space students.

Research with other goal structures has indicated positive effects of experience with peer interaction for a wide range of outcomes, including academic gains, intergroup attitudes, altruism, and self-esteem. Examples of these goal structures include peer tutoring, which typically involves the teacher assigning children to tutor–tutee roles (Allen, 1976); interdependent *Jigsaw* groups in which small teams of children are assigned collaborative roles (Blaney, Stephan, Rosenfield, Aronson, & Sikes, 1977); and cooperative learning groups (Slavin, 1980). So far, however, this work has typically not been concerned with what actually transpires among children as they work, with developmental changes in the interaction patterns or function of these peer experiences, or with the nature of individual differences in effectiveness in peer helping. For example, it would seem useful to identify the characteristics of effective peer tutoring styles, which may differ from the adult model upon which the tutors' training is based.

Our second question about context concerns the range of forms of peer learning that children spontaneously adopt. Because of the traditional constraints on children's interactions in the classroom, we have very little data on this basic question. By observing peer learning among children of different ages, and interviewing teachers who are experienced in fostering a range of peer learning forms across the elementary years, we can begin to understand more clearly the role of adult expectations or goal structures as a context for peer interaction in learning.

Social Perspectives

Within the more egalitarian peer group, and perhaps especially in a more open classroom, fluency in social skills, including role negotiation and conflict resolution, is an advantage in securing access to the resources the peer network offers. Recent work in children's peer relations (Asher & Gottman, 1981; Hartup, 1983; Rubin & Ross, 1982) shows how typical peer interaction patterns during the elementary school years become increasingly differentiated by factors such as age, gender, physical attractiveness, athletic ability, and other qualities. Then too, the basis for friendship develops from an equity or "tit-for-tat" orientation to an awareness of the equivalence of different forms of complementarity (Youniss, 1980). In a classroom, peer learning interactions occur within a network of friends, new acquaintances, and nonfriends. Although the teacher can usually regulate peer contacts to some extent, children's cliques form subsystems that may exclude those who could benefit most from the interaction that occurs within them (Garnica, 1979; Putallaz & Gottman, 1981).

In our work, we have pursued several issues that may be considered as involving the "sociometry of learning." Although conventional sociometric work has focused primarily on popularity, we have been interested in individual differences in children's access to the resources of the peer group for school learning. Our first question concerned developmental patterns in the distribution of children's choices of their classroom working partner and of the most effective helpers in reading and in math. Previous research has indicated that children in open classrooms distribute their friendship choices quite broadly, presumably as a function of their greater opportunities to interact with a range of children and in a range of activity settings (Hallinan, 1981). We were interested in the potential developmental differences in the distributions of children's choices as a measure of their access to support in peer learning and their sensitivity to a hierarchy of competence in the group.

Second, we sought to compare the reflections on the sociometry of learning from interviews with behavioral data. In particular, we were interested in comparing children's and teachers' perceptions of the competence of the children in the group in helping, in math, and in reading in order to assess the convergence of their attributions of competence in the peer helping process.

Cognitive Perspectives

Among the basic changes in cognitive functioning between early and middle childhood is an increase in the capacity to be planful and selective in one's cognitive behavior. The term *strategy,* implying a behavior selected from a repertoire of potential approaches in accordcance with situational requirements, is increasingly used to describe the awareness of means–ends relationships reflected in the behavior of elementary school children (Paris & Lindauer, 1982). These cognitive changes are also reflected in the ways that children help one another. A number of theorists, developing comprehensive accounts of the mechanisms of cognitive change, have suggested that children's peer relations offer a context of special promise for development. Just what these contributions might be, however, has been a matter of differing viewpoints and in some cases disputes. In this section, a number of these suggested and seemingly unrelated modes of peer learning are discussed, a developmental framework is used to organize them, and our own empirical interests in the framework are outlined.

PEERS AS SOURCES OF COGNITIVE CONFLICT

Piaget (1965) suggested that peer exchanges, especially those that bring differing viewpoints into the child's awareness, are likely to play a role in the reduction of egocentrism. Piaget regarded the significance of peer interaction as resting in the opportunity it offers children to experience cognitive conflict. This internal state of disequilibrium he regarded as the most important factor in cognitive development.

A Swiss group, including Mugny, Perret–Clermont, and Doise (e.g., 1981) have conducted an extensive series of studies which provide empirical support for and clarification of Piaget's views. Their key hypothesis is that *intra*individual cognitive structures can develop as a function of *inter*individual interactions. Through a series of studies using Piagetian conservation tasks as well as cooperation games, they have made a number of demonstrations. Among these were that children's interaction with a peer could produce gains that generalize to related tasks (for example, conservation of liquids to conservation of number, matter, and length). Such gains could be distinguished from simple imitation: less advanced children's justifications of their answers were not those they had heard from their partners in over half the cases, and children at intermediate levels of mastery showed progress after interacting with a child of less skill. However, gains of this kind were possible only at certain points in development, when children had prerequisite skills for a particular gain, such as one-to-one correspondence and counting skills for acquiring conservation of number. Further, the experience of cognitive conflict seemed essential, whereas the presentation of a correct or even more nearly correct ("progressive") model was not. Finally, the conflict needed to be a sustained engagement rather than a simple assertion followed by compliance.

Forman (1982) has observed that although peer interaction can foster disequilibrium, it does so only in certain contexts. Those most conducive to cognitive conflict have three characteristics: the children have available to them a rich source of empirical evidence, this evidence can justify at least two different viewpoints, and consensus is viewed as necessary. Although these characteristics apply to the tasks which Mugny and his colleagues have studied, we would argue that there exist a wider range of peer interaction processes that can facilitate learning, and a wider range of tasks for which these processes have been shown to be useful.

PEERS AS PROVIDERS OF COGNITIVE SCAFFOLDING

Prominent among the viewpoints complementing Piaget's emphasis on disequilibrium is that of Vygotsky (1978), who regarded cognitive development as moving from inter- to intrapsychological processes. Vygotsky postulated a "zone of proximal development," the gap between a child's independent problem solving capacity and the level of his or her potential development that could be attained either with the guidance of adults or by means of collaboration with peers who were more skilled (1978, p. 86). This emphasis has stimulated several developmentalists to examine aspects of peer learning interaction that are complementary rather than conflictual. The concept of *scaffolding* (Bruner, 1975), captures the contribution a child (or an adult) can make to another child's learning by observing his or her behaviors, providing hints, guidance, or advice, as well as feedback, correction, or evaluation. Cazden (1983) has also observed that the term *scaffolding* connotes the use of a routine or strategy that is progressively altered by the teacher as the learning child develops, being replaced by one that enhances the mastery of complex behavior of the learner.

BEYOND CONFLICT AND SCAFFOLDING: A DEVELOPMENTAL PERSPECTIVE

In our view, conflict and scaffolding are instances occurring in middle childhood of the doer–doer and knower–doer modes of peer interaction discussed earlier in this chapter. In younger children, who may not have the discourse or cognitive skills to sustain an argument through the resolution of a complex problem (Eisenberg & Garvey, 1981), we have observed that children provide "attentional anchoring" for one another as each works on a problem. In classrooms, this may involve children working alongside one another at two different points in a workbook (we have elsewhere described such "pacing" episodes in more detail [Cooper, Ayers–Lopez, & Marquis, 1982]). Another mode of doer–doer peer learning can be seen in situations in which playful interaction among peers provides a "context for discovery" of a solution that was not known previously by either partner (Bruner, Jolly, & Sylva, 1976).

Along the same developmental lines, the middle childhood skill of scaffolding that may be observed among effective fifth-grade peer tutors of second-grade children (Allen, 1976) may have as precursors less cognitively demanding knower–doer modes such as demonstration, announcing, or narrating. The simpler goal of making one's idea a common or shared one (Higgins, 1980) may typify the knower–doer exchanges of younger pairs.

In our work, we are interested in tracing the modes of peer learning which are typical of older and younger children, and of the more and less effective children at different age levels. Finding such patterns may contribute to an account of the role of peer interaction in cognitive development with greater utility and breadth of application.

Discourse Perspectives

By middle childhood, children have typically mastered the fundamental skills of conversation. With the benefit of increased internal control, including the capacity to develop and utilize plans as well as for interpersonal reciprocity, children show responsiveness to many needs of their listeners. However, the more complex tasks of comprehension monitoring and coordination inherent in guidance and persuasion still present a challenge to many children of this age (Paris & Lindauer, 1982; Shatz, 1983).

As with the study of context, the investigator confronts complex issues concerning the wide diversity of categories for analyzing units and dimensions of discourse. At least three levels of analysis can be seen. At the *utterance* or speech act level, individual statements are classified according to the speaker's presumed intent, such as directives or requests for information (Dore, 1979). By considering an utterance in the context of others adjacent to it, its role and effectiveness in conversation can be evaluated. Finally, at the social level, discourse can be analyzed in terms of its contribution to accomplishing interpersonal goals (Labov & Fanshel, 1977). We should note that others in the area of discourse research are currently working on this very thorny issue of levels and dimensions of analysis (Chapman, 1970; Dore, 1983).

Our interests have focused on what aspects of discourse are predictive of effectiveness in peer learning interaction, measured at the utterance, discourse, and social (as well as cognitive) levels. We have documented the significance of particular utterance types, including attention-focusing statements, directives, questions, as well as responsiveness to these moves (e.g., Cooper, 1980; Cooper, Ayers–Lopez & Marquis, 1982; Cooper, Marquis, Ayers–Lopez, 1982). Patterns of developmental differences have been observed in the use of individual utterance types, both within a single move-response round, as well as across several rounds. For example, kindergarten children tend to use *attention-focusing* or *managing statements,* such as "hey" or "stop it," without other utterance functions. Older children use these together with other moves (such as, "Bill?" "Yes." "Are you busy?")

to gain the attention of the listener, and then to give or ask for additional information. Without these subsequent moves, failure to maintain attention is likely. *Pacing* statements such as "hurry up" or "wait for me" reveal an awareness of the relative rates of progress between speaker and listener; not surprisingly, older children use these more frequently than their younger counterparts.

The degree of *directness* and *referential specificity* in children's peer discourse also shows developmental patterns of interest. For example, requests or offers of help, information, permission or action are often made by younger children to initiate an interaction, whereas older children utilize negotiating or attention-focusing statements prior to these moves. These findings suggest that the form of the move is important to its success. Being indirect reflects an awareness of asymmetry in a relationship, which may improve the chances that an older child will respond to a request, especially one made by a nonfriend. However, younger children often use direct statements with positive results (see also Wilkinson, 1982); perhaps younger listeners need the clarity of direct forms to ensure comprehension and thus compliance. *Evaluative* remarks are often used to mark the closings of an interaction, although many peer learning episodes end without any explicit marking.

The extension of a conversation among children over several rounds of moves and responses, such as in negotiating who will participate in an activity, what the activity will be, what roles the children will assume in carrying it out, as well as its procedures, reflects their more advanced cognitive abilities, such as the awareness of the existence and need to coordinate different viewpoints, as well as the ability to integrate these into a mutually satisfactory arrangement (Flavell, 1977). These negotiations also allow a sense of equity among the participants, particularly when questions, hints, or other mitigators are used rather than directives (Labov & Fanshel, 1977; Youniss, 1980). Our observations have indicated that older elementary children are more skilled than younger ones in both social and cognitive aspects of these negotiations. In the following example, older children often engage in more than one type of negotiation during an episode:

A: Did you finish your work?
B: Yes. After lunch, let's go to the library.
A: Dave told me 'let's go to the library,' but you can come too.
B: Ummm, O.K.

Younger children use these patterns much less frequently, and are more likely to use directives than to negotiate and integrate different viewpoints in the solution.

The study we report in this chapter extends our earlier work by examining the relations between processes in peer discourse to outcomes at the discourse and task levels. In our analyses, the function of each utterance is classified into one of the following groups (see Appendix 1 for entire code, definitions, and examples): focusing or pacing the conversation; instrumentally moving the conversation with directives, predictions, demonstrations, or explanations; responding to a previous utterance; or evaluating the persons, products, or process involved in the task. In addition, the referential specificity of the verbal moves and the use and accuracy of attributes (Cooper, 1980) are coded. Developmental differences in peer learning discourse as well as patterns typical of effective children at each age level can be examined.

A Case Study of Peer Learning in School

In the following pages, preliminary findings from an intensive study of an individual school will be used to address issues from these four perspectives.

METHOD

Subjects

Sixty-nine children, ranging in age from five to twelve years old, participated in the study. They comprised the entire enrollment of a Montessori elementary school which actively encouraged collaborative interaction as a means of accomplishing school learning. The children, who came from primarily white, middle class families, were divided into two groups. The younger group was composed of 37 five- to nine-year-olds, with 22 girls and 15 boys. The older group included 31 seven- to twelve-year-olds, with 18 girls and 13 boys. Age was not the only factor in determining a child's placement in a classroom, since children were moved to the older group when their cognitive and social abilities were commensurate with the rest of the group. Some children were allowed to change classrooms in their daily activities, but only a few did so. This program allowed us an unusual opportunity to study peer learning interactions, since learning with others was an explicit method and goal of the curriculum from the time the children entered the program at age three.

Procedures

Our methods for studying peer interactions in the school involved experimental, observational, and interview methodologies. This work has been based on a number of principles. One is that the complexity of peer learning interactions can best be understood by using multiple methods of data collection and analysis. Also, with each methodological approach, we have sought to obtain data under conditions that would elicit the *optimal,* rather than the typical behavior of children at each age. For example, we observed pairs of "work friends" (i.e., regular partners in classroom learning activities) in the experimental task rather than randomly matching children. We also conducted our naturalistic observations in a school which supported a high level of peer interaction as part of the curriculum. In this way, we could understand what might be possible at different developmental periods.

We conducted naturalistic observations of these children in their classrooms to answer questions concerning spontaneous peer learning. Among these were: In what forms of learning interaction can children of different ages engage? What roles do they assume in such situations?

During key periods of peer learning activity in the daily schedule, we observed the working arrangements of the children in the room so that we could obtain an indication of whom each child might have as potential learning parnters, and which children worked by themselves. In addition, we noted the forms of the working interactions that were spontaneously occurring: both the participants and the forms were recorded by means of time sampling procedures. In addition, we collected samples of spontaneous peer interactions by placing audio tape recorders on children's tables and rugs as they worked together. Pertinent nonverbal and contextual data were also recorded.

In addition, we conducted individual open-ended interviews with the same children we observed in order to examine sociometric issues concerning the children's awareness of both social and cognitive networks in their classrooms. Peer ratings of classmates were obtained through a *sort-and-explain* procedure (following Hallinan, 1981): Children were given the names of classmates, each written on a 3" × 5" card, and were asked to sort the cards into piles to indicate which children were best as work friends, play friends, best helpers in reading and math, and most knowledgeable in reading and math. Each sort was treated separately, and after each one, children were asked to explain their choices. These reponses yielded both a map of the social and learning networks in each class and revealed developmental and competence differences in social constructs.

The teacher or "guide" of each group was also interviewed to obtain information about the principles of teaching that enabled children at each age to use peers as resources in their learning. At the end of the school year, each teacher was also asked to rate each child in his or her class (on a scale from 1 to 10) on a number of dimensions, including competence in reading and math, their progress during the academic year in those areas, and their ability to help others in these skills.

In experimental work, we link process to outcomes in the most systematic way. We examine peer interaction skills under conditions of minimal distraction, and when the roles of cooperating partner, teacher, and learner do not need to be negotiated by the children. The opportunity to standardize tasks and conditions of observation allow us to identify process variables to trace in our naturalistic observational work, and to anchor our examination of process with meaningful outcome measures of effectiveness in peer collaboration (Cooper, Ayers–Lopez, & Marquis, 1982).

For the experimental task (Marquis, in preparation), same-sex pairs of children who had named one another as "work friends" were given a pretest on a balance scale problem adapted from Siegler (1976). Mastery of the problem, which can be demonstrated at different levels, involves the understanding of the interaction of the variables of weight distance from the fulcrum. Children were allowed to interact with their partner for 20 minutes using the materials, and were retested individually on the problem to see if any pretest–posttest changes occurred in their understanding of the problem. During the pretest and posttest, children were asked to provide predictions and explanations about which way the balance scale would tip under various conditions. Each child was asked how he or she knew which way the scale would tip, what might make a difference in the way the scale would tip, and how the scale worked. Children were also allowed to demonstrate their understanding by arranging blocks on the scale. Each phase of the study was videotaped.

RESULTS AND DISCUSSION

Contextual Perspectives

Forms of peer learning. One of the most striking findings of our study concerns the wide range of peer learning forms that we observed in the classroom. At this point, we shall illustrate the range of forms we have observed, ranging from working alone to extended collaborative interactions.

In the following example of *solitary* activity, a child chooses to work alone. Although offered advice, she declines it, thus illustrating that even a child's solitary activity may need to be negotiated within the social system of the classroom.

> Karen is working alone on a string construction.
> Beverly: (Approaches and watches Karen for a few moments) You're supposed to . . .
> Karen: (Holds up her hand to stop Beverly from talking to her) *I* know what to do.
> (Beverly leaves)

Sometimes a child works on a project alone yet allows (as does the teacher) others to watch and make occasional comments or suggestions. We consider this form as *onlooker* because the observers are not engaged in any work of their own. With both younger and older children, the onlooker role can provide a valuable vantage point for observing more skilled children. From our time sampling observations, the children who engaged in this form seemed to be those who were less able to sustain the engagement of collaborative projects, and it was more common among younger than older children (although this may reflect differential tolerance by their teachers). We should note that this onlooker role in academic work settings is rarely tolerated in traditional public schools, where it is called cheating.

When two or more children are each working on their own projects, yet exchange information and perhaps help one another concentrate on and accomplish their individual goals, we consider the form to be *parallel-coordinate*. Often these interactions contain brief exchanges of task-relevant information within a stream of conversation about a range of academic and nonacademic topics, including birthday parties, television programs, social comparisons among classmates, and other personal material. Within this stream occur episodes of concentrated attention:

> Bill and Mark are working on different pages, practicing cursive writing.
> Mark: Remember, let me show you one. There's an F.
> Bill: Capital T's are easy. Here, let me show you.
> Mark: They're almost like F's.

In *guidance,* one child tends to direct the other in accomplishing some activity; overall, one child is the teacher. For example, in teacher–learner exchanges, one child offers to help or teach another:

> Diane: Look, this is how you do it (demonstrating knitting). This around that one and around like this. Pull it very tight, Go under.
> Steve: O.K.
> Diane: It's O.K. if you let it stretch. Go.
> (Steve tries it.)
> Diane: No. Look. Pull this one up and then go under.
> Steve: O.K., I'll try it.
> Diane: Yeah! That's good.

Another form of guidance, learner–teacher, usually is marked by a "learner" requesting help from a "teacher."

> Marshall: What does it say?
> Marie: What does what say?
> Marshall: (reading) "That's everything . . . "
> Marie: (starts reading)

> Marshall: You got it.
> Marie: Yeah.

We have occasionally observed more elaborate forms of guidance in which one child guides another in teaching a third child (*executive guidance*):

> Alice comes to help Betty and Claire work on drawing a map of the United States.
> Alice: What do you need my help for?
> Betty: Because you know how to do it. (to draw a map from puzzle piece)
> Alice: O.K., we'll set it up here. (shows them how to put piece down and draw, then goes to work on own map while Betty and Claire work together)
> Alice leaves, then returns.
> Alice: Why don't you let her do it now? (telling Betty to let Claire do the map on her own) All the pieces fit exactly in here.
> Alice: Look, O.K. there, you'll have to fix it right . . . well I'm going over here . . . You ought to help her.

In *collaborative* interaction, the children share the power of directing the interaction more equally, either through alternating or sharing the teaching role or by not assuming a clear leader–follower pattern. In addition, especially in the older group, we have seen children collaborate on loosely associated projects which accomplish some superordinate goal (*thematic collaboration*) or collaborate on a project but engage in different interrelated tasks that accomplish the shared goal (*differentiated collaboration*). For example, a group of children collaborated on an electricity project in which one child looked for information in reference books, another set up a display of the principles under study, and a third wrote a report on the project. Role assignment was negotiated by the children, who conducted their project over several days. (We should note that to a naive observer, a group of children working on a differentiated collaboration might, at any one time, appear to be engaged in less complex peer interaction forms, including solitary and parallel-coordinate work. The assistance of a member of the class is required to identify the ultimate purpose of some activities.)

Our observation of such a diversity of peer learning forms prompted us to reflect on the relation between decentralization of decision-making power in the classroom and the range of peer interactions that may occur in educational settings. We have summarized this relationship in Table 11.1. In the first column, possible environments for peer learning interaction are ordered from the traditional elementary school classroom in which peer interaction is basically illegal, to a situation (reported in Cooper, Marquis, & Ayers–Lopez, 1982) in which children are permitted to help one another, but where tasks are not shared but are teacher assigned ("peers can help").

Table 11.1

Variations by Setting in Peer Learning Forms Permitted in Classrooms

Classroom setting	Permitted form[a] of peer process in setting	Explanation of form[a]
Traditional classroom (Don't talk to your neighbor)	Solitary	Solitary Individual child works alone
Peers can help[b] with individual assignments	Solitary Onlooker Parallel–Coordinate Simple guidance	Onlooker Child interacts with another who is working on task Parallel–Coordinate Children interact while working on different tasks; "attentional anchoring"
Peer tutoring[c] Peers are assigned helper–learner roles and task		
Jigsaw[d] Peers are assigned roles and task	Differentiated collaborative	Guidance ("Knower-Doer") Simple Child offers or receives help from another on single task including telling, guiding
Cooperative groups[e] Peers negotiate their collaborative roles within mutually competitive groups; teacher-chosen task	Simple and differentiated collaborative	Executive Child helps another child help a learner Referral Child helps another child find a helper
Prepared environment[f] Peers negotiate roles and choose from a range of individual to collabortive tasks with teacher guidance	Solitary, Onlooker, Parallel–Coordinate, Guidance (Simple executive, referral), Collaborative (Simple, Differentiated, Thematic)	Collaboration ("Doer-Doer") Simple Cooperate towards shared goals, taking turns Differentiated Superordinate goal or project, division of labor Thematic Loose association of projects

[a]The studies cited report observations of peer process in respective setting.
[b]Cooper, Marquis, & Ayers-Lopez (1982).
[c]Allen (1976).
[d]Blaney et al. (1977).
[e]Slavin (1980).
[f]Present study.

Other environments include peer tutoring (Allen, 1976), interdependent Jigsaw groups (Blaney, Stephan, Rosenfield, Aronson, & Sikes, 1977), cooperative teams (Slavin, 1980), and the school reported in the present study. In this last setting, we have observed the greatest range of forms of peer interaction, perhaps because children have been taught the complex skills that, over time, increasingly allow them to choose among forms of peer interaction. The range of forms we have considered are listed in the third column, with those permitted within various educational settings suggested in the second.

Thus with regard to the issue of context, it appears that with decentralized decision-making patterns, and with supportive guidance from the teacher, the range of potential forms and complexity of peer interaction may increase.

The role of the teacher in the prepared environment. From interviewing and observing the teachers, we have begun to learn how their actions and expectations influence peer learning patterns in their classrooms. A visitor to the classrooms would be struck by the variety of activities that children are working on. As children arrive in the morning, they are expected to choose some work. The teacher of the older group said:

> They are free to choose their own work, but at this age level, they are not really free *not* to be working during the work period. There are a lot of kids with whom I will set up what kind of things they need to accomplish, if they are behind in skills, and then if they are not doing that, I'll talk with them about it. I may ask "What have you done in the last week (even if I already know all that they have done)?" and "What do you need to be working on?" or if a child doesn't have any work, "Where is your work?" If they say something that they are very good at and do all the time, I say "Yes, that's something that you are very good at. What are some of the things that you haven't spent some time on?" It's a slow progression, and they (ultimately) become quite good at organizing their time.

In the younger group, the teacher provides more structure in helping children set their own goals. For the youngest children in this class, who are typically in their first year in the group, the teacher chooses about half of their work, which is primarily focused on basic reading and math skills. During a child's second year in the group, a majority of the work is self-chosen.

Learning principles of group work. How do teachers promote development in children of the skills of group living that enable such a variety of activities to occur simultaneously? In both groups, explicit lessons in "grace and courtesy" are given during the fall of each year, *grace* referring to individual modes of effective study, and *courtesy* to one's interactions with others. Reminders of these lessons are heard from time to time:

> If you're working with a partner, speak so softly that only your partner can hear you. If you don't have a work partner, there's no need to be talking. Your shoes need to be under your table.

Both teachers emphasize that other principles may be learned best when they are "discovered" by the children:

> The younger kids really learn it (the expectations of the classroom) from the older ones, just by watching. Also I'll kind of direct the space. "What if somebody took their rugs out and took up a huge diagonal, and somebody else came along and wanted to put a bead chain (long strings of beads used in multiplying)," . . . and then they'll say, "We have to set up spaces so that we can walk around people." Or they'll talk about how to walk around rugs so they won't interfere with each other's rugs. This all comes out of the kids. We (the teachers) can direct it a great deal, but it's really integral to the class that the rules aren't rules from the outside . . . When there are 30 to 35 children working in a space that small, it gets very uncomfortable if it gets really loud, if they are bumping into each other or aren't being courteous. Maybe we'll sit down when it's been very comfortable and say "It's sure been nice working together this morning. What are some of the things that made it so comfortable?" But actually it works better in the negative (to consider why things have not gone well). The kids think up all kinds of things: "When there is so much talking going on, we need to look at one another when we talk, because if you're talking while looking off away from someone, you have to talk a lot louder, and then other people besides just the person you are talking to will hear it too."

Channeling the forms of peer learning. The teachers keep in mind a developmental progression of skills in both academic and social areas that are expressed in different forms of peer learning interactions. In the younger group, children who have not mastered basic skills are more dependent upon the teacher for lessons and feedback. With these children, the teacher may channel peer work into practicing skills together, such as cursive writing, in a structured situation, perhaps having children working alongside one another (parallel-coordinate) near the teacher. Simple collaborative games are ordered by how much structure they provide to the children's interaction. If children can work well on a very structured activity, they demonstrate that they have the prerequisite skills for more differentiated and negotiated collaborative roles. Eight-year-olds, for example, may be ready to work with a map puzzle and tectonic plates of the earth's surface, then write a report together. The teacher may give a lesson to a small group of children, then ask one of the more advanced children to take over, thus taking advantage, in one teacher's words, "of both knowledge and friendship.'' The child who is teaching is also "free to express his maturity in a relaxed and spontaneous way.'' Children frequently teach one another various skills spontaneously. When the teacher in the younger group noticed a younger child observing two older children writing stories together, he let this continue. A few months later, the former onlooker began to write his own stories with another younger partner. Or children will "leapfrog" with one another: one child used to help his friend in reading; now the former tutee is getting far enough ahead of his friend in math that he is the teacher.

As in the younger group, older children who have mastered basic skills are encouraged to develop projects more independently. Among the older children, such projects can be quite elaborate, although for the most part, the teacher plays a consultant role.

> At this age, they can take on projects that none of them could or would do alone. Large projects also draw children who would not be able to work this way on their own. There's enough group format and group pressure to help. In a large group activity, I never assign who would do what tasks because I would never be able to do it as well as they do. They will decide who will do the research, who will write it up, who will do the calligraphy, or who will do the art work.

Interventions in peer learning interactions. When the productivity of work friends flags, teachers may intervene. The teacher of the younger group noticed that a trio of girls were not working well together; one child seemed to be manipulating the friendships with her two partners, and this social "agenda" began to predominate in their conversations. The teacher linked each child with other work partners. In the older group, the teacher observed:

> There are times when they work together but they get a lot less done. They get distracted by each other's presence and the social comfort of working together, but they will not get any academic work done. A lot of times when that is going on, I separate them. We will speak to them about whether they are good work partners. I'll say, "I know you are good play partners, but you need to change your habits so you can work together too."

Difficulties in children's pacing their work can also elicit teacher intervention.

> The adults help in setting a goal for the finished product and for a time frame for the plan of work . . . when the children would like to finish, what it would be like when it was finished. So if days have passed, I meet with them and ask "When would you like to go back to working

on the map?'' In a situation like this, the children were complaining, "Oh, we don't want to." I reminded them of their original agreement, and they said, "Oh, did I really say that?" So we worked out they would work on three states a day and finish sometime before lunch, . . . and they finished on schedule.

Social Perspectives

Our findings concerning the sociometry of learning in the children's groups are drawn from two sources: from the interview responses of the children to questions about their work friends and best helpers in reading and math, and from the ratings by the teachers of children's competence in helping one another and in reading and math. By using multiple measures of the group, we could examine the relationships between children's judgments of competence and the views of their teachers.

Sociometric choices. With few exceptions, each child was chosen at least once as a work friend by another child, when sometimes choices were included. In contrast, children showed more selectivity in designating the best helpers in reading and math. Figures 11.1 and 11.2 show histograms of the frequencies with which children in the younger and older groups, each ordered by chronological age, were chosen by their classmates as the best helpers in these two areas.

Several patterns are notable. First, the association between chronological age and frequency of nomination is weak. Although several older children in each group were chosen frequently, several others were among the least frequently chosen, whereas several younger children were seen as very competent. Second, older children were more selective about their choices; in reading, the mean number of nominations made was 8.63 ($N = 32$) for the younger group, compared with 4.83 ($N = 29$) for the older group, $t(59) = 4.02$, $p < .01$. Similarly, in math, the mean number of choices was 8.50 for the younger group, 4.59 for the older children, $t(59) = 4.03$, $p < .01$. It should be noted that many of the choices received by individual children came from different children for reading and math; this was more the case for the younger children (81%) than for older ones (61%). One interpretation of this pattern is that older children are forming more complex and stable attributions of their peers. Perhaps, too, the younger children, in sorting through the name cards, tended to respond less reflectively.

Comparing perceptions of children and their teachers. Children's choices of peers who were the most effective helpers were positively related to the perceptions of their teachers. For the younger and older groups, the number of times each child was named as a work friend, best reading helper, and

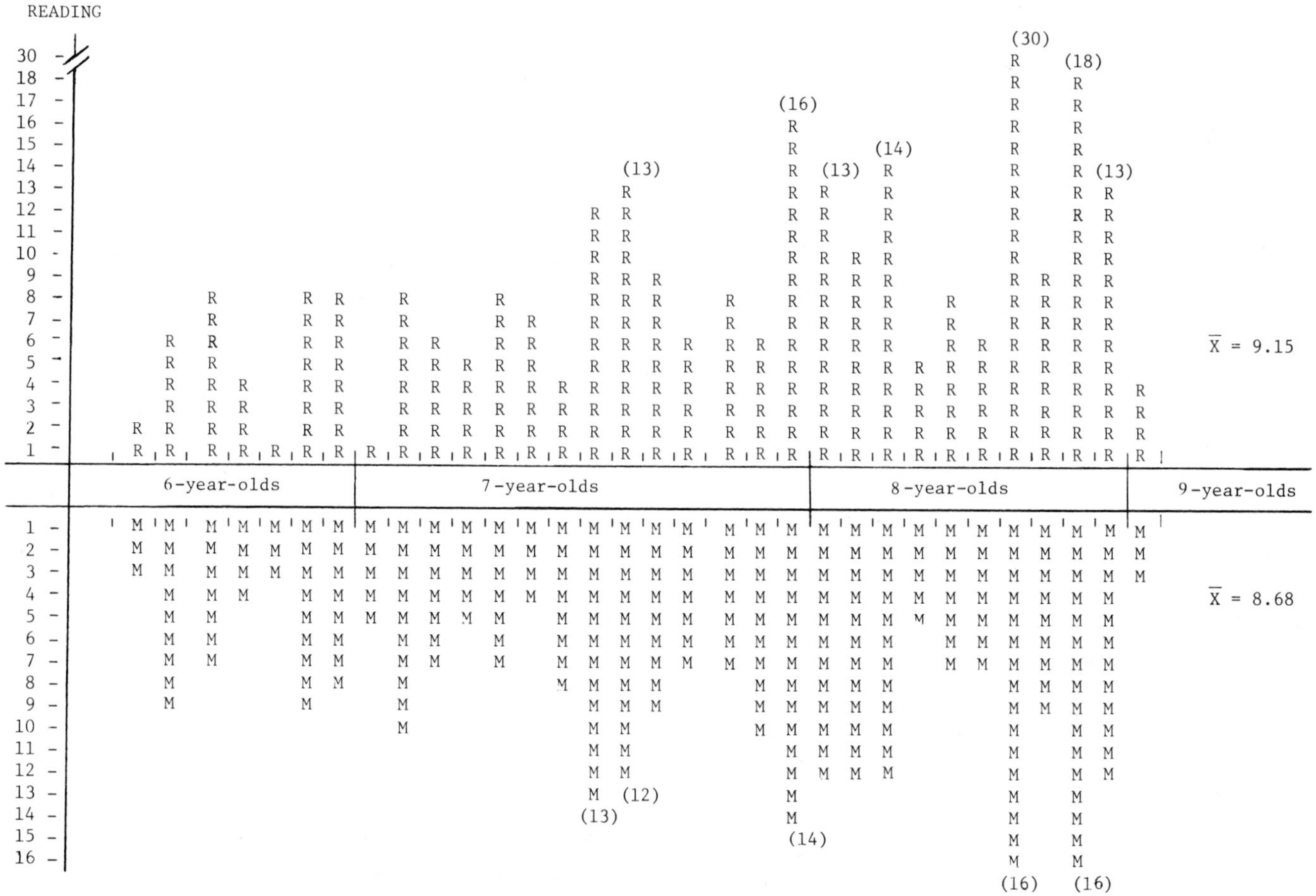

Figure 11.1. Frequencies of nominations of children, ordered by chronological age, as best helpers in reading (R) and math (M): Younger group.

288

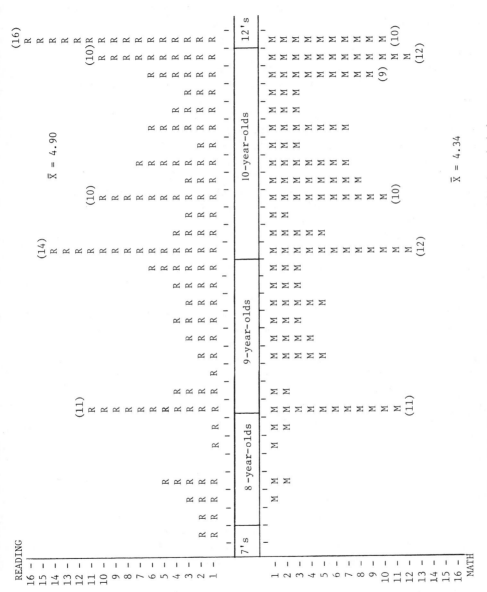

Figure 11.2. Frequencies of nominations of children, ordered by chronological age, as best helpers in reading (R) and math (M): Older group.

289

best math helper were summed and then correlated with the teacher's rating of that child (from 1–10) in response to the question "How effective is this child as a helper?" For the younger group, the Pearson correlation was .64 ($df = 32$, $p < .01$), for the older group, .72 ($df = 27$, $p < .01$). An illuminating comment by the teacher of the older group was that some of the children she regarded as most effective were capable of helping those outside their circle of friends, whereas children she regarded as in the midrange were very helpful within a more limited range of close friends. This pattern may also be reflected in the children's ratings, since the highest scores would depend on a child's effectiveness in helping being known by a larger number of children than one's primary friendship group.

In reading and in math, children's choices of "Who are the best helpers?" and their teachers' ratings (from 1–10) of "How competent is this child in ———?" were also positively correlated for the younger group, reading $r(32) = .57$, $p < .01$; math, $r(32) = .62$, $p < .01$; for the older group, reading $r(27) = .47$, $p < .01$; math, $r(27) = .53$, $p < .01$. The source of these strong associations may lie both in the children and the teachers responding similarly to the signs of competence in the children, and in part in the practice by teachers of making "referrals" to competent children for others needing help. That the patterns are not simply reflections of the latter phenomenon is indicated by the relatively wide distributions of frequencies of children's helper choices, and from remarks made by the teacher of the older group, who commented how advantageous it was to have only herself and an aide for the 32 children in her group (each of whom might be working on a different activity), since children would tire of waiting for her to help them and would turn to their own resources, presumably without a teacher's referral. Thus it seems reasonable that the children and teachers are deriving their attributions of competence in helping and in math and reading from their own experiences with the children of the group.

Cognitive and Discourse Perspectives

For a preliminary investigation of the cognitive and discourse processes involved in peer collaborative interactions, we selected from the experimental session data two pairs of children from each age group: one that was quite effective and one that was less effective. Effectiveness was determined by the number of trials from the beginning of the interaction that were needed for the children to obtain two successes in balancing the scale. We also examined their gains from pretest to posttest in understanding of the principles of the balance scale, as shown by their explanations. Excerpts from the transcripts of the collaborative interaction of these four dyads are given in Appendix 2.

Before examining the relation of discourse processes to task effectiveness and cognitive gains, we must consider these gains from a developmental perspective. From our preliminary analyses, younger children who gained in individual understanding were also effective on the task with their partners. Among older children, the difference between more and less effective subjects was not the amount (the number of levels advanced) as much as the kind of gains (i.e., the nature of the transitions) they made. For example, the less effective older dyad, Lynn and Mary, made gains, but only to a level already attained by many younger children at pretest (that is, in understanding that balance is achieved for equal weights only when they are on the same peg (Klahr, 1980; Siegler, 1976). This gain is not as complex as that attained by Jake, a member of the more effective dyad, for understanding that distance sometimes conflicts with weight, that is, that greater weight on one side will not prevent weights farther out on the other side from tipping the scale. Thus, both how much change and what final level of competence is reached appear to be associated with greater effectiveness in peer interaction. This factor is probably due to a difference across the levels in what skills are necessary to achieve each level, a pattern that occurs not only in this experimental task, but also in academic task sequences such as learning to read.

Although both the younger and older pairs of effective children took only a few trials to obtain two successes in balancing the weights, the process of their interaction differed. It was not only the presence or absence of any single utterance type that distinguished more from less effective children and older from younger ones, but also the patterns of their discourse. For example, the older effective pair, Jake and Keith, made a prediction, then demonstrated that it would hold, explained why it was or was not correct, and demonstrated why it was not correct or what would be necessary to make it so. The younger effective children, Stacy and Judy, exhibited a similar pattern but without using explanations. Although it might appear that explanations were beyond the capabilities of younger children, the *less* effective younger pair, Ed and Carl, did use them yet did not have as much success, either in balancing the scale or in posttest gains in their understanding of the principles of the task. A possible source of this discrepancy is that they did not use demonstrations *with* their explanations, and it may be that demonstrations are more necessary at this age; that is, that "seeing is believing."

The use of several individual utterance types was associated with effectiveness in these examples, and corroborates our earlier findings. Two key instrumental moves seemed useful: the directive and the question. Both direct and indirect forms of directives were effective with older dyads, but for younger children, directness seemed necessary. For the older, less ef-

fective dyad, Lynn and Mary, so little communication transpired that failures here were likely due simply to copying the partner's actions without
talking. However, for the younger children, directness was typical of the
most effective and indirectness with the least effective (Wilkinson, 1982).
Asking questions, either as a Socratic teaching strategy, such as Jake's
"What would be the balance for this?," or to obtain information from the
partner in the course of mutual discovery, was also typical of effective children, whereas less effective pairs did not use questions.

The responsiveness of the listener was also significant. Children in most
dyads complied with their partner's requests, but the effective listeners took
an active role in the communicative process by arguing, adding information, or correcting the partner's statement or action. Less effective children
tended simply to comply with their partners. Particularly for the older less
effective dyad, Lynn and Mary, little responsiveness and simple compliance
or copying of the partner's behavior was associated with little improvement.
For the younger pairs, lack of compliance or responding of any type, or
else incorrect responding was associated with little success.

With regard to referential specificity, it appears that both verbal and nonverbal modes of specifying reference are significant for both age groups,
and the omission of nonverbal cues for older children and verbal cues by
younger ones was associated with less effectiveness. However the use of
nonverbal cues may also benefit younger children, since the less effective
pair, Carl and Ed, used a great deal of nonspecific communication without
either verbally or nonverbally specific messages. Thus nonverbal communication appears helpful for all ages on this task, perhaps because the materials were concrete and so many aspects associated with their manipulation
are important in solving this problem.

What cognitive benefits did effective children provide for one another?
First they planned, organized, and oriented themselves and their partners
as to what strategies they should try. Older children were more likely to
orient their partner whereas younger children directed their partner's activities by telling. Second, effective children utilized their failures to make
gains on the next trial; when the scale did not balance, they did not begin
all over, but rearranged only one weight to see if that would work. In general, the effective children, especially the older ones, did not treat each trial
as an independent effort, but worked toward a superordinate goal across
trials. They helped one another in remembering aspects of the problem,
either with procedural questions such as how to add or remove weights from
the scale, or with substantive matters, such as writing down the results of
their experimentation. Older less effective children tended to treat each trial
as independent, either by taking all the weights off the pegs or by completely rearranging them. These children did not orient one another to the

task or provide mnemonic help, but tended merely to comply with and copy one another. This was not necessarily ineffective for the younger children, since it was more appropriate to the level of understanding they already had, but it did not add as much for the older children. For the younger children, less effectiveness was seen when each child worked as a parallel-coordinate partner, that is, on their own individual task, rather than treating the task as one with a shared goal.

Summary and Conclusions

By examining the processes involved in peer learning in terms of the four perspectives treated in this paper, this study has yielded a more integrated account of the developmental changes in peer relations that occur during middle childhood. Our key conclusions can be summarized as follows:

First, the context in which peer interaction occurs can have profound effects on the form and function of peer process. The teacher may consider peer interaction unacceptable, or may allow tutoring on individual assignments or even collaborative projects. In a classroom in which peer learning is encouraged, a diversity of forms occur, few of which have been studied. Traditional frameworks for categorizing peer interaction in terms of isolate, onlooker, and parallel play (Parten, 1933), which were developed to describe social play in preschool children, now can be supplemented with observations of older children and academic or "work" settings. For example, younger children's onlooker experiences can provide the basis for later academic competence. Children seated adjacent to one another can help sustain attention to work, as well as to provide a source of information or an audience for the announcement of newly discovered knowledge. The variety of patterns of peer learning observed among older children, including referrals to other children as well as complex collaborative forms, suggests that their occurrence depends upon the important interplay of teacher sanction and children's developmental readiness.

A key implication of these findings is that investigators of peer interaction can no longer regard context as a vaguely neutral aspect of this topic. Developmental psychologists, for example, often see as their key task the identification and investigation of variables of developmental significance, separated from situational effects (Wohlwill, 1973). For example, some investigators have sought to excise the study of children's peer relationships from contextual variables by pairing unacquainted children. This chapter has argued that our understanding of the development of peer relationships will benefit from greater sophistication and study of contextual influences on peer interaction.

Second, the process of peer-assisted learning occurs in a social network, which is reflected in the patterns of attribution and of actual choices children make in their collaboration and consultation. Our findings indicate that in a school in which children are able to work together, a remarkable proportion of class members were regarded as resources for learning in math and reading, although older children were more selective in their choices than younger ones. Children and teachers in the school perceived the patterns of skill in helping with striking reliability; this perception suggests that teachers could monitor the degree to which isolated children might be missing the benefit of the peer learning network. As with our earlier work, the findings from this study document the range in degree of involvement in the peer network and presumably in the amount of benefit that children derive from their associations with classmates. Without intervention, it would appear that the rich will continue to become richer.

Third, the preliminary findings concerning discourse and cognitive themes suggest that particular aspects of children's discourse play significant roles in the effectiveness of their exchanges with peers. With our earlier studies (Cooper, 1980; Cooper, Ayers–Lopez, & Marquis, 1982; Cooper, Marquis, & Ayers–Lopez, 1982), these observations offer additional support for the significance of particular features of children's discourse, including directives and questions as well as both verbal and nonverbal means of specifying referents and communicating responsiveness. At a different level of discourse analysis, however, the present study, which involves children who are older than those in much peer interaction research, points out the need to study more abstract and extended conversational strategies such as orienting, negotiating, and guiding that are typical of children in middle childhood. The study of the construction and resolution of collaboration itself, including the negotiation of roles, planning activities, and evaluating outcomes, is in need of further study (Asher & Renshaw, 1982; Stone & Selman, 1982). One notable feature of peer collaborative exchanges is their embeddedness, frequently unmarked, in a stream of conversation covering a great range of school and nonschool topics. Developing the conceptual and analytic frameworks for the study of these episodes involving older children is an important and challenging next step (Cooper & Cooper, 1984).

Fourth, at the level of cognitive mode, our work suggests that the collaborative (doer–doer) and teaching (knower–doer) functions evolve across early and middle childhood, with younger children typically engaging in more symmetrical collaboration and more demonstration and announcement forms of teaching. With increased metacognitive skill, older elementary school classmates can begin to plan more long-term and differentiated collaborative projects, engage in more elaborate and extended arguments, offer more effective orientations, and more progressively adjusted guidance (that is, scaffolding) as teachers. In other words, as children's cognitive and metacognitive skills change, so do their contributions to others.

In closing, it is appropriate to characterize in simple terms the role of peer interaction in children's development. Although claims of the necessity or even sufficiency of peer experience are sometimes addressed (or challenged, e.g., Bates, 1975), a more accurate claim is that experience with peers plays what Flavell (1977) has called a *mediating* role in development—that is, neither necessary nor sufficient, but likely to be of benefit. This chapter documents that although opportunities for peer interaction in school settings may vary a good deal in the United States, teachers can use the peer system in a way that is complementary to the teacher–child relationship. However, in spite of common experience within such a setting, it is notable that the children in the present study showed significant individual differences in peer helping skills. Developmental differences in age and competence levels were noted in cognitive modes and discourse skills involved in peer learning. Further analysis will probe the differential contribution of these factors to gains in cognitive and social domains. Investigation of family origins of these differences would also be fruitful. Finally, the work described in this chapter illustrates the benefit that interdisciplinary perspectives can offer in understanding phenomena as complex as peer relationships.

Appendix 1: Interaction Code for Peer Learning: Definitions and Examples[a]

I. Communication Function
   A. Verbal pacing and focusing:
      1. Attention-getting devices alert or orient another child to the learning task: "Listen!"
      2. Attention management devices direct the behavior of another to focus their behavior on task: "Hurry up."
   B. Verbal instrumental moves:
      1. Request for action (either direct or indirect): "Put that away" or "Can I borrow your pencil?"
      2. Making predictions or hypothesis testing state what the outcome might or should be.
      3. Requesting or offering explanations explain how or why something works or justifies a result.
      4. Offer or request for information. Often an announcement, assertion, or request for some fact: "Weights are heavy," "What side should I put it on?"
      5. Offering or requesting help: "Do you need me to help you?" "Can you help me?"

(Continued)

Appendix 1: Continued

  C. Verbal responses
1. No verbal response (−) is coded when a child makes a move that requires some response, yet none is made.
2. Irrevelant responses or rejections (−) reject the role of listener: "Who cares?", or reject engagement: "No, I won't help you," or make irrelevant comments.
3. Verbal acknowledgements/agreements (+) indicate that the listener is attending without providing any additional information: "This is fun"; "Yeah."
4. Uninformative verbal responses (−) are incomplete answers to an obligating move, or a nonspecific answer: "I don't know"; "You do that."
5. Responses that request information or action (0) seek additional information or action and require a response as well: "Hand me the yellow one"; "Why do you want it?"
6. Arguments, corrections, or disagreements (0) are counterassertions that provide information discrepant from that just given: "The left will tip," "No, the right will."
7. Informative verbal responses (+) are complete answers to a request: "Where does this one go?" "On the third peg."

  D. Verbal evaluations:
1. Evaluations of persons comment about persons involved in the task:
   a. Praising the other child: "You did the right one"; "You're smart."
   b. Praising self: "I'm smart"; "I'm the winner."
   c. Criticizing the other: "You're a dummy"; "You lost."
   d. Criticizing self: "I blew it"; "I can't do these right."
2. Evaluations of the process or procedure involved in the task: "This is hard"; "I'm having fun"; "I like this game."
3. Evaluations of the results or outcome of the task: "It's balancing"; "It's working."

  E. Other
1. Unintelligible utterances
2. Irrelevant utterances—comments that do not pertain to the task but are not responses

II. Referential Specificity
1. Verbal specificity: the child refers to the materials, topics or problem in such a way that the listener probably knows what is needed or being described: "Give me the yellow weight."
2. Refer to text, to something already specified verbally: "Get the yellow weight. Give it to me."
3. No verbal specificity, the child refers to the object or location with deictics: "This," "It."

III. Content
1. Substantive refers to cognitive processes involved with the subject matter under study: "You have to multiply and compare to see if it'll balance."
2. Procedural refers to procedures pertaining to the materials, tasks, or learning: "You should put the blocks underneath to hold the scale up."

[a]Adapted from Cooper, Marquis, & Ayers-Lopez, 1982; Marquis, in preparation.

Appendix 2: Examples from the Experimental Task: Children Work Together on the Balance Scale Problem

OLDER EFFECTIVE PAIR

Jake: The key thing here is to see how it balances. If we put one here (on his fourth peg), what would be the balance, besides this? (pointing to a weight on Keith's fourth peg) This would balance. (demonstrates) What would be the balance for one here? (for one on his fourth peg other than one on Keith's fourth peg)

Keith: Let's try . . .

Jake: Try two here. (points to Keith's third peg)

Keith: (complies by putting two weights on his third peg)

Jake: Take off the outside one. (the weight left on from the first balance attempt)

Keith: (complies)

Jake: Not quite. (it did not balance, but came close)

Keith: Why don't we try putting four there. (on Keith's first peg)

Jake: Four there. That works. (Keith puts the weight on and it balances)

OLDER LESS EFFECTIVE PAIR

With no orientation or negotiation of what they will do, they put weights on the scale and see what happens. They continue without comments other than "OK" for two or three minutes, when Lynn speaks.

Lynn: Let's make it balance.

Mary: (nonverbally complies by putting the same amount of weight on her side and the scale balances)

Then they put five weights on the first peg of each side and balance the scale again, but do not speak. It appears that Mary imitates Lynn's placements of the weights on this and the previous trial, but not on the other six trials, which were not successful.

YOUNGER EFFECTIVE PAIR

Stacy: Now.

Judy: Why don't you put four on this side and I can put four on this side (points to Stacy's first peg)

Stacy: I'll put five on that side.

Judy: No.

Stacy: OK, but it all should balance, we all know it, cause, see . . . Now, take them (the blocks out). See, balance. Now, put them (the blocks) back on.

Stacy: Now, you leave it. (Judy's waits while Stacy rearranges her weights)

Judy: I'll put one. (adds a weight)

Stacy: Uh-uh. Hey. (scale does not balance because of added weight)

Stacy: I have five. 1, 2, 3, 4, 5.

Judy: 1, 2, 3, 4, 5. (both children count their weights on the peg) And let's put the rest (of the weights) on the end (the outermost peg).

Stacy: (complies)

Stacy: I got it. (she removes block to see if scale balances, and is predicting it will balance)

Judy: Hey! (scale balances)

(Continued)

Appendix 2: Continued

LESS EFFECTIVE YOUNGER PAIR

(Nine attempts with two success on the eighth and ninth trials).

    Ed: Ok, let's see how.
    Carl: (removes block, but scale does not balance)

On the next attempt, they do not talk and fail to balance again.

    Ed: Yours is gonna go down, for sure. (Scale does not balance.)

Next trial, no interaction and no success. After they fail to balance on this trial, Ed explains why:

    Ed: Cause you have more on that. (points to Carl's last peg with more weights on it than
        his own peg)
    Ed: Well, I know how. (i.e., how the scale works to balance, although he does not tell
        Carl)
    Ed: And, you put yours on here. (he puts his own weights on and wants Carl to put his
        weights on also, but Ed doesn't indicate where Carl should place his weights)
    Carl: (puts his weights on where he pleases)
    Ed: And mine is heavier. (still no balance)

No communication on this trial and no balance.

    Carl: Let's put, you put just two, put two. (points out where to put weights)
    Ed: (doesn't comply)
    Carl: You put . . .
    Ed: Now, how do I do that?

Acknowledgments

We wish to thank Stephanie Caldwell, Mary Catherine Stevenson, Jeffrey Petruy, and Hunter Traylor for their assistance in data collection and analysis; Robert G. Cooper, Jr. for insightful discussion and feedback; and especially the children, guides, parents, and staff of the school, who so generously helped us in this work.

References

Allen, V. (1976). *Children as teachers*. New York: Academic Press.

Asher, S. R., & Gottman, J. M. (Eds.). (1981). *The development of children's friendships*. New York: Cambridge University Press.

Bates, E. (1975). Peer relations and the acquisition of language. In M. Lewis & L. A. Rosenblum (Eds.). *Friendship and peer relations.* New York: Wiley.

Blaney, N. T., Stephan, C., Rosenfield, D., Aronson, E., & Sikes, J. (1977). Interdependence in the classroom: A field study. *Journal of Education, 69,* 121–128.

Bruner, J. S. (1975). The ontogenesis of speech acts. *Journal of Child Language, 2,* 1–19.

Bruner, J. S., Jolly, A., & Sylva, K. (Eds.). (1976). *Play: Its role in development and evolution*. New York: Basic Books.

Cazden, B. (1983). Peekaboo as an instructional model: Discourse development at school and at home. In B. Bain (Ed.), *The sociogenesis of language and human conduct: A multidisciplinary book of readings.* New York: Plenum.

Chapman, R. S. (1980). Exploring children's communicative intents. In J. F. Miller (Ed.), *Assessing language production in children.* Baltimore: University Park Press.

Cook–Gumperz, J., & Corsaro, W. A. (1976). Social-ecological constraints on children's communicative strategies. U.C. Berkeley Language Behavior Research Lab Working Paper #46.

Cooper, C. R. (1980). Development of collaborative problem solving among preschool children. *Developmental Psychology, 16,* 433–440.

Cooper, C. R., Ayers–Lopez, S., & Marquis, A. (1982). Children's discourse during peer learning in experimental and naturalistic situations. *Discourse Processes, 5,* 177–191.

Cooper, C. R., Marquis, A., & Ayers–Lopez, S. (1982). Peer learning in the classroom: Tracing developmental patterns and consequences of children's spontaneous interactions. In L. C. Wilkinson (Ed.), *Communicating in the classroom.* New York: Academic Press.

Cooper, C. R., & Cooper, R. G. (1984). Peer learning discourse: What develops? In S. Kuczaj (Ed.), *Children's discourse.* New York: Springer–Verlag.

Coulthard, M. (1977). *An introduction to discourse analysis.* Essex, England: Longman House.

Dore, J. (1979). Conversational acts and the acquisition of language. In E. Ochs & B. B. Schieffelin (Eds.), *Developmental pragmatics.* New York: Academic Press.

Dore, J. (February, 1983). The development of conversational competence. Address to Child Language Research Group, University of Texas at Austin.

Downing, L. L., & Bothwell, K. H. (1979). Open-space schools: Anticipation of peer interaction and development of cooperative independence. *Journal of Educational Psychology, 71,* 478–484.

Eisenberg, A. R., & Garvey, C. (1981). Children's use of verbal strategies in resolving conflicts. *Discourse Processes, 4,* 149–170.

Flavell, J. H. (1977). *Cognitive development,* Englewood Cliffs, NJ: Prentice–Hall.

Forman, E. A. (1982). Understanding the role of peer interaction in development: The contribution of Piaget and Vygotsky. Paper presented at Jean Piaget Society, Philadelphia.

Garnica, O. (1979). Social dominance and conversational interaction: The Omega child in the classroom. In J. Green & C. Wallat (Eds.), *Ethnographic approaches to face-to-face interactions.* New York: Ablex.

Garvey, C., & Baldwin, T. (1970). *Studies in convergent communication: I. Analysis of verbal interaction.* (Report No. 88). Baltimore, MD: Center for the Study of Social Organization of Schools, Johns Hopkins University.

Green, J., & Wallat, C. (Eds.). (1981). *Ethnography and language in educational settings.* Norwood, NJ: Ablex.

Greenfield, P., & Lave, J. (1982). Cognitive aspects of informal education. In D. A. Wagner & H. W. Stevenson (Eds.), *Cultural perspectives on child development.* San Francisco: Freeman.

Hallinan, M. T. (1981). Recent advances in sociometry. In S. R. Asher & J. M. Gottman (Eds.), *The development of children's friendships.* Cambridge: Cambridge University Press.

Hartup, W. W. (1983). The peer system. In E. M. Hetherington (Ed.), *Handbook of child psychology (Vol. 4). Social development.* New York: Wiley.

Higgins, E. T. (1980). Rules and roles: Speaker–listener processes of the "communication game." In W. P. Dickson (Ed.), *Children's oral communication skills,* New York: Academic Press.

Klahr, D. (1980). Information-processing models of intellectual development. In K. Kluwe & H. Spada (Eds.), *Developmental models of thinking.* New York: Academic Press.

Labov, W., & Fanshel, D. (1977). *Therapeutic discourse.* New York: Academic Press.

Marquis, A. L. (in preparation). *The relationship of verbal and nonverbal processes of children's peer interaction to cognitive outcomes.* Doctoral dissertation, University of Texas at Austin.

Merritt, M. (1982). Distributing and directing attention in primary classrooms. In L. C. Wilkinson (Ed.), *Communication in the classroom.* New York: Academic Press.

Michaels, S., & Cook–Gumprez, J. (1979). A study of sharing time with first grade students. Discourse narratives in the classroom. *Proceedings of the fifth annual meetings of the Berkeley Linguistics Society.*

Mugny, G., Perret-Clermont, A. N., & Doise, W. (1981). Interpersonal coordinations and sociological differences in the construction of the intellect. In G. M. Stephenson & J. M. Davis (Eds.), *Progress in applied social psychology* (Vol. 1). New York: Wiley.

Ochs, E., & Schiefflin, B. B. (1979). *Developmental pragmatics.* New York: Academic Press.

Paris, S. G., & Lindauer, B. K. (1982). The development of cognitive skills during childhood. In B. B. Wolman (Ed.), *Handbook of developmental psychology.* Englewood Cliffs, NJ: Prentice-Hall.

Parton, M. B. (1933). Social play among preschool children. *Journal of Abnormal and Social Psychology, 28,* 136–147.

Piaget, J. (1965). *The moral judgment of the child.* New York: The Free Press.

Putallaz, M., & Gottman, J. M. (1981). Social skills and group acceptance. In S. R. Asher & J. M. Gottman (Eds.), *The development of children's friendships.* Cambridge: Cambridge University Press.

Renshaw, P. D., & Asher, S. R. (1982). Social competence and peer status: the distinction between goals and strategies. In K. H. Rubin & H. S. Ross (Eds.), *Peer relationships and social skills in childhood.* New York: Springer–Verlag.

Rubin, K., & Ross, H. (Eds.). (1982) *Peer relationships and social skills in childhood.* New York: Springer–Verlag.

Shatz, M. (1983). Communication. In J. H. Flavell & E. Markman (Eds.), *Handbook of child psychology. (Vol. 3). Cognitive development.* New York: Wiley.

Siegler, R. S. (1976). Three aspects of cognitive development. *Cognitive Psychology, 8,* 481–520.

Slavin, R. (1980). Coooperative learning. *Review of Educational Research, 50,* 315–342.

Stone, C. R., & Selman, R. L. (1982). A structural approach to research on the development of interpersonal behavior among grade school children. In K. H. Rubin & H. S. Ross (Eds.), *Peer relationships and social skills in childhood.* New York: Springer–Verlag.

Youniss, J. (1980). *Parents and peers in social development: A Sullivan–Piaget perspective.* Chicago: University of Chicago Press.

Vygotsky, L. S. (1978). *Mind in society.* M. Cole, V. John-Steiner, S. Scribner, & E. Souberman (Eds.), Cambridge, MA: Harvard University Press.

Wilkinson, L. C. (Ed.). (1982). *Communicating in the classroom.* New York: Academic Press.

Wohlwill, J. F. (1973). *The study of behavioral development.* New York: Academic Press.

Problem Solving in Children's Management of Instruction*

Shari Ellis and Barbara Rogoff

Introduction

Children frequently encounter tasks that they complete with the assistance of others. At times, children function as collaborative partners in problem solving, each offering opinions, hypotheses, and special expertise (Beaudichon, 1981; Bos, 1937; Cooper, 1980; Mugny & Doise, 1978; Perret-Clermont, 1980). Or, children may approach the problem possessing unequal amounts of task-relevant information, thus creating a didactic interaction in which the more knowledgeable child teaches the other. Findings of several lines of developmental research suggest that experience in joint problem solving with other children may be influential in children's cognitive growth. Work in the Piagetian tradition has focused on how conflict of opinion among peers may induce disequilibrium and encourage cognitive development (Mugny & Doise, 1978; Perret-Clermont, 1980). As children coordinate plans in play and problem solving, they seem to learn about their own and each other's cognitive activities (Forbes & Lubin, 1979; Gearhart, 1979; Gearhart & Newman, 1980; Goldman & Ross, 1978; Lomov, 1978). And the literature on peer tutoring suggests that children can be effective

*Preparation of this chapter was partially supported by the University of Utah Research Fund and by a grant from the National Institute of Health, Biomedical Research Support Grant No. 507–RR07092.

301

teachers of other children (Allen, 1976; Cazden, Cox, Dickinson, Steinberg, & Stone, 1979; Cicirelli, 1976; Steward & Steward, 1974).

Studies of peer instruction suggest that children teach differently than do adults, that is, children rely more on demonstration and modeling of tasks and use less complex chains of verbal instruction (Ellis & Rogoff, 1982; Jordan, 1978; Mehan, 1977; Steward & Steward, 1974). Although some authors argue that the instructional communication of adults and children may be functionally equivalent (Jordan, 1978; Mehan, 1977), we found that on complex laboratory classification tasks children were less effective instructors than were adults (Ellis & Rogoff, 1982). The problems the child teachers had in providing effective instruction seemed to be due to difficulty in coordinating the numerous demands involved in managing the instructional task. In this paper, we will compare the strategies used by adult and child teachers in accomplishing the cognitive task of instruction, adopting the perspective that managing instruction itself is a problem-solving task.

The tasks for which we examined instructional interaction involved the classification of either grocery items or photographs of common objects into groups located on kitchen shelves or in colored boxes, respectively. Adult and child teachers were familiar with the organization of items and were given the task of preparing child learners to classify independently the teaching items and some new ones. To manage the instruction in our tasks effectively, teachers needed (1) to physically sort the items into their appropriate locations, (2) to assist the learner in understanding the underlying classification scheme organizing the items, and (3) to take primary responsibility for managing the social relations between themselves and their learners.

Children may respond to complex tasks by distributing their limited cognitive resources to allow successful resolution of the immediate task demands, while neglecting less immediate aspects of the task (Shatz, 1978). Ellis and Rogoff (1982) speculated that the child teachers in their classification tasks dealt with the complexity of the tasks by focusing on two immediate demands, that is, item placement and managing the social interaction, and by neglecting to assist the learner in understanding the classification system. One obvious question is whether the child teachers themselves understood the classification system. When interviewed following the instructional session, the 9-year-old teachers were able to label or describe virtually all of the categories and presumably knew the relevance of categorization for memory performance (Kreutzer, Leonard, & Flavell, 1975). However, the simultaneous tasks of communicating category information, directing item placement, refining the nature of categories, and managing social interaction may have been too demanding for the young teachers.

In this paper, we examine the possibility that the child teachers' relative

ineffectiveness as teachers in this complex task may be due to a focus on the immediate, rather than longer range, demands of the task. Our study uses transcripts made in a subsequent analysis of Ellis and Rogoff's data. We argue that while all the child teachers were successful in physically sorting items, and most managed the interpersonal aspects of the task well, the child teachers neglected to provide category information or to determine how well the learners understood the basis for grouping items—activities necessary to ensure that learners were prepared for the memory test. We present evidence that the child teachers did not prepare the learners for the long-term goal of handling the organization of items independently. They did not involve the learners at a comfortable level allowing the learner some degree of participation without requiring the learner to do too much alone prematurely. Child teachers may have difficulty working in this "zone of proximal development" or "region of sensitivity" to optimal instruction (Vygotsky, 1978; Wertsch, 1978; Wood & Middleton, 1975). They may be insensitive to the learner's current state of understanding when forced to devote considerable attention to organizing the interaction or solving the classification problem. And, even if aware of learner needs, child teachers may have difficulty determining the appropriate level at which to provide support for the learner to profitably engage in the task, especially since effective instruction requires adjusting support over the course of the session, as the learner progresses from ignorance to varying levels of skill in the classification.

We argue that instructional interaction is a problem-solving situation for both teacher and learner. In addition to the immediate task of classifying items, the child teachers needed to discover effective means of communicating instructions, assessing learner needs, and organizing the instruction such that both the immediate and long-term goals of the task would be met. To prepare for the test, the learners were required to discern the category scheme underlying the item organization, sometimes by structuring the teacher's communication of information. We suggest that, through practice coordinating problem solving in communication, children progress toward the skills demonstrated by adult-child dyads in the same tasks.

We should note that the difficulties experienced by child teachers in this study are likely to be somewhat limited to tasks of this nature. Readers should not conclude that children are ineffective teachers in general. We assume that our observations reflect the children's response to the extensive social and cognitive demands of these tasks (like most laboratory tasks). Instruction by children may appear much different in tasks that are simpler or more familiar to children (Flavell, 1977; Goldstein & Kose, 1978), or in tasks that are undertaken with friends, or in a familiar classroom where collaboration with peers is sanctioned (Cooper, Marquis, & Edward, Chapter 11, this volume). Observations of interaction on these tasks do, however, suggest where children's weaknesses as teachers may lie, as well as offer a glimpse into the process by which children begin to formulate instruction when faced with complex simultaneous demands.

After describing the experimental tasks and the participants, we will compare adult and child teachers on three components of instruction, that is, orientation to the nature of the classification task, explanation of the category structure of the items, and preparation for the learner's test. We will then focus on the teachers' attempts to involve the learner at a comfortable, yet challenging, level in the classification task.

The Participants and Classification Teaching Problems

Dyads consisting of 32 middle-class adult-child and child-child pairs participated in one of two classification tasks resembling home and school activities. "Teachers" were 16 8-9-year-old children and 16 women with children of the same age as the learners. "Learners" were 6-7-year-old children unrelated to their teacher. The child-child dyads were composed of same-sex children who attended the same school but were not regular playmates. Equal numbers of boys and girls participated in the study.

The "home" classification task involved putting 18 grocery items on 6 shelves (corresponding to condiments, snacks, sandwich spreads, fruits, baking goods, and dry goods). The "school" task took place in the same mock laboratory kitchen and involved sorting 18 color photographs into a tray divided into 6 colored compartments (corresponding to machines, cutting tools, table settings, hygiene articles, baking utensils, and cleaning tools). After instruction, the learners sorted 8 of the original items and 12 new items, which were introduced to test generalization of the category structure.

The experimenter asked the teacher to study the items (either the groceries or photographs) in their locations until the teacher felt she knew the organization. We did not point out the category structure of the items to the teacher but provided a cue sheet illustrating the items in their correct locations, for the teacher to use if necessary during instruction. The teacher was told to use whatever teaching method she liked to help the child learn the location of items, save showing the child the cue sheet. We encouraged the teacher to teach the way she would at home when putting groceries away (home task) or helping with homework (school task).

Both teacher and learner were informed that it was important for the learner to know the organization of items because after a short delay, the learner would return to the kitchen to place some old and new items in their proper locations. The dyad began the videotaped instructional phase with the items placed in a standard order, the groceries in two brown sacks and the photographs in a single stack. Time was unlimited for both the instructional and assessment phases; the entire procedure averaged 20–30 minutes.

Preparation of the Learner
for Independent Classification

In this section, we analyze the means by which the teachers oriented the learners to the nature of the classification task, whether and how an explanation of the category structure of the items was provided, and the preparation of the learner for the upcoming test. While child and adult teachers were all successful in sorting items into their proper locations, the adult, but not the child, teachers focused on the less tangible goal of teaching: ensuring the learner's understanding of the organization of items so that they would be able to classify independently.

We will describe each aspect of instruction in turn and refer the reader to Tables 12.1 and 12.2, which provide the data for each dyad, and Table 12.3, which summarizes the data for child versus adult teachers in the two tasks. Two observers coded one-third of the transcripts for the presence of each variable listed in the tables. Interscorer reliabilities reached an effective percentage agreement of 88% or above on 12 of the 14 variables (the other 2 reliabilities were 67%).

ORIENTATION TO THE NATURE OF
THE CLASSIFICATION TASK

Orientation involved providing any introductory statement prior to the placement of items. When orientation did not occur, the teacher simply placed an item in its location. Of particular interest is any reference to the fact that the task involved classifying or sorting items (this is the "notes need to sort items" variable in the Tables).

Variation in task orientation is influenced both by the teacher's assessment of what the learner must know to begin working on the task effectively and by the teacher's assumptions regarding the learner's prior knowledge from experience with similar tasks. In our procedure, the experimenter reviewed the task instructions in the presence of both the teacher and learner, assigned teacher and learner roles, encouraged a pretense, and noted that the object of the task was to put items away and prepare the learner for a test. The teachers could initiate instruction in one of three ways. (1) The teachers could assume that the learners understood the point of the task because the experimenter had just mentioned the task goals. Thus the teach-

Table 12.1

Instruction in Individual Child–Child and Adult–Child Dyads in the School Task

Instructional Component	Adult–child dyads											Child–child dyads				
	#16	#17	#19	#20	#33	#9	#21	#22	#2	#18	#23	#15	#29	#3	#8	#28
Orientation provided	X		X	X	X	X	X	X	X		X			X	X	X
Notes need to sort items			X	X	X	X	X	X	X					X	X	X
Provision of category structure																
Item X Item (No category)									X	X	X		X	X	X	12
Item X Item (Category)						X										6
Categories Marked	X		X									X				
Category X Category				X	X		X	X								
Preparation for test																
Mnemonics		X							X					X		
Rehearsal–Replacement		X				X	X	X								
Rehearsal–Verbal		X		X	X	X		X								
Remind about test; "study"	X							X	X				X			
Balance of responsibility																
T. places without explanation	X					X	X		X							
T. places with explanation		X						X		X			X			
L. places w/teacher explanation	X		X	X	X						X	X		X	X	X
L. places w/o teacher explanation												X			X	X
Learner test score (max. = 20)	9	18	13	19	9	16	17	18	12	11	10	16	4	13	11	1[a]

[a] This child received such a low score because only one location was correct; he did group all items but only one correctly.

306

Table 12.2

Instruction in Individual Child–Child and Adult–Child Dyads in the Kitchen Task

Instructional Component	Adult-child dyads								Child-child dyads							
	#27	#14	#13	#4	#32	#31	#30	#1	#5	#24	#12	#6	#26	#25	#10	#11
Orientation provided	X	X	X	M	X	X	X	X				X			X	X
Notes need to sort items	X		X					X								
Provision of category structure																
Item X Item (No category)		X	X						X	X	X		X	X	X	X
Item X Item (Category)				X			X									
Categories Marked								X								
Category X Category	X				X	X	X					X				
Preparation for test																
Mnemonics																
Rehearsal–Replacement	X			X	X			X							X	
Rehearsal–Verbal			X	X	X				X	X			X		X	
Remind about test; "Study"						X										
Balance of responsibility																
T. places without explanation			X		X	X	X	X	X	X	X		X	X	X	X
T. places with explanation				X												
L. places with teacher explanation	X	X	X	X	X	X	X	X				X				
L. places w/o teacher explanation																
Learner test score (max. = 20)	14	5	11	14	9	16	14	15	11	10	5	15	9	3	8	5

M = missing data.

307

Table 12.3

Instruction in Adult–Child and Child–Child Dyads in Kitchen and School Tasks[a]

Instructional Component	Kitchen		School	
	Adult–Child	Child–Child	Adult–Child	Child–Child
Orientation provided	7	3	7	4
Notes need to sort items	3	0	5	3
Provision of category structure				
Item X Item (no category)	1	7	0	7
Item X Item (category)	3	0	2	1
Categories Marked	1	0	3	1
Category X Category	4	1	3	0
Preparation for test				
Mnemonics	1	0	2	0
Rehearsal–Replacement	0	0	1	2
Rehearsal–verbal	4	1	6	0
Remind about test; "study"	3	5	5	2
Balance of responsibility				
T. places w/out explanation	0	7	0	3
T. places with explanation	1	0	4	0
L. places w/teacher explanation	8	1	4	2
L. places w/o teacher explanation	0	0	0	5
Learner test score (max. = 20)	12	8	15	10

[a] N = 8 dyads per condition.

ers could launch directly into placing items using the experimenter's directions as orientation. (2) The teachers could repeat the experimenter's instructions, reiterating the teacher and learner role assignment and the need to put items away and prepare for the learner's test. (3) Or, they could expand upon the experimenter's instructions to explain a rationale for organizing the items in their locations.

Child and adult teachers differed widely in the provision of orientation. While 14 of the 16 adult teachers initiated their instruction with an orientation, only 7 of the 16 child teachers did so ($X^2[1] = 4.99$, $p < .05$). Of the child teachers who did not provide an orientation, 7 simply placed the items themselves and the remaining 2 began the task by asking the learner (after an uncomfortable pause), "Now where do you think that (the photograph) goes?". The child teachers who omitted an orientation phase seemed to either ignore their learner or assume that the learner, who had just heard the experimenter's instructions, understood the task sufficiently to begin.

The child and adult teachers differed in their provision of orientation to the classification aspect of the task. In these tasks, knowledge of the categorization scheme assists learners in both item placement and test performance. The difference between adult and child teachers in orienting the learner to the nature of the categorization task was not significant ($X^2[1] = 2.22$), though 8 of the 16 adult teachers referred to the sorting aspect of the task as they began instruction and only 3 of the 16 child teachers mentioned the grouping of items. All but one adult eventually referred to categorization: An additional 7 of the adult teachers (none of the child teachers) referred to categorization later in the instruction, during item placement.

The child teachers who did recognize the importance of communicating that the items were organized by a categorization scheme had difficulty formulating the idea, for example:

> Okay, now what we're trying to do . . . (picks up the photographs). You see
> these pictures? Well, we're going to try and get—like there's *three*
> pictures (points to photographs)—then we're gonna take *three* pictures
> and we'll take them and 'spoze like there was, um, a *cup,* a *razor,* and a
> *toothbrush* in here . . . well, you'd take the tooth- . . . then—you'd take those
> three and you kinda put 'em in a box. Okay now what you're going to try
> to do is put these in the right order and I'm gonna help you, okay?

This example contrasts with the skillful communication of two adults who began the task by placing the task of classification in a context familiar to young children—the classification games and songs of "Sesame Street." For example:

> We're gonna put *three* of these in each box. And some of these things go
> together. Remember on "Sesame Street" when they would ask, "Which of these
> things go together?"

Provision of a familiar context for the task may assist the learner in applying familiar skills to the novel laboratory problem (Rogoff & Gardner, in press).

The differences in the guidance provided by the child and adult teachers regarding the classification aspect of the task become even more apparent in instruction regarding the category structure during item placement.

EXPLANATION OF CATEGORY STRUCTURE DURING ITEM PLACEMENT

As items were placed, dyads varied in the extent to which the teacher provided information elaborating the rationale for grouping items together. Placement of the photographs or groceries that followed an "item-by-item with no category information" pattern focused on finding the correct location for each item but did not include information that would relate items to one another. Placement that followed the "item-by-item with category" pattern also focused on the correct placement of individual items but included information such as category labels or description of item functions that would assist in relating items to one another. The placement strategy of "marking" categories involved the teacher placing one item in each category location as she labeled the category, therby "marking" the group and location. Subsequent items were then compared to the marked items and other items that began to fill up the groups. Teachers who instructed "category-by-category" completed instruction on all the items in one category before proceeding to the next. These instructional strategies were not mutually exclusive; a strategy was scored if used on at least 3 of the 18 items (only one teacher, a child in the school task, shifted strategies over the course of the session).

The instruction provided by child and adult teachers differed strikingly in the extent to which it included a rationale for organizing items. All but one of the adult teachers organized instruction around a categorization scheme, while only 3 of the 16 child teachers provided a rationale for grouping items ($X^2[1] = 15.36, p < .01$).

For a teacher to use the classification scheme in her instruction required understanding the scheme and recognizing its usefulness to the learner. While the child teachers were able to identify an average of 5.8 of the 6 categories when interviewed following the instructional session, they appeared to be developing the category rationales *during* the instruction. In these tasks, the two strategies used for communicating category structure, that is, category-by-category and marking, required teachers to plan their instruction at least a bit in advance. The category-by-category strategy required teachers to decide on their organization ahead of time and to select items sequentially that match with their plan for grouping. Seven of the adult teachers and one of the child teachers proceeded in the category-by-category fashion. Teachers who marked categories did not necessarily have a plan prior to placing the items but developed the marking notion and subsequent comparison process early in the session as they encountered items belonging to each of the six categories. Four adult teachers and one child teacher used the strategy of marking categories. Developing category rationales while planning instruction based on those rationales appears to have been too difficult for the majority of the child teachers.

It is noteworthy that learners paired with child teachers who communicated the categorization scheme in a systematic fashion (by marking or by communicating category-by-category) attained excellent scores on the posttest—16 and 15 items correct out of 20. These scores contrast with a mean of 8.6 items placed correctly by the 13 learners whose teachers failed to provide a rationale for the grouping of items.

The difficulty of planning such systematic communication regarding category structure is apparent in the contrast between the one child who used the marking strategy and the adults who marked categories. The child frequently switched her category labels, while the adults stayed with the same label or reinforced the label by elaborating further information. The child's shifting of labels suggests continual modification of both her understanding of the classification system and her teaching plan. It also supports the notion that the task of instruction on this complex task required active problem solving on the part of the child teacher. Over the course of the instructional session, the child's formulation of the grouping rationale improved as she actively sought the most encompassing label for each category. In one category, her first label did not provide category information (she referred to the box in the tray where the popcorn popper was placed as the "high cupboard"). She shifted to a category label, "mechanical things," when placing the typewriter. For another group, her label underwent a progressive revision to make it fit subsequent items. She referred to placement of the scissors in "the sewing room," but when she needed to include the paring knife in this group, she revised the grouping rationale to a reference to the common function of the group—"it cuts." The determination and communication of category structure was clearly a demanding problem-solving task for this child, and was perhaps too demanding for the other child teachers.

The 5 adult teachers and 1 child teacher who used the "item-by-item/category" strategy built an organizational structure less systematically: As an item appeared at the top of the deck of photographs or sack of groceries, the teacher would identify its relation to a category or to other items already placed. The one child who built an organization rationale for the items in this manner reveals again the active problem-solving activity required for a child to communicate the category structure. The child teacher began the session by noting that the items were to be sorted into groups and he struggled for a time with a variety of hints to the learner. For example, his hint for placing the scissors was to ask "What do they cut?" The learner replied, "paper," and the teacher continued, "What color is paper?," prompting placement in the cutting box, which happened to be white. The learner used the "what does it cut" hint to determine placement of the next item, for which it unfortunately did not apply. Eventually the teacher began to use category information in his hints. After several false starts with the photograph of the bucket, the teacher attempted to direct the learner's attention to the item's function and its relationship with other items:

> Well . . . now . . . this (points at photograph) looks like—what would you use to clean this out? Do you use a knife to clean this out?
> > (takes card from teacher)
> Would you use a toothbrush?
> > Hose.
> No, not a hose. Would you use *that* (points to spoon)? Would you use a spoon to clean it out?
> > (shakes head no)
> Would you use a *brush* to clean it out?
> > Uh-uh (no).
> No . . . you . . . let me (takes card from learner).
> Umkay, now this looks like (examining card) this right here (points to broom already placed in box) looks like it fits right here (points to bucket) Doesn't it? Wouldn't it? (holds card over cleaning box)
> > Yeah.
> So, where do you think this would go?
> > (places in cleaning box)
> RIGHT!

It was clearly difficult for this child to develop a means of communicating the organization of items. For most child teachers, communication of the categorization scheme may have been too difficult to attempt. The learner working with this teacher did perform relatively well on the memory test; while he confused all category locations, he properly grouped all items except one.

The organization of instruction around the category scheme was important for the learner to understand the categorization of items but not necessary for the placement of individual items. Thus provision of a rationale organizing the items implies a concern with the learner's preparation for the upcoming memory test, in which placement of the new test items would be exceedingly difficult without understanding of the organization of items. Many of the adult teachers explicitly used the category structure to prepare the learner for the upcoming test through rehearsal of category names (see the section entitled "Preparation for the Learner's Memory Test"). In contrast, not one of the three child teachers who provided category rationales during item placement conducted any subsequent preparation for the memory test. The child teachers may have thought provision of the rationale to be sufficient preparation for the test or may have provided the category structure as an aid in placing items rather than as preparation for the test. We compare the child and adult teachers' explicit preparation for the learner's memory test in the next section.

PREPARATION FOR THE LEARNER'S MEMORY TEST

Teachers provided four types of explicit preparation for the learner's upcoming test of memory and generalization of items: *Mnemonics* were hints explicitly provided to assist in the memory of items, e.g., "you can remember that the snacks go down on this bottom shelf because that's where they're the easiest to reach". *Rehearsal-replacement* involved removing all items from their locations and replacing them as practice for the upcoming test. *Rehearsal-verbal* involved either the teacher or the learner reciting the item names or category labels out loud. *Remind about the test* involved any reference to the upcoming test, including admonishments to study. These categories of test preparation are not mutually exclusive.

Most of the adult teachers (11 out of 16) prepared their learners for the memory test through rehearsal and mnemonics, while only 3 of the child teachers guided their learners through test preparation ($X^2[1] = 6.22$, $p <$ .05). Child teachers did, however, indicate that they were aware that the learner needed to be ready for the test; half of the child teachers (8 out of 16) referred to the upcoming test in some way, primarily by admonishing the learner to study. This suggests that, rather than forgetting about the existence of the test, the child teachers simply had difficulty guiding another's study behavior.

The most challenging strategy of test preparation, requiring coordination of category rationales and associated locations, was to develop a system of mnemonics linking categories and locations that would be simple. One adult teacher developed a coherent system to help the learner remember item relationships and their locations and two adults used mnemonics sporadically.

Not surprisingly, none of the child teachers developed a system of mnemonics.

The most effortful strategy used in preparation for the test (not necessarily the most effective) involved physically replacing each item in its proper location after all items had already been placed once. One adult teacher and two child teachers used this "dry run" strategy, all in the school task. (In the home task, the logistics of removing and replacing the bulky grocery items may have discouraged the use of the dry run rehearsal strategy.)

Most of the adult teachers (10 out of 16) and only one of the child teachers engaged the learners in verbal rehearsal of the categories and locations. Verbal rehearsal was sometimes structured as a quiz for the learner, as with the following adult-child dyad:

What is the blue box for?

> It's for . . . uh . . . things you use to
> keep the house clean.

(nods encouragingly) Good!
Why don't you say that to me
one more time. The blue
box is for . . . .

Other adults repeated the category labels themselves, often speaking slowly to provide the learner with the opportunity to jump in and provide the category label. A number of the adult teachers used several forms of rehearsal, repeatedly preparing the learner for the test (at times exhausting the learner!)

The one child teacher who attempted to prepare the learner for the test through verbal rehearsal had not used a category scheme during item placement. At the time of the rehearsal, the child teacher began to use container characteristics as cues for rehearsing items and their locations. These cues evolved into a categorization scheme based on container size and form (package, box, bag, can). Unfortunately for this dyad, this categorization scheme had been designed *not* to fit the organization of items and thus was not effective preparation for the test. The dyad ran into difficulty rehearsing according to size and form of containers, since most groups involved several types of container. Again, this child teacher reveals the active problem-solving nature of trying to prepare the learner for the test. The child teacher was simultaneously trying to prepare the learner for the test, formulate a categorization scheme, and communicate the scheme. Adult teachers appeared not to struggle with complex problems to be solved simultaneously. Even when confused about the classification scheme, adult teachers were usually able to recognize discrepancies, cover their errors, redirect instruction, and communicate strategies for learning and test preparation.

Involving the Learners in Solving the Problem

Another facet of instruction that reveals the child teachers' difficulty in managing the various task agendas concerns the involvement of the learner in the task solution at a level that is comfortable, yet challenging. Adults encouraged the learner's understanding of the organization of items and their locations by having the learners play a role in decisions regarding category membership or by rehearsing the learner for the test. In contrast, the child teachers often appeared insensitive to the learner's need for involvement by not including the learner in the task, by requiring the learner to perform the task with minimal guidance, or failing to interject useful information at the level the learner needed.

Rogoff (in press; Rogoff & Gardner, in press) has argued that effective instruction occurs through the guided participation of the learner in the activity. The teacher does not carry out the task with the learner as a passive observer, nor does the learner solve the problem without the teacher's assistance. Instead, the learner is involved in the task, contributing at a comfortable yet challenging level, with the teacher's support facilitating gains in knowledge and skill. To involve the learner effectively requires attention to the learner's performance. As the learner gains understanding of the task (e.g., understanding the classification scheme), the teacher must adjust the support to fit the learner's changing needs. This results in a transfer of responsibility for task management from the teacher to the learner over the course of the session. With adult teachers, this is often a subtle process, involving successive attempts to determine the learner's readiness for greater responsibility and negotiations of the division of problem-solving labor by both or either participant.

Our data suggest that the child teachers had great difficulty with involving the learner at an appropriate level in the task. They differed from the adult teachers in the general level of involving the learner in the task—tending either toward no involvement or great involvement without support. They also differed in skill in adjusting and fine-tuning hints in immediate situations where it was clear the learner needed a change in level of involvement. We will first describe the differences between child and adult teachers in the general level of learner involvement. We will then discuss their sensitivity and their skills in adjusting the level of involvement over the session. Finally, we will argue that the child teachers' relative lack of skill in providing the learner with guided participation increased the likelihood of the learner taking a more active role in forcing an appropriate level of involvement.

GENERAL LEVEL OF INVOLVEMENT
IN PROBLEM-SOLVING

We differentiated the balance of involvement of teacher and learner in item categorization as follows: The teacher placed items without explaining the rationale or involving the learner in the placement; the teacher placed items while providing an explanation to support the placement; the learner placed items while the teacher provided an explanation of the rationale for placement; or the learner placed the items without the benefit of an explanation for the placement, that is, guessed locations for the items. In dyads in which the teacher utilized more than one pattern of instruction on at least three items, both patterns were scored. Tables 12.1, 12.2, and 12.3 provide the scores for each dyad and summary scores comparing child and adult teachers in the two tasks.

These data provide a contrast in the involvement of the learner when paired with a child versus adult teacher. All of the adult teachers in both tasks involved the learner to an intermediate degree—either the learner was involved in determining the placement of items with the adult assisting by providing an explanation to guide placement, or the adult determined the placement of items and the learner was asked to provide an explanation of the rationale for item placement. Not only were adult teachers more likely to provide a categorization scheme, but the learners were involved in an ongoing fashion with the categorization scheme as it developed.

Learners with child teachers were not integrated in using or developing a rationale for grouping items. While the child teachers were effective in getting all the items placed, they often accomplished this immediate goal at the expense of any learner involvement or guidance that would clarify the categorization scheme. The two most common strategies of the child teachers were (1) to place all the items themselves without explaining the placement of items (10 of 16 child teachers), often without even looking to see if the learner was watching, or (2) to require the learner to guess the placement of items with minimal guidance regarding the category structure (5 out of 16 child teachers). Three of the child teachers provided an intermediate level of involvement on at least some of the items, having the learner place items with guidance regarding the rationale.

While the child teachers' strategy of simply placing the items themselves was the most efficient way to complete item placement, it did not allow the learners any participation in solving the classification problem and, therefore, was unlikely to prepare them for the subsequent memory test. In the kitchen task, it was not uncommon for the child teacher to simply begin by placing groceries on shelves, to continue item placement while the learner fidgeted, and to conclude the session with a comment such as, "OK, we're done," or an attempt to finally prepare the learner, "You got it?" As we will later discuss, some of the learners intervened under these circumstances to seek more involvement in understanding the classification scheme.

The child teachers' strategy of having the learner place items without benefit of explanation regarding the grouping of items was also effective in actually getting the items placed but ineffective in transmitting information regarding the organization of items. The resulting guessing strategy resembles the game where a child is attempting to answer a question or find an object, with clues limited to "you're getting warmer . . . colder . . . warmer." There was some variation among children using this strategy. Some gave feedback involving only correctness of successive guesses ("pretty close . . . no, pretty close . . . nope . . . OK"), and others provided guarded hints, such as clues regarding the general location of the correct box (e.g., whether it is in the top or bottom row in the tray). It is interesting that this guessing-game strategy appeared with 5 of 8 child teachers in the school task and not in the home task, nor for adult teachers in either task. The child teachers may have interpreted the school-like nature of the task to imply constraints on the amount and type of help that legally could be provided to the learner. In school, direct assistance between children on homework is regarded as cheating. Furthermore, the instruction children receive in school may often be perceived as a series of hints which do not necessarily explain a concept, as teachers attempt to lead children to figure out the solution to a problem "by themselves."

Some child teachers did provide specific clues for individual item placement, but these hints were not effective for placing the next item in the group, nor for the long-term goal of communicating the category structure in preparation for the memory test. For example, one child teacher gave a hint for placing an item in the white box by pointing to the background of the photograph and asking, "What does it got around it?" While the learner quickly placed the item in the correct compartment, the information regarding background color would not be effective for the next items in that group nor for test performance. During the placement of the next item, the child teacher attempted to extend his use of the color hint strategy for item placement in the blue box:

What is your favorite color
in the world?
                                    Ummm . . . purple.
Unh-unh, that won't help.

(none of the boxes are purple)
What color is closer than purple?
                                    Purple.
(just looks at learner)
                                    Red? (looking at teacher)
(shakes head) No.
(slightly later)
Red and green—no, Red and
what make purple?

                                    Red, ohhh (looks at ceiling)
                                    Red and green—no—red and . . .
                                    yellow? (looks at teacher)
(shakes head no)

                                    Red and . . . (looks at teacher)
                                    (looks at tray of boxes)
       BLUE!

                                    (looks at teacher, startled)

The contrast between child and adult teachers in level of involvement of the learners is also apparent when we examine specific points in the interaction where dyads negotiated the appropriate level of involvement of the learner.

ADJUSTING TEACHER'S AND LEARNER'S RESPONSIBILITY FOR THE TASK

Teacher's Adjustment

It was common for adult teachers to play a dominant role in the early phase of item placement, as they labeled the categories or provided a marker for each category. Then, after the teacher had provided the rationale for grouping and had perhaps given an example or two, the learner played a greater role in decisions concerning item placement. For example, after marking each compartment in the school task, the teacher would label the next item according to category and ask the learner where it belonged, directing the learner to find the compartment already containing an item of that category. The learner would examine the six marker items already placed and determine which one fit the same category as the new item.

The adult teachers' adjustment of the learner's involvement allowed the learner to participate in the task. It also provided the teacher with an assessment of the learner's current level of understanding, allowing fine tuning of the level of involvement and the opportunity to intervene if more information was needed. The fine-tuning of the level of involvement and the assessment of the learner's understanding often occurred in a subtle fashion, with the adult teacher permitting the learner to function somewhat independently but with the teacher ready to increase the support again if the problem remained beyond the learner's current skill.

We will illustrate how adult teachers attempted to gauge the appropriate level of intervention by periodic withdrawal of support to test whether the learner could function without it, and how the adult teachers reconstructed the support when the learner indicated difficulty, using an example of an adult teacher assisting a learner with three successive items. The teacher began work on the electric mixer by having the learner identify the item. The learner hesitantly began to place it (incorrectly) in the machine's box. The teacher intervened, asking what the mixer might be used for and simultaneously rearranging the only card in the baking box, thus providing a subtle nonverbal cue to the answer to both her question and the placement of the item. The learner took the hint, withdrawing the card from over the incorrect box and moving it to the correct baking box. The teacher answered her own question, labeling the function of the item, "to . . . bake with?," and confirming the child's move with a point to the baking box.

On the next item (the paring knife), the teacher no longer asked the learner to identify the item. She asked the child to label the function of the item rather than providing it for the learner. The learner labeled the item function correctly (cuts) but began to place the item in a plausible but incorrect box (the table settings). The teacher intervened with more information about the correct category by pointing to the cutting box and commenting that the knife's sharpness makes it fit the cutting rather than the table setting category. As the learner still appeared uncertain of placement, the teacher provided more concrete directions, telling the child to put the item "with the scissors that cut."

For the next item (the bowl) the teacher initiated instruction at the same level at which she began instruction for the knife, that is, asking the learner about the item's function. The learner correctly identified the functional category (eating) and the teacher hinted at the location by holding the card toward its correct placement. The learner, however, did not use the cue to place the item—he took the card but moved it away from above the table settings box, looking around at the other boxes. Here, the teacher refrained from providing the learner with more information even though the learner was hesitating. Instead, she repeated her previous clue by asking the learner to find another eating utensil and looking at the table settings box. The learner began to place the item incorrectly in the baking box, and the teacher again repeated her directive to "find another eating utensil," while looking at the table box. At this point, the child correctly placed the item, confirming the teacher's assessment that the learner was ready to determine placement more independently.

The child teachers were not as skilled in constructing and withdrawing support for the learner in accord with the learner's current understanding. In fact, the child teacher's strategy of placing all the groceries themselves in the home task often did not even involve particular attention to the learner. However, in the school task, the child teachers often realized when the learner needed more information, as when the learner hesitated and/or sometimes made errors. The child teachers in the school task tried to modify their instruction to be more helpful, within the constraints they seemed to allow themselves (i.e., the guessing game script seemed to limit the directness with which the child teachers could provide support when the learner had difficulty). For example, one child teacher attempted to assist the learner first by providing some encouragement and prodding and then by providing an unclear hint apparently meant to draw attention to two boxes that did not yet contain any items ("OK now, what color is bugging you?"). The child teacher proceeded to clarify this hint, first by asking, "What two boxes don't have any cards in them?" and when the learner indicated he still did not catch on, the teacher pointed specifically at the two boxes in question. Note that this teacher narrowed the guessing game to two boxes with some adjustment to the learner's state of understanding.

Child teachers using the guessing game script appeared to avoid hints that would "give it away." Well-placed hints regarding the categorization scheme seemed to be actively avoided, with the goal of eliciting independent problem solution by the learner. For example, in the interaction described above, the child teacher not only failed to provide category information but also avoided pointing to the correct box, mentioning the color of the correct box, or placing the photograph himself. Child teachers in the school task apparently believed that the learner should carry primary responsibility for the task; they had difficulty formulating hints that were useful but still allowed the learner some independence in solving the problem. In other words, the child teachers had difficulty working in the region of sensitivity, providing hints involving just enough information.

It did appear that the child teachers developed more skill in adjusting their instruction to the learner's region of sensitivity over the course of the session. For example, instruction became more specific as the interaction proceeded. While adults began to remove their support of the learner as the session progressed, allowing the learner increasing responsibility for the task, the child teachers in the school task began the session allowing the learner too much independence and then created more structure as the instruction continued and the child teacher presumably gained skill in understanding the learner's needs. For example, one child teacher initially used a pure guessing game script, "Now where does this go?. . . . Nope, try again. . . . Unh-unh. . . . (shakes head no). . . . No. Think a little bit, think a little, don't just guess. Which one do you think this will go with?" On the next item, the child teacher provided more structure to his suggestion to compare the item with those already placed. First, he suggested, "Now don't just guess on it. Look around for a second." He then indicated three boxes by tapping them and asked, "Which do you think that would go with?" The learner leaned forward and sighed heavily. So the teacher volunteered, "Here, let me help you," and took the card and physically structured the comparison process by putting the item in a possible box, "Do you think it will match with this?" The teacher progressively added more structure to the comparison process, but notably did not add information on which to base the comparisons to aid the learner in inducing the category structure. Again, the active problem-solving nature of the child teacher's instruction is apparent as this child teacher attempted to adjust the level of support and involvement of the learner.

Learner's Adjustments

It is instructive to examine what learners contribute to the joint problem-solving involved in classification and the communication of information when they are with child versus adult teachers. Mehan and Riel (1982) observe that learners working with child teachers play a more active role in the instructional process than do those working with adult teachers, who simply wait for the teacher to teach.

Because the child teachers in the kitchen task largely ignored their learners while placing the groceries themselves, learners who wanted to be involved in the task were forced to initiate their own participation. This behavior stands in contrast to their behavior with the adult teachers in either task and with the child teachers in the school task, where the degree to which the learner participated was largely managed by the teacher. While the learners working with the child teachers in the school task were compliant and shy, 6 of the 8 learners working with child teachers in the kitchen task attempted to get involved in the task or at least to gain the child teacher's attention.

Some learners had a difficult time even getting the child teachers to notice them. One girl seemed to exhaust her social repertoire in her attempt to elicit a response from her teacher. First she danced around and made faces at the camera, which the child teacher acknowledged with a smile. She then attempted to engage the teacher in a discussion of food likes and dislikes, building on the items the teacher was placing, perhaps in an indirect assay at getting involved with the task materials. Unfortunately, the child teacher put an end to this discussion by commenting, "I don't eat any of these things." Subsequently, the learner tried to elicit a conversation about the Batman drawing on the refrigerator (to no avail), attempted to discuss the task (with no response), tried to discuss the camera, offered a suggestion concerning item placement, commented again about the room decorations, and finally resigned herself to singing and dancing for the camera.

Other children were somewhat more successful in becoming involved in the task using the strategy of beginning a conversation regarding preferences for or familiarity with the grocery items the teacher was placing. On occasion, this strategy led eventually to the learner offering opinions on where the items should be placed.

Two learners working with child teachers in the kitchen task focused more directly on the aim of achieving an understanding of the rationale for placing items. They told their teachers that they did not understand the task, but the teachers did not respond with additional information. Here is one interaction:

	Do you have to put them in the same order?
(nods)	
	Oh, gosh.
This is easy. (While placing grocery items)	
	I don't think I can see how you could put them in the same order. (Shakes head and throws arms up in desperation.) Was it hard to remember what kind of order you're supposed to put them in?
(doesn't respond)	

This casual interaction contrasts markedly with the adult teachers' concern for the children's readiness for the test, and their attempts to involve the children in determining whether they were ready. Some adult teachers explicitly asked the learners how confident they were about the task: "Now, you can look at these. Do you think you can put them back together in different places? (Learner shakes head no.) Which ones are you going to have problems with?" In such a case, the learner did not need to initiate involvement in order to ensure preparation for the test. Learners who were very concerned about their test performance but who were paired with teachers who ignored their interest were forced to initiate their own test preparation. One child working with an adult and two working with children actually sought additional study time.

Summary

In a complex classification task requiring the communication of the category structure of a set of items to a younger child, child teachers apparently overlooked the less immediate goal of making sure the learner understood the rationale for organization in preparation for a test and focused instead on accomplishing the immediate goal of placing items in their correct locations. The child teachers, as compared to adults, were unlikely to orient the learners to the task, seldom explained the category rationale that organized the items, rarely assisted the learner in preparing for the test, and did not involve the learners in a comfortable but challenging role in the classification task. The child teachers appeared relatively unskilled at guiding instruction within the learner's region of sensitivity to instruction. Child teachers in the school task tended to assign learners too much responsibility for deciding how the items were organized, without guiding them through explanation of the rationale for classification. Child teachers in the kitchen task did not allow their learners sufficient participation in the task; they completed the sorting themselves without concern for the learner's involvement. The child teachers seemed to be aware, to some extent, of their learner's need for more information and guidance. In the school task, some child teachers began to construct more instructional support as the task progressed. And some learners in the kitchen task attempted to influence their child teachers to provide more guidance.

In this challenging classification and communication task, the peer instructional context places heavy problem-solving demands on both the child teacher and on the child learner. The child teacher must manage the immediate task demand of devising a categorization scheme and sorting objects and the less immediate task demand of ensuring understanding by the learner. The child learner is responsible for both learning the classification information and inducing the teacher to provide it.

It would be informative to compare child and adult instruction using tasks in which the children are expert in the material to be taught to ascertain whether such difficulties in peer instruction are limited, as we expect, to tasks that overload the child teacher with information to be learned as well as transmitted. We do not, however, think that our findings are limited to the specific tasks, age groups, or middle class population we used. We are finding a similar pattern with 9-year-old Navajo reservation children instructing familiar 6- and 7-year-old children in playing a board game of finding routes past obstacles (Ellis, in preparation). And we have recently learned of McLane's dissertation work (1981), in which 5-½-year-olds and mothers taught 3-½-year-olds how to put a puzzle together, with results remarkably similar to ours: The young teachers focused more on the completion of the puzzle than on ensuring that the learner participated in an increasingly independent fashion. And, like our child teachers, the children had difficulty determining the optimal amount of assistance to provide. The child teachers provided too much "assistance" by carrying out the task themselves or by involving the learners in completing concrete steps without understanding the overall goal, as occurred with our child teachers in the kitchen task. Or, McLane's child teachers often provided too little assistance, expecting the young learners to carry out the task without guidance. Their discourse closely resembled the guessing-game script we observed with child teachers in the school task. McLane (1981) reports one poignant teaching interaction between a 3-½- and a 5-½-year-old with which we will conclude our arguments: The 3-year-old would place a puzzle piece and then look at the 5-year-old teacher who would often respond "wrong place" or "that's wrong" until the young learner placed it correctly in the puzzle. Eventually, it got so the learner would select a puzzle piece and while placing it look at the tutor and expectantly ask, "wrong piece?"

Acknowledgments

We gratefully acknowledge the help of Ensign School children and their parents, teachers, principal, and PTA. We are also thankful to C. Cooper, M. Gauvain, and B. Radziszewski for their comments on drafts of the paper.

References

Allen, V. L. (1976). Children helping children: Psychological processes in tutoring. In J. R. Levin & V. L. Allen (Eds.), *Cognitive learning in children: Theories and strategies.* New York: Academic Press.

Beaudichon, J. (1981). Problem-solving, communication and complex information transmission in groups. In W. P. Dickinson (Ed.), *Children's oral communication skills.* New York: Academic Press.

Bos, M. C. (1937). Experimental study of productive collaboration. *Acta Psychologica, 3,* 315–426.

Cazden, C. B., Cox, M., Dickinson, D., Steinberg, Z., & Stone, C. (1979). "You all gonna hafta listen": Peer teaching in a primary classroom. In W. A. Collins (Ed.), *Children's language and communication: The Minnesota symposia on child psychology* (Vol. 12). Hillsdale, NJ: Erlbaum.

Cicirelli, V. G. (1976). Siblings teach siblings. In V. L. Allen (Ed.), *Children as teachers; Theory and research on tutoring.* New York: Academic Press.

Cooper, C. R. (1980). Collaboration in children: Dyadic interaction skills in problem solving. *Developmental Psychology, 16,* 433–440.

Ellis, S. (in preparation). *Impact of collaboration on children's instructional problem solving.*

Ellis, S., & Rogoff, B., (1982). The strategies and efficacy of child vs. adult teachers. *Child Development, 53,* 730–735.

Flavell, J. H. (1977). *Cognitive development.* Englewood Cliffs, NJ: Prentice-Hall.

Forbes, D., & Lubin, D. (1979, September). Reasoning and behavior in children's friendly interactions. Paper presented at the meetings of the American Psychological Association, New York.

Gearhart, M. (1979, March). Social planning: Role play in a novel situation. Paper presented at the meetings of the Society for Research in Child Development, San Francisco.

Gearhart, M., & Newman, D. (1980). Learning to draw a picture: The social context of individual activity. *Discourse Processes, 3,* 169–184.

Goldman, B. D., & Ross, H. S. (1978). Social skills in action: An analysis of early peer games. In J. Glick & A. K. Clarke-Stewart (Eds.), *The development of social understanding.* NY: Gardner.

Goldstein, D., & Kose, G. (1978). Familiarity and children's communication. *Perceptual and Motor Skills, 47,* 19–24.

Jordan, C. (1978, February). Hawaiian peer interaction and the classroom context. Paper presented at the meeting of the Society for Cross-Cultural Research, New Haven.

Kreutzer, M. A., Leonard, C., & Flavell, J. H. (1975). An interview study of children's knowledge about memory. *Monographs of the Society for Research in Child Development, 40,* 159.

Lomov, B. F. (1978). Psychological processes and communication. *Soviet Psychology, 17,* 3–22.

McLane, J. B. (1981). Dyadic problem solving: A comparison of child-child and mother-child interaction. Unpublished doctoral dissertation, Northwestern University.

Mehan, H. (1977). Students formulating practices and instructional strategies. *Annals of the New York Academy of Sciences, 285,* 451–475.

Mehan, H., & Riel, M. M. (1982). Teachers' and students' instructional strategies. In L. L. Adler (Ed.), *Cross-cultural research at issue.* New York: Academic Press.

Mugny, G., & Doise, W. (1978). Socio-cognitive conflict and structure of individual and collective performances. *European Journal of Social Psychology, 8,* 181–192.

Perret-Clermont, A. N. (1980). *Social interaction and cognitive development in children.* London: Academic Press.

Rogoff, B. (in press). Social guidance of development. In E. Gollin (Ed.), *Social context and human development.* New York: Academic Press.

Rogoff, B., & Gardner, W. P. (in press). Developing cognitive skills in social interaction. In B. Rogoff & J. Lave (Eds.), *Everyday cognition: Its development in social context.* Cambridge, MA: Harvard University Press.

Shatz, M. (1978). The relationship between cognitive processes and the development of communication skills. In C. B. Keasey (Ed.), *Nebraska Symposium on Motivation* (Vol. 26). Lincoln: University of Nebraska Press.

Steward, M., & Steward, D. (1974). Parents and siblings as teachers. In E. J. Mash, L. C. Handy, & L. A. Hamerlynck (Eds.), *Behavior modification approaches to parenting.* New York: Brunner/Mazel Publishers.

Vygotsky, L. S. (1978). *Mind in society.* Cambridge, MA: Harvard University Press.

Wertsch, J. V. (1978). Adult-child interaction and the roots of metacognition. *The Quarterly Newsletter of the Institute for Comparative Human Development, 2,* 15–18.

Wood, D., & Middleton, D. (1975). A study of assisted problem solving. *British Journal of Psychology, 66,* 181–191.

PART VI

REFLECTIONS
AND NEW DIRECTIONS

In "Peer Relations and the Growth of Communication," (Chapter 13, this volume) Garvey reviews the chapters of the volume and offers insight on their central questions concerning process, development, context, and outcome. She uses Hinde's approach to the study of relationships to differentiate process in terms of interaction, relationships, and social group. The chapters of the volume address these different levels of relational functioning. Some chapters focus on patterns of interaction, drawing upon speech act and sociolinguistic theory to analyze patterns of peer communication. Other chapters focus on the more enduring bonds of collaborations, friendships, and other relationships. Still others concern the level of the social group, as the child's sociometric standing and cultural socialization are analyzed.

Garvey's discussion of the developmental changes in peer relationships also offers a useful perspective on the contributions of the volume. She traces a progression of peer interaction skills beginning with the preverbal repertoire of toddlers, who are establishing an orderly procedure for communication. By the preschool years, children begin

327

to use their verbal skills to negotiate pretend play as well as literal issues of space and time. Older school-age children, with greater metacognitive skills, can negotiate more effectively in both play and academic contexts.

In considering the contextual variables in peer relations, she differentiates the task or goal of the interaction from other dimensions of context such as the persons involved, their role expectations, and the qualities of objects, location, and time. Regularities in children's experiences in interactional contexts enable them to develop scripts or expectations concerning normative behavior.

Garvey formulates the key developmental outcome of peer experience for children as the "ability to do things with words with particular persons," that is, to engage in the process of establishing, maintaining, evaluating, and refocusing social reality. Unlike conventional parent–child or teacher–child relationships, in which children may depend on the structure and support of the adult, the world of peer relations requires and enhances children's capacity to engage in the negotiation of social reality, an accomplishment that influences their language, cognitive, social, and affective development.

Peer Relations and the Growth of Communication

Catherine Garvey

Introduction

The aim of the study group was to examine children's peer relations and to inquire what the consequences of such contacts might be for development. In cultures such as ours which arrange for and require same-age groupings of individuals from the play group or nursery school, through higher educational institutions, in job markets, and beyond to senior citizens' groups and nursing homes, the study of peer interaction and relations requires no justification. Hinde (1976) pointed out that the interactions of individuals, repeated or continued over time, become relationships, and relationships themselves exist in the still more extended and abstract structures of social groups and social institutions. One important insight to be gained from the papers in this volume, considering them all together, is that whatever the emphasis of the research, all three levels of organization must be considered.

There is bidirectionality of effect from one level of organization to another. For example, interactions contribute to the formation of a relationship as when some children in a play group become friends. At the same time, a given relationship, for example, friendship, may foster certain types of interactions, like expressive fantasy play. Certain types of group or family structure may facilitate or impede the formation of agemate relationships (Whiting, Chapter 4, this volume). The social organization of the

Process and Outcome
in Peer Relationships

329

school or classroom provides either opportunities or obstacles to students' potential for influencing peers, and thereby, for influencing learning outcomes (Epstein, Chapter 6, this volume). It is likely that peer group processes may also feed back to maintain or change the character of the school. Although no single paper examined the dynamics of peer relations across the three levels proposed by Hinde, pointing out the transitive and the reciprocal influences of interactions, relationships, and groups, a number of the papers did recognize that factors operating at one level produce results at another.

It is somewhat surprising that one particular outcome of peer interactions, or peer relations, was not stressed by any of the participants. That is, that peer relations, for the most part, lead to further peer relations and often to peer relationships such as friendship or the complementary statuses of leader and follower in a group. There is overwhelming evidence that the ability to get along with peers, to play, to share, to cooperate or compete with agemates, is of vital importance in our culture to social adaptations not only in childhood, but in youth and in maturity. While specific friendships may not endure over a long period of time in early childhood, the ability to form friendships and to take part in changing structures of informal groupings of playmates and classmates has long lasting significance for the individual child. Further, from the play group on in time, the preference for association with peers grows, and the frequency of contact with peers increases to comprise the dominant social activity of children and young people. Research supporting the adaptive significance of peer relations, the preference for and actual contact with peers has been recently reviewed by Hartup (1983).

The probable importance of experience with peers as a prerequisite for further peer relations derives from the complexity of the skills and knowledge required for those relations. The papers in this volume that attempt to describe the social activities of children and to determine the competence that underlies those activities suggest the extent of the interactive abilities and shared understandings that children must utilize in peer relations. The contingency of responses and, particularly, the sequenced structure of the interactions themselves challenge our powers of description and analysis. There is little doubt that many factors beyond the child's control (e.g., physical appearance, handicaps, even personal name) influence the child's potential for achieving satisfactory peer relations. Nonetheless, many aspects of peer contact demand a considerable amount of learning and practice. Successsful strategies for bargaining and negotiation, techniques for entry into an informal group, the conventions for structuring pretend play, and the tacit rules governing possession or disposition of objects, of space, of rights to carry out certain actions are among the classes of knowledge to be acquired. Adults may attempt to inculcate certain relevant skills, teaching conventional means for solving interpersonal problems, for example, "You can take turns on the swing," or "Why don't you ask Johnny nicely if you can play with his truck?" Further, adults can probably facilitate the acquisition of some special skills by their attitudes or by actual coaching, and Jacobson, Tianen, Wille, and Aytch (Chapter 3, this volume) hypothesize that the nature of a child's attachment relationship with the mother may influence the nature of the child's peer relations. It would seem likely that the mother whose child has achieved a secure attachment relationship is also a mother who facilitates the child's self-confident participation in peer activities. But given these considerations, it is still probable that the child must learn by experience the variants of behavior that are successful in peer activities, the skills required for peer relations, and the contents typical of peer engagement at different age periods.

Developing Procedures for Interaction

Some indication of the variety and complexity of these skills, of the interactive abilities and the shared understandings the child must utilize in peer relations is provided in this volume. Among the first is the ability to develop standardized procedures for communication with another person. Most young children bring to their first peer relations the prior experience of having engaged in standardized interactions with adults. (By "standardized procedures" I mean regular, predictable ways of accomplishing some mutually recognized objective, i.e., ways of "doing a thing that we often do together.") Children have learned to detect and even to anticipate the multimodal cues that signal and then regulate the steps in such a procedure as "having a game of peek-a-boo" or "we're getting dressed to go outdoors." The cues and procedures are, for the child at least, not conventional, but have been built up together with the adult. Establishing procedures with less familiar partners and partners not expert in the redundant and systematic signaling of intentions and in the interpretation of one's own state and gestures, is one of the first tasks in early peer relations. The preverbal toddlers described by Stambak and Verba (Chapter 9, this volume) and by Brenner and Mueller (1982) have achieved standardized procedures for creating play episodes and for sharing and modifying a theme, although they have yet to integrate verbal communication with these abilities. Mueller and Cohen (Chapter 7, this volume) provide a deeply disturbing picture of two unhappy children's mutual understanding of the meaning of threat and insult, where the aggressor and victim are perfectly coordinated in the acceptance of their complementation in the relationship and recognize the nonverbal cues that signal imminent attack and submission. Second, the preschoolers observed by Shugar and Bokus (Chapter 8, this volume) have added another vital component to their relations. They have integrated verbal communication in the sharing of their activities and have differentiated these messages according to both spatial and attentional features of the dyadic interactions. Underlying the observed behavior is a shared conceptualization of the distribution of personal and interpersonal space, which is a component of the vastly complex constructs of possession and of the "territories of the self" (Goffman, 1971). They are further able to convey these understandings to a third party by conventional means. That they were able to convey these understandings to an adult depended to a large degree on the ingenuity of the investigators who arranged the conditions under which this metacommunication was possible.

Even clearer evidence of the use of conventional means (language) to realize the content of peer play is provided by Forbes, Katz, and Paul (Chapter 10, this volume). These 5- and 7-year-old children communicate an extremely complex set of understandings concerning the possible permutations of imaginary scenes and acceptable rationales for dramatic action. They are actually manipulating their ongoing interpersonal relations (e.g., directing, persuading, joining, excluding another person, presenting the self as a knowledgeable member of the group) and, at the same time, jointly constructing the action of the pretend scenarios. We see here the application of conventional constructs to the interpretation of social action in, for example, justifying demands, and in "explaining" motives, and we see them applied not only to the interpersonal relations, but applied to the imaginary scenarios as well. There is, in these examples, evidence of a further achievement in shared understanding, that is, the fluent use of the conventions of pretend play such as the formulae and other techniques for indicating in which persona the actor is speaking. Although the very early stages of learning these conventions have been documented in children younger than three years of age (Garvey, 1982), the skillful use of these techniques with either familiar or unfamiliar partners and in more and more complex imaginary dramas continues to develop through the preschool period. The examples provided by Forbes et al. illustrate the agile shifting between the pretend and the nonpretend frames. This ability also appears in the interactions of younger children and becomes more and more sophisticated as the content of pretend play begins to include fantasy, material from fairy tales, and science fiction themes, and as pretend play extends beyond the dyad to larger groupings of children, for example, "teams" of cowboys and indians or of Earthlings and extraterrestrial beings.

The report by Cooper, Marquis, and Edward (Chapter 11, this volume) describes children who work together in a school that encourages the interaction of classmates. These children cooperating, or teaching and learning from one another, have developed a number of specialized procedures for assessing one another's ability and willingness to collaborate in goal-directed activities. They have learned how and when to offer or refuse help or information to a classmate and they share an understanding of the functional roles in the interpersonal orientations of teaching-learning and of joint collaboration on a task. The way such roles are realized between or among agemates differs from the way the functional roles are realized when the child is working with an adult (Gumperz & Herasimchuk, 1972).

Interaction in Role Relationships

One product of peer relations, then, is learning how to do things (and eventually, learning how to do things with words) *with particular kinds of persons.* Associations with agemates provides a set of opportunities and demands for the child which extend the world beyond that of the family or of other nurturant or controlling adults such as teachers, or doctors. Peers can be defined as near agemates to whom the child does not stand in an a priori dependent or subordinate relationship (nor in a superordinate relationship as would be the case with a younger sibling). Relations with such persons and the types of relationships that emerge among such persons necessarily challenge development as a new interpersonal orientation. The potential cognitive advantages of the discovery and exploration of relations based on equality of status were proposed by Piaget and have been elegantly elaborated by Musatti (Chapter 2, this volume). I would like to stress some of the opportunities and demands for social action that relations with peers as particular kinds of persons impose. Research is now beginning to appear that has the potential for delineating just what it means, in terms of communicating behavior, to be equal or unequal in status to another person.

Particular role relationships are characterized by particular styles of interaction, and the types that the child has experienced are influenced by his or her culture (Whiting, Chapter 4, this volume). Particular relationships assign responsibilities to persons. At a more global, descriptive level, we might summarize the adult-child relationship as that of nurturance-dependence. In analyses of the day-to-day and moment-by-moment behavior of parent and child, the asymmetricality of the relationship is realized in a multitude of ways. The parent feeds, controls, teaches, comforts, and entertains the child, who is either the passive or demanding recipient of these actions. Given a situation in which a child is grouped with several children and adults, the child does not hesitate in selecting the person to repair a toy, settle a quarrel, tell how an unfamiliar object works, or fix a cut finger. Children are acute respectors of persons and especially of their functions or uses in relation to themselves. They are aware of the relational aspects of persons, as is amply demonstrated in the pretend role enactments of 2- and 3-year-olds. A young girl will enact the role relationship of mother to baby with a doll or with a partner child who is willing to adopt the role of baby, while treating the actual partner, if that partner is not "in role," in quite a different way (Garvey, 1979, 1982). The enactment represents the role relationship in specific detailed behaviors, and it is especially in speech and in the use of "motherese," that the understanding of the role relationship is most clearly revealed. Further, talk, as speech act theorists have stressed, is a type of social action. We might expect that the types and variants of speech acts that are associated with particular role relationships be used appropriately not only in real life, but in pretend role play as well, and this is indeed the case. The same young girl who, in the role of "mother," offers her "baby" food and sternly warns her to stay away from the hot stove, will, in the role of "baby," whine, ask for help, and make only self-referencing demands, for example, "I want my cereal."

Role Relationship and Speech

Talk, as sociolinguists have shown, is extremely sensitive to differences in status between or among interactants. In some instances, the differentiation of interpersonal relations is built directly into the linguistic code, for example, different pronouns must be selected to indicate or affirm relationships of power or solidarity. In other instances, the selection of titles, forms of personal names and/or variant forms of speech acts can be used, often in combination, to indicate or affirm the particular social relationship existing between speaker and addressee. In talk interactions, even the timing and deployment of turns-at-speaking may reflect subtle differences in the relationships of the participants since the access to conversational activity is a valued social resource (Merritt, 1982). In their talk engagements, then, children reveal much of their knowledge of the practical implications of equality or inequality of social status. They may further discriminate between the component of authority, or power, and the component of intimacy, or solidarity, and indeed, even among degrees of authority or of intimacy, as Emihovich's study (1981) of the use of personal names among playmates suggests. It would be interesting to examine the talk of pairs of friends and other peers in Berndt's (Chapter 5, this volume) tasks to determine whether, even under conditions that elicit competitive behavior, the friends verbally marked their interpersonal orientation of familiarity or solidarity.

The young child begins his or her learning of interpersonal communication under conditions of intense intimacy and lack of authority in relation to the power and responsibility of the adult. This relationship is reflected in child-adult discourse at virtually every level of its organization. Characteristics of this discourse have been exhaustively described. It is asymmetrical in most respects, the adult assuming the responsibility for determining what it is the child wishes to communicate and for accepting or correcting the child's expressions. And it is the adult who primarily assumes the responsibility for keeping the conversation going (Kaye & Charney, 1981) usually by asking further questions of the child on the topic that sometimes the adult, but perhaps more frequently the child, has initiated. Engagements with a peer present the child with radically different conversational demands. In such engagements, the child must assume some of the responsibility for maintaining and extending the topic that he or she has raised and must detect and repair any hitches or misunderstandings that occur. Equality of status in respect to conversational engagement means taking a more active role in regulating and extending the talk. Is there any evidence that very young children do assume a greater responsiblity for management of the conversation with peers than with adults? We have found that 2-year-olds do indeed adopt greater responsibility for the conduct of conversations with their "best friends" than with their mothers.

Some Differences in Peer and Child–Adult Conversation

In a study in progress, we are examining the questions and question-asking behavior of young children in the two partner settings. When a distinction was made between questions that are dependent on prior text and questions that are independent of prior text, it was found that the children issued significantly more dependent questions in the child–child engagements than in the mother–child setting. Conversely, the children issued significantly more independent questions in the mother–child setting than in the child–child setting. Mothers, as expected from the results of prior research, issued more dependent questions than their children, and children asked more independent questions than their mothers when the children and mothers were engaged. Since dependent questions are addressed to the partners' prior message, and function either to elaborate and extend that message or to correct or clarify it, these results suggest that when engaged with a peer, children are, indeed, trying harder. Further, while mothers answered ("answer" being defined as the response requested by the question) both the dependent and independent questions of their children approximately equally, children were more successful in obtaining answers from their peers to their dependent questions than to their independent ones. This finding suggests that in the peer setting, children learn to apply successful and appropriate conversational strategies for that partner setting. In this process, one requirement is that they attend carefully not only to the partner's utterances but to his or her intended meaning as well. That they do, indeed, do so is revealed in the variety of dependent questions which are addressed to the form, the function, the content, or even to the manner of speaking.

Another indication that peer conversation is more demanding of the child's abilities to regulate on-going talk was found in the use of a notice-missing-response strategy. This strategy, in which a child notices that the partner has not replied and then repeats or paraphrases his or her prior message in a second (or third or fourth) attempt to obtain a response, was described by Garvey and Berninger (1981) for 3- to 5-year-old children. In our present study of 2-year-olds, we have found frequent use of this technique by children in the peer setting, some use of it by mothers in the mother-child setting, but very few instances of it by children in the mother-child setting. Similarly, the use of tags appended to declarative messages (forms that make explicit the speaker's expectation of a response), for example, "I'll fix it, OK?," was found more frequently in the children's talk with peers than with their mothers. These findings indicate that children must and do work at regulating and maintaining talk with peers, sometimes using techniques that are infrequently required by the child in engagements with adults.

The important point is that with a change in role relationship, there is also a change in conversational style and in the respective conversational rights and obligations of the interactants. Although the techniques for maintaining or regulating conversation described above are certainly familiar to the child, who in adult-child interactions is the frequent recipient of dependent questions, requests for repeats or clarification, and tag questions, the child has little opportunity to use these techniques in his or her own speech with adults and thus has probably not integrated them into his or her active conversational repertoire. In child-child interactions, the child can and does begin to use these techniques. The portrayal of social roles in pretend play provides a similar opportunity. A child, in adopting the role of mother vis-a-vis a doll or child partner, employs an array of interpersonal acts and displays an interactional style that have, in the child's real life, been only observed and rarely, if ever, executed. Such acts as warning, scolding, comforting, are acts usually directed from superordinate status to a subordinate one. In fact, deployment of such acts toward the role complements displays and affirms the pretend role relationship.

Yet another aspect of verbal interaction that differs in child-child and mother-child engagements is that of timing. Mothers in interaction with their children assume primary responsibility for maintaining the temporal integration of conversational episodes, and the temporal segregation of one topical episode from another (Messer, 1980). Contrasting the duration of the pause in the exchange of turns-at-speaking (switching pause) between mother and 2-year-old child, we (Garvey & Rae, 1983) have found that mothers respond more quickly to the child's message than does the child to the mother, and that the difference is highly significant, $p > .001$. Mothers were also more consistent than the children; the range of variability in time taken to respond to the child's message was less than the comparable measure for the child. Among the child-child dyads, the switching pauses in coherent conversational exchanges were somewhat longer and more variable than in the mother-child dyads. There was a (nonsignificant) tendency for the children to respond more quickly to a child partner than to the adult. The results for the comparison of pause durations between topical episodes (i.e., the points at which semantic and pragmatic links were absent) were comparable. There were briefer pauses in mother-child conversations between coherent topical episodes than in the child-child dyads, and the range of variability was less in the former than in the latter. In the temporal regulation of talk, the mother appears, again, to bear the primary responsibility for rapid and efficient turn exchange, for temporal cohesion in talk about a topic, and for temporal segregation of episodes built on different topics. In talk engagements with a peer, the child must begin to assume a greater share of that responsibility. The child must learn, for example, how long he or she must wait for a conversational response from a peer before taking steps to repair the interaction by repeating or paraphrasing the message and must learn that a prompt response is expected and that in delaying, the partner's attention or interest may be lost. If interruptions are to be avoided in a conversation in which both partners are eagerly involved, then the child must also learn to determine whether a pause signals an intended exchange of turn-at-speaking or that the speaker will resume the turn him or herself.

Developing Responsibility in Peer Communication

Such findings as those described briefly above make quite explicit and precise the notion of equality and inequality in interpersonal relations. They also suggest a few of the vast number of adaptations the child must make in moving from interactions with supportive adults to relations with peers. In this sense, peer relations can be seen as an arena for the extension and elaboration of communicative activity. To further support this perspective, I believe that we need studies that contrast specific interactive behavior of the same child in different partner settings, as well as studies that focus on the different types of behavior that are characteristic of different partner groupings. One excellent study (Martlew, Connolly & McCleod, 1978) provided an analysis of the play of one child in three different settings: alone, with the mother, and with a same-age friend. Behavior in the three settings showed clear contrasts on measures of linguistic complexity, measures of speech functions, length of episodes, and the nature of the play, that is, whether fantasy or factual-realistic. The effect of the partner was pervasive. Martlew, et al. (1978), attribute the differences to the demands of the role relationships: the child "did not use what he conceived to be an adult's way of speaking when talking with his mother. Rather he assumed the role of a child being instructed in the ways of conducting discourse and learning about the social world or the world of objects" (1978, p. 90).

Children demonstrate in their communicative behavior their understanding of their role relationships with other persons, and they do this long before they are able to comment on the nature of those relationships. In the process of "surviving as a child," the child adds to his or her concept of self as that self changes in relationship to other persons or other types of persons. The opportunities for and constraints on social behavior and interpersonal attitudes in the role position of child to parent are very different than those in effect in the position of child to child. Though the relationships may change with development, they nevertheless remain in contrast for a number of years. To understand the significance of peer relations, we will need, I believe, to contrast these relations with contacts with other persons who will differentially constrain or provide opportunities for the child in specific realms of social action. Concrete manifestations of a relationship of "equality"/"inequality" may be seen in such diverse conversational functions as the right to join an on-going conversation, the obligation to respond to a question even though the questioner already knows the answer, the right to reject a topic raised by another person, introduce a new topic, and the obligation to assure that one's message has been interpreted as intended. Shugar and Bokus (Chapter 8, this volume) have suggested that in peer interactions, the child comes to exercise and becomes aware of his or her own agency, that is, taking the responsibility for one's own actions. A very concrete example of such assumption of responsibility in conversation is the repetition or repair of a failed message or the rejection of a response that indicates misunderstanding of one's prior message.

Other Influences on Social Behavior

To this point in the discussion, I have been primarily concerned with the child's relations with persons, the balance, or symmetry, of relationships, and the effects of these factors on interpersonal communication. Peer relations, it was suggested, provide a different set of rights and obligations and favor different types of interactional styles than do relations with adults.

There are, however, other factors that influence social behavior. Most of the papers in this volume recognize two very important areas of influence, although differences in terminology among the papers may have obscured, to some extent, their common concerns. The first factor is that of "task"; the second is that of "context." These terms have wide ranges of application and sometimes their usage overlaps, as in Berndt (Chapter 5, this volume) where the nature of the task is discussed as the context in which friends will or will not display competitive behavior.

Beginning with the notion of "task," I would like to suggest a way that this important influence on behavior may operate from the perspective of the child actor.

"Task" is a term used by psychologists to refer to what it is a subject is expected to do, that is, an objective to be accomplished by some steps or procedure. Developmental psychologists have become increasingly aware of the possibility that the "task" as perceived and executed by the subject may not be the same as the "task" defined or intended by the investigator. In observational studies of naturally occurring behavior, that is, situations in which the subjects define their own tasks, the observer attempts to determine what is going on, usually in order to assign a code to some unit of behavior. The observer will ask, for example, whether the children were behaving aggressively or whether they were joking, and on the basis of that decision will code a gesture or larger unit as "hit" or "fight" on the one hand or "play-hit" or "rough and tumble" on the other hand. That there are serious problems here for the investigator is not news. Many researchers now feel the need to bring more closely into line the definition of the task held by the subjects and that held by the investigator. What I would like to suggest is a concept of "task" as a vital influence on the behavior of the actors (or subjects) themselves, be it in an experimental or naturalistic setting. It may be that children themselves conceive of certain segments of action in their world in a way which is similar to the notion of task, that is, as "something I undertake to do." In peer engagements, it would be necessary that the participants were able to communicate their own objectives and to infer those of the partner. The types of tasks that playmates undertake are likely to differ in some respects from those that dominate child-adult interactions.

In an influential article, Grice (1975) formulated "The Co-operative Principle" and listed its "Maxims." In essence the principle, which is as relevant to nonverbal as to verbal social action, states that participants are expected to make their contributions to an interaction appropriate to the "purpose-at-hand," and should do so honestly, promptly, and efficiently. The principle implies that participants (or observers) of an interaction can generally detect (though perhaps cannot express precisely in words) "what it is that we are doing" (or, "what it is that is going on"). In successful interactions, participants are more or less agreed on "what it is that we are doing," for example trying to finish the report before midnight, making a loaf of bread, resolving a disagreement, just horsing around, having a snack before nap time. On the level of verbal exchange, the principle is observed in answering a question by providing just the information requested and required by the "purpose-at-hand." For example, depending on the "purpose-at-hand" and the persons engaged in the exchange, the question, "Where do you live?" might be cooperatively answered by any of the following responses: "In the U.S.A.," "In Boston," "516 Oak Street," "In a dormitory," "Right above you," "Not far from here." To ask and answer the question, the participants take into account not only their physical location and whatever personal history of the interactants is known, but also the probable objective of the exchange, for example, to offer a ride home, to send the other person a package, to initiate a friendly conversation, to learn more about the other's social status. A working definition of the purpose-at-hand, (which may, of course, be revised as the action unfolds) influences the interpretation of the question and thus, the selection of a response.

Participants have a vested interest in determining the purpose-at-hand in an interaction. Its identification has an immediate bearing on the behavior of the participant, since his or her next move is contingent on it. Ascertaining what a coparticipant is doing or is going to do is essential to a decision to join in, to assist, to disrupt, or to permit. Mothers and children devote a fair proportion of their communications to determining the purpose-at-hand that one or the other has initiated. Once agreed upon, the purpose is frequently referenced by both participants as long as that task and its objective serve to organize their action and attention. Examples of typical exchanges that serve to determine or reaffirm what it is that is going on are the following from a mother-child play session: M. "What are you going to do with the baby doll?" C. "I'm going to put her to bed." M. "Shouldn't you burp her before you put her down?" C. "She has to go to bed right now." In mother-initiated tasks, such as baking bread or doing the washing, the mother usually states the purpose and relates subgoals to the objective, for example, M. "We're going to make some bread." C. "Are you going to roll it?" M. "No, we don't use the rolling pin to make bread," (later in episode) C. "What are you doing now?" M. "Now we're going to put in the yeast beasties. They're what makes the bread rise. Remember?" C. "Can I do that?" M. "Sure, just pour it slowly." In a recent study of 18, 24- and 30-month-old children's helping behavior (Rheingold, 1982), the children were observed to "help" both parents and an unfamiliar adult perform common household tasks. They did so quickly, spontaneously, and appropriately; their behavior and verbalizations indicated that they correctly identified the task in which the adult was engaged, for example, sweeping the floor, setting the table, putting the groceries away, and could contribute appropriate moves, and knew when the task was completed.

When our 2½-year-old friends (whose question-asking behavior was described above) were alone in the laboratory playroom, they also exhibited a need to know what was going on. If one child had not previously announced what was happening or going to happen but was engaged in what the partner took to be purposive action, the partner would inquire. For example, as Child A pulled out a box of toy dishes, Child B asked, "What are you going to do?" Child A. "Gonna set the table." Child B. "Are we gonna have a tea party?" Child A. "Yes, we are." Child B examines the cups and says, "Can I have this one?" Child A assents and Child B sits down at the little table and waits while Child A completes the subordinate task of distributing the tea things. They both seemed to understand and share a common purpose. In this episode, which continued through the enactment of a pretend tea party, we cannot say with certainty that Child A intended to prepare for a tea party when she began to take out the dishes. Child B's request for an identification of what was going on and his suggestion of a possible thing to do did lead, however, to a definition of the action toward which both children's subsequent activity was directed. That this type of joint definition can be achieved by peers before the onset of language is nicely demonstrated in the peek-a-boo game described by Stambak and Verba (Chapter 9, this volume). In that game, the children came to mesh their behavior in a common undertaking once the proposed purpose-at-hand was grasped.

While a number of students of mother-child interaction have observed mothers' tendency to request or provide a verbal encoding of the task that either the child or the child and mother together are undertaking, it is my impression that young children also are concerned with identifying, and naming, if possible, what is going on. Most young children in solitary or in social play provide a running commentary on what they are doing. In play with a partner, this commentary allows the partner to interpret and follow the action and participate in it if he or she so desires (Garvey, 1982). In pretend play, the communicative function of this speech is quite clear; objects and actions may not be what they appear to be, and thus must be identified. What appears to be a sofa, for example, may, in the make-believe scenario, be a train that takes one "all over the world." Do children exhibit this tendency in nonplay activities? Do they attempt to name or otherwise identify what it is that they or another person is doing? If they do, what types of information or cues do they utilize in categorizing the purpose-at-hand and what are the categories of "communicable tasks" that they recognize as things that they can do together? in trying to answer such questions, we may uncover further differences and similarities between adult-child and child-child relations. To exemplify one type of interpersonal task that children spontaneously undertake and one which seems to be widely recognized among children as a type of intelligible action, I will briefly describe what might be called "the distribution task." It is a procedure that most of the children we have observed in dyadic or triadic interaction sessions have undertaken. When there are two or more items of a similar type or function, the children seem to feel that they should be distributed between the participants. Now, they may be distribued for some specific purpose, such as putting out a complete place setting for each person for a tea party, or they may be just distributed as a justifiable undertaking in its own right. This distribution task is not directly named by the children, but is cued, often by such phrases as, "One for you, one for me." It continues until all the items have been distributed, more or less to everyone's satisfaction, and, of course, there can be a great deal of talk devoted to each step. There does not seem, however, to be any doubt or confusion as to what the purpose-at-hand really is. If adults have previously suggested or modeled such a task to a child (which is very likely), it is, nonetheless, one that children often undertake spontaneously and elaborate or extend beyond what adults are likely to have suggested, for example, once every item has been distributed, all may be lumped together and distributed once again. Whatever its origins, distribution is something that children do together, either as an end in itself or as a subgoal for some other objective.

To repeat with a different emphasis what was said above: One product of peer relations is learning how to do things with words with particular kinds of persons. The particular kinds of interpersonal tasks that children undertake among themselves are among those things child interactants must learn.

Context

The term "context" is used in this and many other volumes to select a great variety of different referents. All behavior, of course, is situated. There is, in effect, no such thing as neutral or zero context. Factors influencing our understanding, or interpretation of a social act are present in the situation in which the act is observed or experienced. What counts as context cannot be defined in any general or absolute sense because what counts as context depends on what, in any given investigation is selected as text, that is, the behavior which is the object of interest. What is not text is then examined as a source of possible influence on the particular forms or content of the text. Further, what at one point is considered as text may, at another point, become context for text. Some disciplines, notably, discourse analysis, literary criticism, and sociolinguistics have been forced, necessarily, to propose systems for distinguishing types and levels, or orders, of factors that are likely to function as context in relation to verbal text. Developmental psychologists have not proceeded as systematically in this respect; perhaps because they have been less concerned with communication and verbal behavior, which are highly sensitive to context. There has been, however, a marked increase in their awareness of situational factors and their potential influence.

As Ochs (1979) has pointed out, not all entities in a physical space constitute context. Context consists, rather, of those features of the environment that form part of the actor's universe, his or her apperceptive mass. With few exceptions, the papers in this volume display the relatively new interest in determining what features of the context of behavior influence children's relations with other children. Psychological variables as well as physical variables have been included. The authors have looked to such disparate factors as the attitudes of teachers toward peer teaching, organizational features of the school, the type of toys or objects available to the children, the relationships or prior experience of the children as friends, acquaintances, or strangers, demands or structure of an experimental task, the amount of adult participation in the children's activities, and the number of children present in an area. All of these factors appear to exert some influence on children's interpersonal relations with other children.

The parameters of whatever is considered as context do not, of course, occur in isolation. In any social experience, there are persons (with whom the actor stands in particular relation by virtue of age, sex, prior experience, etc.) and in those persons' roles there are particular things to be done (along with usually predictable or familiar procedures for doing those things); there are objects and arrangements of objects; and there are locations and times. These various potential components of situations, or of the environment, or of the context, tend to cluster in typical ways to create regular configurations which sometimes, though not always, can be named, for example, Sunday school, class, bedtime, visit to the doctor, party. Some of the obstacles to creating a taxonomy of contexts have been summarized by Cooper, Marquis, and Edward (Chapter 11, this volume). Children's behavior, however, indicates a tendency to type-categorize configurations of the various components into standardized or conventional events for which certain expectations and predictions are operative. In cases that involve conventional events, the knowledge of events can be described as "scriptal" (Nelson & Gruendel, 1979). Expectations concerning parts of the configuration of events may at times be made quite explicit. For example, in our own research, children were introduced in pairs into a laboratory "playroom." They were told they could stay there until their teacher finished some work she had to do with us. One pair of 4-year-old boys looked around the room and one asked the other, "This is the playroom?" and the other replied, "Yes, what do you want to play?" A pair of 3-year-old girls commented, "Is this the playroom?"—"Yes."—"Well, where's the baby doll?," as if this particular prop was a necessary part of the playroom where one expects to play at mothering, which the two girls promptly began to do when the doll was located. Similar comments concerning the locale and props for a number of other pretend events indicated that time, place, and objects or instruments were closely associated with particular person roles and activities appropriate to those persons.

We also observed a striking change in the children's communication with each other when alone in the playroom and during "interim" activities when the teacher or one of the investigators was present. While getting coats on and off, going to the restroom, waiting in the hall, or driving back and forth to the nursery school, no conversation was recorded between the children, though each child conversed with the adults. When the children had been left alone in the playroom, most dyads immediately began to scan the room, locate something of interest and start either a play event or a discussion about the room, objects in it, or the experience of being left there alone. Not all pairs of children actually played in the playroom, but no dyad failed to conduct one or more conversations.

Conclusion

To highlight the suggestion made above in peer relations, children are learning how to do things with words with particular kinds of persons, under particular conditions and in particular settings. One future task for students of peer relations is to investigate how communication among child peers differs from communication with adults and communication with siblings or other persons outside the peer relationship.

References

Brenner, J., & Mueller, E. (1982). Shared meaning in boy toddlers' peer relations. *Child Development, 53,* 380-391.

Emihovich, C. (1981). The intimacy of address: Friendship markers in children's social play. *Language in Society, 10,* 189-199.

Garvey. C. (1979, October). An approach to the study of children's role play. *The Quarterly Newsletter of the Laboratory of Comparative Human Cognition.*

Garvey, C. (1982). Communication and the development of social role play. In D. Forbes and

M. Greenberg (Eds.), *New directions in child development: The development of playful behavior in children.* San Francisco: Jossey-Bass.

Garvey, C., & Rae, G. (1983). *Temporal patterns in child-child and mother-child dialogues.* Unpublished manuscript.

Garvey, C., & Berninger, G. (1981). Timing and turn-taking in children's conversations. *Discourse Processes, 4,* 27–57.

Grice, H. P. (1975). Logic and conversation. In P. Cole & J. Morgan (Eds.), *Speech acts.* New York: Seminar Press.

Goffman, E. (1971). *Relations in public.* New York: Harper and Row.

Gumperz, J., & Herasimchuk (1972). The conversational analysis of social meaning: A study of classroom interaction. In R. Shuy (Ed.), *Sociolinguistics: Current trends and prospects* (pp. 99–134). Washington, DC: Georgetown University Press.

Hartup, W. W. (1983). Peer Relations. In P. H. Mussen (Ed.-in-chief) and E. M. Hetherington (Ed.), *Carmichael's Manual of Child Psychology* (Vol. 4, 4th ed.) New York: Wiley.

Hinde, R. (1976). On describing relationships. *Journal of Child Psychology and Psychiatry, 17,* 1–19.

Kaye, K., & Charney, R. (1981). Conversational asymmetry between mothers and children. *Journal of Child Language, 8,* 35–50.

Martlew, M., Connolly, K., & McCleod, C. (1978). Language use, role and context in a five-year-old. *Journal of Child Language, 5,* 81–99.

Merritt, M. (1982). Repeats and reformulations in primary classrooms as windows of the nature of talk engagement. *Discourse Processes, 5,* 127–145.

Messer, D. (1980). The episodic structure of maternal speech to young children. *Journal of Child Language, 7,* 29–40.

Nelson, K., & Gruendel, J. M. (1979). "At morning its lunchtime": A scriptal view of children's dialogues. *Discourse Processes, 2,* 73–94.

Ochs, E. (1979). Introduction: What child language can contribute to pragmatics. In E. Ochs and B. Schieffelin (Eds.), *Developmental pragmatics.* New York: Academic Press.

Rheingold, H. (1982). Little children's participation in the work of adults, a nascent prosocial behavior. *Child Development, 53,* 114–125.

AUTHOR INDEX

Numbers in italics show the page on which the complete reference is cited.

SUBJECT INDEX

A

Action fields
  accessibility, 219
  common, 212
  control, 219
  linguistic component, 212–213
  nonverbal presentation, 216–219
  physical object content, 216
  proxemic component, 212–215
  separate, 212
  verbal presentation, 219–221
Action lines
  duration, 208–211
  individual, 209–211
  interpenetration, 223
  joint, 209–211
  mutual accommodation, 211–212
Actions
  dimensions, 222
  mutual meaning, 224
  plans, 252
Activities
  coordination, 46
  object-centered, 231
  and parental goals, 86–87
  peer, 189–228
  social versus solitary, 207
  as spatial-temporal organization, 221
Adolescents, 9, 55, 113 ff., 130–160
Adult–child relations, 230, 333
Adults, as instructors, 301–315
Affect
  style, 60–62
  transformations, 169–170

Age, see also Development
  altruism, 113–116
  communication skills, 277, 291
  cross-race friendships, 141
Agency, 11, 185, 190, 193, 194, 207, 209, 211, 222–224, 338
Altruism
  and age, 113–116
  consequences, 116–123
  toward friends, 113–116
  generalization, 117–119
  reasoning about, 125
  versus self-interested behavior, 109, 111–112
Anality, 172–173
Apperceptive mass, 343
Attachment
  infant–parent, 58–66, 173, 331
  peer, 12, 60–62, 74–76, 176
Attention, 11, 270, 275
Autonomy, 175, 181, 189, 222

B

Behavior
  affective, 45
  altruistic, 109, 113–123
  versus character, 10
  codes
    discrete, 57, 63–64, 66
    transcultural, 87–90
  cognitive, 25, 26, 45
  composite measures, 66
  contextual variation, 62, 76, 124
  imitative, 193